CGS

Tosiyasu L. Kunii
Yoshihisa Shinagawa (Eds.)

Modern Geometric Computing for Visualization

With 131 Figures, Including 13 in Color

Springer-Verlag Tokyo Berlin Heidelberg New York
London Paris Hong Kong Barcelona Budapest

Tosiyasu L. Kunii
Professor
Yoshihisa Shinagawa
Research Associate
Department of Information Science
Faculty of Science, The University of Tokyo
7-3-1, Hongo, Bunkyo-ku, Tokyo, 113 Japan

ISBN-13: 978-4-431-68209-7 e-ISBN-13: 978-4-431-68207-3
DOI: 10.1007/978-4-431-68207-3

Softcover reprint of the hardcover 1st edition 1992

Preface

This volume is on "modern geometric computing for visualization" which is at the forefront of multi-disciplinary advanced research areas. This area is attracting intensive research interest across many application fields: singularity in cosmology, turbulence in ocean engineering, high energy physics, molecular dynamics, environmental problems, modern mathematics, computer graphics, and pattern recognition. Visualization requires the computation of displayable shapes which are becoming more and more complex in proportion to the complexity of the objects and phenomena visualized. Fast computation requires information locality. Attaining information locality is achieved through characterizing the shapes in geometry and topology, and the large amount of computation required through the use of supercomputers.

This volume contains the initial results of our efforts to satisfy these requirements by inviting experts and selecting new research works through review processes. To be more specific, this book presents the proceedings of the International Workshop on Modern Geometric Computing for Visualization held at Kogakuin University, Tokyo, Japan, June 29-30, 1992 organized by the Computer Graphics Society, Japan Personal Computer Software Association, Kogakuin University, and the Department of Information Science, Faculty of Science, The University of Tokyo. We received extremely high-quality papers for review from five different countries, one from Australia, one from Italy, four from Japan, one from Singapore and three from the United States, and we accepted eight papers and rejected two. Also distinguished international leading researchers working in the subject areas mentioned above contributed important research results on our invitation. These papers are grouped into four chapters entitled as follows: Basic Tools for Modern Geometric Computing; Analyses of Visual Information; Applications of Modern Geometry; and Supercomputing for Modern Geometry.

The volume concludes with a listing of the workshop committee, our staff, cooperating societies, sponsors, and the technical reviewers. The efforts, support, and contributions of all these individuals and organizations are gratefully acknowledged. Special thanks are due to Mr. Robert Bishop, the President of Silicon Graphics International, Mr. Atsuyasu Takagi, the Chairman of the Board of Directors of the Aizu Area Foundation for the Promotion of Education and Science and Mr. Muneyuki Yamaguchi of Kubota Corporation for their support to the Workshop, and to Ms. Hiromi Yamamura for secretarial work in compiling the proceedings.

Tosiyasu L. Kunii
Yoshihisa Shinagawa

Contents

Chapter 1
Basic Tools for Modern Geometric Computing

Computer Geometry and Topological Classification of Integrable Hamiltonian Differential Equations: Visualization of Concrete Physical Examples

Anatory T. Fomenko

ABSTRACT

The work contains new results in computer geometry, Hamiltonian mechanics and simplectic topology. Topological classification of integrable Hamiltonian dynamical systems with two degrees of freedom. Visualization of the evolution of the solutions for integrable systems. Computer experiments, real physical integrable systems and their place in the Table of all "mathematically existing" integrable Hamiltonian systems. There exists the algorithm of recognition of topologically equivalent (and topologically non-equivalent) systems.

Keywords: Integrable Hamiltonian systems, Topological classification, Computer experiments, Algorithmical recognizability, Visualization

The paper contains new results which are obtained on the basis of the theory constructed by the author (Fomenko 1991b) (Fomenko 1988) and developed by his colleagues (Bolsinov, Matveev and Fomenko 1990) (Fomenko 1991a) . At first we recall some fundamental facts of the theory and then formulate the new results.

1. HAMILTONIAN SYSTEMS OF DIFFERENTIAL EQUATIONS

Each Hamiltonian vector field on a smooth four-dimensional phase space M^4 (where M^4 is some symplectic manifold) can be considered as Hamiltonian system of differential equations on M (and conversely). such systems can be written (in corresponding symplectic coordinates) in the form:

$$\frac{dp_i}{dt} = \frac{\partial H}{dq_i}, \frac{dq_i}{dt} = -\frac{\partial H}{dp_i}$$

The corresponding vector field is denoted $sgradH$, where H is the Hamiltonian *(the energy function).*

2. ISOENERGY SURFACES OF INTEGRABLE SYSTEM

Let $v = sgradH$ be a Hamiltonian system, having a second supplementary independent smooth integral f. We will study the integrability of the systems on a single isolated constant-energy surface $Q^3 = \{H = const\}$.

Since H is an integral of the system v, it follows that the field v may be restricted to an invariant three-dimensional isoenergy surface Q. Consider noncritical level surface Q, that is, such surface on which $sgradH \neq 0$. We will denote by T common level surface given by a system of equations $H(x) = h, f(x) = a$. Suppose that on this surface the functions H and f are independent. Then (Liouville theorem):

1. If level surface T is connected and compact, it is diffeomorphic to a 2-dimensional torus T^2, invariant with respect to v.

2. The vector field v has the simplest form on the torus T^2 in special coordinates; its components are constant, and its integral trajectories set a rectilinear winding of the torus. that is to say, almost periodic motion along the torus.

3. BOTT INTEGRALS

Definition (see Fomenko 1991b). We will call a smooth integral f a *Bott integral* on a isoenergy surface Q if the critical points of the function f form on Q nondegenerate critical smooth submanifolds.

Important "experimental fact": the investigation of physical integrable systems has shown that the overwhelming majority of the discovered integrals in concrete mechanical and physical systems are Bott integrals on almost all regular isoenergy surfaces Q^3 in M^4.

Definition. The subdivision of the phase space M^4 and the isoenergy surface Q^3 into the union of the Liouville tori and the connected components of the critical surfaces of the Bott integral f will be called *Liouville foliation on M and Q.*

4. NON-RESONANT INTEGRABLE HAMILTONIAN SYSTEMS

Definition. Let us call the Hamiltonian H and the system $v = sgradH$ *non-resonant* on a given isoenergy surface *($H = const$)* if in this surface there are everywhere dense irrational winding.

The experience of the study of concrete known physical systems on M^4 shows that on four-dimensional manifolds Hamiltonians are mainly non-resonant ones on almost all surfaces Q^3. We will assume in our paper that all considered Hamiltonian systems have Bott integrals and are non-resonant.

5. TOPOLOGICAL EQUIVALENCE OF INTEGRABLE HAMILTONIAN DIFFERENTIAL EQUATIONS

Definition. We call two integrable nonresonance Hamiltonian systems v_1 and v_2 on the isoenergy surfaces Q_1 and Q_2 *topologically equivalent* if there exists the diffeomorphism $\tau : Q_1 \rightarrow Q_2$, which preserves the orientation of the isoenergy manifolds, transforms the Liouville foliation of the system v_1 into the Liouville foliation of the system v_2 and preserves the orientation of all isolated critical circles of the integrals.

6. FORMULATIONS OF THE ALGORITHMICAL PROBLEMS

1. **Enumeration problem.** *Does there exist an algorithm which enumerate all integrable Hamiltonian systems up to topological equivalence ?*

2. **Recognition problem.** *Does there exist an algorithm which solves the problem: are two integrable Hamiltonian systems topologically equivalent or not ?*

3. **Problem of algorithmical classification of all integrable Hamiltonian systems of general position up to topological equivalence.** *Does there exist such effective algorithm which can be realized on the computer ?*

We prove that all these problems have the positive answers (Bolsinov, Matveev and Fomenko 1990).

Theorem 1

1) *There exists the algorithm of enumeration of all classes of topologically equivalent integrable Hamiltonian systems (of general position and with two degrees of freedom).*

2) *There exists the algorithm of topologically equivalent (and topologically non-equivalent) integrable Hamiltonian systems.*

3) *There exists the algorithmical classification of all integral Hamiltonian systems up to topological equivalence.*

7. VISUALIZATION OF INTEGRABILITY. CODING OF INTEGRABLE SYSTEMS

Let us consider the Liouville foliation of the three-dimensional manifold Q. Let us cut the manifold Q along some Liouville torus T and then glue the two copies of torus T (which appear after cutting) using some diffeomorphism (preserving the orientation). We obtain some new three-dimensional manifold Q_1 with some new Liouville foliation. We will say that *foliation on Q_1 is obtained by the twisting from the foliation on Q.*

Definition. Let us call two integrable Hamiltonian systems *roughly equivalent* if their Liouville foliations are obtained one from another by some twisting along Liouville tori.

Definition. We will call the class of all systems roughly equivalent to a given system the *(abstract) skeleton of a system.*

Definition. *Molecule* is the pair *(P, K)*, where P is the compact closed orientable two-dimensional surface and K is the graph in P. The graph K is as follows:

1) Each vertex of the graph K is either isolated or has the degree 2 or 4.

2) The surface $P - K$ (the complement to K in P) is homeomorphic to the union of several open rings $S^1 \times (0,1)$.

3) The set of boundary circles of the rings can be separated in two parts: positive circles and negative ones, in such a way that exactly one positive and exactly one negative circle are glued to each edge of the graph K.

4) The graph K does not contain loops without vertices, except in the case when P is the torus and K is one circle without vertices.

Two molecules are considered as identical if they are homeomorphic as two topological spaces (with preserved orientation).

Theorem 2 *There exists the natural one-to-one correspondence between the set of all molecules and the set of all skeletons of integrable Hamiltonian systems.*

8. COMPLEXITY AND ITS VISUALIZATION

Let v be the integrable Hamiltonian system on Q with some Bott integral f. Denote by m the total number of all minimal, maximal and saddle critical circles of the integral. Let us remove from the manifold all isolated critical circles and connected components of all critical level surfaces of f containing the saddle circles. In other words, we remove all singular fibers of corresponding Liouville foliation. As a result, the manifold Q goes to pieces, transforms into the union of finite number of open manifolds homeomorphic to the direct product $S^1 \times S^1 \times (0,1)$. Let us denote the total number of such manifolds by n.
Definition. The pair of nonnegative integer numbers (m,n) will be called *complexity* of a given integrable Hamiltonian systems v.

The complexities of two roughly equivalent integrable Hamiltonian systems coincide. Thus, the complexity is the *invariant of the skeleton* of the system. The complexity of the *molecule (P, K)* is the pair (m,n), where m is the number of the vertices of the graph K and n is the number of the connected components of the manifold $P - K$.

Theorem 3

a) *The number of different molecules of a given fixed complexity (m, n) is finite.*

b) *The set of all topologically non-equivalent integrable Hamiltonian systems with the same molecule of the complexity (m, n) is parameterized by independent parameters*

$$r_i,\ \varepsilon_i,\ n_k,\ 1 \ll i \ll n,\ 1 \ll k \ll s,$$

where r_i are the rational numbers, $0 \ll r_i < 1$ or $r_i = \infty$, then $\varepsilon_i = \pm 1$; n_k are the integer numbers and $s \ll m$.

Thus, we can say that integrable Hamiltonian system can be uniquely defined (up to topological equivalence) by the *framed molecule.* Conversely, each *framed molecule* is the molecule of some integrable Hamiltonian system.

Theorem 4 *There exists the natural one-to-one correspondence between the set of all framed molecules and the set of all integrable Hamiltonian systems (considered up to topological equivalence.)*

9. COMPUTER EXPERIMENT. THE LIST OF ALL INTEGRABLE HAMILTONIAN SYSTEMS OF LOW COMPLEXITY

We need in some procedure of the coding of the integrable systems. Let us separate the piece of the *molecule* (P,K) on the pieces of two types: a) the regular neighborhoods of the connected components of the graph K, b) the remaining rings. Let us call the regular neighborhood of the graph K *letters-atoms.* The complexity of the *letter-atom* is equal to the number of the vertices in its *spine.* The *spine* is the connected component of the graph K, which is the deformation retract of the letter-atom.

The list of all letter-atoms of complexity no more than 3 see in the Table 1 in (Bolsinov, Matveev and Fomenko 1990) . (All Tables were calculated on computer).

The rings (which form the manifold $P - K$) can be interpreted as segments-edges-connections in some new object which can be called *word-molecule.* Word-molecule is formed by several letters-atoms connected by edges (which correspond to the rings). The word-molecule defines the molecule of integrable Hamiltonian system. Table 3 in (Bolsinov, Matveev and Fomenko 1990) shows the list of all words-molecules corresponding to the integrable Hamiltonian systems of complexity (m, n), where $m \leq 2$. Let us denote by $\lambda(m, n)$ the total number of all molecules of integrable Hamiltonian systems of a given complexity (m, n). This number is finite. The list of the values of the function $\lambda(m, n)$, where $m \leq 4$, is given in Table 4 in (Bolsinov, Matveev and Fomenko 1990) .

We calculate the number $\Lambda(m)$, where $\Lambda(m)$ is the upper bound of all numbers n such that $\lambda(m, n) \neq 0$ and m is fixed: $\Lambda(m) = \{sup\ n : \lambda(m, n) \neq 0\}$. It turned out that $\Lambda(m) = [\frac{3m}{2}]$.

10. NEW RESULTS: REAL PHYSICAL SYSTEMS AND THEIR PLACE IN THE CLASSIFICATION TABLE OF ALL INTEGRABLE HAMILTONIAN SYSTEMS

It is extremely interesting and important to calculate the cells (m, n) in our table which contain the real mechanical and physical integrable systems. A.T.Fomenko, A.A.Oshemkov, A.V.Bolsinov, L.S.Polyakova, E.N.Selivanoa, E.V.Anoshkina, B.S. Kruglikov calculated the words–moleculas for the following important physical systems: integrable cases of the equations of the rigid body motion (Kovalevskaya case, Goryachev-Chaplygin case, Sretenskii case, Clebsch case, Euler case, Lagrange case); some integrable cases in Toda lattice, integrable cases for the motion equations of the four-dimensional rigid body (the system on the Lie group $SO(4)$) and so on.

In previous discussion we assumed that the isoenergy surface Q was fixed. But indeed we need in the consideration of all isoenergy surfaces of a given integrable system which correspond to different values of the energy function (Hamiltonian) H. This problem arises naturally when we study real physical system. It is natural to start from the minimum of the Hamiltonian H and move then in direction of its maximum. The change of the Hamiltonian's value changes the isoenergy surface Q. It is natural to correct all types of surfaces Q which appear in this process. This set of integrable surfaces represents the total topology of a given integrable system.

Thus, we obtain "one-parametric" family of words-molecules. Let us represent these molecules by the points in corresponding cells of the plane (each such cell corresponds to the concrete complexity (m, n)). Then let us connect each two consecutive points by a segment. As a result, we obtain some curve on the plane (m, n). The curve corresponds to the motion of the value of Hamiltonian from the minimum to maximum. Thus, each real physical system is represented by some curve on the plane (m, n). Figs.1-2 shows these curves for the following famous integrability cases in dynamics of 3-dimensional rigid body: Clebsch and Zhukovskii cases. Fig.3 shows three examples from the dynamics of 4-dimensional rigid body.

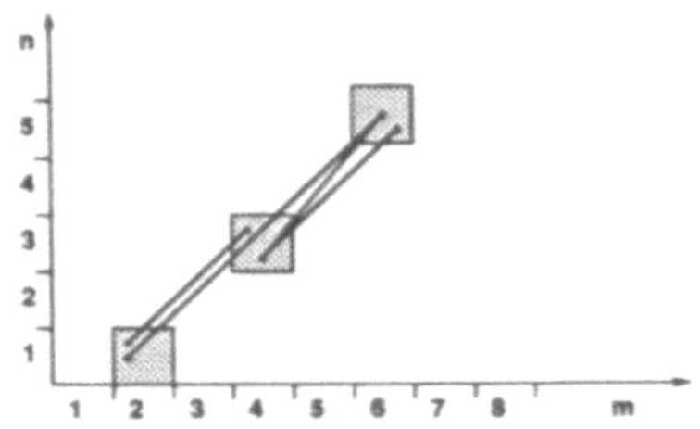

Fig. 1. Zhukovskiy's case

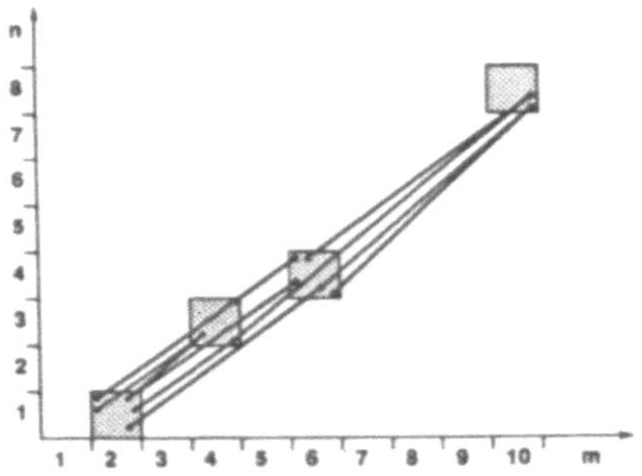

Fig. 2. Clebsch's case

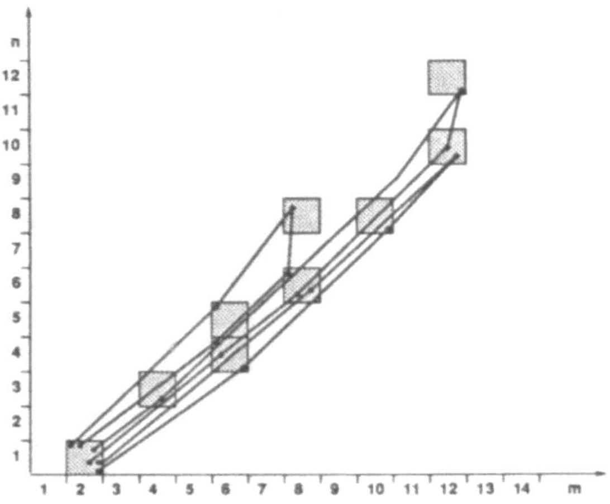

Fig. 3. Four-dimensional rigid body (three examples)

Fig.4 shows the "physical zone" which is formed by the following important physical cases of integrability: a) the cases in dynamics of 3-dimensional rigid body (Euler, Lagrange. Kovalevskaya, Zhukovskii, Goryachev-Chaplygin-Sreteskii, Clebsch, Steklov), b) all known integrability cases for 4-dimensional rigid body, c) Toda lattices. We indicated in each cell the number of different molecules with a given complexity. The reader can see that "physical zone" has "regular character". Fig.5 is author's artistic representation of Liouville tori bifurcation.

It is clear that the farther analysis of another real mechanical systems will fill some new cells on the plane. We obtain, as a result, some remarkable "general physical zone". Important problem: to describe "the form" of this zone. Where are located "all physical integrable systems"?

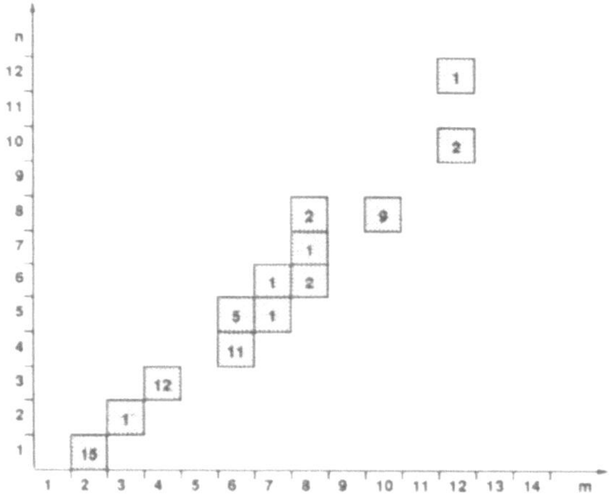

Fig. 4: "Physical zone". Complexity of integrable cases of Euler, Euler, Lagrange. Kovalevskaya, Zhukovskii, Goryachev-Chaplygin-Sreteskii, Clebsch, Steklov, and 4-dimensional rigid body; Toda lattices. (integers in the cells indicate the numbers of integrable cases with given complexity)

REFERENCES

Bolsinov AV, Matveev SV, Fomenko AT (1990) Topological classification of integrable hamiltonian systems of small complexity. *Russian Math. Surveys*, 45(2).

Fomenko AT (1988) *Integrability and Nonintegrability in Geometry and Mechanics.* Kluwer Academic Publishers.

Fomenko AT (1989) Visual and hidden symmetry in geometry. *Computers Math. Applic.*, 17(1–3).

Fomenko AT, editor (1991) *Advances in Soviet Mathematics*, volume 6. American Math. Soc, Providence. see "Topological classification of Integrable Hamiltonian systems".

Fomenko AT (1991) Topological classification of all hamiltonian differential equations of general type with two degrees of freedom. In: *The Geometry of Hamiltonian systems, Proceedings of a Workshop Held June 5-16, 1989*, Springer–Verlag. NewYork, pp. 131–339.

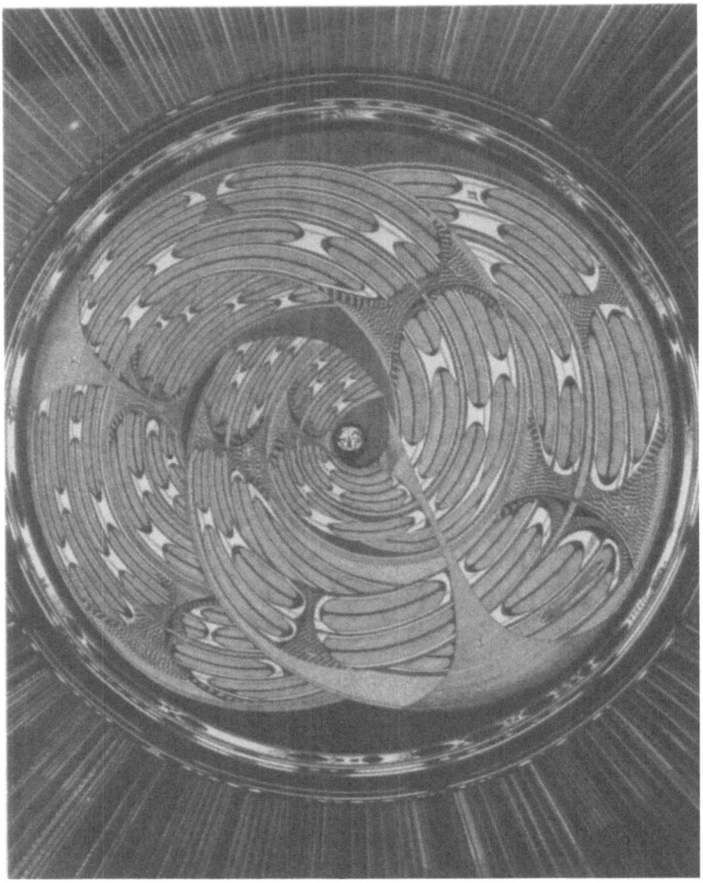

Fig.5

AUTHOR BIOGRAPHY

Anatory T. Fomenko, born on March 13, 1945, UKrainian city Donetsk, USSR. Education: Math.Dept. of Moscow State Univ. In 1969: the defense of dissertation "Totally Geodesic Models of the Homology Cycles in Homogeneous Riemannian Manifolds"; in 1972: the defense of doctoral dissertation "Minimal Surfaces and Solution of the Multidimensional Plateau Problem in the Special Bordism Classes on Riemannian Manifolds". In 1974: Prize of Moscow Math.Society; in 1987 - Prize of the Presidium of the Academy of Science of USSR for the new theory of topological classification of integrable equations. In 1990 was elected as Associated Member of Sci.Academy of USSR. The author of 17 books in geometry, topology, calculus of variations, Hamiltonian mechanics.

Address: Dept. of Geometry and Topology, Faculty of Math. and Mech. Moscow State Univ., Moscow, 119899, USSR.
E-mail:anatoly@fomenko.mian.su

Interdisciplinary Techniques, Toolkits and Models for Scientific Visualization

Rae A. Earnshaw

ABSTRACT

Scientific visualization is concerned with the processing and display of large amounts of data in such a way as to facilitate assimilation of the information in an efficient and effective manner. Many disciplines and application have common requirements. This paper summarises current work in this area in the UK and the range of tools and techniques currently available.

A Scientific Visualization Workshop in the UK in 1991 examined the areas of framework models, visualization techniques, data facilities, human-computer interface aspects, applications, and products. Studies were also done in the area of enabling technologies - hardware, software, toolkits, database systems, and generic data formats. This work has been published as *'Scientific Visualization - Techniques and Applications'*, Springer-Verlag, 1992. This paper summarises the key results from this work.

An inter-disciplinary Scientific Visualization Group was formed at the University of Leeds in October 1990 to facilitate and coordinate campus-wide developments in area of tools and methodologies for visualization. We summarise the current work and objectives of the group in interdisciplinary application areas, and also current studies in methodologies for visualization via networks. Experiments are being set in place to study the partitioning of the visualization pipeline across different facilities (e.g. parallel processor, supercomputer, graphics workstation) and investigate interactive response times and network bandwidth requirements. Optimum configurations should enable local users to utilize high-powered facilities via network access. Desk top visualization is part of the required user toolset for the 1990's.

KEYWORDS: visualization, computer graphics, modelling, interdisciplinary techniques, remote visualization, nework-based tools, desk-top visualization, visualization environments, virtual reality.

1. INTRODUCTION

Scientific Visualization is concerned with exploring data and information in such a way as to gain understanding and insight into the data.

"The purpose of computing is insight, not numbers", wrote the much cited Richard Hamming in *'Numerical Methods for Scientists and Engineers'* McGraw-Hill, 1962. Scientific visualization is an amalgam of tools and techniques that seeks to promote new dimensions of insight into problem solving using current technology.

Visualization utilises aspects in the areas of computer graphics, userinterface, image processing, design, and signal processing. Formerly these were independent fields, but convergence is being brought about by the use of analogous techniques in the different areas.

Visualization highlights applications and application areas because it is concerned to provide leverage in these areas to enable the user to achieve greater exploitation of the computing tools now available. In a number of instances visualization has been used to analyse and display large volumes of multi-dimensional data in such a way as to allow the user to extract significant features and results quickly and easily. Tools and techniques in this area are therefore concerned with data analysis and data display, with perhaps provision for the display of data changes with respect to time.

Such tools benefit by the availability of modern workstations with good performance, large amounts of memory and disk, and with powerful graphics facilities - both in terms of range of colours available and also speed of display by the workstation. This close coupling of graphics and raw computation power is a powerful combination for those areas where visual insight is an important part of the problem-solving capability.

Such workstations now offer substantial computation power coupled with high speed 3D graphics. These facilities can be exploited to significant advantage in application areas such as modelling, simulation, and animation. Real-time dynamical simulation can involve the processing and display of large amounts of data, and often the only effective analysis of the performance or validity of the model is through visual observation.

Such workstations provide the computation power to process the data, and the high speed graphics pipeline can transform this into graphical images, often in real time. In those cases where additional computational resource is required, the calculation can be off-loaded on to a supercomputer, or other advanced workstations with spare capacity, and the resulting image down-loaded for viewing (and perhaps even interaction) when it is ready.

These advances will allow mathematical models and simulations to become increasingly complex and detailed. This results in a closer approximation to reality, thus enhancing the possibility of acquiring new knowledge and understanding. Scientific visualization is concerned with methods of generating and presenting large collections of numerical values containing a great deal of information. The scientist has to be able to make effective use of this information for analytic purposes.

A further aspect is that increases in computer performance allow 3D problems in simulation and design to be done interactively. In addition, processes that formerly separated out simulation and design can now bring them together (e.g. in CAD, design of new drugs etc). This in turn moves the user into a new era of methods of design.

Control over fine simulations, interactivity, and computer performance mean that vast amounts of multidimensional data can be generated. Super workstations allow this data to be displayed in optimum ways. These features and capabilities are driving the current wave of interest in scientific visualization.

A further current trend is to make software tools for visualization more user-friendly and accessible to a wide variety of application areas, thus increasing their potential and usability.

Nielson at al (1990) contains a wide variety of current applications of scientific visualization and also an excellent bibliography of scientific papers. A 2-hour video tape can be obtained with the book.

Frenkel (1988) provides a general introduction to basic visualization techniques.

Thalmann (1990) contains a number of papers in the areas of scientific visualization and graphical simulation.

2. HISTORY AND BACKGROUND

A Report published in 1987 (McCormick et al, 1987) recommended a series of short term and long-term initiatives. A further Report (McCormick et al, 1989) by the same authors detailed the progress made between 1987 and 1989. The authors (Bruce McCormick, Tom DeFanti, and Maxine Brown) reported the outcome of a Workshop on 'Visualization in Scientific Computing' held 9-10 February 1987 as a result of an earlier Panel Meeting on 'Graphics, Image Processing and Workstations' sponsored by the Division of Advanced Scientific Computing of the National Science Foundation (NSF).

The Workshop was attended by representatives of Academia, Industry, and Government Research Laboratories.

McCormick et al (1987) summarises the conclusions and recommendations.

Here are a number of the principal conclusions -

(i) **High Volume Data Sources**
Data sources such as supercomputers, satellites, spacecraft, radio astronomy arrays, instrument arrays and medical scanners all produce large volumes of data to be analysed. The numbers and density of such data sources are expected to increase as technology moves forward. Satellites have resolutions 10-100 times higher than a few years ago. Terabyte data sets are becoming increasingly common in all systems concerned with real-time recording of data.
Scientific visualization is the only way to effectively handle such large amounts of data.

(ii) **The Value of Interdisciplinary Teams**
Systems concerned with scientific visualization benefited from having collaborating disciplines. For example, computational scientists and engineers could combine in areas such as fluid dynamics and molecular modelling; visualization scientists and engineers could combine in areas concerned with visualization software, hardware, and networking. Artists and cognitive scientists could ensure that the best forms of visual communication were used - colour, composition, visual representation, visual perception, etc.

(iii) **Visualization Issues for Tool Makers**
The following areas were identified as needing development and support for the future -

- o Interactive steering of computations and simulations
- o Workstation-driven use of supercomputers
- o Graphics-oriented programming environments
- o Visualization of higher dimensional scalar, vector, and tensor fields
- o Dynamic visualization of fields and flows
- o High bandwidth networks for pictures
- o Handling terabyte data sets - for signal and image processing
- o Vectorised and parallelised algorithms

o Specialised architectures for graphics and image processing
o Establishing a framework for international standards in scientific visualization

(iv) Benefits of Scientific Visualization
The following potential benefits were identified -

o Integrated set of portable tools
o Increase scientific progress and collaboration
o Increase scientific productivity
o Standardisation of tools
o Improve market competitiveness
o Improve the overall usefulness of advanced computing facilities

The following were some of the principal recommendations of the Report -

(i) Develop new and useful tools for the future
(ii) Distribute tools to provide opportunities for use
(iii) Greater funding support needed (e.g. as % of national spend)
(iv) Fund both research (tool users) and technology (tool makers)
(v) Fund immediate and long term provision
(vi) Enhance scientific and engineering opportunities
(vii) Recognise the short-term potential of visualization environments
(viii) Address the long term goals of visualization environments
(ix) Address the issue of industrial competitiveness

In addition, a range of application areas in science, engineering, and medicine were presented as illustrative of the current uses of scientific visualization tools.

3. CURRENT ACTIVITIES IN SCIENTIFIC VISUALIZATION

3.1 USA

The principal recommendations of the McCormick Report were that national funding should be provided for short and long term provision of tools and environments to support scientific visualization, and to make these available to the scientific and engineering community at large. Such provision was considered to be essential if the ennabling tools were to be effectively harnessed by current and future scientists and engineers.

Such tools often require access to significant computation resources. A natural focal point for these developments has been the funding of Supercomputer Centres - to provide both the facilities and access to them by the community.

An example of this at the San Diego Supercomputer Center is the development of network-based general purpose visualization tools. These are accessed by 2800 users with 350 different applications. Such users access the facility by a variety of different routes including dial-in lines, national networks, and dedicated high-speed links. In addition to this broad range of provision there are also more specialised tools for high-end applications (e.g. molecular modelling, computational fluid dynamics).

Similar provision has also been made at other Supercomputer Centers at Cornell, Pittsburgh, and the University of Illinois at UrbanaChampaign.

Workshops on Scientific Visualization have been established by ACM SIGGRAPH and IEEE to address specific aspects such as Data Facilities (to facilitate ueas of use and transfer of information), and Volume Visualization (to enable representation of real 3D information and to give inside views). Representatives from the Department of Defense and the Department of Energy have initiated a Working Group to define a Visualization Reference Model.

In addition, a large number of major Universities are establishing Visualization Laboratories, and often such installations receive supplementary funding for further proposals in specific application areas. Funding is provided by such bodies as NSF, DARPA, and NASA. State Supercomputers and associated Visualization facilities exist in Ohio, North Carolina, Minnesota, Utah, Alaska, and Florida.

To provide a forum for the presentation and discussion of the latest advances in Scientific Visualization, the IEEE Technical Committee on Computer Graphics has established an international Visualization conference, which is held on an annual basis.

In addition, the National Science Foundation is providing funds for the support and promotion of educational initiatives in Scientific Visualization by means of Institutes, Workshops, and Summer Schools.

Fast networks are required for distributed and remote visualization. Developments in networking infrastructure are planned to provide faster communication, interconnection, and the ability to aggregate computing resources at different locations on to one particular problem. For example, the CASA test bed project is funded by the NSF to develop a 1 Gbit/sec network link between Los Alamos National Laboratory, California Institute of Technology, and San Diego Supercomputer Center, to enable all three resources to be concentrated on one application simultaneously.

A recent multi-million dollar grant has recently been awarded by NSF to California Institute of Technology, Brown University, University of Utah, Cornell University, and the University of North Carolina at Chapel Hill, to explore the foundations of computer graphics and visualization.

3.2 UK

A number of centres in UK academic institutions are concerned with application areas such as molecular modelling and computational fluid dynamics (CFD). There are a number of collaborative projects between academia and industry in the areas of parallel processing and scientific visualization. One example, GRASPARC, a Graphical Environment for Supporting Parallel Computing, is a joint project between NAG Ltd, the University of Leeds (School of Computer Studies), and Quintek Ltd. The major objective of the work is to improve the interaction between the numerical analyst and the parallel computer through the development of interactive visualization software.

The IBM UK Scientific Centre in Winchester is primarily concerned with scientific visualization and has a Visualization Group, a European Visualization Group, a Medical Imaging Group, and a Parallel Programming and Visualization Group. There are a number of collaborative projects with academia and industry in the areas of parallel processing, user-interface aspects, and medical informatics.

NERC has a Visualization Advisory Group concerned with evaluating products for the areas of geological surveys and oceanography. SERC Engineering Board has evaluated super workstations in the areas of hardware and software. A Workshop on Scientific Visualization was held in February 1991, and arose out of an initiative by the Computer Board and the Advisory Group on Computer Graphics.

The Rutherford Appleton Laboratory, Central Computing Division, has developed a video facility for use by the academic and research community in the UK, and is involved in projects in the areas of oceanography, atmospheric physics, laser design, mechanical engineering, ecological simulation, and CFD.

3.3 Europe

IBM has a number of European centres actively involved in projects involving Scientific Visualization. These include the European Petroleum Applications Centre (EPAC) in Bergen, the Paris Scientific Centre which is involved in visualization in the medical area, and the European Scientific Centre in Rome which is involved in engineering and modelling turbulent flow. IBM also has a joint project with the Centre of Competence in Visualization at the University of Aix-Marseilles.

FhG-AGD in Darmstadt is working on a number of areas, including tools for volume visualization on a variety of platforms, and handling different kinds of data sets.

Eurographics arranged a Workshop on Scientific Visualization in April 1990. The proceedings will be available from Springer-Verlag. A further workshop is planned for April 1991.

3.4 Recent UK Activities

The Advisory Group on Computer Graphics (AGOCG) has been set up to play a number of roles in the academic and research community in the UK. Its terms of reference are:

- to advise the Computer Board and the Research Councils on all aspects of computer graphics

- to be aware of advances in computer graphics in both the standards area and in innovative new technology in both hardware and software

- to liase with the community to help identify requirements in the area of computer graphics

- to recommend to all relevant funding bodies options for purchase, support and development that would improve the environment available to the academic community in the area of computer graphics

- to ensure that facilities for education and training are provided to the community on the benefits arising from the use of computer graphics including standards.

A Worksop on Scientific Visualization was arranged 22-25 February 1991 which was supported by the Computer Board and Eurographics UK. This brought together 29 experts from UK academic and research establishments The participants came from a range of disciplines and from research and support environments. This led to a very useful exchange of ideas.

A management report has been produced from the Workshop. In addition, based on work commenced at the Workshop two volumes have been produced. The first is a reference work and the second an introductory guide.

The purpose of the "*An Introductory Guide to Scientific Visualization*", R. A. Earnshaw and N. Wiseman, Springer-Verlag, pp100 is to explain in simple terms what scientific visualization is and what it can do, and give illustrations and explanations of the technical terms in a way the non-specialist can understand. This volume is intended for readers new to the field and who require a quick and easy-to-read summary. Written in a popular and journalistic style with many illustrations it will enable readers to appreciate the benefits of scientific visualization and how current tools can be exploited in many application areas.

In addition, a comprehensive technical summary of the state of the art in the field of scientific visualization has been produced and is entitled "*Scientific Visualization - Techniques and Applications*", Eds K. W. Brodlie, L. A. Carpenter, R. A. Earnshaw, J. R. Gallop, R. J. Hubbold, A. M. Mumford, C. D. Osland, P. Quarendon, Springer-Verlag, 300 pp. It is intended as a reference volume and contains chapters on Framework, Visualization Techniques, Data Facilities, Human Computer Interface, Applications, and Products. An Introduction gives an overview of the field, and a final chapter summarises the conclusions. There is also a Glossary of Terms, a comprehensive Bibliography, and a summary of Enabling Technologies.

3.5 Recommendations of the Workshop

The major recommendations of the workshop were twofold:

- Scientific visualization systems should be made widely available to a range of disciplines in the UK academic and research community.

- The concepts and benefits of scientific visualization should be made widely understood in the UK academic and research community.

These two recommendations lead to a set of specific recommendations concerning product evaluation, purchase and education and training to enable these to be implemented. These are:

a) Evaluations Leading to Proposals for the UK

Further evaluations and investigations are required to advise AGOCG on the solutions available for the provision to the community of scientific visualization in the short, medium and long term. The workshop set the framework for such evaluations and specific work needs to be addressed by AGOCG. This includes:

(i) Further work should be undertaken on the viability, merits, operational environments of the various distributed strategies for visualization systems. The results of this work should be distributed widely via an AGOCG Technical Report. The study should investigate the different hardware/software scenarios: this would include the use of dataflow systems (such as AVS, Khoros and apE) in distributed computing environments for different applications and the use and accessibility of supercomputer facilities, particularly from remote sites.

(ii) Recognising that parallel systems are becoming widely available, through at least the HPDS initiative, work should be undertaken to make the current visualization systems available on these machines. Further research into graphics and visualization systems for parallel applications is needed.

(iii) Evaluation of the various formats for generic application data and image transfer needs to be made and recommendations made.

(iv) Following the evaluations described in these recommendations AGOCG should extend the current Graphics Operational requirement to include the needs of scientific visualization which are addressed by the other recommendations of this workshop.

(v) There is a need to investigate how scientists solve their problems and how scientific visualization can assist.

(vi) Studies should be undertaken to consider alternative methods for interaction in relation to scientific visualization, for example, alternative ways to process multi-modal, multi-device dialogues.

b) Support, Education and Awareness

(i) Support needs to be given to this area and it is recommended that both the Computer Board and the SERC allocate one man year per year for 3 years to support general queries about systems and developments in this area. Other research councils and funding bodies are encouraged to allocate resources to this effort. Close working between these support people is essential.

(ii) It will be necessary to provide education in the use of these systems. AGOCG should recommend Computer Board funding within their Training Initiative for training, information exchange and development of training materials based on purchases and recommendations made over the period of the post in this area.

c) General

(i) There were both academic and industrial representatives at the workshop. There is a clear need to foster these links and to continue the exchange of insights and knowledge in this area in future collaborative work which should be encouraged and fostered by all parties.

(ii) In the light of the considerable implications of scientific visualization for networking, it is recommended that AGOCG forward the workshop report to the Joint Network Team (JNT) for their comments.

4. SCIENTIFIC VISUALIZATION TOOLS AND TECHNIQUES

4.1 Techniques

The schemata in Figure 4.1.1 outlines some of the current representation techniques.

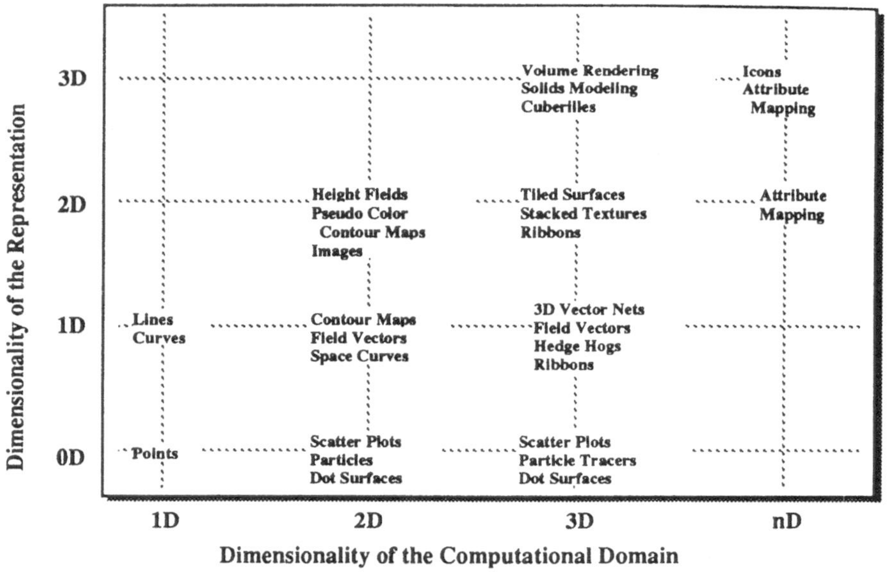

Fig 4.1.1 The visualization Mapping Space: the mapping from the computational domain into the visualization domain (Courtesy of Craig Upson)

The origin of several visualization techniques can be traced back to line-based two-dimensional contour maps. These extensions result in higher dimensional or more continuous representations as shown in Figure 4.1.2.

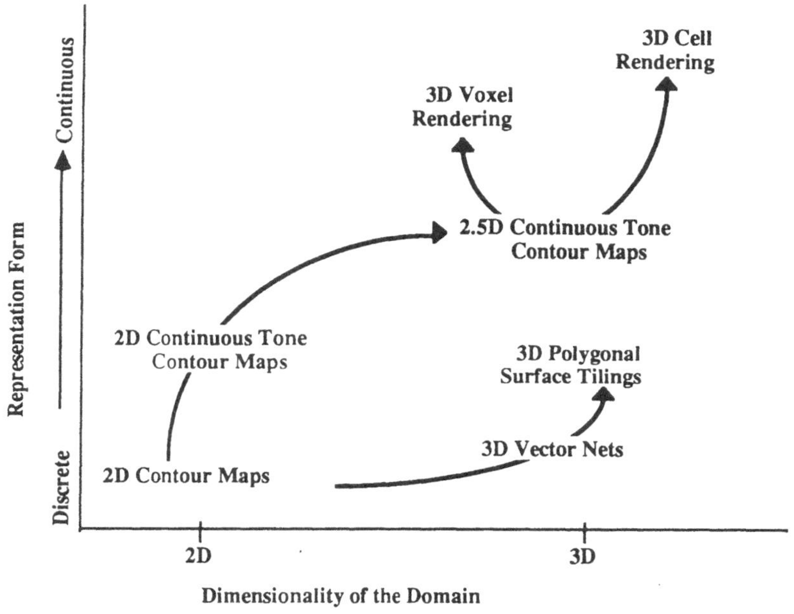

Fig 4.1.2 Three dimensional extensions of contouring

(Courtesy of Craig Upson)

Each technique can typically be modelled as three separate processes: a model building step, in which a continuous model is constructed from the discrete data; a step in which the best means of visualising the model is selected; and finally a rendering step. Traditionally the model building step has been the construction of an interpolant to fill out the data. Today however the increasing prevalence of large quantities of data to be analysed is focussing more attention on filtering and smoothing of data rather than on interpolation.

It should be noted that the current trend is to embed these techniques in an integrated, multi-functional system (the 'application builders' described in the Section 4.2), and so some related issues are also involved: image processing, animation, interaction and perception.

Volume rendering is used to view 3D data without the usual intermediate step of deriving a geometric representation which is then rendered. The volume representation uses voxels (volume elements) to determine visual properties, such as opacity, colour, and shading at each point in the computational domain. Several images are created by slicing the volume perpendicular to the viewing axis at a regular interval and compositing together the contributing images from back to front, thus summing voxel opacities and colours at each pixel. By rapidly changing the colour and opacity transfer functions, various structures are interactively revealed in the spatial domain.

A number of projects in the USA have demonstrated the benefits to medical and surgical planning from volume visualization techniques. Further information may be found in Frenkel (1989), Kaufman (1990), and Upson (1991).

4.2 Toolkits for Scientific Visualization

4.2.1 A Hierarchy of Tools

A variety of software tools for scientific visualization are now available, ranging from low-level graphics libraries, through tools and vision libraries, up to high-level applications builders (Fig 4.2.1). In the latter area, users are offered a variety of functional modules which they can aggregate together to produce a customised application. Such applications builders are available for the high-end of the workstation market and include products such as Stardent AVS, Wavefront Visualization software, Silicon Graphics Explorer, apE (University of New Mexico) and Khoros (University of New Mexico).

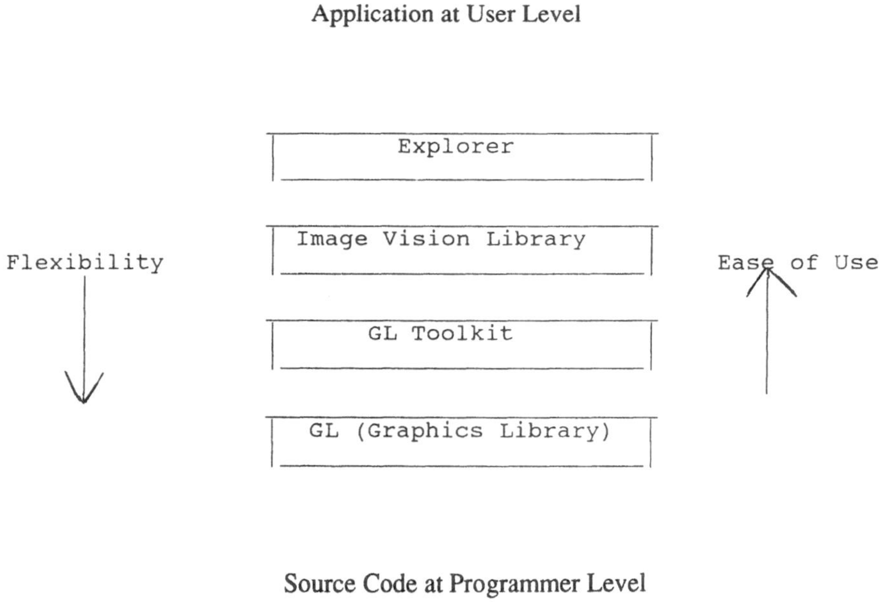

Figure 4.2.1 Levels of Software Function

4.2.2 Current Trends

The majority of current visualization systems are what are usually referred to as turnkey applications. They provide an improved user interface and in many cases a good match with certain specific applications. However, the user interface is often not very flexible nor extensible.

Application builders offer much improved flexibility and the promise of being applicable to a wide range of applications. However, at present most practical uses of visualization centre around turnkey systems, or one-off packages that are built out of component parts.

It is anticipated there there will be further developments in the following areas -

(i) Application builder products hold considerable promise, but their coverage of visualization techniques is sparse when compared with the sum of application needs. Exposure to real applications is needed in order to build up experience and an improved tools set.

(ii) Although most of the application builder products allow modules to be distributed, this capability is not well proven in real applications. Practical considerations of resource distribution and cost give rise to the need to carry out trials on specific practical distributed combinations.

(iii) Some components supporting visualization are becoming available on parallel hardware, but there are few signs at present that a complete visualization system can be easily tailored to exploit the capabilities of parallel hardware.

(iv) Validation of a visualization system is vital, but has hardly been considered in a systematic way. How do we know that that the visualization system is producing the correct response, or providing correct information?

(v) The extent to which application builders are easy to use has yet to be evaluated.

4.3 Applications of Scientific Visualization

Areas such as molecular modelling, computational fluid dynamics, oil exploration, and architectural modelling have already made significant advances by the use of visualization tools and techniques. These are areas where there is significant computation requirement and also substantial benefits from the use of visual information display and user interaction. There are many other potential application areas which have these as common requirements.

Visualization promotes new ways of looking at problems and fosters the use of inter-disciplinary approaches. Kunii and Enomoto (1991) demonstrate the use of an interactive tree model, FOREST, for visualizing the growth and development of forests over their life cycle. It also possible to use the model to investigate the effect of perturbation factors on the normal growth of the forest. This in turn has implications for the ecological environment.

Such models and their visualization can be thus used to increase our understanding of the growth processes in nature and the way these processes can be affected by apparently minor disturbances in the environment. For example, forestation affects the percentage of carbon dioxide in the atmosphere, which in turn affects global warming, which in turn affects the total area of deserts. Understanding these effects and the relationship between the variables is the key to understanding how to influence the future of the planet. Visualization can play a significant role in furthering this understanding

Kunii and Shinagawa (1991) summarise the way in which visualization concepts and techniques can be used to integrate diverse application areas.

5. DATA FACILITIES

Handling large volumes of data is an important aspect of scientific visualization. This has increased the strategic importance of data standards, data exchange utilities, and data management. HDF and netCDF are examples of current work in this area and the wide interest in them is indicative of the real need for adequate and efficient data handling tools. Commercial database suppliers are increasingly targetting products at the scientific market, in order to provide solutions to current needs and expected future requirements.

There is a multiplicity of current data formats in use and many of these have been summarised. A categorisation of data formats has been outlined e.g. generic, application-specific, and image. However, it is unrealistic to expect all existing data to be converted for input into a visualization system. What is needed is the ability to handle the more common formats such as CGM, GIF, TIFF, XDF, HDF and PostScript. Toolkits for data format conversion are becoming increasingly available (e.g. PBMPLUS and SDSC) although further work is needed in this area.

Agreed standards for data transfer are becoming highly desirable, particularly in the area of data compression.

Because of the way in which standardization efforts tend to arise from discipline-specific areas, the standards that are produced can be too restrictive in functionality or domain of applicability. At the same time, data has wide coverage across all disciplines and there are clearly advantages to wider coordination and collaboration across disparate areas. Here are some examples of data standards that have arisen from particular constituent areas, but are nevertheless of relevance to a wider field: CGM (computer graphics metafile), raster interchange formats (image processing), STEP (CAD/CAM data exchange), ASN.1 (encoding standards). Visual computing tends to bring together areas that have been historically separated such as computer graphics and image processing, graphics data and modelling data. Hopefully the current work in scientific visualization will encourage greater cross-disciplinary efforts that will be to the scientists' mutual advantage.

The development of image storage and picture compression standards such as JPEG are becoming increasingly important as the use of video becomes the norm for interchange of data and results. Such standards are already being embedded in products (e.g. the colour NeXT workstation). Other workstation vendors are also moving in this direction.

6. SCIENTIFIC VISUALIZATION INITIATIVES AT THE UNIVERSITY OF LEEDS

6.1 Introduction

The Scientific Visualization Group at the University of Leeds was formed on 2 October 1990 with the following objectives -

- o Get the most out of new equipment - Silicon Graphics Advanced Workstations, and the Silicon Graphics Computationally Intensive Facility
- o Coordinate developments that may be required in the area
- o Exchange experiences in different application areas
- o Facilitate planning and discussion
- o Share common software tools, where available
- o Address common problems
- o Disseminate information
- o Assist with teaching materials for courses U/G and P/G
- o Plan for any new products that may be needed
- o Establish electronic links between Workstations and the TV Centre
- o Investigate alternative methods for storing picture information

There have been nine meetings of the Scientific Visualization Group to date, and a number of sub-groups have been set up which in turn have had their own meetings.

Although most members of the Group are from science and engineering departments, links with the arts departments are currently being explored. The Department of Fine Art is interested to use visualization tools for creative applications. It is hoped that, in turn such creative and artistic talents will be of benefit to the scientific visualization community in the presentation of their images. Such cross-disciplinary ideas should be to the benefit of all.

6.2 Current Activities

Current activities of the Group are as follows:

- o An introductory document on Scientific Visualization has being compiled.
- o A survey of current work in the University is being done.
- o Details of visualization software available in the public domain have been obtained.
- o We have obtained Khoros from the University of New Mexico.
- o We have obtained apE from Ohio Supercomputer Center.
- o Details on how to best handle video have been obtained (University of Calgary, RMIT, University of Otago, RAL etc).
- o Methods for visualizing statistical and multi-dimensional data are being looked at.
- o CD Rom is being investigated.
- o Multi-media is being investigated.
- o Seminars on scientific visualization topics have been set in place.
- o New items of information are circulated to the Group by electronic mail.
- o New members are joining the Group as they realise the potential of the tools available.
- o Visualization software is being evaluated and procured.
- o Plans for setting up a video facility have been brought forward

6.3 Recent Work

A recent seminar in the University of Leeds brought together 9 key researchers to present their latest results using visualization tools. This has been written up as a separate report and a video is also being produced. Live demonstrations during the seminar enabled the audience to observe visualizations in real time. Application areas covered included computational fluid dynamics, chemical analysis, geophysics, ship hull design, image analysis, and general applications. A video consisting of the key points arising out of this seminar has been made.

6.4 Remote Visualization

Experiments are currently being set in place to investigate the viability of visualization across high speed networks (2 Mbit/sec and greater). We wish to determine optimum allocation of computational processes, so that users can do visualization from modest and low powered equipment on their desks. The visualization pipeline consists of the following processes -

APPLICATION → FILTER → MAP → RENDER
Raw data Data Geometry Display

We can arrange to put different processes on different machines and observe how the total system performs from the user viewpoint. For example, the Application can be run on a specialist parallel processor, the result can be fed to a local supercomputer for the Mapping, and then the image displayed on a local workstation. Alternatively, more of the computation and transformation could be done remote from the user and the image sent to the user's station in compressed format. Data compression and de-compression chips are now available for handling large images.

It is not clear what kind of interactive response would be obtained for networked visualization, nor the optimum kinds of configuration for different applications. The objective of our work is to do experimental measurements, and investigate the viability of low-cost user access to networked-based visualization tools.

7. RECENT TRENDS IN THE USA

A 3-day Workshop st Stanford University and NASA Ames in 1990 reviewed current developments and trends in scientific visualization, survey current hardware and software tools and capabilities, address current problems and issues, and plan for future developments to meet emerging requirements. It was the second Workshop in the series; the first being at the Jet Propulsion Laboratory in 1988.

The first day consisted of a review of current hardware and software offerings in the market place, presented primarily by vendors and technical developers. This included Stardent, Intelligent Light, United Technology, SUN, Visual Edge, Apple, SGI, and NASA Ames.

The second day surveyed issues, problems, and solutions from a University perspective and also from a laboratory perspective. The former were addressed by presentations from San Diego Supercomputer Centre, Pittsburg Supercomputer Centre, Ohio Supercomputer Centre, Stanford University, Rutgers University, University of Texas, and University of Lowell. The latter were addressed by Los Alamos Lab, Lawrence Livermore Lab, RIACS, and JPL.

The third day consisted of 5 Working Groups at NASA Ames. These had the following themes - Scientist's Environment, Shareable Environments, Representation of Complex Systems, Education, and Standards.

Some of the most significant matters which were raised were as follows -

- o It is apparent that there is wide range of emerging tools
- o Such tools are moving down-market to encompass high end Mac's and PC's, as well as up-market on to faster platforms
- o Development of 3D style guides, and dialogue management
- o How to integrate or resolve conflicting requirements in visualization
- o Multi-media systems
- o Development of appropriate standards
- o Data management and filtering (for terabytes of data)
- o Volume visualization

- o Taxonomy of concepts, operations, data types
- o Visumetrics
- o High speed networking aspects
- o Educational aspects

8. SOURCES OF FURTHER INFORMATION

This paper has presented a distillation of current techniques and applications of scientific visualization. The coverage is not exhaustive, but the tools and techniques that are described are representative of current practices in these areas. Further work is continuing on many of the topics highlighted in this paper.

A number of journals and societies are addressing the topic of scientific visualization, both from a theoretical and a practical point of view. Interested readers should consult the relevant literature such as IEEE Computer Graphics and its Applications, ACM Computer Graphics (and the Proceedings of the annual ACM SIGGRAPH conference), and the Proceedings of the recently established (1990) Visualization Conference organised by the IEEE Computer Society Technical Committee on Computer Graphics. The Visual Computer (published by Springer-Verlag) is the journal of the Computer Graphics Society (CGS) and publishes papers in the areas of computer vision, graphics, imaging, and applications. It includes detection and communication of visual data, intermediate data structures and processing techniques for visual data and computer graphics, and graphical representations of images. The Journal of Visualization and Computer Animation (published by Wiley) started in 1990 and publishes papers in the areas of animation and visualization techniques. Computer Graphics Forum is the journal of Eurographics and presents papers on the theory and practice of computer graphics. Its primary objectives are the dissemination of research results and of engineering developments to academic and industrial groups and individuals; reporting standardization activities; and reporting on events related to computer graphics. The British Computer Society has a special interest group on Computer Graphics and Displays that covers the general areas of vision, design, computer graphics, displays, human factors, and applications. A further journal, the Supercomputing Review, contains useful information on aspects of supercomputing. The journal Computers and Graphics (published by Pergamon Press) presents papers on computer graphics.

9. CONCLUSIONS

This paper has provided a summary of current progress in the area of scientific visualization and its current and prospective applications.

9.1 Applications

At present, applications mainly use special purpose solutions and software. The more general purpose packages have yet to replace these. This is probably due to the current investment of time and effort in particular applications areas to develop specialised programs which do what is currently required. These become the base lines from which further developments are made. Moving to a more general software platform will probably not be perceived to be advantageous until the following conditions are satisfied -

(i) Easy access to high power computation facilities so that there are no performance or interaction limitations.

(ii) Easy migration paths to enable users to specify their required functionality using general purpose software.

(iii) Successful use of visualization tools by pioneering scientists in particular disciplines, so that use of them spreads because of their reputation and functional advantages.

(iv) Easy to use facilities for exploiting the new hardware facilities that are increasingly becoming the norm, e.g. producing video output, utilizing multi-media interfaces, and effective utilization of supercomputer facilities across networks.

Techniques and products concentrating on three-dimensional visualization are readily available, since this is a common requirement across a number of application areas. Thus application areas requiring this are well catered for.

Other areas such as two-dimensional data sets with variable visualizations and data sets with a larger number of dimensions are less well covered, and further developments are required in these areas.

9.2 Infrastructure Support for Scientific Visualization

The current High Performance Computing and Communications Initiative in the USA has been formulated to provide a major upgrade in the computational resource available to scientists and engineers. The objective is to provide an enabling resource for previously unsolved problems in disciplines such as chemistry, meteorology, and astronomy. One such proposed project is the Eos earth observation satellite system which will produce 10 exp 12 bits of information every day. A typical supercomputer centre in the USA currently has only built up around 2 terabytes of information in its user files in the past five years. Thus projects such as Eos will generate data at a rate considerably greater than current experience! In order to facilitate network access to supercomputer facilities to provide the resource to process such data, a National Research and Education Network is proposed. This would consist of fibre optic cables capable of carrying information at rates over 1 Mbit per sec.

Such considerations in the area of infrastructure support need to made in other countries on a national basis, in order to be able to plan for the facilities that are required.

9.3 Other uses of Visualization Tools

Tools such as those described in this volume can be also used by those whose primary interest is not in the scientific content of the information presented, but rather the creative or aesthetic value. Barlow et al (1990) outlines how artists create effects and explores issues at the interface between art and science.

Artists and sculptors have been using computer-assisted tools for a number of years (Lansdown and Earnshaw, 1989) and these tools often promote new and unexpected ways of creating and developing images and objects. Thus visualization tools are not confined to scientific visualization but can be used in all areas where the user is seeking to create and manipulate information via visual means.

9.4 Virtual Reality Systems

Virtual reality is a set of hardware and software technologies to enable the user's body and senses to be translated into the information space to be examined. For example, a data glove can enable a user's hand to be projected into a 3D environment. By manipulating the glove the user interacts with the virtual world and can 'handle' or 'move' objects and issue commands. Alternative forms of interaction include body suits and data helmets with built-in stereoscopic viewscreens to enable the user to 'enter' the virtual world. It is clear that these environments offer considerable potential in applications where the user has to interact in real time with objects in the viewing space, or develop an understanding of spatial relationships, or receive training in some particular procedure. Such techniques could be practised in the virtual world without the risk of expensive and dangerous mistakes. As such, they are developments and generalisations of procedures and techniques that have been used in flight simulators for years. However, flight simulators are expensive and usually only available to corporations such as airlines with the revenue to afford them! Current trends in visualization systems are to provide similar functionality but at much lower cost and for more generalised applications.

Such systems are capable of displaying large amounts of 3D information. It is possible to conceive of a scenario where a scientific visualization system interfaced to the user in a way that most suited the user's requirements. Such requirements could be to explore large data sets; look for similarities in structure or appearance of objects; investigate spatial relationships; or run simulations and observe the results directly.

Accessing information in large data sets has analogues with hypertext systems, where the user is provided with facilities for exploring data often using multi-media tools. It is anticipated that the development of interfaces for multi-media systems will also have benefits for visualization systems. Fairchild et al (1988) describe the use of a 3D navigator to access a large hypermedia network and display the results.

9.5 Importance of Scientific Visualization

The increasing occurrence of large volumes of data, high-powered workstations, new styles of interaction and user interfaces, fast networks, and new techniques for data display are all changing the nature of computing and what the user can expect from the tools now available. Scientific visualization encompasses all these areas and significant developments are expected in the future (Thalmann et al, 1991; Upson,1991)

10. REFERENCES

Selected Bibliography

Barlow H., C. Blakemore, M. Weston-Smith (Eds), "Images and Understanding: Thoughts about Images, Ideas and Understanding" Cambridge University Press, 1990.

Brodlie K. W., L. A. Carpenter, R. A. Earnshaw, J. R. Gallop, R. J. Hubbold, A. M. Mumford, C. D. Osland, P. Quarendon (Eds) "Scientific Visualization - Techniques and Applications" Springer-Verlag, 284 pp, 1992.

Dyer D. S., "A Dataflow Toolkit for Visualization", IEEE Computer Graphics & Applications, Vol 10, No 4, pp 60-69, July 1990.

Earnshaw R. A. and N. Wiseman "An Introductory Guide to Scientific Visualization", Springer-Verlag, pp100, to be published 1992.

Fairchild K. M., S. E. Poltrock, G. W. Furnas "Semnet: 3D graphics representations of large knowledge bases", in Guindon R (Ed), 'Cognitive Science and Its Applications for Human Computer Interaction', Lawrence Erlbaum Associates,1988

Frenkel K. A., "The Art and Science of Visualizing Data", Communications of the ACM, Vol 31, No 2, pp 110-121, 1988.

Frenkel K. A., "Volume Rendering" Communications of the ACM, Vol 32, No 4, pp 426-435, 1989

Kaufman A. (Ed), "Volume Visualization", IEEE Press, 1990

Kunii T. L. and H. Enomoto, "Forest: An Interacting Tree Model for Visualizing Forest Formation Processes by Algorithmic Computer Animation", Computer Animation 91, N. Magnenat-Thalmann and D. Thalmann (Eds), pp 191-213, Springer-Verlag, 1991

Kunii T. L. and Y. Shinagawa, "Visualization: New Concepts and Techniques to Integrate Diverse Application Areas" "Scientific Visualization of Physical Phenomena", N. M. Patrikalakis (Ed), pp 3-25, Springer-Verlag, 1991

Lansdown R. J., R. A. Earnshaw (Eds), "Computers in Art, Design and Animation", Springer-Verlag, 1989.

McCormick B. H., T. A. DeFanti, M. D. Brown (Eds), "Visualization in Scientific Computing" ACM SIGGRAPH Computer Graphics, Vol 21, No 6, Nov 1987

McCormick B. H., T. A. DeFanti, M. D. Brown (Eds), "Visualization in Scientific Computing", IEEE Computer, Vol 23, No 8, Aug 1989

Nielson G. M., B. Shriver, L. Rosenblum, (Eds) "Visualization in Scientific Computing", IEEE Press, 1990.

Patrikalakis N. M. (Ed) "Scientific Visualization of Physical Phenomena", Springer-Verlag, pp 690, 1991

Thalmann D. (Ed), "Scientific Visualization and Graphics Simulation" Wiley, 1990.

Magnenat Thalmann N. and D. Thalmann (Eds) "New Trends in Animation and Visualization", Wiley, 1991

Tufte E. R., "The Visual Display of Quantitative Data" Graphics Press, USA

Tufte E.R., "Envisioning Information", Graphics Press, USA, 1990

Upson C., T. Faulhaber, D. Kamins, D. Laidlaw, D. Schlegel, J. Vroom, R. Gurwitz, A. van Dam, "The Application Visualization System: A Computational Environment for Scientific Visualization", IEEE Computer Graphics & Applications, Vol 9, No 4, pp 30-42, 1989

Upson C., "Volumetric Visualization Techniques" in "State of the Art in Computer Graphics - Visualization and Modelling", Eds D. F. Rogers, R. A. Earnshaw, Springer-Verlag, 1991

AUTHOR BIOGRAPHY

Rae Earnshaw is Head of Computer Graphics at the University of Leeds, with interests in graphics algorithms, scientific visualization, display technology, CAD/CAM, and human-computer interface issues. He has been a Visiting Professor at Illinois Institute of Technology, Chicago, USA, Northwestern Polytechnical University, China, and George Washington University, Washington DC, USA. He was a Director of the NATO Advanced Study Institute on "Fundamental Algorithms for Computer Graphics" held in Italy, England, in 1985, a Co-Chair of the BCS/ACM International Summer Institute on "State of the Art in Computer Graphics" held in Scotland in 1986, and a Director of of the NATO Advanced Study Institute on "Theoretical Foundations of Computer Graphics and CAD" held in Italy in 1987. He is a member of ACM, IEEE, CGS, EG, and a Fellow of the British Computer Society.

Dr Earnshaw has authored and edited 12 books on graphics algorithms, computer graphics, and associated topics, and published numerous papers in these areas.

Dr Earnshaw Chairs the Scientific Visualization Group at the University of Leeds, is a member of the Editorial Board of The Visual Computer, a Committee Member of the board of the Computer Graphics Society, and Chair of the British Computer Society Computer Graphics and Displays Group.

Address: Head of Graphics, University of Leeds, Leeds LS2 9JT, England.

Topology and Visualization: From Generic Singularities to Combinatorial Shape Modelling

Yannick L. Kergosien

ABSTRACT

Differential topology permits analysing qualitatively how interactive continuous controls modify the views in a visualization system. In realistic visualization, data usually have differential structures that permit studying their topologies by means of singularities (e.g. with Morse theory). Objects can be simplified and modelled with graphs (e.g. Reeb graphs) or complexes to allow algebraic topology for computer assisted comparison. Singularity theory permits describing the generic effects of control in relation with some classical geometric properties of the visualized object. Generic patterns seen on particular views provide clues about the effects of control. Bifurcation diagrams in control space also provide shape coding. The results about controlled projections and controlled sections of smooth surfaces cover many of the situations arising in medical imaging.

Keywords: Topology, Singularity, Generic, Morse, Shape, Surface, Medical Imaging. Computer graphics.

1. INTRODUCTION

Visualization can use very different levels of abstraction, from the simple display of images (simulating the physical vision of real objects) to the graphical conceptualization of a relation (simplifying a complex set of data). Topology can also apply to very different kinds of mathematical objects, from classical smooth surfaces in 3-D space (with induced coordinate systems, differential structure and particular metric), to combinatorial objects like complexes of all kinds (e.g. graphs or abstract polyhedra defined only by incidence relations between set elements called vertices, edges, and faces, independently of any spatial representation). Topology relates these different levels of generality : for instance, using differential topology and the generic properties of singularities on an object like a differentiable surface, tools like Morse theory can get some combinatorial model of it and extract even more general information pertaining to algebraic topology. Precisely one can also classify in terms of levels of generality the tasks for which the users of visualization systems would often like some computer assistance : (1) analysis (e.g. of images) usually consists of some abstraction from complex data; (2) model specification and building calls for the manipulation of conceptual objects and the exchange of limited amounts of selected information between the operator and the system; (3)synthethizing some concrete instanciations of conceptual models can be required for visualizing them under realistic presentations.

We shall take concrete medical imaging situations to examine the use of topology in visualization. This will lead us to emphasize the role of interactivity and control in visualization and more generally in shape understanding or coding; to take control into account we shall embed it in the visualization structure. Especially for such level of reality as sonographic sections or radiologic projections, the control has continuous structure and topology is fundamental to the conceptualization necessary for the user to interpret the display and select proper views from the visualization system. There, the sign systems taken from differential topology can easily be used directly by the human operator and also be implemented as machine algorithms. This possibility for topological concepts to be used both by man and machines is certainly a major property : One can hope use them as the basis for man machine communication languages as universal icons, and perhaps also, with increasing processing unit complexity, eventually for more general inter-system communication.

2. VISUALIZATION, CONTROL, AND TOPOLOGY

2.1 The Place Of Control In Visualization

We shall consider visualization to be an interactive process where a set of data is mapped to the attributes of a screen, the characteristics of this mapping being partly controlled by some input parameters. Visualization systems thus output screens to a human operator upon input commands from him a bit like a database outputs answers upon queries. Visualization can use data and produce displays at very different levels of abstraction and can make use of different degrees of processing, from the simple display of realistic images (either recorded from real data or synthesized from a model) to the graphical conceptualization of some relations (either recorded or to be extracted from some complex data).

We shall focus on visualizations that remain close to physical presentations, taking examples from medical imaging. Contrary to common databases the input parameters which control the presentation can approximate continuous variables and have continuous effect on the visual outputs instead of being of some discrete conceptual type. In medicine, for instance, even with digital imaging visualization still reproduces physical processes like anatomical sections or radiologic projection with the screen representing a piece of physical space. Processing uses mostly linear transforms with limited and homogeneous information loss. The control on angles, slice positions, or filter characteristics also remains continuous and can be very problematic for the user. Interestingly, since much of the processing (the associative and conceptual part) is left to another system (a brain), designers must care for inter-system cooperation and communication. One should not think of visualization only as a temporary alternative to fully automated processing but also as a way of conveying complex information to man through channels broader than text interfaces. The broadest channel can be the input channel, like in a movement teaching system where limited output can guide the search for complex motor patterns. Similarly, for instance in sonography just as in tactile perception, the difficulty of shape analysis can lie more in understanding how the control modifies the view than in the analysis of isolated views.

2.2. The Need For Topology

Accepting to restrict processing and outputing views that still need some human interpretation, one should interface with the tasks that brains can most easily perform. Man is good at visual detection of qualitative patterns. He can be helped by being taught what visual patterns to look for and how to relate them to control decisions. One should thus view as part of a visualization system any set of visual rules that can enable man to use it. Looking for them can be part of the design effort. As these patterns should not include precise quantitative relations, it is natural to look for some sort of topological features.

Artificial image processing systems can also use topology. Using a particular kind of geometry to study a given object amounts to selecting part of the information relative to it. A first reason to use topology and the related strong simplification can be of algorithmic nature, to render tractable such tasks as comparison or matching. From a rich set of data, it can thus be desirable to be able to extract and maintain models with different degrees of simplification adapted to the tasks to be performed, with a hierarchical structure for the whole set of representations. Several levels of the same structure can interact just as in multiresolution image processing or in multiscale numerical analysis.

A second reason is communicational : Even if the objects to be processed by a visualization system are known with great accuracy, they must often be related to coarser representations such as the knowledge that human experts can have of them, that can happen to be only topological. A database can thus have to maintain more or less conceptual objects for which the base level is not complete. These objects will call for instanciation tools to hierarchically provide default specifications for visualization (instances can be produced deterministically using added constraints such as optimality, or randomly to enable statistical analysis and inference). Conceptual layers of objects are also important for output, e.g. to give conceptual explanations on internal objects, what can consist of the display of simplified models like polyhedra or graphs. With the development of simulation, a greater need is growing for data understanding, organizing and selection, what calls for such automated explanations, and more generally interaction assistance.

3. SINGULARITY THEORY AND THE FORMALISM OF MAPPING CONTROLS.

To qualitatively understand how he controls the views, an operator can explore the space of available controls and record the values for which he notices a qualitative change in the view. Singularity theory provides a mathematical formalism adapted to this setting. What we are going to describe is close to the formalism of Elementary Catastrophe Theory (Thom 1972), but here the control space will be structured according to morphological criteria like the types of general mappings (not only functions) instead of relying on the states of gradient dynamical systems.

3.1. Singularity Theory : Basic Concepts.

Differentiable manifolds. The spaces on which singularity theory is applied are differentiable manifolds; we shall only consider finite dimensional manifolds. Given an integer n, a n-dimensional *manifold* is a topological space such that any neighbourhood of a point can be mapped in a one-to-one way onto an open subset of the n-dimensional space R^n. Such a mapping is called a *chart* and provides coordinates for the points in the domain of the chart. For the manifold to be p times differentiable (i.e. of class C^p), one requires that for points in the range of two different charts, the transformation from one coordinate system to the other should be p times differentiable. A manifold can thus be seen as being made of pieces of R^n overlapping in a differentiable way. For instance, a circle can be given the structure of a 1-dimensional manifold (using at least two charts onto line segments), the surface of a sphere can be made a 2-manifold (using two charts onto disks), or the surface of a torus a 2-manifold (using four charts on rectangles). Removing knotted circles from R^3 gives examples of 3-manifolds (charts onto cubes) with non trivial global properties, and higher dimensional manifolds appear for instance as configuration spaces of robot arms (for which boundaries must be introduced with charts to half spaces).

Differentiable mappings, singularities. By means of charts, a mapping from a p-manifold to a n-manifold can be numerically expressed piecewise using mappings from pieces of R^p to pieces of R^n (i.e. n functions of p variables for each one of these mappings). A mapping is of class C^k if once expressed using charts and coordinates its components are k times continuously differentiable. Still with local coordinates, one can compute a jacobian matrix at each point. Its rank is at most min(n, p); points at which the rank of the jacobian matrix reaches this maximal value are called *regular*, the others are called *singular* or *critical* and the points on which they are mapped are called *singular values*.For instance, functions of a single variable are singular where their graph has a horizontal tangent. One often speaks loosely of a *singularity* to mean either the mapping, its graph or its behaviour near a singular point.

Mapping equivalence. The C^p *type* of a mapping is the precise notion for what we shall call the "qualitative features of a mapping". Two mappings f, g, from a C^p manifold M (the source space) to a C^p manifold N (the target space) are defined to be C^p equivalent (fig. 1) if there exist h, a C^p diffeomorphism of M, and k, a C^p diffeomorphism of N, such that for any x in M : $k(f(x))=g(h(x))$, what means that f can be transformed into g using coordinate changes in the source and the target. This constitutes an equivalence relation on the set $C^p(M, N)$ of C^p mappings from M to N, and two equivalent mappings are said to have the same C^p type.

Stability. A mapping is *stable* when it has in $C^p(M, N)$ a whole neighbourhood of equivalent mappings, with the Whitney topology on $C^p(M, N)$ (involving the higher derivatives up to order p). This means that its qualitative features resist small perturbations as long as these remain small enough, i.e. the graph of the function is neither moved too much nor locally deformed in a too sharp way (fig.2). For instance, the function $f(x)=x^3$ is not stable (fig.3) since adding to it a perturbation $g(x)=ax$ will change its type whatever the smallness of a. In fact, the perturbed function x^3+ax takes a different type according to the sign of a. On the other hand, $f(x)=x^2$ resists small C^2 perturbations, taking into account the crucial fact that to be small in the topology of $C^2(R,R)$, a perturbing function should also have small first and second order derivatives. In order to check the stability of a mapping, one needs only study its singularities.

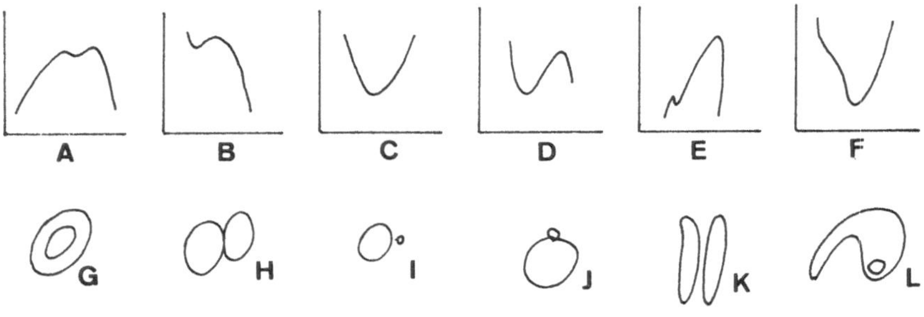

Fig. 1 : Equivalence of functions and patterns. Equivalent couples are A-E, B-D, C-F for functions (top), and G-L, H-J, I-K for plane patterns (image sets of mappings from two circles to the plane).

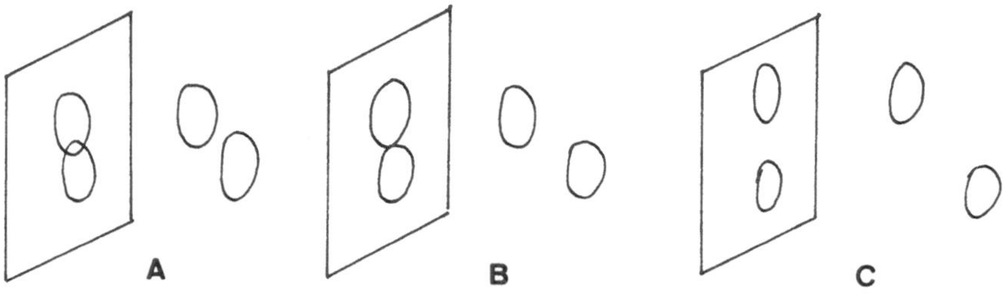

Fig. 2 : Projections A and C are stable, B is not.

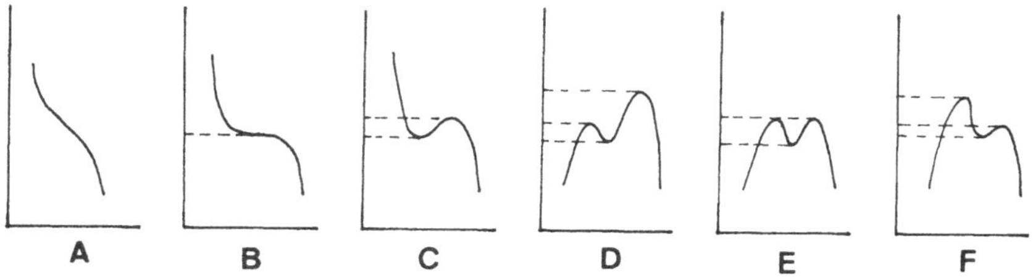

Fig. 3 : A, C, D, F are stable, B is locally unstable, E is multi-locally unstable .

Genericity. *Genericity* is a topological way of defining the set of exceptions to a property to be negligible. A property is generic if, given a topology on the set of objects on which this property makes sense, the set of objects which have the property is open and dense. In many cases, the genericity of a property implies probabilistic almost certainty (i.e. the probability of drawing at random an object that does not have the considered generic property is zero). This equivalence depends on the kind of probability model which generates the random objects under study. Genericity theorems typically relie on converting properties into geometric transversality conditions in spaces of higher derivatives, using (Thom 1956); see Hirsch (1976) and Golubitsky-Guillemin (1973) as introductory textbooks on singularity theory.

3.2. From Patterns To Types of Mappings.

We shall consider anatomical surfaces modelled as 2-manifolds embedded in 3-D space. The patterns visualized on screen will be attached to certain mappings defined on the embedded surface : cross sections are the counter-images of a height function defined on it, and projection patterns are sets of singular values when projecting the surface to a plane. Two patterns (as subsets of the plane) can be defined as qualitatively equivalent if they can be transformed into each other using a C^p diffeomorphism of the plane. Equivalence of patterns (and families of patterns) will however be studied by looking for the C^p equivalence (or some extension of it) of the associated mappings. This is to involve the way the patterns are produced (stability has to refer to such conditions) and to account for the correspondence between the patterns and what they represent. As a simpler case, if two plane curves (possibly with self-intersections or cusps) are the images of a circle under two C^p equivalent mappings f and g, then they are C^p equivalent (the diffeomorphism of the source circle cares for the arbitrariness of parameterizing). There may be some difficulties translating some natural visual equivalences in the C^p formalism. For instance, four curves crossing at the same point cannot in general be transformed into four other curves crossing at the same point by a diffeomorphism, due to the linear invariant called cross-ratio. On the other hand, taking homeomorphisms ($p=0$) does not permit to recognize angles on curves. This however can be solved technically both in a mathematical and image analysis settings.

To be observable, the changes of the C^p type should not be chaotic. Stability of a C^p type guarantees that once observed it will persist for slighly different controls and operating conditions, i.e. for a whole region of the control space, whatever the uncontrolled slight perturbations. The stability of a mapping depends only on its singularities and stability generally corresponds to a kind of simplicity of the mapping at its critical points and singular values. There is generally a finite list of local types of singularities for the stable mappings. Stability also eliminates such particular situations as the coincidence of two curves in the plane. In the favorable cases, the theory typically produces theorems saying that any mapping can be approximated by a stable one. One can thus untangle the situation by a slight perturbation and use the list of corresponding singularities to deduce important geometrical facts, such as producing a small number of candidate equivalent polynomial models of the mapping just from observing the qualitative features of its sets of critical points or singular values. Often, also, one can prove that stability is a generic property, so that in many probabilistic settings one can consider with probability equal to one that a random mapping is already stable.

3.3. Mapping Controls

To study the transitions between stable C^p types under some control, one has to introduce similar concepts of equivalence, type, and stability, for objects that embed the whole control structure and that we call mapping controls. A mapping control is a mapping from the space $A \dot{\times} C$ (A : source or object space; C : control space; $A \dot{\times} C$: product space or fiber bundle over C) to the space $B \dot{\times} C$ (B : target or screen space; $B \dot{\times} C$: product space or fiber bundle over C). Equivalence between mapping controls is defined as for mappings, except that the diffeomorphisms of $A \dot{\times} C$ and $B \dot{\times} C$ are required to respect the bundle structures over C, i.e. to commute with the projections on C. This means that two controls are equivalent if there is a diffeomorphism between the control spaces so as to get the same topological types of views (mappings from A to B) for corresponding values of the control. Here again stability can sometimes be proven to be generic and a finite list of all the stable transitions be described. One can then describe the set of values of the control that produce a transition. It is a kind of bifurcation set in the control space, separating regions leading to different stable view types. The related organization of the control space in open sets, curves and points, generalizes into the so-called obturation (or collimation) stratification. The corresponding transitional singularities on the view can be described and serve as clues on the screen to detect qualitative changes. The points of A that produce these transitions constitute the so-called singular set, in fact a whole singular stratification in correspondence with the obturation stratification. According to the number of points of A that are involved in transitional singularities, one distinguished local transitions (one point) and multi-local singularities (several points).

We shall use these concepts to study the structure of view control in two cases : In the case of controlled plane sections of a surface we take as controlled mappings the height functions on the surface (the level lines of which are the cross-sections by horizontal planes), with the control rotating the surface in space (in fact we shall consider an equivalent setting). In the case of parallel ray projections of a surface the control also rotates the surface in space. The studies in these two cases relie on the generic properties of the points on the surface that are responsible for the unstability of the controlled mapping.

4. THE GENERIC STRUCTURE OF VIEW CONTROL FOR SECTIONS OF SMOOTH SURFACES.

4.1. Sectional Imaging in Medicine.

Sectional images physically appear in microscopic imaging, and are diigitally reconstructed in sonography (ultrasound) and C.A.T., M.R.I., or P.E.T. scanners. They are often used as reference presentations for precise analysis since choosing the right cross-section permits isolating any point in space somewhere on the screen. The 3-D body region to be studied is made of anatomical compartments separated by smooth surfaces. The compartments have approximately constant but different densities or textures on the cross-sectional image, so that after segmentation one can reduce the problem of reconstructing the body in space to that of reconstrucing the separation surface in space. Choosing the proper cross-sections for image analysis may however be difficult, especially in sonography where the slice is chosen by manually positioning the probe on the patient's skin and where the organs can move under it. In other cases, such as for C.A.T. scanner, a single common axis can be chosen with precision for all the cross sections, so that only the levels of the slices have to be chosen. In that case we shall speak of a family of parallel sections. In that case also, positioning the level of a cross-section is generally guided by viewing projections on a plane parallel to the axis (scout views).

We shall successively consider different visualization structures, progressively extending the control available on section position. The generic effects of the control on the views will thus be described in the case of single sections, in the case of single families of parallel sections, and in the case of completely controlled sections (families of parallel sections with control on the direction of the common axis). The first two cases only apply results from Morse theory.

4.2. Morse's Lemma

Morse theory (Morse-Cairns 1969, Bott 1960, Milnor 1963, Hirsch 1976) was historically the first instance of a scheme that we shall use repeatedly. One uses differential structures to study the topology of a space. Some topological transitions are studied on polynomial local models, i.e. the Taylor approximations at singular points of a differentiable mapping. For these changes to be simple enough one has to consider mappings with simple enough singularities and one proves that any mapping can be approximated by such a mapping ("genericity untangles the situation"). Morse theory deals with the simpler case of functions from a manifold to R (think of our surface as the manifold). Morse's Lemma gives such approximation theorem and tells what system of simple singularities is enough to account for the topological features of a function of several variables.

Hessian matrix, index of a singularity, Morse function : For a mapping from a n-manifold to R (we shall call such mappings : Functions on a manifold), a point is *critical* if and only if all partial derivatives are null. At such a point the function is thus approximated by a quadratic form based on second order partial derivatives, the matrix of which is called the *Hessian matrix* and has terms $h[i,j]=d^2f/dx^i dx^j$. The maximum dimension of a space on which this quadratic form is negative definite is called the *index* of the singularity (it is also the number of minus signs in the reduced form). A singularity is *non degenerate* at a critical point $(a_1,..,a_p)$ if the hessian matrix has rank n there. In a neighbourhood of that point a mapping equivalence permits to write the function as

$$f(a_1+x_1,.., a_p+x_p)=f(a_1,..,a_p) - x_1^2 - ... - x_i^2 + x_{i+1}^2 + ... + x_p^2,$$

where i is the index of the singularity. A function on a manifold is called a *Morse function* if none of its singularities are degenerate.

The key result is Morse's lemma, saying any function can be approximated by a Morse function. Near a singularity, a surface in space can be represented in Monge's form as the graph of a height function : $z= f(x,y)$, and approximating the function is equivalent to approximating the surface. Singularity of the height function corresponds for the surface to having horizontal tangent plane, i.e. tangential cross-section by a horizontal plane. Morse's lemma means that after slight perturbation of the surface, any singularity of the height function will correspond to only one of the three following local models of surface :

$$z= x^2 + y^2 \text{ (index=0)}; \quad z = x^2 - y^2 \text{ (index=1)}; \quad z = - x^2 - y^2 \text{ (index=2)}.$$

Each one of these local shapes can be recognized either from the type of cross section (a crossing for index 1, a point for the others) and the characteristics of neighbouring slices (closed curve above for index 0, beneath for index 2, fig. 4). The critical points of a Morse function are isolated, so that for a compact manifold, there are only a finite number of them.

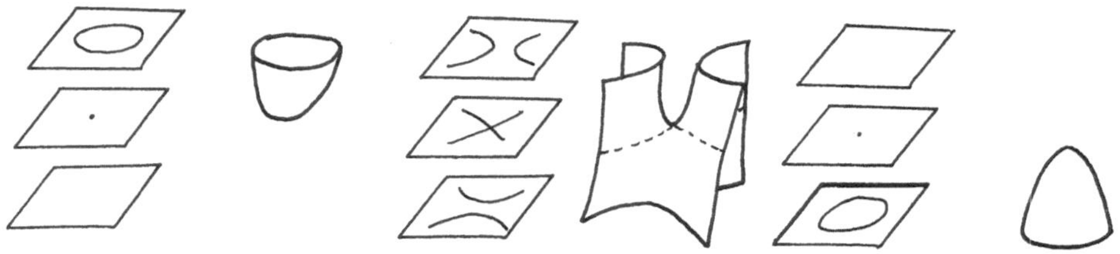

Fig. 4 : The three local models of Morse singularities and their sections at, above, and below the critical level.

The whole theory is nowadays interpreted in the more general theory of singularities of differentiable mappings : Requiring further for Morse functions that no two singular values are equal, one gets the stable functions on the manifold, and the approximation result can be strengthened into "the stability of functions on a manifold is a generic property" (the result does not extend to all kinds of mappings, see Mather 1972). Genericity provides a probabilistic justification for assuming a priori, in some settings, that the original height function is (almost surely) already Morse. For instance, if the embedded surfaces are randomly drawn using splines with absolutely continuous distributions, the probability for the height function to be Morse and stable is equal to one.

4.3. Single cross-section of a surface.

Generically a function defined on a compact manifold is Morse with a finite number of singular values. The level of a single horizontal cross-section is thus generically different from any of the singular values so that the cross-section of the surface is transversal, i.e. the cross-section is made of disjoint closed curves. Of course the topology of such cross-section depends on the level, but it is stable under small changes of the level.

4.4. Generic family of parallel cross-sections

One can assume the planes to be horizontal. The intersections of a surface by the family of horizontal planes are the level curves (like topographic contours) of its height function, which is generically Morse. Morse theory says that the topological type of the cross section does not change between two critical levels. The topological behaviour of the cross-sectional pattern near a critical level is found by studying the local model of the singularity of the same index. Crossing a critical level results in the appearance or disappearance of a closed curve (for index 0 or 2), or the merging of two curves (index 1)(fig. 4). For visualization and from the user's point of view, one can guarantee the reliability of the equivalence between crossing a particular type of critical level, recording a corresponding topological change in the sequence of sections and observing the corresponding transitional pattern (point or crossing) if precisely stabilized by the operator.

The index of each singularity relates to classical geometric properties of the surface at the (critical) point where the sectional plane is tangent : indices 0 and 2 occur at elliptic points (i.e. where the Gaussian curvature is positive, like on an ellipsoid) and index 1 occurs at hyperbolic points (negative Gaussian curvature, like on a saddle).

4.5. Controlled family of parallel cross-sections (generic surface)

We shall now consider full control on the sectional plane, like in sonography where the effects of moving the probe are instantly apparent on the screen and where it is precisely from what he sees on the screen that the operator decides how to control the position of the probe. A plane in space can be specified by one of the two oriented lines perpendicular to it from the origin (we call it axis) and the signed abcissa of the intersection on that axis. With this convention, a family of parallel planes is an oriented stack of planes (with top and bottom) and the different oriented stacks correspond bijectively (diffeomorphically) to the points of a sphere (the oriented directions in space). We shall consider a given surface and identify each set of parallel cross sections of it with the corresponding height function. The control of the sectional plane is thus decomposed into a control on the section level within the family of parallel planes plus a control on the axis of the family within the directions on the sphere.

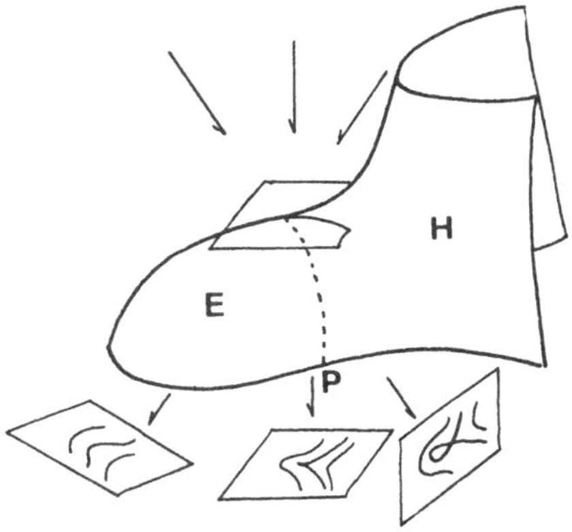

Fig. 5 : The family of sections parallel to tangent plane at a parabolic point is unstable and intermediary between families tangent at elliptic points and hyperbolic points (E : elliptic , P : parabolic, H : hyperbolic).

To study the structure of this view control, one looks for the axis directions that produce a qualitativre change in the height function (i.e. in the sequence of corresponding cross-sections). This amounts to considering the sphere as control space and recording on it the control values that produce qualitative change. The theory of mapping controls (Kergosien 1981, 1983) permits to show that such changes occur only when one of the critical points of the height function is a parabolic point on the surface (fig.5). It has been proven (Kergosien-Thom 1980) that generically the set of parabolic points of a smoothly embedded surface consists of smooth curves, with a limited number of possible local models for the surface at each of its points. As the axis has to be perpendicular to the surface at a critical point, it easy to compute from a given surface the set of axis directions that will produce a qualitative change in the sequence of parallel sections of a smooth surface. One computes first the curves of parabolic points from the equations of the surface (e.g. solving $rt-s^2=0$ in Monge's form) and then one maps them to the sphere using the local normal directions. The simplest non-trivial case (the "fossette" dent, the projections of which we shall also study) shows for the bifurcation diagram on the sphere a "Napoleon hat" curve with two cusps corresponding to the "godrons" of the surface (fig. 6).

The transitional directions correspond to the appearance of some definite cross-sectional patterns in the stack of cross-sections (at one of the critical levels fig. 5-6). This permits to detect from screen what kind of qualitative change is occuring in the stack. Most of these patterns consist of a sectional cusp (with tip on the parabolic curve). They can be interpreted as a topological transitions between stable sectional patterns : They cancel at the same time a crossing and a closed curve. Visualizing them is relatively easy as one should only cross a curve in control space. Some exceptional patterns correspond to sections tangent at some 2-codimensional (isolated) points on the parabolic lines (the "godrons") and need the precise control of two parameters to be observed (one should reach the isolated cusp points on the sphere of controls).

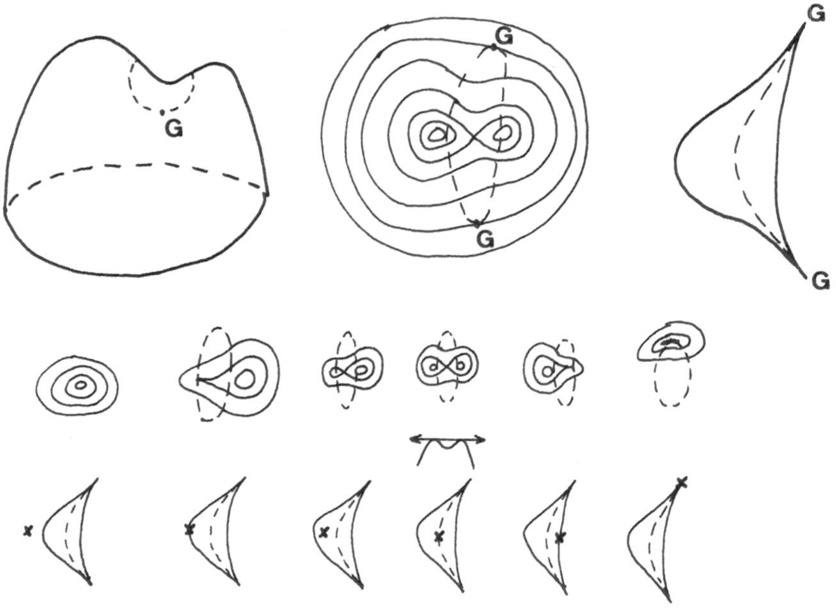

Fig. 6 : Fossette surface. Top left and middle : Perspective view and topographic contours (dotted lines: parabolic curve, G : godron). Top right : bifurcation set on the sphere of directions (dotted line : multi-local stratum). Bottom : sequences of cross-sections at the different strata of the bifurcation diagram.

Other changes relate to the global structure of the sections. Height functions and the related section stacks are unstable if two peaks have the same height. Such transitions are called multi-local. They occur when one of the sectional planes in the stack is tangent to the surface at two different points. The corresponding directions constitute the multi-local stratum, a piece of curve between the cusps of the local bifurcation stratum (fig. 6). The tangency points (multi-local singular set) constitute a smooth curve tangent to the parabolic curve, two points of that set being mapped on the same bifurcation point of the control space.

5. THE STRUCTURE OF VIEW CONTROL IN PROJECTION IMAGING

5.1. Radiologic Projection Imaging : Contrast Curves As Singular Values.

Radiology started with projection imaging and analogic recording on photographic films. Projection imaging is progressively getting digital; it remains important besides sectional imaging or as a preliminary examination because of qualities such as synthetic power for screening purposes and high definition. It is even extending to non X-ray 3-D imaging such as sonography as a synthetized presentation to help shape understanding. In standard radiology X-rays are emitted from an approximately punctual source. The rays cross the examined body along straight lines with some absorption depending on the kind of tissues then cross. Using some transduction, possible amplification, and processing, the image is recorded from the residual photons as an optical density on a plane film or in an array of sensors (fig. 7).

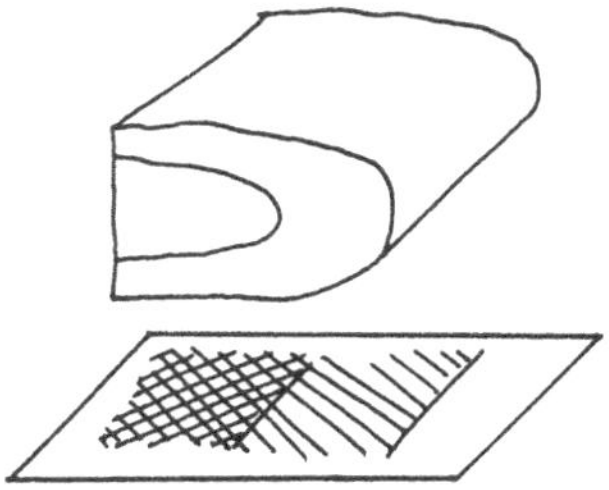

Fig. 7 : Formation of radiologic contrast curves on film from anatomical contrast surfaces in space.

As in sectional imaging, the body in space is partitionned in regions within which the absorbing power is approximately constant. These regions are unions of anatomical compartments and are limited by smoothly embedded manifolds called contrast surfaces. Standard radiologic interpretation aims at retrieving facts about the shape of the contrast surfaces in space from the optical density on film. In fact man has poor performance to measure slowly varying shades of gray. Radiologists base most of their interpretations on the contast curves that their eyes and brains see on the film in place of the sharp variations of optical density, and they often describe these contrast curves as boundary curves between regions of approximately constant densities.

To relate the contrast curves on film to the contrast surfaces in space it is known that the sharp variations that produce the curves come from X-rays tangent to the contrast surface (from sharp transition between rays that cross a region and rays that do not; it is known from psychophysiological experiments that the curves are seen on the film a little besides the location corresponding to the tangent ray). Mathematically we can thus consider the contrast curves as the set of singular values of the conical radiologic projection of the contrast surface to the plane of the film. For simplification we shall assume the source to be infinitely remote and the rays parallel, orthogonal to the film. We shall start with a single projection before allowing control to rotate the surface to be projected. The problem is now to retrieve some facts about the shape of a surface in space from the singular set of one of its orthogonal projections on a plane, in a way accessible to human qualitative reasoning. As for sections and Morse theory, qualitative inference ultimately relies on some genericity and stability results for such mappings.

5.2. Classical Whitney Results

Whitney (1955, see also Thom 1955, and Haefliger 1960 for the extension to orthogonal projections of surfaces from space) proved that in the space of C^p mappings from a plane to a plane, stability is generic, and that stable mappings have only one of the three following local types of singularities (fig.8) : (1) the fold, (2) the transversal superposition of two folds (their sets of singular values cross transversely); (3): the cusp. Taking u and v as parametric coordinates on the surface in (x,y,z) space and projecting on the (x,z) plane along y-axis, the fold is locally equivalent to $(u = x^2;\ v = y)$ and the cusp to $(u = x - xy;\ v = y)$.

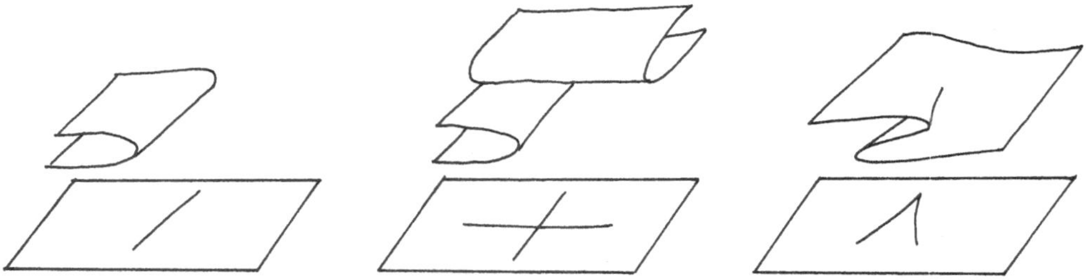

Fig. 8 : The three stable local singularities, local signs for radiologic interpretation.

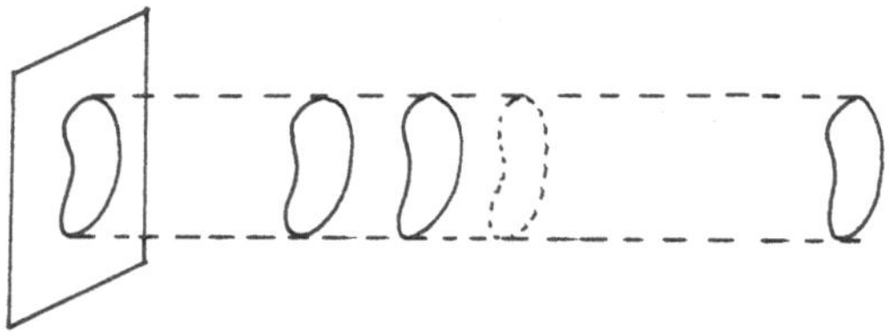

Fig. 9 : For (unprobable) unstable situations, many configurations can lead to the same set of contrast curves.

5.3. Generic Single Projection : The Three Local Signs.

Interpreting projections from the sets of contrast curves can lead to untractably ambiguous cases (fig.9). Using genericity, however, one can assume with negligible risk that the mapping to be interpreted is stable, thus combining only the three former local types of singularities. One can then reconstruct locally the qualitative behaviour of the surface near the ray tangency from the qualitative type of the contrast curve. The rules can be viewed as a generic system of signs (fig.8) : (1) a simple curve comes from the projection of a fold of the surface, (2) a transverse crossing comes from the projection of two superposed two folds of the surface, (3) a cusp on the contrast curve comes from a projected "pleat" of the surface. There are still some ambiguities from symmetries, but most of them can be eliminated from other knowledge or global considerations especially to enable patching these local models into a global one.

These signs are the basis for many deductions in Radiology . The second one has been extensively used former to this theory as the silhouette sign (Felson 1973). The cusp sign has also found some practical applications. Using them amounts to a Bayesian inference where one discards the bad cases as too exceptionnal (see Kergosien 1977, 1983, 1988, 1991 for further discussions).

5.4. Controlled family of projections (generic surface)

Let us now assume interactive control on the direction of the projection, as in fluoroscopy. As in the case of sections we can expect to stabilize new patterns as transitions between the stable ones we already know. Limiting these to a short list of simple cases again relies on a stability property for the view control. Surfaces that lead to stable control of projections under rotations are called multiprojectively stable (Kergosien 1981, 1983). A general principle in using singularity theory is that of assuming genericity regarding the uncontrolled operating conditions. Including some of these conditions in the control leads to richer singularities (which need dimension to "unfold" and appear). For instance, single view examination could have already been interpreted as detection of sharp variations under two dimensional control of the position of the detector on the film, itself an extension from scanning the film along a generic line. It is thus not surprising to progressively find the singularities described in Elementary Catastrophe Theory in ascending codimensional order. However the control considered may include some constraints on the mappings it produces and lead to other singularities than those of catastrophe theory. This is pecisely the case for surface projections under controlled rotations.

In the formalism of mapping controls, C can be taken to be the sphere of oriented directions in space, A to be the surface and B the plane of projection (to avoid orientability problems on the projective space P^2, we shall not try to identify projections for opposite directions). Multi-projective stability (i.e. stability of this mapping control) can be proved to be generic for smoothly embedded surface (after some modifications of the equivalence relation to avoid cross-ratios), and a list of local singularities of the control described : For each type of stable transition of the projection under controlled rotation, one can know the shape of the bifurcation set in control space (here called obturation set), and the associated transitional projection pattern together with the patterns obtained for neighbouring values of the control. The 1-codimensional patterns (fig. 10) correspond to curves on the sphere of controls. They are easily obtained as transitions between stable combinations of the Whitney patterns. They were known in E.C.T. as "beak-to beak", "lip", and "swallow-tail". But understanding the global structure of view control requires knowing also the 2-codimensional patterns "godron", "gouttière" (fig. 11) and "papilllon", two of which are new and come from the special action of rotations on projections. Like for controlled sections, the results are based on the study of the generic properties of the points on the surface which are responsible for the projection's unstability. Among these points, there are again the curves of parabolic points (with relations between the transitional sections and transitional projections) but also swallow-tail curves related to some local properties of the asymptotic lines. Other cases of unstability are related to special coincidences such as tangencies (on the film) of contrast curves generated by different parts of the surface. They are called multi-local and have also been classified (Kergosien 1981).

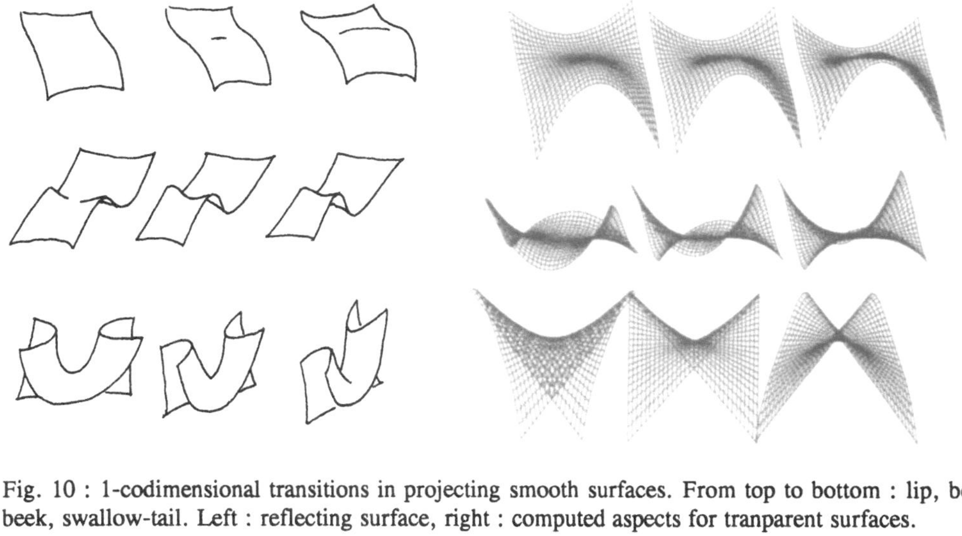

Fig. 10 : 1-codimensional transitions in projecting smooth surfaces. From top to bottom : lip, beek to beek, swallow-tail. Left : reflecting surface, right : computed aspects for tranparent surfaces.

For a given surface in space, the structure of view control in this case can be summarized by a stratification of the sphere into (1) regions of stability, limited by (2) curves of 1-codimentional transitions, on which one finds (3) isolated points of 2-codimentional transitions, together with (4) a labeling of the strata by the corresponding types of singularity. Knowing the curves is enough to find the regions, and also the 2-codimensional points since these occur at special morphological accidents of the curves such as cusps or tangencies. The curves of this stratification can easily be computed a bit like in the case of sections : From the equations of the surface one computes the parabolic and swallow-tail lines; one then maps them on the sphere using at each point the direction of instability (it is the common asymptotic direction for parabolic points, and one of the asymptoitc directions for swallow-tails). Figures 11-12 show the structure of view control for the same simplest example of non trivial set of projections (Kergosien 1983).

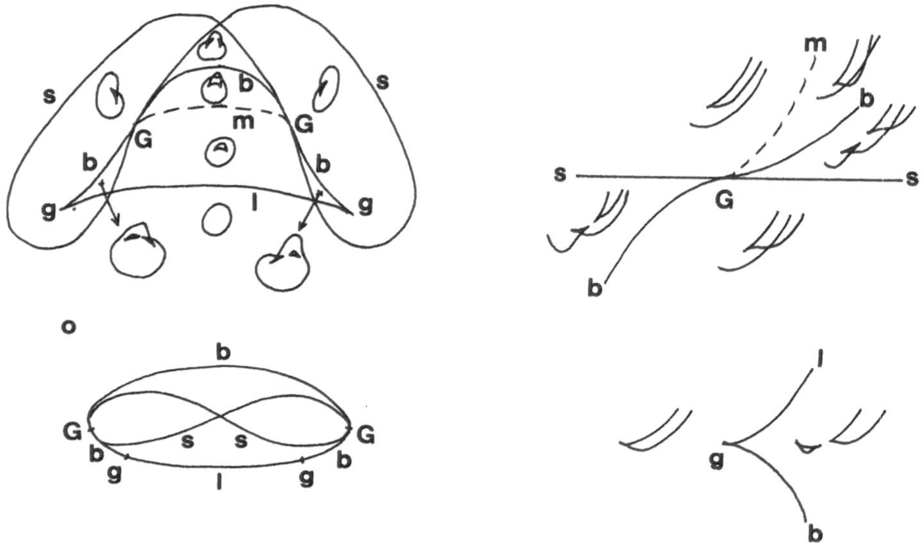

Fig. 11 : The obturation set of a bean shaped "fossette" surface accounts for the changes in its projections when rotated. Stable types of contours are drawn in the corresponding regions. Curves b: beek to beek; l : lip; s : swallow-tail; m : multi-local. Points G : godron; g : gouttiere. Bottom : corresponding singular set on the surface (b, l, G, and g consitute the set of parabolic points). Left : details for godron and gouttiere.

Among the applications of these results, one should first mention the relations between transitional view patterns and local control structure available as a set of signs for the operator to predict the effects of control. For instance it has been empirically known to radiologists in which direction to rotate a patient in order to supress a swallow tail pattern when it appears during digestive examinations; this direction is deduced from the position of the pattern on film or control screen.

Another kind of application relates to synthesis and identification. To compute directly the contrast curves from a surface model, one should first track the set of critical points on the surface (nullifying the jacobian of the projection) and then project it. The first step is a difficult search as the topological structure of the critical set and thus its data structure (such as the number of components) is not known. If one already knows the stratification of the sphere from the model of the surface, one can locate on it the proposed direction of projection and deduce the topological structure of the critical set (which is the same for all the controls of each stratum) to facilitate search. It is also possible to use the fact that when crossing a bifurcation curve on the control sphere, the related topological changes of the critical set on the surface occur at the precise point on the surface (on parabolic or swallow-tail curve) to which the bifurcation point corresponds by normal vector mapping (fig. 13). These procedures also apply to the topology of contrast lines for the difficult problem of angle identification from projection image.

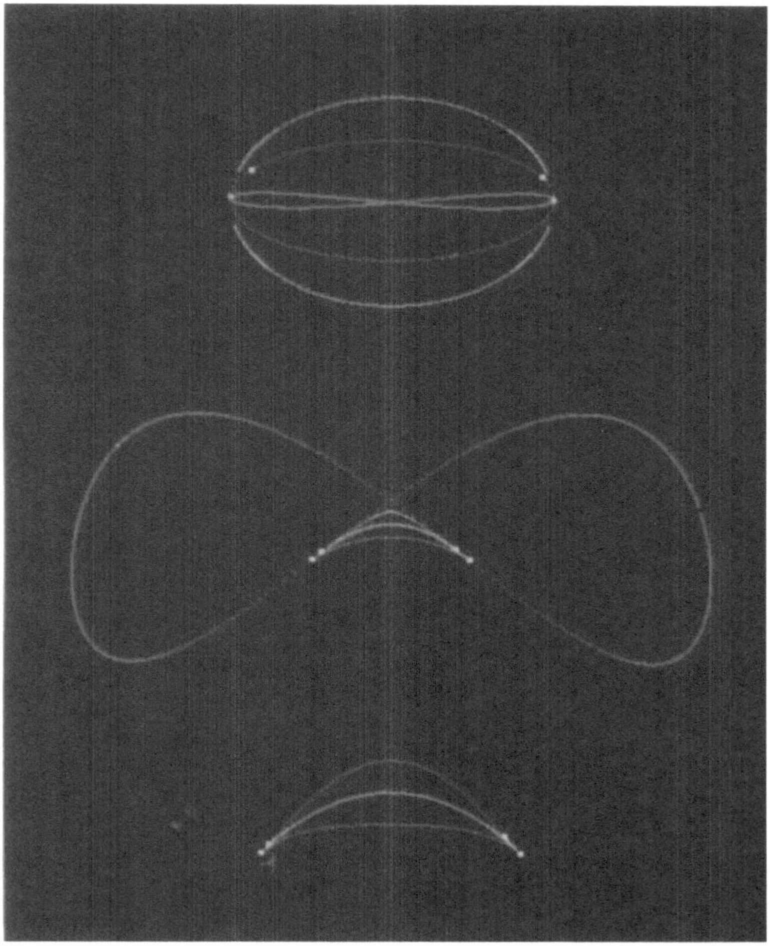

Fig. 12 : Top : Computed singular set for the same fossette surface as in fig. 6. Blue : swallow-tail curves; red : parabolic curves; green : multilocal strata; white dots : godrons; yellow dots : gouttieres. Middle : corresponding computed obturation set, same colors. Notice that contrary to sections, godrons relate to flex points of the obturation set and gouttieres to cusps. Bottom : Bifurcation set for sections.

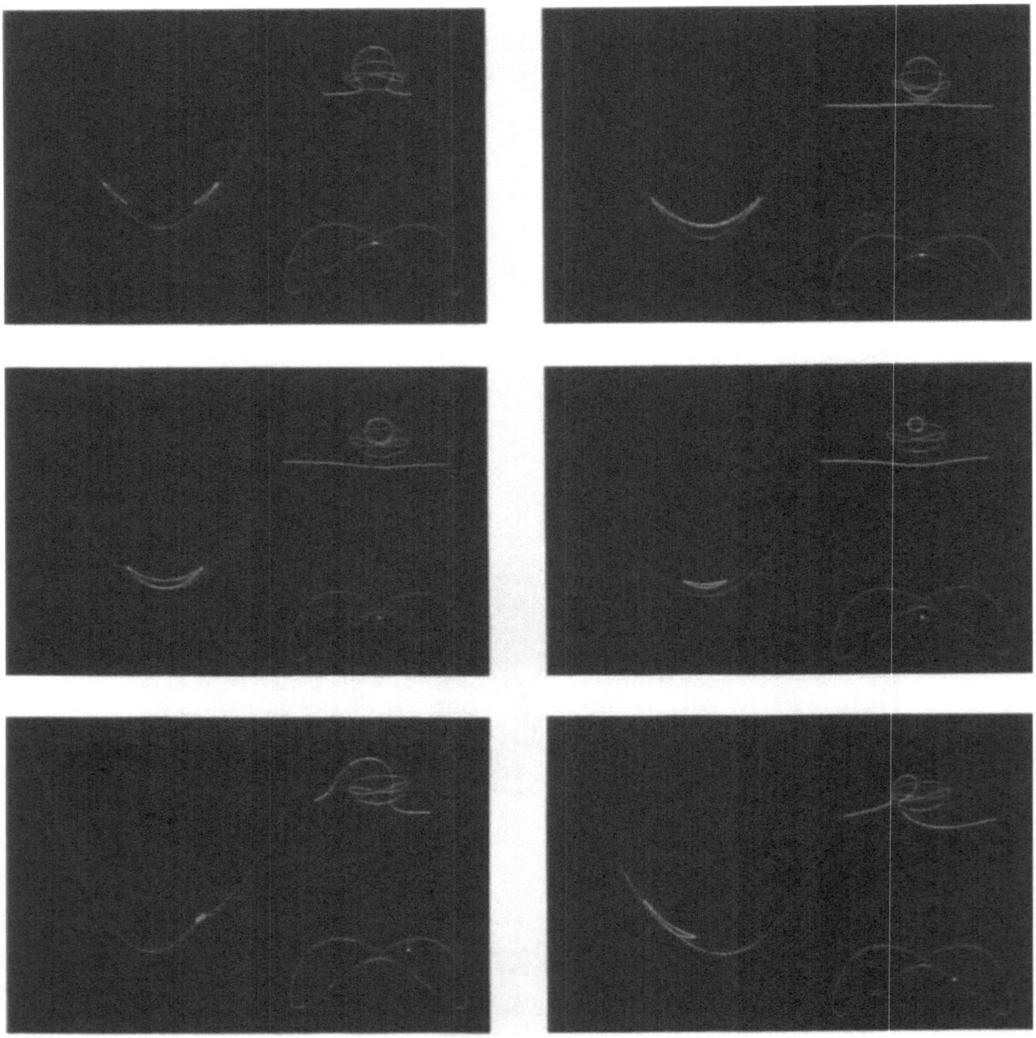

Fig. 13 : Same surface. Using the obturation set (lower right) to predict the types of projections (left, green) and the topology of critical sets (upper right). Color conventions for obturation and singular strata are as in fig. 12. Each slide corresponds to a different angle of the surface (white dot visible in the area of the obturation set). For each control angle the critical and singular set are shown rotated so that cusps always correspond to vertical tangencies of the critical set. As the dot crosses the obturation strata, corresponding changes are observed in the projection pattern and the topology of the critical set. Notice that the changes in the latter are generated at the corresponding points of the singular set.

6. SHAPE CODING AND CONTROL STRUCTURE.

6.1. The problems of coding; the place of control.

Coding the shape of a surface in space amounts to representing it by a finite object, for instance a sequence of symbols. In coding one can oppose two demands : (1) The description requirement asks for keeping as much relevant information as possible from the object. It could be met by a finite element approximation of the surface embedding to be described, but then arises (2) the comparison problem : Can one decide from the codings alone if two given embedded manifolds are equivalent ? (For diverse given kinds of equivalence, like homeomorphism, homeomorphism of the ambiant space, etc...). For instance, the same surface can have very different presentations if known from slices along different axes. Mathematics have so far emphasized the comparison problem, known as potentially very difficult, even for linear codings (some problems have been shown to be undecidable), so that they prefered using simplified presentation, at the cost of incomplete description. This is why one often uses algebraic topology to compute from topological spaces and their finite models some even coarser data such as homotopy, cohomology and homology groups for which comparison is easier. Such methods can of course be translated into computer algorithms, what supports the demand for combinatorial modelling.

For graphics and design purposes, one is usually interested in the precise description of surfaces or solids for which existing mathematical classifications may appear unsufficient. We suggested (Shinagawa 1991) that mathematical descriptions can still be used as starting points if complemented by additional information, providing the basic format of the description and pointing out some of the topological facts to be recorded in the coding. On top of this format should come more precise data, in a hierarchical way.

In another research direction we shall see how including in the coding the topological effects of some controlled transformations (in the case of Morse coding, rotating the axis of slices) provides some solution to the problem of invariance. It is not surprising that control can be relevant to shape coding considering for instance how using a stick and poor sensitive information permits structuring a rich control space and retrieving the shape of objects from proprioception.

6.2. Surface Codings Based on Morse Theory

6.2.1 Combinatorial modelling from the parallel sections of a surface : Structure.

Morse theory simplifies studying how the part of a surface which is below a certain level changes topologically as the level increases. That object is combinatorially modelled as a cell complex. One shows on the known local models of singularities that the topological change in that complex when crossing a critical level can be reproduced using an operation called attaching a k-cell, where k is the index of the singularity. As the height axis is scanned, the topology of the complex does not change between two sucessive singular values, but each time a critical value is crossed, the cell complex is updated by attaching a k-cell to the former complex, where k is the index of the singularity (fig. 14). One can thus construct a complete model of the surface that is shown to have the same homotopy type as the surface. This procedure extends to higher dimensions. Some topological invariants of the surface such as the Euler characteristic can be computed from the simple sequence of indices, but for building an equivalent complex, one should keep track of which connected components of the cross section are to be involved in attaching each cell.

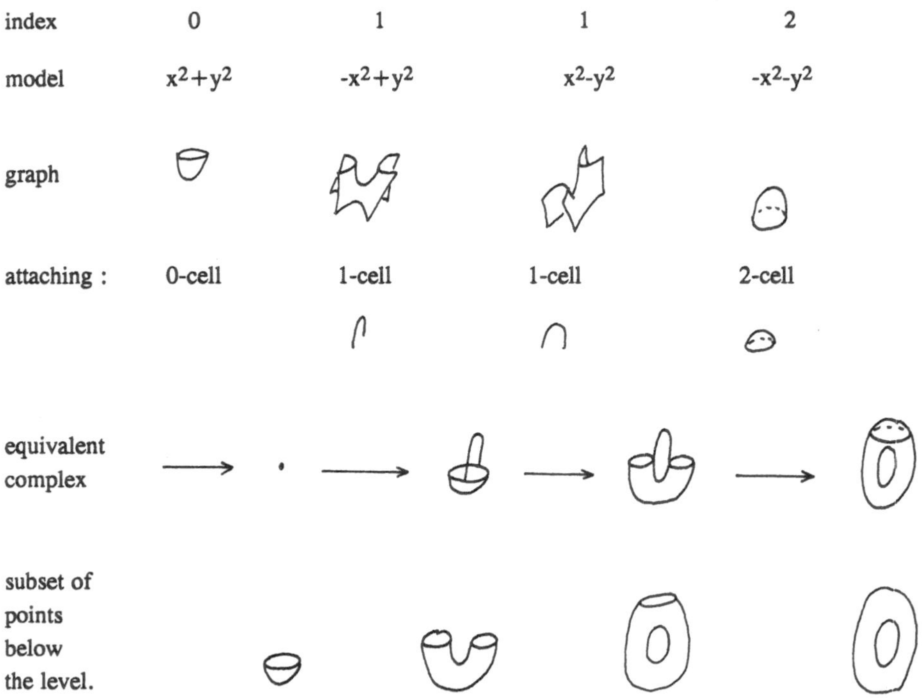

Fig. 14 : Each time the sectional plane crosses a critical height, the topology of the set of points below the threshold changes. This change is topologically equivalent to attaching a k-cell, k being the index of the singularity crossed (after Bott 1960).

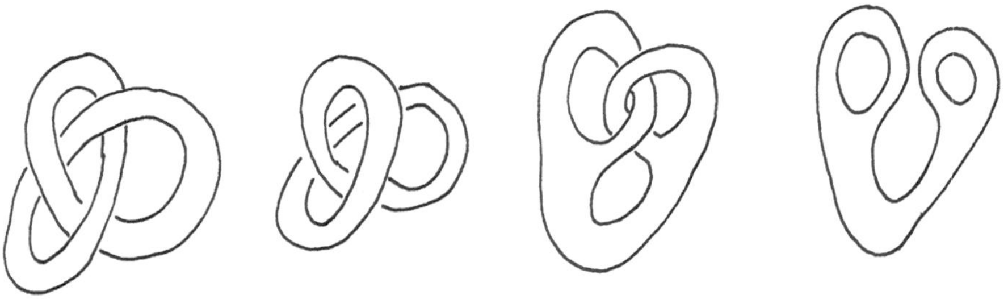

Fig. 15 : Two pairs of embeddings that are not distinguished by straight Morse coding.

It is important to realize that using Morse theory in this classical way permits to recover only the intrinsic topological properties of the manifold. The way the manifold is embedded in space in not coded by the sequence of attaching cells. For instance one cannot know whether an embedded torus is knotted in space or not; the existence of links is another feature skipped by simple Morse coding (fig.15). These two problems have motivated much mathematical work in the form of Knot theory or the theory of braids, where the research is still active. In designing a surface in space, one designs at the same time a 2-dimensional manifold and its embedding in space. Some constraints on the complex have to be met for embeddability or if the surface has to bound a solid. The problem of building a richer model on top of a Morse based format and checking such constraints was addressed in (Shinagawa Kunii Kergosien 1991).

6.2.3. Further abstraction : The Reeb graph of a manifold.

Reeb (1946) proposed to conceptualize further the sliced object by considering a graph obtained as a topological quotient space : One identifies in the manifold (assumed to be compact) all the points which give the same to the considered Morse function and which are in the same connected component of the corresponding cross-section (fig. 16). The connected components of the part of the manifold that is situated strictly between two critical levels are thus represented by separate line segments, i.e. edges of the graph, and each singularity corresponds to a vertex of the graph. Calling order of a vertex the number of edges incident to it, Reeb proved that the order of vertices of index 0 or n is 1, and that in the case of a surface, the order of vertices of index 1 is 2, 3, or 4. This Reeb graph (as refered to by Thom) is quite expressive as an icon and can be used to conceptually visualize higher dimensional objects.

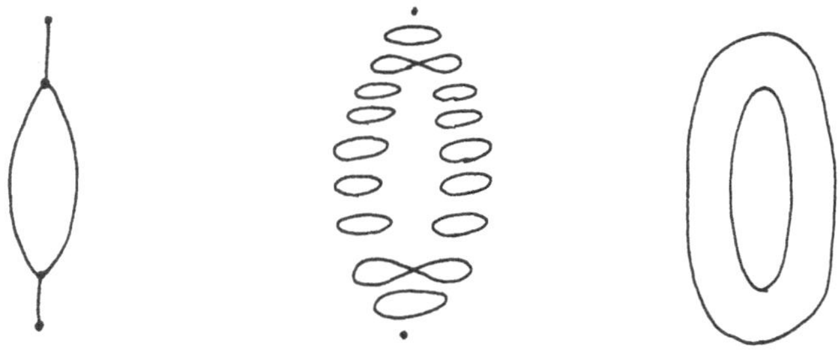

Fig. 16 : Constructing the Reeb graph of a manifold by identification.

6.2.4. Including the structure of angle control : Shape.

Morse codings of a surface usually depend on the axis used for the sections and deciding whether two codings refer to the same surface is difficult. A way of addressing the problem is to code the whole qualitative structure of the sectional view control. One has to record the qualitative organization of the control sphere into regions together with the associated Morse codings. This can make use of complex and some region labelling to model the stratification we mentionned. Matching can then be performed on such objects and use their hierarchical structure to decrease computational overhead. This structure can also serve to find the initial conditions from which to start quantitative matching methods for section identification (the cross-section being given, to find its position on the surface).

6.3. Sequences of maps

Artificially generating singularities is a way to build synthetic views and summarize data, on the model of projection imaging. A sequence of functions defined on a plane can be qualitatively coded considering the control of these mappings from $A=R^2$ to $B=R$ by time ($C=R$). What we again call the diagram of contours is the plot against time of the singular values of each function, i.e. the heights of its peaks, wells and saddles. Under some conditions this diagram displays only cusps and crossings and one can use these patterns as signs to recontitute some of the topological changes in the topographic contours of the functions (fig. 17). The presentation proved to be quite efficient as a format to screen long sequences of electric potential maps in cardiology (500 maps per second). This is due especially to the analogies between that format and E.C.G., but also to its low sensitivity to noise, and to the fact that it is very difficult to understand the evolution of isopotential maps on 2-D animations due to the complex moves of the peaks wells and saddles around the chest in a single cycle.

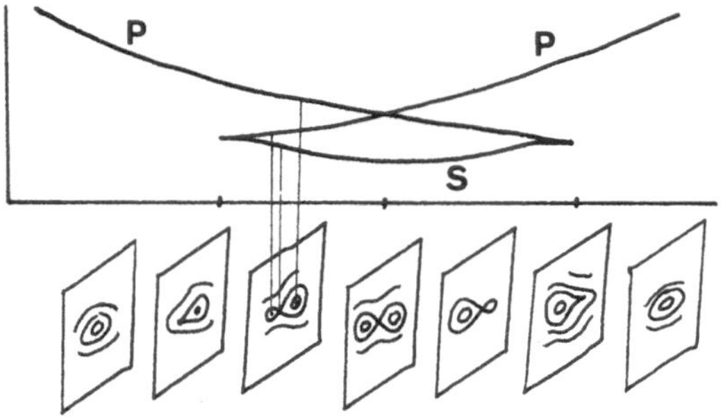

Fig. 17 : Plotting against time the singular values of potential maps helps retrieving the qualitative of the sequence, which appear as cusps and crossings on the diagram (P : peak values; S saddle values).

As a more general remark, accepting to use non-obvious display conventions and a set of signs to understand their meanings permits concentrating much information in a single view and reducing the complexity of control search.

6.4. Multi-projective Types and the Shape of Plane Curves

Multi-projective stability also applies to the orthogonal projections of a plane curve on lines in different directions. In the formalism of mapping controls, A is the curve, C the circle of directions, and B a line. We proposed in (Kergosien 1983) using the structure of this control as a way of coding the shape. This control is much easier to study than the one we considered for surfaces. It is convenient to build the so called "diagram of contours" which records all the singular values of the projection for all the possible angles (fig. 18). It has to be drawn on a on a Moebius strip if one wants to identify opposite directions; it can then be viewed as a dual representation of the curve, each point corresponding to a tangent to the curve (drawing it on a cylinder doubles the diagram but enables using orientation for coding). Generically a smoothly embedded curve has a diagram consisting of a curve with only cusps and crossings as special accidents. Stability of the control also forbids two curve accidents two have the same abcissa; it is generic. A cusp occurs for each inflection point of the curve and its abcissa on the diagram is the direction of the tangent at that point (there are thus generically an even number of cusps). A crossing corresponds to a double tangent to the curve. From the dual correspondence one can parameterize the diagram with the closed curve. The topological structure of the diagram is invariant under translations, rotations, and perspective transformations of the plane curve.

A similar scheme makes use of the evolute to associate to a convex curve a diagram made of an immersion with cusps. It can be formalized using the function defined on the curve as the distance to a point in plane, that function being controlled by the position of the point in plane (Kergosien 83) One then gets a very fine classification for convex curves, some simple quanitative versions of which have been applied to the classification of eggs in Zoology.

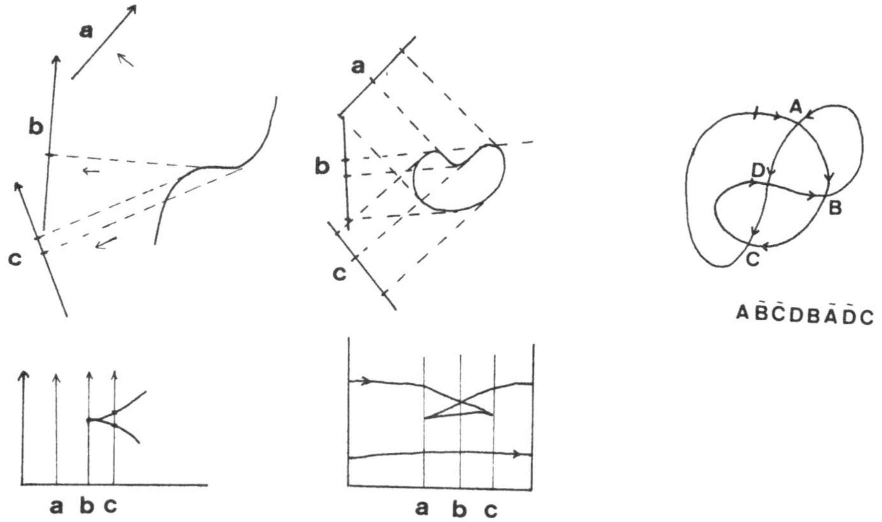

Fig. 18 : Drawing the diagram of contours, i.e. plotting the singular values against the angle of projection (left) and coding a curve immersion with letters and priority rule (right).

Coding the diagram is easy and provides a very fine coding for shape. Several degrees of precision are available, from the exact coding of the control type to coarser classifications. One can for instance code the topology of the contour diagram labelling the cusps and crossings with letters and signs for orientation and writing the circular sequence of letters as one describes the diagram in correspondence with the curve. As circular permutations are quickly computed, rotation invariant recognition is tractable. Interestingly, substrings correspond to shape subpatterns and can be searched in an efficient way that easily outperforms human pattern extraction.

6.5. Syntactic shape generation from generic dents.

Another advantage of this coding in the case of plane curves is its capability of translating syntactically morphological changes in the curve ("dents", fig. 19). The generic singularities of 1-dimensional families of plane curves are easily classified. For instance they include swallow-tails which introduce or cancel on the diagram one crossing and two cusps; also a cusp of the diagram can cross another part of the curve, or a triple point occur (triple tangent), and so on. The effects of these dents can be written as syntactic transformations (there are however some relations that call for rewriting rules), what provides a morphologic distance to compare curves.

This procedure is very general and addresses the problem of constraint validation in design. When designing a surface with a view to its sections or projections, it is difficult to know and meet all the topological constraints that relate the diffferent sections or projections. A way of dodging this difficulty is to progressively modify the shape from one that is known and validated, like a sphere. Using singularity theory and genericity one can produce a finite list of shape transitions, together witht the related effects on the structure of section control or projection control, so as to be able to generate any stable shape. The "fossette" shape analysed in figures 11-13 is an instance of a shape that one can get from a sphere with a single generic dent.

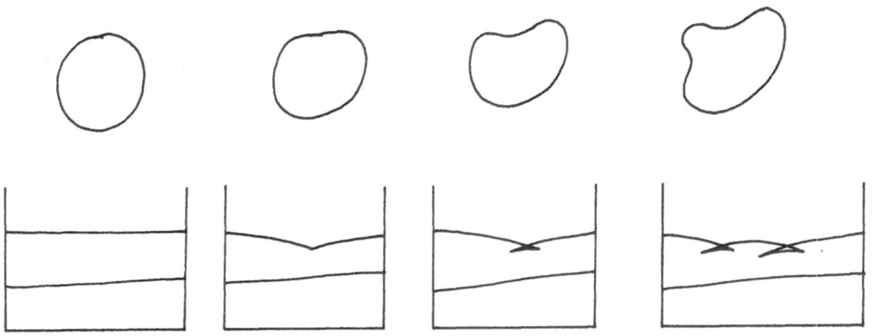

Fig. 19 : Denting the plane curve generates swallow-tails or other 1-codimentional singularities in the diagram of contours.

7. PROSPECTS : SELF-EXPLANATORY VISUAL SYSTEMS AND BEYOND.

To cope with ever increasing data collected from either natural or simulated phenomena, man has to delegate more intelligence to machines and interact with more autonomous systems. Human interfaces are clearly a bottleneck and new ways of inputting man's orders are developing (e.g. in virtual reality). But output to man is also a major problem. The difficulty of globally validating opaque systems is an obstacle to their acceptance, especially in medicine where responsability issues could ask for empirical assessment just as in the case of drugs. To provide some monitoring for the processing and the inferences of the system partially solves the problem, most of the responsibility being transfered to the user. Practically one should aim at systems able to cooperate with the inquirer, understanding his concerns and providing explanations at different levels of abstraction. For intelligent image analysis systems, part of the machine rhetorics can be based upon the choice of adequate views from the data, just as some radiologic images "speak for themselves" to experts. Similarly, alarm raising systems that are sought to help tumor screening (within usually non interpreted data) should choose the proper image presentations to support their proposed conclusions, with a possible comment in graphical form. This level of communication should certainly benefit from the topological approaches of the former sections and develop in the direction of graphical (iconic) rhetorics rather than verbal interfaces. More generally, as simulation improves and reproduces better the natural phenomena, the need for some understanding not only remains, but even increases. Assistance is needed for exploring, organizing, and guiding the control of complex phenomena, calling for a kind of computer assisted experimental method. There again, all the tools of topology such as identifying qualitatively equivalent regions of the control, building models, computing invariants, building new spaces, or finding special subsets, should be available to the operator or autonomously used by the system to extract conceptual information.

Topology has been recognized to be the fundamental level to explain many phenomena in mathematics, even if in richer settings (differential equations, partial differential equations, complex variables...). In the same way the most important information required to control a dynamical system is often of topological nature. For instance, topologically different initial configurations usualy relate to different local minima in the gradient descent used for pattern matching or identification, and an operator may be required to input such information with a pointing device modifying the state of the evolving structure : Man inputs qualitative data at the basic level of the hierarchical structure and lets the system adjust the higher levels. Besides such specialized channel for input, however, more "natural" channels of communications can be used. In the case of a vision system one can temporary modify the image input by the camera to bias the evolution in desired directions (Kergosien 1986). Similarly,

neural networks show interesting behaviour upon "hints" (Suddarth Kergosien 1990): Instead of accessing directly their inner layers, one can add to their learning tasks some added tasks that interact and guide the original ones. One interesting feature of this, besides modularity, is the possibility of understanding these controls in functional terms, whereas weight structures are poorly understood. Back to vision systems, one can ask what visual signs could apply in a rather universal way to guide certain tasks. Such visual signs could then be output by the systems themselves to communicate together through visual channels in a modular way and with the possibility of human monitoring.

8. CONCLUSION.

Singularity theory permits formalizing the same qualitative geometric reasoning as used by human use for interpreting medical images (sections and projections of surfaces). Genericity arguments justify using only a small number of simple models. The topological structure of geometric objects like smooth surfaces can be reduced to combinatorial data involving these simple models. Introducing a continuous control on the way different sections or projections are formed from a fixed surface, many precise facts about the shape of the surface appear as qualitative characteristics of the control. They are also related to some classical geometric properties of the surface, especially the structure of its set of parabolic points. Generically these structures combine models from a known finite list. The combinatorial types of control structures can serve as shape coding. In the case of plane curves the codings record the structure an intermediary plane diagram and permit automatic syntactic analysis. The procedure has been extended to the design of special displays to screen rapidly the topological changes within sequences of plane maps.

9. REFERENCES

BOTT R (1960) : *Lectures on Morse Theory*. Mimeographed notes by A Van de Ven, University of Bonn.

FELSON B (1973) : *Chest Roentgenology*, W.B. Saunders Company.

GOLUBITSKY M, GUILLEMIN V (1973): *Stable Mappings and their Singularities*. Springer.

HAEFLIGER A (1960): Quelques remarques sur les applications differentiables d'une surface dans le plan. *Ann. Inst. Fourier, Grenoble*, Vol.10, 47-60.

HIRSCH M W (1976) : *Differential Topology*. Springer.

KERGOSIEN Y L (1977) : *Introduction de la Topologie en Médecine*, Thèse de Doctorat d'Etat en Médecine, C.H.U. Necker-Enfants Malades, Paris, 152 pages.

KERGOSIEN Y L , THOM R. (1980) : Sur les points paraboliques des surfaces. *Comptes Rendus Acad. Sc. Paris*, t.290, Série A-705-710.

KERGOSIEN Y L (1981) : La famille des projections orthogonales d'une surface et ses singularités. *ComptesRendus Acad. Sc. Paris*, t.292, Série I-929-932.

KERGOSIEN Y L (1983) : Medical exploration of some rythmic phenomena, *Rythms in Biology* (Proceedings C.I.R.M. colloquium, Luminy Sept. 1981), M.COSNARD, J.DEMONGEOT, M. LEBRETON ed., Lecture Notes in Biomathematics Vol 49, Springer Verlag.

KERGOSIEN Y L (1986) : Local versus global minima, hysteresis, multiple meanings. *Disordered systems and biological organisation*. Proceedings of the NATO ASI (Les Houches Feb. 1985), series F, vol.20, E.BIENENSTOCK, F.FOGELMAN-SOULIE, G.WEISBUCH ed., Springer.

KERGOSIEN Y L (1987) : Projections of smooth surfaces : stable primitives. *Actes du colloque Cognitiva-MARI* (Paris, May 1987), CESTA, Paris.

KERGOSIEN Y L (1988) : *Les signes locaux stables, contribution à l'étude du trait radiologique*. Mémoire pour le C.E.S. de Radiodiagnostic, Faculté de Médecine Cochin-Port-Royal, Paris.

KERGOSIEN Y L (1989) : Topological methods for the analysis and synthesis of medical images/Méthodes topologiques pour l'analyse et la synthèse d'images médicales. *Proceedings VISUDA 89* (Paris, June 1989).
KERGOSIEN Y L (1991) : Generic sign systems in medical imaging. *IEEE CG&A*, Vol. 11, No 5, pp. 46-65.
MATHER J N (1972) : Stability of smooth mappings, VI : The nice dimensions, *Liverpool Singularities Symposium I*, pp. 207-253, Springer.
MILNOR J (1963) : *Morse theory*, Annals of Math. Studies 51, Princeton University Press.
MORSE M, CAIRNS S S (1969) : *Critical point theory in global analysis and differential topology*. Academic Press.
REEB, G (1946) : "Sur les points singuliers d'une forme de Pfaff complètement intégrable ou d'une fonction numérique". *Comptes Rendus Acad. Sciences Paris*, vol. 222, pp. 847-849.
SHINAGAWA Y, KUNII T L, KERGOSIEN Y L (1991): Surface codings based on Morse theory. *IEEE CG&A* ,Vol 11, No 5, pp. 66-78.
SUDDARTH S C , KERGOSIEN Y L (1990) : Rule-injection hints as a means of improving network performance and learning time. *Neural Networks*, Proc. EURASIP Workshop (Sesimbra Portugal 1990), Springer Lecture Notes in Computer Science 412.
THOM R (1956) : Un lemme sur les applications differentiables, *Bol. Soc. Math. Mexicana*, pp. 59-71.
THOM R (1955): Les singularites des applications differentiables. *Ann. Inst. Fourier*, t.6 p. 43-87.
THOM R (1972) : *Stabilité Structurelle et Morphogénèse*. Benjamin.
WHITNEY H (1955) : On Singularities of Mappings of Euclidean Spaces. I : Mappings of the Plane into the Plane. *Annals of Math.*, Vol 62, pp.374-410.

AUTHOR BIOGRAPHY

Y.L. Kergosien is Maître de Conférences in mathematics at Université de Paris-Sud in Orsay (France). He is also a medical doctor and a trained radiologist. His interests include the applications of mathematics (topology, singularities, catastrophe theory, generic properties of surfaces) to medicine (medical imaging, psychiatry), theoretical biology (morphogenesis, adaptive ramification, neural networks), epistemology, and semiotics.

KERGOSIEN got a D.E.A. in pure mathematics from Université Paris VII and a M.D. from University Paris V.

Address : Department of Mathematics, Bât. 425, Université de Paris-Sud, 91405 Orsay, France.

Chapter 2
Analyses of Visual Information

Polyhedral Surface Decomposition Based on Curvature Analysis

Bianca Falcidieno and Michela Spagnuolo

ABSTRACT

This paper describes a method to characterize the shape of a generic surface approximated with a triangulation. Combining classical topological techniques and differential geometry provides simple methods for evaluating several shape descriptors. Based on this idea a qualitative analysis is defined to estimate the curvature "along" edges and "around" triangles in order to identify regions whose shape is classified as *concave, convex, plane* or *saddle*. The proposed curvature regions are defined as connected components of the graph surface model and give rise to a unique surface decomposition which is suitable for parallel implementation and has a linear computational complexity.

Key words: shape decomposition, surface modeling, topology, differential geometry.

1. INTRODUCTION

Much of the potential of contemporary geometric modelling resides in its techniques for synthesizing, providing means to easily describe complex shapes as arrangements of simpler ones. In particular, the problem addressed by shape decomposition is the reduction of a generic surface to a compact symbolic description which picks out the essential information about the surface structure and leaves out low level details.

In many fields it is necessary to handle very large and complex shape data. For example, many industrial and navigational robotics tasks definitely benefit from an explicit and effective representation of the information contained in range or intensity images. Indeed, a symbolic description based on characteristic shape elements can be used to perform high level pattern or object recognition by matching the description with pre-computed sample scenes (Besl et al. 1986, Medioni et al. 1984, Haralick et al. 1983, Watson et al. 1985).
Spatial data handling is another context where surface characterization is desirable. Natural terrains are usually represented by large number of low level geometric primitives and the availability of abstraction mechanisms could be very useful to define generalized models based on morphological features (Falcidieno et al. 1992, Weibel et al. 1990).

There are several ways of solving the problem of shape decomposition.
Mathematical morphology is gaining increasing attention for being pleasingly neat and suitable for image processing (Pitas et al. 1990).
Classical methods use concepts from differential geometry or analysis to subdivide a surface into regions having equivalent mathematical characteristics. The shape operators, i.e. Gaussian and mean curvature, are widely used and considered satisfactory especially in image processing (Besl et al. 1986).

Nackman (1984) has proposed the concept of *Critical Point Configuration Graph* for surface description. A critical point on the surface is one where the first partial derivatives are zero and, similarly, slope lines are computed as the zero crossing of the first partial derivatives. Slope lines connecting critical points define a graph whose minimal cycles bound the so-called slope districts. Slope districts, together with the curvature districts proposed in (Nackman 1985), can be used for surface characterization.

The method presented in this paper is based on the idea that combining classical topological techniques with well-known differential geometry can provide simple methods, suitable for computer implementation for evaluating several shape descriptors. Originally, we approached the problem of shape decomposition in the context of natural surface modelling, where a terrain can be regarded as a set of sampling points of a bivariate function (Falcidieno et al. 1991). The method has a wider applicability and the problem of shape decomposition is here more generally formulated in the following way: we want to represent and characterize a three-dimensional shape whose boundary is a surface S on which a set of points are known by their three coordinates. The first step is the definition of a piecewise approximation of the underlying surface, which is constructed as a triangulation of the data points. Then, a graph-based model is defined which makes explicit the geometric relationships between triangular facets. A kind of qualitative analysis is proposed to estimate the curvature "along" edges and "around" triangles in order to identify regions whose shape can be classified as *concave, convex, plane* or *saddle*. Curvature regions are defined as particular connected components of the graph surface model and give rise to a unique surface decomposition. Finally, a relational structure is defined which encodes the decomposition of the surface by making explicit the adjacency relationships between curvature regions.
The remainder of this paper is organized as follows. First, the classical Gaussian and mean curvature are briefly reported, both in the continuous and discrete statement. Second, our approach to shape decomposition is outlined and the concept of curvature regions is defined. Next, the decomposition algorithm is presented which is simple and intuitive. Some experimental results are shown, compared with those obtained using the techniques defined in (Lin et al. 1982).

2. Curvature of Piecewise Linear Surfaces

As well as speed, curvature and torsion uniquely determine the shape of a curve in the space, similar characteristics can be defined which uniquely determine and quantify general smooth surfaces. The two basic descriptors considered in the classical analysis of smooth surfaces are referred to as the *first* and *second fundamental forms,* whose definition is briefly reported. For more details on this topic see (Lipschutz 1969 or O'Neil 1969).

Let $\mathbf{X} = \mathbf{X}(u,v) = (x_1(u,v), x_2(u,v), x_3(u,v))$ be a coordinate patch on a surface of class C^m, $m \geq 1$, and consider the differential of $\mathbf{X}$ defined by

$$d\mathbf{X} = \mathbf{X}_u\,du + \mathbf{X}_v\,dv$$

which maps the vectors (du, dv) in the plane uv onto the vectors $\mathbf{X}_u du + \mathbf{X}_v dv$ parallel to the tangent plane at $\mathbf{X}(u,v)$. The differential may be considered as the first order approximation to the vector $\mathbf{X}(u+du,v+dv) - \mathbf{X}(u,v)$.

The *first fundamental form* I of $\mathbf{X}(u,v)$ is defined by

$$I = dX \bullet dX = (X_u\,du + X_v\,dv)\,(X_u\,du + X_v\,dv) =$$
$$= (X_u \bullet X_u)du^2 + 2(X_u \bullet X_v)dudv + (X_v \bullet X_v)dv^2$$
$$= E\,du^2 + 2\,Fdudv + G\,dv^2$$

where $E = (X_u \bullet X_u)$, $F = (X_u \bullet X_v)$ and $G = (X_v \bullet X_v)$. The first fundamental form measures the small amount of movement $|dX|^2$ on a surface at a point *(u,v)* for a small amount of movement in the parameter space *(du,dv)* (see figure 1) and it can be shown that it depends only on the surface itself and not on the particular parametrization chosen.

The second fundamental form measures the relation between the change in the surface position **dX** and the change in the normal vector **dN**, defined as

$$N = \frac{X_u \times X_u}{|X_u \times X_u|}$$

Then, the *second fundamental form* **II** is defined by the following quantity

$$II = -\,dX \bullet dN = -\,(X_u\,du + X_v\,dv) \bullet (N_u\,du + N_v\,dv) =$$
$$= -\,(X_u \bullet N_u)\,du^2 - (X_u \bullet N_v + X_v \bullet N_u)\,dudv - (X_v \bullet N_v)\,dv^2 =$$
$$= L\,du^2 + 2\,M\,dudv + N\,dv^2 =$$

where $L = -\,(X_u \bullet N)$, $M = -\,1/2\,(X_u \bullet N_v + X_v \bullet N_u)$ and $G = -\,(X_v \bullet N)$. It can be shown that **II** is invariant for parameter transformation which preserves the direction of the vector **N**, otherwise **II** changes its sign.

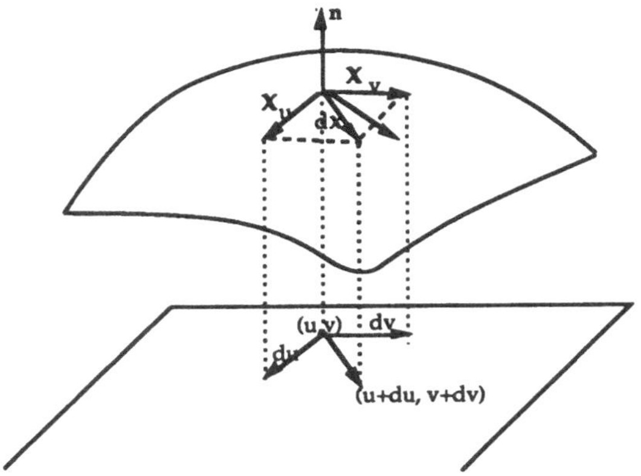

Fig.1 Differential and normal vector at a point *(u,v)*.

Based on the first and second fundamental forms, the mean curvature H and the Gaussian curvature K of a surface at a point are defined as follows:

$$H = \frac{EN + GL - 2FM}{2(EG - F^2)} \qquad K = \frac{LN - M^2}{EG - F^2}$$

Both mean and Gaussian curvature have a more intuitive interpretation as, respectively, the average and the product of the maximum and minimum principal curvature

(Lipschutz 1969). Knowledge of these quantities permits to classify the shape of a smooth surface in several surface types (Besl et al. 1986).

When dealing with discrete surface models it is obviously impossible a straightforward use of the continuum scheme outlined before and different approaches may be used, depending on the knowledge available about the surface. Techniques devised for discrete surfaces can be roughly classified into two categories: those computing explicit derivative estimates and those using a discrete version of the curvature concept. The first class of methods requires the computation of a continuous differentiable function that "best" fits the data, the computation of its derivatives and then their evaluation at the data points. This problem is computationally discouraging and should be used only if no simpler methods work. This technique have been successfully applied in all cases where an approximation of class at least C^2 can be easily constructed, for example when dealing with images, which represent bivariate surfaces sampled on a regular network. Indeed, the formulae for Gaussian and mean curvature are simplified for graph surfaces and smooth approximation can be easily derived when a regular sampling is available. Many examples can be found in the literature, concerning image processing or pattern recognition (Besl et al. 1986, Medioni et al. 1984, Haralick et al. 1983, Watson et al. 1985). In contrast to this rich bibliography, only few authors have attempted to adapt the continuum definitions to a discrete domain. When the surface is known as a set of irregularly distributed sampling points, the computation of continuous differentiable patches preserving smoothness along adjacent boundaries can be very awkward. A better and lighter solution is to perform a discrete version of the curvature analysis on a piecewise linear approximation, which is much easier to construct. In particular, a triangulation of the data points is a quite easy and versatile choice because it is suitable for curvature analysis, it adapts to any kind of spatial distribution of the data points, and any given surface can be well approximated by arbitrarily fine triangulations.
The concept of curvature for piecewise flat surfaces can be formulated as shown in (Mortenson 1985; Abelson et al. 1986), and it derives from the theory concerning polygonal subdivision of curved surfaces. The curvature of a surface subdivided in polygons can be studied and computed on the basis of the *angle excess* associated with the polygonal paths of the subdivision. The angle excess is defined as the rotation that an indicator of orientation undergoes when moved along the path. Using the closed-path theorem, the angle excess E of a simple closed path on an arbitrary surface, can be written in terms of the total turning T along the path as $E+T=2\pi$ (see figure 2). Angle excess is additive, meaning that the excess of any polygon is the sum of the excesses of any polygonal subdivision of the polygon itself.

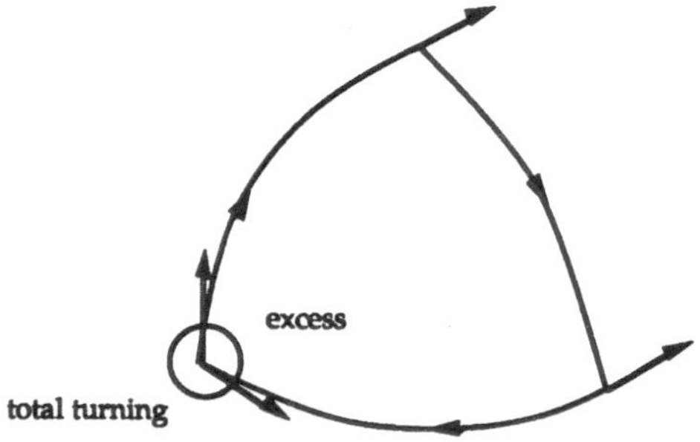

Fig. 2 Angle excess associated with a closed path.

Based on the angle excess, both a local and a global form of curvature can be defined. The local quantity, called *curvature density,* tells how curved is the surface and is defined at a point on the surface as the excess per unit area of a small patch of surface around the point.

The global quantity is called *total curvature* and, given a region on an arbitrary surface subdivided in polygons, the total curvature is the sum of the excesses computed for each polygonal path of the subdivision (Abelson et al. 1986). The total curvature is well defined, meaning that it is independent of the particular subdivision chosen. Moreover, it can be shown that the total curvature for a closed surface is a topological invariant, while for surfaces with boundary, the total curvature does not change for topological deformation not affecting the boundary.

Given a polygonal and generally curved subdivision of a generic curved surface, the definition of local and global curvature can be effectively used to study the curvature of the surface. The same results hold for piecewise flat surfaces, that is, surfaces formed by planar polygons glued along the edges. For this kind of surfaces, the curvature analysis is simpler because the surface will be flat everywhere except possibly along the edges, and if edges are straight then the curvature will be concentrated at the vertices. As well as for generic polygonal subdivisions, the total curvature of a piecewise flat surface can be computed by summing up the angle excess of small paths around each of the vertices. Moreover, another interesting result derives from the Gauss-Bonnet theorem, which is fundamental in differential geometry: the *total* curvature of closed surface is equal to $2\pi\chi$, where χ is the Euler characteristic of the surface. As far as polyhedral surfaces are concerned, the Euler characteristic can be more precisely written as $\chi = V-E+F$, where V is the number of vertices, E is the number of edges and F the number of faces. Thus, the total curvature of a closed polyhedral surface could be computed by simply counting the number of geometric primitives defining the surface.

In the context of triangulated surfaces, Lin and Perry in (Lin et al. 1982) have proposed several formulae to compute some shape descriptors. For each vertex of the surface a classification is proposed based on the angle excess which is used to define the so called angle deficit. With reference to figure 3, let v be a vertex of the triangulated surface, T_i, $i=1 \ldots n$, the triangles incident to v and θ_i, $i=1 \ldots n$, the angle on T_i subtended at v. Intuitively, the curvature can be analyzed by imagining to "cut" the surface around vertex v along one of the edges incident to it. Then, the surface is unwrapped onto the plane and triangles are checked to see if they overlap, after being developed.

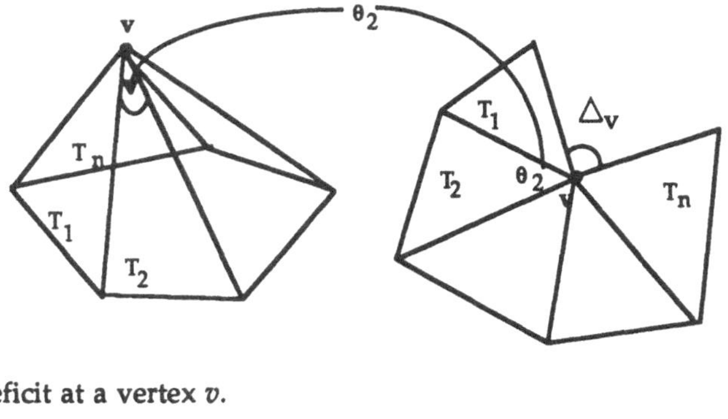

Fig. 3 The angle deficit at a vertex v.

The deficit angle is defined by $\Delta_v = 2\pi - \sum \theta_i$, and if triangles do not overlap, i.e. $\Delta_v > 0$, then the surface has positive curvature like a sphere. If triangles already belong to the same plane, i.e. $\Delta_v = 0$, then the surface is obviously flat around v. Finally, if triangles do overlap, i.e. $\Delta_v < 0$, then the surface has negative curvature like an hyperboloid. Notice that only the edge lengths are needed, not the coordinates of the extremes, to compute θ_i and consequently the curvature. Always based on the angle deficit, the Ricci scalar can be computed, which is defined as R=2/{Gaussian curvature}, using the following :

$$R_v = \frac{3\,\Delta_v}{\Sigma A_i}$$

where A_i is the area of the ith triangle incident to vertex v.

3. The Surface Curvature Regions

The method proposed in this paper approaches the problem of finding a surface characterization by a geometrical and topological point of view. Our solution has been originally devised in the context of bivariate surfaces, but the method can be applied to any surfaces, even closed ones, and it will be explained more precisely within this section.

With regard to the choice of the surface approximation, if the sampling points are randomly distributed a triangulation offers effective advantages because it can represent the surface at a variable resolution, it is independent of the point spatial distribution, thus adapting to the local changes of the surface morphology (Boissonnat 1984; De Floriani et al. 1985). Moreover, a triangulation can be easily updated permitting the inclusion of additional points to locally refine the approximation. Among all the triangulations feasible, we have considered the *Delaunay* triangulation, which is widely considered satisfactory for approximation problems as it is the one in which most of the triangles are as equiangular as possible (Preparata et al. 1985; Falcidieno et al. 1991). However, the following definitions are independent of the particular type of triangulation chosen.

Let *S* be a set of sampling points of a surface, and *T(S)* a triangulation of S, that is, a simplicial polyhedron with vertices at the data points and with triangular faces. The adopted surface model is defined as a relational graph which makes the adjacency relationships between triangular facets explicit. Moreover a geometric classification of the triangulation primitives is performed, in order to assign geometric attributes to edges, according to the following definition.

Definition 1 *: The dihedral angle α subtended by two adjacent triangles t_1, t_2 is said* convex (concave) *if for any two points $p_1 \in t_1$, $p_2 \in t_2$ the straight line segment p_1p_2 lies completely* below (above) *the surface, otherwise it is* plane *(see figure 4). Then, to each arc* e = (t_1, t_2) *of the surface graph model an attribute is assigned in the set* convex, concave, plane *according to the type of the corresponding angle.*

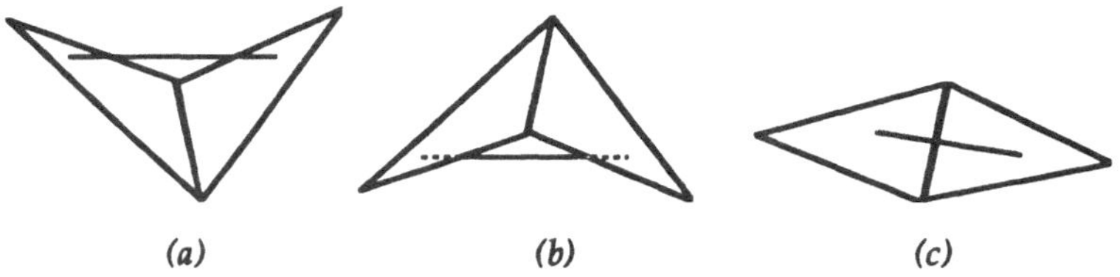

Fig. 4 Examples of concave (a) , convex (b) and plane angle (c).

Formally, the geometric model of S is defined as a labelled and attributed graph $G_S = (N, A, A_a)$, where N is the set of nodes and A is the set of arcs and A_a the set of attributes of arcs, such that:

- the node set is $N = \{ t \mid t$ is a triangle of T(S) $\}$ and for every triangle t in T(S) a unique node in N exists, which is labelled t;
- the arc set is $A = \{ (t_i, t_j) \mid t_i, t_j$ share a common edge in T(S) $\}$ and for every edge e in T(S), shared by two triangles t_1, t_2, a unique arc in A exists joining the two nodes t_1, t_2 in N, which is labelled e;
- to each arc $e \in A$, corresponding to a pair (t_i, t_j) an attribute $q \in A_a = \{$ *concave, convex, plane* $\}$ is assigned according to definition 1.

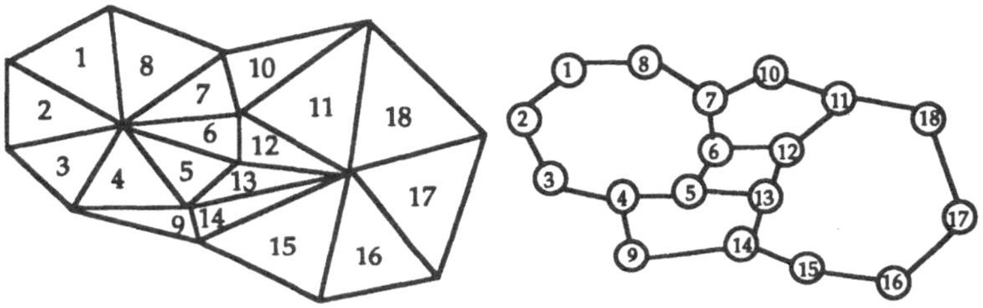

Fig. 5 A triangulation and the corresponding graph model.

The next step is the definition of the structural components used to decompose the surface. These components should be mathematically well defined and should be regarded as "simpler" shape components with respect to the complex surface shape, so that the symbolic description coding the decomposition definitely represents a simplification of the surface shape.

Two levels of decomposition are proposed respectively based on *strong* and *weak* curvature regions, which can be alternatively used in order to perform a characterization which is either closer to a precise analytical description or which aims at the recognition of *global* shape properties. Both classes of regions are formally defined as particular connected components of the surface graph model and are obtained on the basis of a classification which takes into account the curvature around triangles.

As far as strong curvature regions are concerned, the classification of triangles follows these rules.

Definition 2 *: A triangle t is said to be* convex (concave, plane) *if all its edges are of type* convex (concave, plane), saddle *if all its edges are of different type,* hybrid *in the remaining cases (see figure 6).*

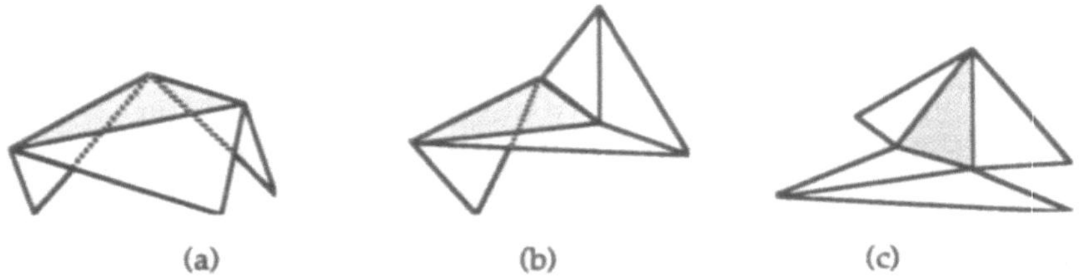

Fig. 6 Examples of convex triangle (a), saddle triangle (b) and hybrid triangle (c).

Beside the triangle attributes, for the set of arcs of the surface graph model G_S a property is defined which is used to test the *connection* between triangular facets induced by the type of arcs and triangles.

Definition 3 *: Let* type *be the function returning the type of a triangle and* q ∈ {concave, convex, plane, saddle, hybrid}. *Then, an arc* $(t_i, t_j) \in A$ *is said to be* q-connected *if and only if* type(t_i) = type (t_j) = q.

This connection property is well defined over the set of arcs *A*, as it is a single-valued property. The reason for introducing this property is to give a rule for traversing the graph G_S meaning that it is possible to walk form a node t_i to a node t_j only if they are of the same type, that is, if there is a similar curvature "around" triangles.

Following this classification, strong characteristic regions on a triangulated surface are defined as follows:

Definition 4 *: Let* q ∈ { concave, convex, plane, saddle, hybrid }, *and GS be the graph surface model of S. A* strong curvature region *of S is any connected component of* G_S *obtained removing from* G_S *all arcs not complying with the q-connection property.*

In terms of triangulation, curvature regions identify connected and partially disjoint sets of triangles, whose boundary is defined by one or more closed sequences of edges which do not comply with the *q*-connection property. Definition 4 guarantees that the resulting surface decomposition is *unique*. Indeed, as the *q*-connection property is well defined, the uniqueness directly results from the definition of connected component of a graph. Obviously, each shape component can be unambiguously classified according to the type of its interior triangles, and strong curvature regions of type convex, concave, planar and saddle correspond to areas where the total curvature has the same sign when computed at interior vertices using the rules given in the previous section. Indeed, since all edges belonging to a strong convex (concave, planar) region are of type convex (concave, planar), it follows that at each vertex in the interior of the region the curvature will be non negative. According to the proposed characterization the meaning of areas defined as saddle regions can be explained considering the possible configurations of adjacency type around a vertex internal to a saddle region. With reference to figure 7, two consecutive edges, incident to a vertex v in a saddle region, cannot be of the same type since saddle regions are formed by triangles having all edges of different type. In other words, moving around vertex v one would pass from a convex to a concave edge possibly through a plane one. These changes in shape justify the use of the term saddle to identify sets of triangles whose edge types are not homogeneous. Thus, saddle regions are "qualitatively" saddle-like although nothing can be said locally about the sign of the curvature at individual internal vertices.

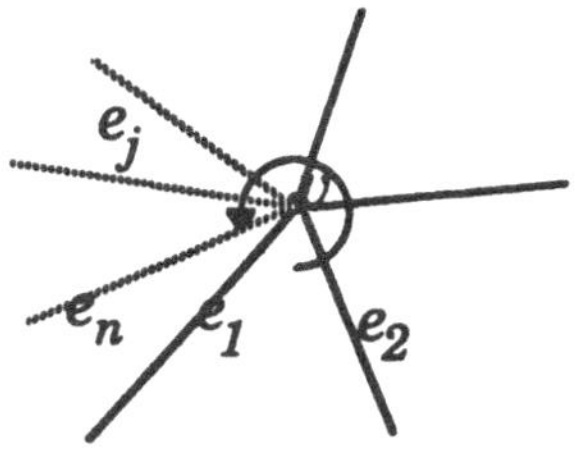

Fig. 7 A vertex v and the edges incident to it.

As well as for saddle regions, nothing can be said locally about the sign of the curvature at a vertex internal to a hybrid region, meaning that no precise shape information can be derived by checking the adjacency type of triangles and different configurations may occur. Strong curvature regions have a well defined mathematical meaning and can be used to extract global and local shape information. However, when only a rough sketch of the surface shape is needed, the strong characterization proposed is rather rigid and a more flexible analysis can be more appropriate. Thus, a kind of tolerance on the shape is introduced, leading to the definition of weak curvature regions. The concept of tolerance on the shape concerns the extraction of global information, meaning that one could use the term "convex" to point to an overall convex area even if containing small concavities along edges. Thus, a second set of shape components is introduced, called the *weak curvature regions*, whose definition requires a new classification of triangles and a new version of the q-connection property.

Definition 5 *: A triangle* t *is said to be* convex (concave, plane) *if at least two of its edges are of type* convex (concave, plane), *it is termed* saddle *otherwise.*

Notice that hybrid triangles do not appear in the *weak* classification scheme.

Definition 6 : *Let* q ∈ { concave, convex, plane, saddle}, attr *be the function returning the attribute of an arc and* type *be the function returning the type of a triangle. Then:*

- *if* q ≠ saddle *then an arc* $(t_i, t_j) \in A$ *is* weakly-q-connected *if and only if* type(t_i) = type (t_j) = q *and* attr((t_i, t_j)) = q;
- *if* q = saddle *then an arc* $(t_i, t_j) \in A$ *is* weakly-q-connected *if and only if* type(t_i) = type (t_j) = q .

Weak curvature regions are always defined in terms of connected component of the surface graph model, as follows.

Definition 7 : *Let* q ∈ { concave, convex, plane, saddle }, *and* G_S *be the graph surface model of S. A* weak curvature region *of S is any connected component of* G_S *obtained removing from* G_S *all arcs not complying with the* weak-q-connection *property.*

The difference with respect to strong curvature regions is that the requirements to classify triangles are weakened, while the rule for walking from a triangle to an adjacent one requires triangles compatible with the adjacency type. This implies that in a weak curvature region of type q it is possible to move from one triangle to any other one through edges of type q. Weak curvature regions of type convex, concave and planar identify global shapes of the surface, meaning that in the interior of a region type q adjacencies will predominate although chains of non-q edges may exist. Local information about the sign of the total curvature cannot be derived due to the global meaning of weak curvature regions.

Obviously, strong curvature regions of type convex, concave and planar are contained in the set of weak curvature regions of the corresponding type. Saddle regions extracted using a weak characterization correspond to saddle regions extracted using the strong one, as in both cases they are connected components formed by triangles with three edges of different type. In figure 8 an example of strong and weak characterization is shown, applied to the same surface. The strong convex region is depicted in figure 8(a) and the concave one in figure 8(b), whereas the weak convex regions are depicted in figure 8(c) and the concave one in figure 8(d). By the point of view of shape information, the weak characterization covers the complete surface, because no hybrid regions result.

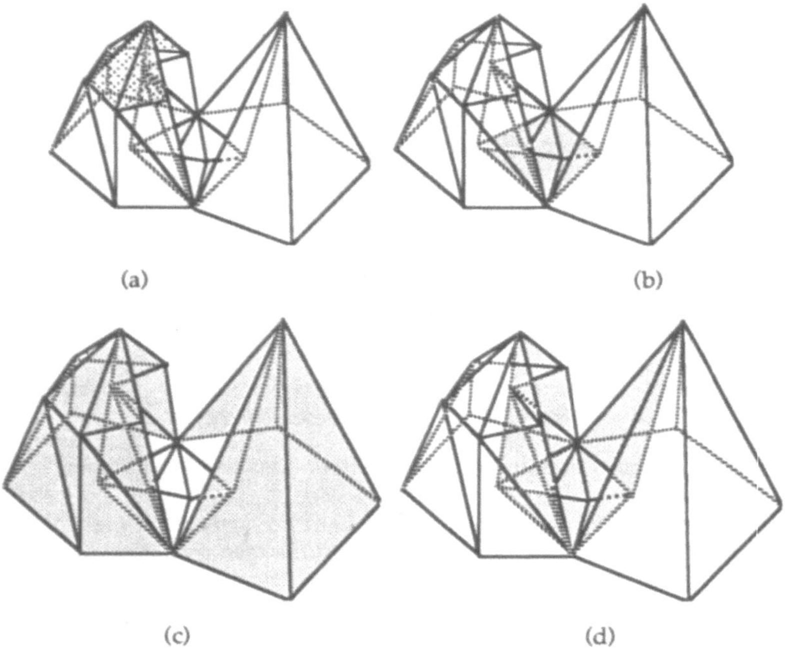

Fig. 8 Example of strong and weak characterization. A strong convex region is highlighted in (a), a strong concave region in (b), while two weak convex regions in (c) and a weak concave region in (d).

The *region adjacency graph* is a suitable structure to encode the surface decomposition and consists of a relational structure where each node corresponds to a consistent curvature region and two nodes are connected by an arc if their corresponding regions have overlapping boundaries. Thus, the structure called *Characteristic Region Configuration*

Graph (CRCG) has been defined, which is more precisely a hypergraph representation of the surface decomposition.
Since the surface decomposition is unique, the node set of the CRCG is unambiguously identified by the set of the surface curvature regions. Since two regions are partially disjoint they can intersect only at their bounding contours. These intersections are called the surface *characteristic lines* and define the arc set of the CRCG, which makes explicit the adjacency relationship between pair of curvature regions. The adjacency between more than two regions is represented by the concept of hyperarc. Again, since two curvature regions may intersect only at their bounding contours, it follows that more than two regions may intersect only at one point of their contours. Differently stated, characteristic lines may intersect only at their endpoints. These intersection points are called the surface *characteristic points* and define the hyperarc set of the CRCG, where one hyperarc is defined for every n-uple of regions adjacent through a point. A formal definition of the CRCG can be found in (Falcidieno et al. 1991)
The CRCG has the advantage of maintaining the spatial relationships among primal shape describers, thus being suitable for further surface analysis requiring to examine neighbouring regions. Moreover, properties of the graph translate directly into relationships among primitives. For example, a cut-node corresponds to a region which completely surrounds other regions.

4. THE SURFACE DECOMPOSITION

The shape elements previously defined can be used to decompose a polyhedral surface and the resulting high level description can be coded in the Characteristic Region Configuration Graph. Since two sets of curvature regions have been defined, at least three schemes of characterization can be used to decompose the surface.

The first possibility is to perform a strong characterization on the whole surface. On the one side, this kind of decomposition gives the possibility to identify areas where the surface curvature has the same sign, thus yielding a result which should be consistent with classical analysis. On the other side, it has the drawback of producing a partially complete characterization, because hybrid regions do not contain precise information about the surface shape.

The second possibility is to perform a weak characterization which aims to the recognition of *globally* uniform areas. This decomposition scheme has the advantage of assigning a morphological meaning to each surface part, thus resulting in a complete shape characterization.

The third approach corresponds to a mixed use of strong and weak curvature regions, by applying at first a strong characterization and performing a weak characterization on the set of the already isolated hybrid regions. In this way, the characterization obtained with strong curvature regions is completed by giving a morphological label to hybrid regions too.

Weak curvature regions play already the role of tolerance on the shape, but the characterization may be used in an even more flexible manner by introducing another tolerance parameter which should formalize the concept of "scale" of characterization. Instead of considering a context of nominal geometry, one could imagine to look at the surface at a certain distance. From a far viewpoint small angles appear "nearly" flat, while from a near viewpoint small variations could be sensibly considered too. Thus, the definition of plane angle is weakened with the introduction of a parameter that represents the tolerance within which an angle must be considered plane. This parameter could be used to tune the characterization to a particular level required, using the tolerance as a selective filter to detect shape properties of interest and possibly varying it to refine locally the recognition of shape elements (Falcidieno et al. 1991).

Given the surface graph model, chosen the set of curvature regions and possibly chosen a tolerance, the algorithm for the shape decomposition consists of four main steps:

Algorithm Shape Decomposition
Edge_classification (tolerance);
Triangle_classification (strong or weak);
Q_connection_test (strong or weak);
Connected_component_extraction;

The first three steps are the core of the proposed method whereas the fourth one is independent of the previous steps and of the set of curvature regions chosen.

The first step assigns geometric attributes to the arc set, using a given tolerance for the classification of plane angles. For every arc, the two normals of the triangles sharing the corresponding edge are needed and their product is checked to classify the subtended angle. Note that only in this step numerical computation is required, whereas the remaining steps simply consists of evaluating the type of other graph elements by "counting" the number of geometric attributes of the adjacent elements.

The second step performs a triangle processing to assign attributes to the node set, according to the chosen set of curvature regions, i.e. strong or weak. During the third step, labels are given to all those arcs not complying with the q-connection property, either in the strong or weak formulation according to the selected level of characterization. Finally, the q-connected components of the graph are extracted, i.e. the curvature regions are recognized.

The computational complexity of these steps can be expressed in terms of the total number of nodes in the graph surface model: being a planar graph, if N denotes the number of nodes (i.e. triangles) then the number of arcs (i.e. inner edges) is at most 3N-6.

Thus, the first step of edge classification has a O(3N) complexity, while the triangle classification is O(N) complex. Again, the q-connection test is linear in the number of arcs, that is, it has a O(3N) complexity. Observe that the operation required in these three steps are "intrinsically" local, meaning that they could be performed in parallel.

5. Concluding Remarks

Triangular meshes for surface approximation is a quite general and versatile choice and the proposed method is an efficient tool for identifying regions with uniform curvature properties. The method can be applied to any set of irregularly distributed data points and has a natural implementation in sequential and parallel models of computation. The recognition of the primal shape elements can be performed in parallel with respect to their type and the decomposition can be obtained by removing the non-*q*-connected arcs from the surface graph model. In other words, the surface decomposition is reduced to the solution of the arc labelling subproblem, whose computational complexity is linear.

The surface decomposition yields a simplification of the shape which is useful in computer graphics applications. For example, the method proposed has been successfully applied in the context of surface approximation for the reconstruction of natural landscapes using a set of data points and morphological constraints as start points (Falcidieno et al. 1990; Falcidieno et al. 1992).

An example of decomposition is shown in figure 9, where the recognized convex regions are coloured in white, the concave ones in dark green, the plane regions in pale green and the saddle ones in red.

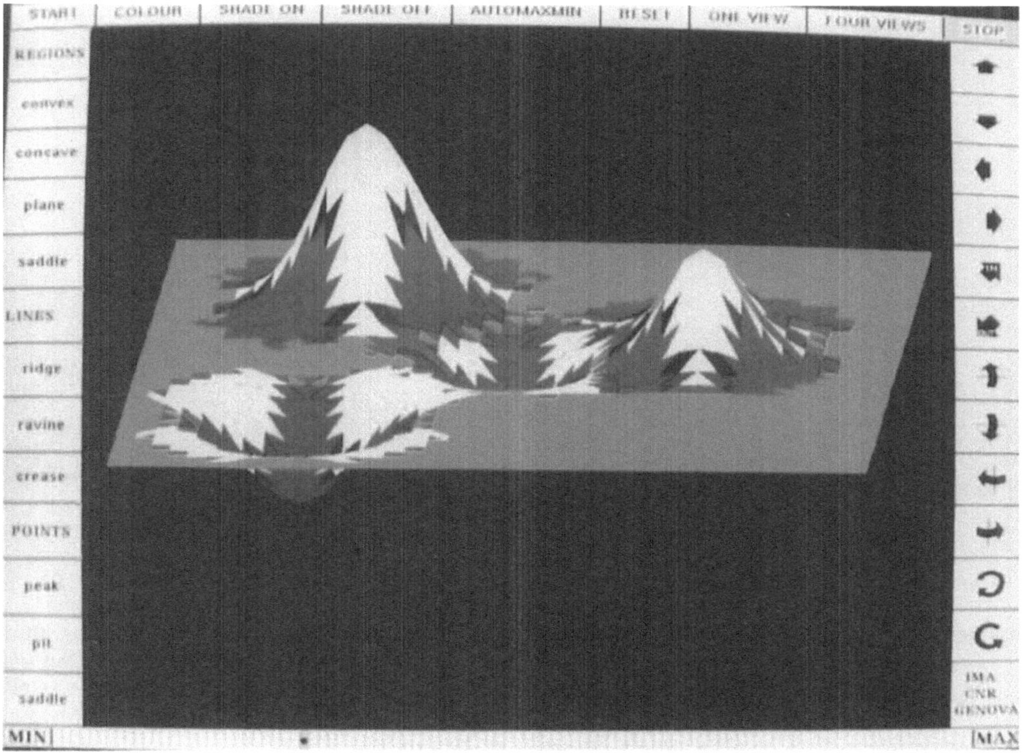

Fig. 9 An example of the proposed shape decomposition.

Some comparison between our method and that proposed in (Lin et al. 1982) can be made. The main difference is that the latter method does not care about "how" the surface is folded around a vertex. Indeed, with reference to figure 10(a), the angle deficit is positive at vertex v, thus the total curvature is positive. If the surface is folded as depicted in figure 10(b) or as depicted in figure 10(c) the classification remains unchanged. This result is consistent with the meaning of Gaussian curvature, which is independent of the embedding of the surface in the space.

When our method is applied to the same example, a different characterization will be obtained according to the different folding of the surface. In the first case a characterization with only one convex region will be produced, as depicted in figure 10(d), while in the second case a decomposition into one convex and one concave region will be obtained (figure 10(e)). Thus, our method makes distinction between the different manners in which the surface can be folded around a vertex and by this point of view could be somehow considered as a discrete counterpart of an analysis of the mean curvature of the surface.

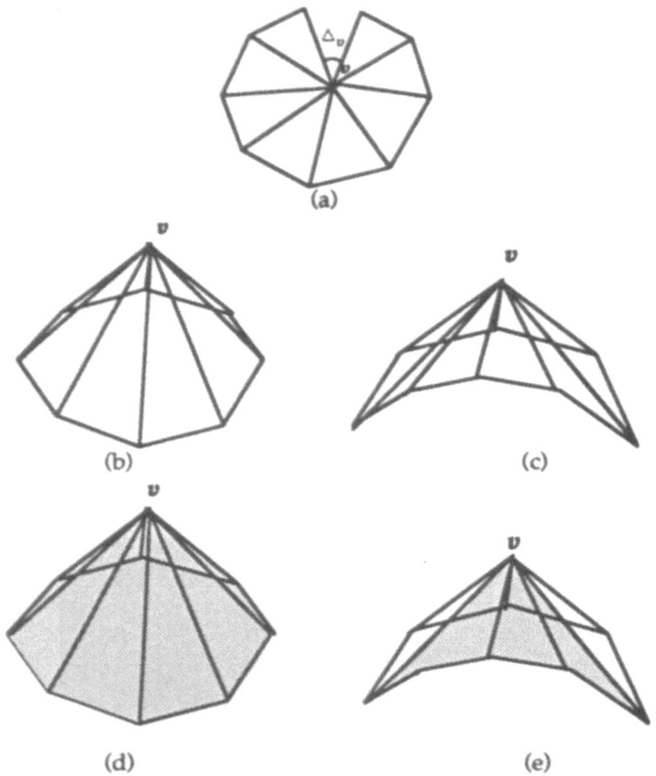

Fig.10 The triangles incident to a vertex v are unwrapped on the plane and the corresponding angle excesses give a positive total curvature (a). Different folding of the triangles around the vertex v can be constructed ((b) and (c)) preserving the total curvature at v. Our method of characterization produces two different decompositions as respectively depicted in (d) and (e).

References

Abelson,H., Disessa,A. (1986) *La geometria della tartaruga,* Franco Muzzio & c. Editors, Padova

Besl,P.J., Jain,R.C., (1986) Invariant surface characteristics for 3D object recognition in range images, *Computer Vision, Graphics and Image Processing* , No 33

Boissonnat,J.D., (1984) Geometric structures for three-dimensional shape representation, *ACM Transactions on Graphics,* Vol. 3, No. 4

De Floriani,L., Falcidieno,B., Pienovi,C., (1985) Delaunay-based representation of surfaces defined over arbitrarily shaped domains, *Computer Vision, Graphics and Image Processing* , 32

Falcidieno,B., Pienovi,C., (1990) Natural surface approximation by constrained stochastic interpolation, *Computer-Aided Design*, 22, 3

Falcidieno,B., Spagnuolo,M., (1991) A new method for the characterization of topographic surfaces, *International Journal of Geographical Information Systems*, vol. 5, No. 4

Falcidieno,B., Pienovi,C., Spagnuolo,M., (1992) Discrete surface models: constraint-based generation and understanding, In: B. Falcidieno, I. Herman, C. Pienovi (eds.) *Computer Graphics and Mathematics*, EUROGRAPHICS SEMINARS Series, *Springer-Verlag* (to appear)

Haralick,R.M., Laffey,T.J., Watson,L.T., (1983) The topographic primal sketch, *Int. J. Robotics Res.* 2, 1 (Spring)

Lin,C., Perry,M.J., (1982) Surface description using surface triangulation, *Proceedings of the Workshop in Computer Vision: Representation and Control,* (Rindge, N.H. August 1982)

Lipschutz, M.M., *Differential Geometry* , McGraw-Hill, New York 1969

Medioni,G., Nevatia,R., Description of 3-D surfaces using curvature properties, in *Proceedings of Image Understanding Workshop,* New Orleans, La., October 1984, DARPA

Mortenson,M.E., (1985) *Geometric Modeling* , John Wiley & Sons, New York

Nackman,L.R., (1984) Two-dimensional critical point configuration graph, *IEEE Transactions on Pattern Analysis and Machine Intelligence,* PAMI-6

Nackman,L.R., Pizer,S.M., (1985) Three-dimensional shape description using the symmetric axis transform I: theory, *IEEE Transactions on Pattern Analysis and Machine Intelligence,* PAMI-7, No. 2

O'Neill,B., (1966) *Elementary Differential Geometry,* Academic Press, New York

Pitas,I.,Venetsanopoulos,A.N., (1990) Morphological shape decomposition, *IEEE Transactions on Pattern Analysis and Machine Intelligence,* vol. 12, No 1

Preparata,F.P., Shamos,M.I., (1985) *Computational Geometry,* New York , Springer Verlag

Weibel,R., Heller,M., (1990) A framework for digital terrain modeling, *Proceedings of Spatial Data Handling,* K. Brassel and K. Kishimoto eds.

Watson,L.T., Laffey,T.J., and Haralick, R.M., (1985) Topographic classification of digital image intensity surfaces using general splines and the discrete cosine transformation, *Computer Vision, Graphics and Image Processing,* 29

AUTHORS BIOGRAPHIES

Bianca Falcidieno is currently director of research at the Istituto per la Matematica Applicata, an institute belonging to the National Research Council of Italy.
She started to work there since 1974 and now acts as head of the Computer Graphics Group and as leader of national and international projects on Computer Graphics and its applications.
She has written more than 70 refereed technical publications on subjects related to these areas. She is a member of the Editorial Board of Computer and Graphics and Computer Graphics Forum, and coeditor for the Technical Report series in EUROGRAPHICS. As a member of various societies and associations (EUROGRAPHICS, ACM, AICA, IEEE, IFIP, etc...) she served on numerous program committees for several international conferences, in particular she has been program co-chair for the EUROGRAPHICS Workshop on Computer Graphics and Mathematics in 1991.
She coordinates of the national activity in Computer Graphics of the Italian Association for Computer Science (AICA) since 1986 and is member of the EUROGRAPHICS Executive Committee since 1990.
Her research interests include Geometric Modelling, Computational Geometry and Graphics Standards.

Michela Spagnuolo graduated from the Department of Mathematics, University of Genova, in 1989.
Since then, she holds a Research Fellowship at the Istituto per la Matematica Applicata of the National Research Council, in Genova.
Her research interests include Surface Modelling and Geometric Modelling for CAD/CAM applications.

Address
Istituto per la Matematica Applicata del C.N.R.
Via L.B. Alberti, 4 - 16132 Genova (Italy)
Phone: +39-10-515510
Fax: +39-10-517801
Email:FALCIDIENO@IMAGE.GE.CNR.IT
SPAGNUOLO@IMAGE.GE.CNR.IT

The Conjugate Classification of the Kernel Form of the Hexagonal Grid

Zhijie Zheng and Anthony J. Maeder

ABSTRACT

The *conjugate* classification, a new classification of the *kernel form* which defines the spatial structure of binary data on the hexagonal grid, is presented in the paper. The seven points of the kernel form on the hexagonal grid have a state set of 128 states and the conjugate classification arranges the state set in a five level hierarchy. The state set is divided into 2 conjugate sets, 14 groups, 22 clusters, 28 classes and 128 states in the five levels respectively. Using information theory, the conjugate classification is proved to be an optimal structure, in the sense that it has the minimum number of variables and the shortest whole bit length for each variable on each level. When using the new representation, it is necessary to process both conjugate sets in same pass as both sets have equivalent importance. The new classification is potentially useful for cellular automata and mathematical morphology operations in different practical application areas.

Keyword: cellular automata, connectivity analysis, computational geometry, digital topology, information theory, mathematical morphology.

1 INTRODUCTION

1.1 The Hexagonal Grid and Visual Computing

The hexagonal grid plays a significant role in visual computing. Many natural and artificial instances of hexagonal grids exist, such as insect eyes [Weyl 1952], display screens [Dubois 1985], halftone pictures [Stevenson and Arce 1985], plane tilings [Loeb 1971] and mammal retinas [Walters 1986]. Different optimal problems, such as minimum length, maximum area, tightest arrangement, lightest structure [Steinhaus 1960] and simplest plan nets [Wells 1977] are intrinsically solved with the hexagonal grid [Luczak and Rosenfeld 1989, Mersereau 1979, Horn 1986]. Analysis of geometric and topological properties on the hexagonal grid has proved an efficient way [Kong and Rosenfeld 1989, Horn 1986, Gray 1971, Dubois 1985, Steinhaus 1960] for investigating various related subjects, from biological morphology to visual computing [Serra 1982, Preston and Duff 1984]. Considering any point on the hexagonal grid, there are six neighbour points around it, all of which are an equal distance from the given point. Because the whole grid can be generated by repeating this seven point structure, it is called the *kernel form* of the hexagonal grid. A fixed value of the points of the kernel form is called a *state*. If each point is either 0 or 1, there are in total 128 possible states making up the *state set* of the kernel form. Grouping these states into subsets with some similar properties constructs a classification of states useful, when describing certain shape and topological properties of collections of points on the grid.

0 0	1 0	1 1	1 1	1 1
0 x 0	0 x 0	0 x 0	0 x 1	1 x 1
0 0	0 0	0 0	0 0	0 0
$<0,1>$	$<1,6>$	$<2,5>$	$<3,4>$	$<4,3>$
1 1	1 1	1 0	1 1	1 1
1 x 1	1 x 1	0 x 1	0 x 0	0 x 0
0 1	1 1	1 0	0 1	1 0
$<5,2>$	$<6,7>$	$<7,14>$	$<8,11>$	$<9,10>$
1 1	1 0	0 0	1 1	
0 x 1	0 x 1	1 x 1	0 x 0	
1 0	0 0	0 0	1 1	
$<10,12>$	$<11,9>$	$<12,8>$	$<13,13>$	

Here x can be either 0 or 1 and the $< i,j >$ value associated with each state shown indicates i for Golay-Preston and j for Serra numbering for each specific group in the classification.

Figure 1: Two Numbering Systems for the Golay Transformation

1.2 Cellular Automata and The Golay Transformation

In the past three decades, investigations of the hexagonal grid have been conducted in the research area of Cellular Automata for digital image analysis, image processing and pattern recognition. Cellular Automata [Preston and Duff 1984, Kunii and Takai 1989] is an active branch of computational techniques invented in 1948 by von Neumann and Ulam. In 1969 Golay [Golay 1969] proposed a classification of the state set - the *Golay transformation* - for the kernel form of the hexagonal grid to be 14 groups, using a rotational symmetry policy and ignoring the value at the central point in the kernel form. He gave each group in the classification an integer number(0-13) [Preston and Duff 1984, p45]. Following his number system, Preston [Ingram and Preston 1970, Preston 1971] made use of this numbering system for work on a series of cellular automata machines and Serra [Serra 1982, p186] gave another different numbering system(1-14) for the Golay transformation in Mathematical Morphology. We call the two numbering systems the Golay-Preston system and the Serra system respectively, as shown in Figure 1.

The transformation is also known as an *alphabet table* on the hexagonal grid. Only the last group has the same number in both systems; all other $< i,j >$ pairs in the numberings are different. Following Golay's original research, theories, methods and specific cellular automata computers were subsequently developed using his classification for describing the key functions [Preston and Duff 1984].

1.3 The Game of Life, Mathematical Morphology and Machines

The invention of Conway's game *life* in 1971 [Gardner 1971] gave cellular automata a role in an interesting visualization of dynamical properties on geometric grids. Using the number of 1-elements in a state as the parameter, transforming rules have been investigated for many grids and applications from microscopically physical processes to social and economical behavior in complicated macroscopic systems.

To investigate geometric and topological properties of digital images, Mathematical Morphology invented in 1964 by Matheron deepens the results of Cellular Automata [Serra 1982]. After Serra and others developed transformations such as 'Hit' and 'Miss', 'Dilation' and 'Erosion', 'Opening' and 'Closing', Boolean valued models have become a useful terminology for visual computing. Mathematical Morphology accepted the Golay transformation and Conway rules as the foundations for higher level image analysis. Its results [Preston 1971, Preston and Duff 1984, Serra 1982, Deutsch 1970, Deutsch 1972, Luczak and Rosenfeld 1989, Kong and Rosenfeld 1989, Dubois 1985, Gray 1971] have been widely applied in different branches of visual computing and connected with many theoretical questions and practical applications.

Besides different theories and methods, a series of cellular automata machines [Preston and Duff 1984] have been constructed in the past three decades. Starting from CELLSCAN (1961), CLIP4, DAP and MPP [Preston and Duff 1984] are three examples of full array cellular automata now in existence. Using up-to-date VLSI techniques, more cellular automata machines are being developed currently [Preston and Duff 1984]. Cellular automata machines can easily and naturally support high speed arithmetic and logic operations on 2-D digital images. Due to the close correspondence with matrix computations, they offer efficient architectures for visual computing.

1.4 Weaknesses of Traditional Schemes

The numbering of groups in the Golay transformation has no intrinsic meaning connected to the group, so the numbering system can be replaced by any set of 14 symbols without loss of generality. It would be an advantage, if it were possible to calculate the group number from a state directly. Look-up tables and Boolean logic programming are the two main techniques used for finding group numbers in today's cellular automata machines. The look-up table scheme is mainly used for arithmetic operations and logic operations, and the Boolean logic programming scheme is used for logic operations.

From geometric and topological considerations, the Golay transformation is only dependent on rotational symmetry with one parameter. There are more properties of geometric symmetry than rotation for the kernel form of the hexagonal grid, such as *conjugate* and *reflective* [Weyl 1952]. Different properties of topological invariants such as number of connections, branches and crossings are also important to represent invariants on the hexagonal grid. Considering the Golay transformation from the point of view of rotational symmetry alone, each one of the 14 groups in the transformation can consist of 2, 4 or 12 states. With 14 groups for 128 states in the Golay system, the average number of states in one group is $128/14 \approx 9$. Because two values can be assigned to the center point and only six directions of rotation on neighbours are possible, each group contains more properties than rotation alone. If we want to analyse other properties for a state, then extra information has to be extracted from the state.

For analysing topological properties on the hexagonal grid, Gray [Gray 1971] in 1971 proposed *Differentials* on square and hexagonal grids. He reverses the center point from 1 to 0 or 0 to 1 to extract the useful information of connectivity relationships on the state.

The Conway rules use a classification in which the states with the same number of points with a value of 1 are collected in a group. His system is equivalent to a Boolean system with seven variables. The k-th group with k points having a value of 1, is composed of $\binom{7}{k}$ states, $0 \leq k \leq 7$. Each of the eight groups contains 1, 7, 21 or 35 states respectively. For eight groups and 128 states, the average number of states in one group of the Conway rules is $128/8 = 16$.

1.5 A Calculable Classification

A new classification scheme of the kernel form on the hexagonal grid is proposed in this paper. We use a collection of geometric and topological properties as parameters to give each state a directly calculable classification i.e. the parameter values can be used to calculate the group number for a given state. Three parameters, *conjugate* (reversing all point values from 1 to 0 or 0 to 1) , *connection* (number of neighbours with the same value as the center point) and *branch* (number of neighbour runs with the same value as the center point i.e half the number of neighbour crossings) together provide the fundamental collection of parameters. For example, let X_1, X_2, X_3, X_4 be four states of the kernel form.

$$X_1 = \begin{array}{ccc} & 0 \quad 1 & \\ 0 & 1 & 0 \\ & 1 \quad 1 & \end{array}, \quad X_2 = \begin{array}{ccc} & 1 \quad 0 & \\ 1 & 0 & 1 \\ & 0 \quad 0 & \end{array}, \quad X_3 = \begin{array}{ccc} & 0 \quad 1 & \\ 1 & 1 & 0 \\ & 1 \quad 1 & \end{array}, \quad X_4 = \begin{array}{ccc} & 0 \quad 1 & \\ 1 & 0 & 0 \\ & 1 \quad 1 & \end{array},$$

X_2 is a *conjugate* state of X_1, since both of them have 3 connections and 2 branches(or 4 crossings). X_4 is a *differential* state of X_3, since X_3 has 4 connections and 2 branches while X_4 has 2 connections and 2 branches.

Using these three parameters, a total of 22 groups in two conjugate sets can be identified. Each set contains 11 groups and each group contains 1, 2, 6, 9 or 12 states respectively. The groups in these conjugate sets can be arranged as two corresponding triangles, which provides a stronger organization than with the relatively unstructured Golay transformation. For this conjugate classification, two additional parameters are used for uniquely distinguishing every state. They are termed *spin* and em rotation parameters.

1.6 The Balanced Policy

The new classification scheme, using conjugation and connectivity conditions, has direct meaning in terms of topological properties. Traditional image analysis on binary images divides an image in two complementary parts, foreground and background. It is convenient to concentrate further analysis on one of them, which is deemed more important than its complement part. Using recent techniques of Mathematical Morphology, it is usual to identify this part with Hit or Miss transformations. Using a one pass procedure on a matrix, one and only one result is generated for a class of matching operations. Normally, if the contours separating foreground and background are smooth, then it is usually reliable to use classical techniques for analysis. However, if the contours have intrinsic properties of discontinuity or non-smoothness, then it is more complex for further analysis to be undertaken properly. *Opening* and *Closing* are effective operations for this kind of non-smooth situations. Although 'Opening' and 'Closing' are balanced operations which affect both foreground and background, their atoms, 'Dilation' and 'Erosion', operate only on either foreground or background. For the new representation proposed here, it is not sufficient to process only one part. The two complementary parts have to be managed and transformed in the same pass since both parts have equivalent importance.

2 CONJUGATION AND CONNECTIVITY

It is necessary to give some fundamental definitions for conjugation and connectivity properties on the hexagonal grid before discussing the conjugate classification scheme in detail.

2.1 The Kernel Form, State Sets and Operations

The hexagonal grid is an important lattice in 2-D geometry because all six neighbours of any point on the grid are at the same distance from it (and from their neighbours in turn). Because the whole grid can be generated by repeating this seven point structure, we call it the *kernel form* of

x_0 x_1

x_5 x_6 x_2

x_4 x_3

Figure 2: The Kernel Form of The Hexagonal Grid

the hexagonal grid. Let a given state X of the kernel form be $X = \{x_0, x_1, x_2, x_3, x_4, x_5, x_6\}$. This state is shown in Figure 2. For a given state, each x_i has a certain value. Collecting all different states, the *state set* Y of the kernel form is created.

For any state X, each $x_i \in X$ is a Boolean variable, if the grid is used to represent only binary images. The state set is thus a Boolean system with seven variables:

$$Y = \{X | x_i \in \{0,1\}, 0 \leq i \leq 6\}. \tag{1}$$

There are in total $2^7 = 128$ states in this system. Because each x_i is a Boolean variable, a set of operations can be performed on X. In this paper, we use the following five fundamental Boolean operations: { NOT, AND, OR, XOR, NAND } denoted by $\{^-, \cap, \cup, \oplus, \odot\}$ respectively. Note that $x \oplus y = \overline{x} \cap y \cup x \cap \overline{y}$ and $x \odot y = \overline{x} \cap \overline{y} \cup x \cap y$.

Let $\tilde{}$ be the *conjugate* operation, which reverses the value of all Boolean variables in X from 0 to 1 or 1 to 0 and keeps other binary operations invariant. i.e. f or $f(X)$ is a function of X,

$$\tilde{f} = \tilde{f}(X) = f(\overline{X}).$$

For example,

$$\begin{aligned} f(x,y) &= (x \cap y) + (\overline{x} \odot y), x, y \in \{0,1\} \\ \tilde{f}(x,y) &= f(\overline{x}, \overline{y}) \\ &= (\overline{x} \cap \overline{y}) + (x \odot \overline{y}). \end{aligned}$$

Generally speaking, if f is a Boolean function, $\overline{f} \neq \tilde{f}$. For example,

$$\begin{aligned} f(x,y) &= x \cap \overline{y} \\ \overline{f}(x,y) &= \overline{x \cap \overline{y}} \\ &= \overline{x} \cup y; \\ \tilde{f}(x,y) &= f(\overline{x}, \overline{y}) \\ &= \overline{x} \cap y. \end{aligned}$$

The center element x_6 of the kernel form plays the key role in determining the structure properties of X, as there is a fixed distance between any $x_i, 0 \leq i \leq 5$ and x_6. However, only $x_{i-1 \pmod 6}$ and $x_{i+1 \pmod 6}$ have the same property with respect to x_i for $0 \leq i \leq 5$. Because of this difference, it is convenient to separate the kernel form into two parts i.e. the center x_6 and neighbours $\{x_i\}_{i=0}^{5}$. For any state $X \in Y$, there is a unique conjugate state in the state set Y too. It can be generated by performing the NOT operation on all $x_i \in X$. Let $\overline{X}$ denote the *conjugate state* of X, $\overline{X} = \{\overline{x}_i\}_{i=0}^{6}$.

The fact that each state X has a unique conjugate state $\overline{X}$ provides a property useful in the classification scheme. If we collect a subset of states dependent on x_6's value of each state, then Y

can be divided into two *conjugate sets* of states and denoted by G and $\tilde{G}$ in which all $X \in G, x_6 = 1$ and all $X \in \tilde{G}, x_6 = 0$.

$$\begin{aligned} G &= \{X | X \in Y \text{ AND } x_6 = 1\} &(2)\\ \tilde{G} &= \{X | X \in Y \text{ AND } x_6 = 0\} &(3)\\ Y &= G \cup \tilde{G} &(4)\\ \emptyset &= G \cap \tilde{G} &(5)\end{aligned}$$

Each of the sets G and $\tilde{G}$ contains a total of 64 states.

2.2 Connection and Branch Number

If $\exists x_i$ such that $x_6 = x_i, 0 \leq i \leq 5$, then there is said to be a *connection* between x_6 and x_i. For any given state X, the number of connections from x_6 is equal to the number of neighbours with the same value as x_6. We call this number the *connection number*, denoted by p. p is an integer $p \in \{0, 1, \cdots, 6\}$. Let the conjugate connection number of p be $\tilde{p}$, then we have following equations:

$$\begin{aligned} p &= p(X) \\ &= \sum_{i=0}^{5} x_i \odot x_6 \\ &= \sum_{i=0}^{5} \overline{x}_i \odot \overline{x}_6 \\ &= p(\overline{X}) \\ &= \tilde{p}(X) = \tilde{p} &(6)\end{aligned}$$

For a regular state, the maximum value of p is 6. However if x_6 is in a *broken* state in which only part of $x_i, 0 \leq i \leq 5$ can be defined (such as at a border position of an image), it is convenient to define p_X be the *maximum number* of connections from x_6 to all neighbour variables.

Let $\overline{p}$ be a *complement connection number* of p, p_X be the *maximum number* of connections on X, $\tilde{\overline{p}}$ be the *complement number* of $\tilde{p}$ and $\tilde{p}_X$ be the *conjugate connection number* of p_X then we have following equations:

$$\begin{aligned} \overline{p} &= \overline{p}(X) \\ &= \sum_{i=0}^{5} \overline{x}_i \odot x_6 \\ &= \sum_{i=0}^{5} x_i \odot \overline{x}_6 \\ &= \overline{p}(\overline{X}) = \tilde{\overline{p}} &(7)\\ p_X &= p + \overline{p} \\ &= \tilde{p} + \tilde{\overline{p}} = \tilde{p}_X &(8)\end{aligned}$$

By the above equations, we always have $p = \tilde{p}, \overline{p} = \tilde{\overline{p}}$ and $p_X = \tilde{p}_X$, but p and $\overline{p}$ are different and complement each other.

The elements $x_i, i \neq 6$, accessed in sequence with increasing (or decreasing) i, make up a cycle around x_6. If any two successive neighbour elements in the cycle have the same value, they are said to be *linked*. It is usual to find a specific linked structure called a *run* which is a maximum sequence of elements with the same value. Because each point itself could form a run, there are at most six runs composed of $\{x_i\}_{i=0}^{5}$. The number of runs is even for any multi-run state and in these cases only half the runs can be of the same value as the center element. Each such run can be regarded as a *branch* from the center point, so there are between 0 and 3 branches for any state. If there is only one run around x_6, either x_6 is an isolated point without a branch or an inner point also without a branch (since the run does not end). The number of such branch connections is denoted by q, $q \in \{0, 1, 2, 3\}$.

For any X and $\overline{X}$, the branch number q and its *conjugate branch number* $\tilde{q}$ can be calculated by following equations:

$$\begin{aligned} q &= q(X) \\ &= \frac{1}{2}\sum_{i=0}^{5} x_i \oplus x_{i+1} \pmod 6 \\ &= \frac{1}{2}\sum_{i=0}^{5} \overline{x}_i \oplus \overline{x}_{i+1} \pmod 6 \\ &= q(\overline{X}) \\ &= \tilde{q}(X) = \tilde{q} \end{aligned} \tag{9}$$

The equations for q and $\tilde{q}$ are independent of x_6, since the branch number is invariant for either x_6 or $\overline{x}_6$.

For example,

$$X_1 = \begin{array}{ccccc} & 1 & & 0 & \\ 0 & & 1 & & 1 \\ & 1 & & 0 & \end{array},\ \begin{array}{c} p = 3 \\ \overline{p} = 3 \\ p_X = 6 \end{array},q = 3; \quad \overline{X}_1 = \begin{array}{ccccc} & 0 & & 1 & \\ 1 & & 0 & & 0 \\ & 0 & & 1 & \end{array},\ \begin{array}{c} \tilde{p} = 3 \\ \tilde{\overline{p}} = 3 \\ \tilde{p}_X = 6 \end{array},q = 3;$$

$$X_2 = \begin{array}{ccccc} & 0 & & 0 & \\ 0 & & 0 & & 1 \\ & 1 & & 0 & \end{array},\ \begin{array}{c} p = 4 \\ \overline{p} = 2 \\ p_X = 6 \end{array},q = 2; \quad \overline{X}_2 = \begin{array}{ccccc} & 1 & & 1 & \\ 1 & & 1 & & 0 \\ & 0 & & 1 & \end{array},\ \begin{array}{c} \tilde{p} = 4 \\ \tilde{\overline{p}} = 2 \\ \tilde{p}_X = 6 \end{array},q = 2;$$

$$X_3 = \begin{array}{ccccc} & 1 & & 0 & \\ 0 & & 0 & & 1 \\ & 1 & & 1 & \end{array},\ \begin{array}{c} p = 2 \\ \overline{p} = 4 \\ p_X = 6 \end{array},q = 2; \quad \overline{X}_3 = \begin{array}{ccccc} & 0 & & 1 & \\ 1 & & 1 & & 0 \\ & 0 & & 0 & \end{array},\ \begin{array}{c} \tilde{p} = 2 \\ \tilde{\overline{p}} = 4 \\ \tilde{p}_X = 6 \end{array},q = 2;$$

$$X_4 = \begin{array}{ccccc} & 1 & & 1 & \\ 1 & & 1 & & 1 \\ & 1 & & 0 & \end{array},\ \begin{array}{c} p = 5 \\ \overline{p} = 1 \\ p_X = 6 \end{array},q = 1; \quad \overline{X}_4 = \begin{array}{ccccc} & 0 & & 0 & \\ 0 & & 0 & & 0 \\ & 0 & & 1 & \end{array},\ \begin{array}{c} \tilde{p} = 5 \\ \tilde{\overline{p}} = 1 \\ \tilde{p}_X = 6 \end{array},q = 1;$$

$$X_5 = \begin{array}{ccccc} & 0 & & & \\ 1 & & 1 & & 0 \\ & & & 1 & \end{array},\ \begin{array}{c} p = 2 \\ \overline{p} = 2 \\ p_X = 4 \end{array},q = 2; \quad \overline{X}_5 = \begin{array}{ccccc} & 1 & & & \\ 0 & & 0 & & 1 \\ & & & 0 & \end{array},\ \begin{array}{c} \tilde{p} = 2 \\ \tilde{\overline{p}} = 2 \\ \tilde{p}_X = 4 \end{array},q = 2;$$

X_5 and $\overline{X}_5$ are two broken states and for both of them $p_X = 4$.

3 THE CONJUGATE CLASSIFICATION

Each state X has been described by three numbers in the above cases i.e. x_6, p and q. Therefore a prospective classification of the state set of the kernel form has been provided. When we transform $x_j = x_i$ from $\{x_i\}_{i=0}^5$ to $\{x_j\}_{j=0}^5, j = i+1$ or $i-1 \pmod 6$ cyclically, p and q are invariant, in other words, they have a rotation invariant property. This collection of numbers corresponding to the conjugation, point and branch connections has obvious topological meaning. We need to investigate the properties of this classification and demonstrate that it is useful for purpose of practical topological analysis.

3.1 The Fundamental Structure

Let ${}_p^qG$ be a subset termed *cluster* of states in G with p connections and q branches, and ${}_p^q\tilde{G}$ be the *conjugate cluster* of states in $\tilde{G}$ with the same p and q. In each cluster, only one state in a rotation invariant *class* which contains all rotation invariant states needs to be chosen as a representative. We call a classification composed of $\{{}_p^qG\}$ and $\{{}_p^q\tilde{G}\}$ the *fundamental structure*, shown in Figure 3 and Figure 4 respectively.

This fundamental structure is composed of 22 clusters in two conjugate sets laid out in a symmetric arrangement of two conjugate triangles, for which the three clusters ${}_0^0G, {}_6^0G$ and ${}_3^3G$ (and their conjugates) are the vertices. Each set contains 11 distinguishable clusters. A cluster has 1 ($q = 0$), 2 ($q = 3$), 6 ($q = 1$), 9 ($p = 2, 4$ and $q = 2$) or 12 ($p = 3, q = 2$) states respectively. Except for $q = 2$ clusters, a cluster contains only one rotation invariant class. A cluster of $q = 2$ is composed of two classes of rotation invariant states, which cannot be distinguished further in the fundamental structure.

3.2 The Fundamental Structure and the Golay Transformation

Since most clusters in the fundamental structure contain one rotation invariant class, we have a foundation for a comparison with the Golay transformation i.e. with the Golay-Preston and Serra systems described in section 1.2. It is attractive to list the three number schemes together as in Figure 5. For each cluster, a $< i, j >$ parameter is listed under each ${}_p^qG$ or ${}_p^q\tilde{G}$ cluster where i denotes the i-th group of Golay-Preston system and j denotes the j-th group of Serra system.

Comparing the two classifications, it is clear that the Golay transformation does not cater for conjugate relations. Except for $p = 3$ clusters, a Golay group contains two non-conjugate clusters. Considering the importance of conjugate relations in a Boolean system, this is an unfortunate weakness. Though there are two non-rotationally equivalent classes in $p = 2$ clusters, the conjugate relation has separated states sufficiently to give only 9 or 12 states in each cluster. Considering that there are 12 states in most groups of the Golay transformation, our clusters are generally smaller than Golay groups.

3.3 Spin and Rotation

The fundamental structure is not a complete classification. Analysing the states in $q = 2$ clusters, there is reflection symmetry in $p = 3$ cluster in which one state in a rotation invariant class has a reflection state in another rotation invariant class. However, the states in $p = 2$ and $p = 4$ clusters do not have a similar reflection symmetry between them in which the reflection of a state is contained in the same class. It is useful to borrow the concept of *spin* from the terminology of modern Physics, to provide a new parameter (denoted by s) for distinguishing different directions between 'left' and 'right' rotations. Only two classes need to be distinguished from each other, so s can be a Boolean value. After adding this parameter, the fundamental structure is extended to a four variable classification in which a total of 28 classes in two conjugate sets can be identified.

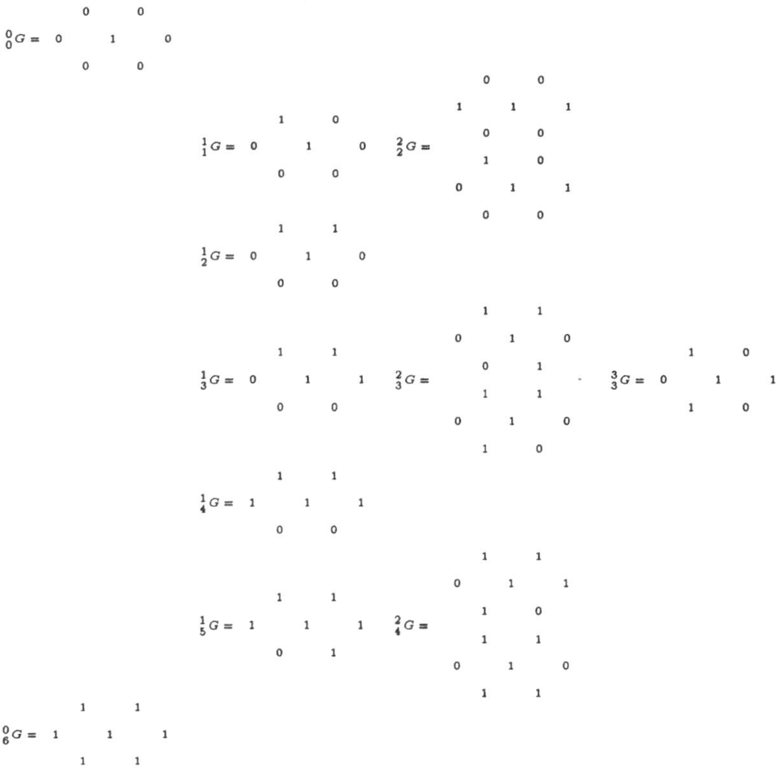

Each cluster contains one state from a rotation invariant class as a representative.

Figure 3: The Clusters of G Set of The Fundamental Structure on the Kernel Form

Another additional parameter termed *rotation* (denoted by r) must be used for distinguishing rotational positions in a class. For any class with more than one state, we can define a state as *initial* starting from the position of x_0. Relative to this position at most 6 positions can be distinguished. For a class only with one state, this can be defined as the invariant position. Seven rotation positions can thus be identified and they can be indicated by $r \in \{0, 1, \cdots, 6\}$ for one invariant operation and six circumrotation operations.

Using this five parameter collection, it is possible to give any state of the kernel form a proper classification. From the historical point of view, our solution is similar to classifying isotopes in Nuclear Physics in the early years of the 20-th century. Because it is not sufficient to use number of electrons or protons in isotopes as atomic number for distinction, another atomic number of mass or neutrons had to be introduced. For instance ${}^{131}_{54}Xe$ denoted an atomic species whose nucleus contains 54 protons (atomic number) and 131 protons-plus-neutrons (mass number) i.e. 77 neutrons. Isotopes can be well identified by the same atomic number but different mass number.

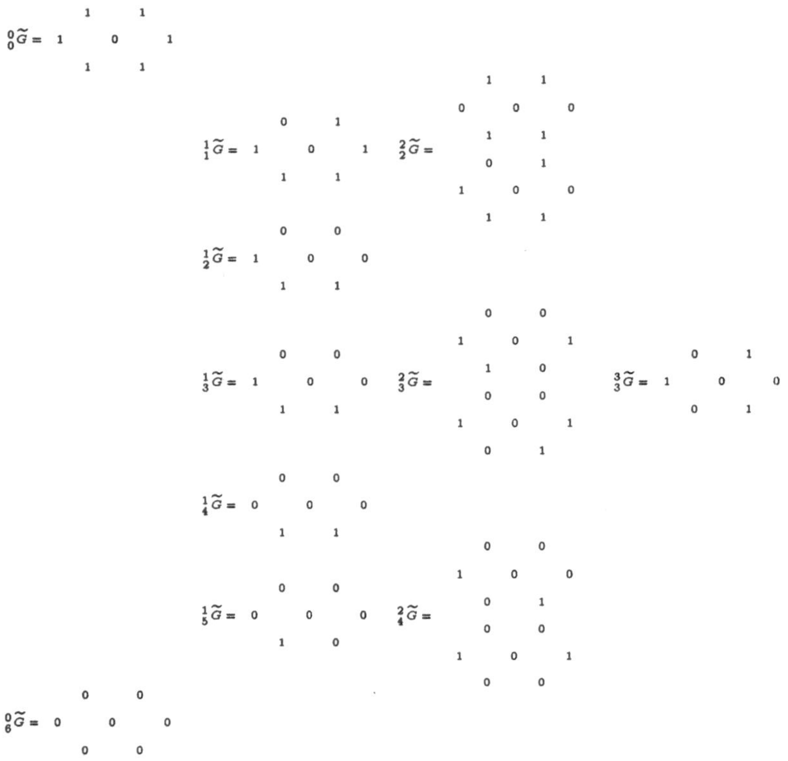

Each cluster contains one state from a rotation invariant class as a representative.

Figure 4: The Clusters of $\tilde{G}$ Set of The Fundamental Structure on the Kernel Form

3.4 The Complete Conjugate Classification

Our classification system uses a five variable collection of Boolean-plus-arithmetic numbers to represent a seven Boolean variable system on the hexagonal grid. Because each of our variables has clear geometric or topological meaning and is directly calculable from the state values, the new classification should be an efficient approach to performing geometric and topological analysis on binary data represented using the hexagonal grid. Considering that the conjugate concept plays a key role in our scheme, it is reasonable to name the classification the *conjugate classification.* We describe the properties of the conjugate classification in the following theorems and corollaries.

Let p be the number of connections, q be the number of branches, s be the spin and r be the rotation. Let ${}^q_pG^s_r$ be a representation for a state in G and ${}^q_p\tilde{G}^s_r$ be a representation for a state in $\tilde{G}$. For convenience, we call each $\{G, \tilde{G}\}$ a *set*, each $\{{}_pG, {}_p\tilde{G}\}$ a *group*, each $\{{}^q_pG, {}^q_p\tilde{G}\}$ a *cluster*, each $\{{}^q_pG^s, {}^q_p\tilde{G}^s\}$ a *class* and each $\{{}^q_pG^s_r, {}^q_p\tilde{G}^s_r\}$ a *state*. The two main structures of the conjugate classification can be summarized as follows.

Theorem 3.4.1 *The fundamental structure of the kernel form of the hexagonal grid divides the state set Y into two conjugate sets G and $\tilde{G}$ for which each set contains 11 clusters. A cluster can*

${}^{0}_{0}G$ $<0,1>$ ${}^{0}_{6}G$ $<6,7>$

${}^{1}_{1}G$ $<1,6>$ ${}^{1}_{2}G$ $<2,5>$ ${}^{1}_{3}G$ $<3,4>$ ${}^{1}_{4}G$ $<4,3>$ ${}^{1}_{5}G$ $<5,2>$

${}^{2}_{2}G$ $<11,8>,<12,9>$ ${}^{2}_{3}G$ $<8,10>,<9,11>$ ${}^{2}_{4}G$ $<10,12>,<13,13>$

${}^{3}_{3}G$ $<7,14>$

${}^{0}_{0}\widetilde{G}$ $<6,7>$ ${}^{0}_{6}\widetilde{G}$ $<0,1>$

${}^{1}_{1}\widetilde{G}$ $<5,2>$ ${}^{1}_{2}\widetilde{G}$ $<4,3>$ ${}^{1}_{3}\widetilde{G}$ $<3,4>$ ${}^{1}_{4}\widetilde{G}$ $<2,5>$ ${}^{1}_{5}\widetilde{G}$ $<1,6>$

${}^{2}_{2}\widetilde{G}$ $<10,12>,<13,13>$ ${}^{2}_{3}\widetilde{G}$ $<8,10>,<9,11>$ ${}^{2}_{4}\widetilde{G}$ $<11,8>,<12,9>$

${}^{3}_{3}\widetilde{G}$ $<7,14>$

Figure 5: The Fundamental Structure and the Golay Transformation

be represented by ${}^{q}_{p}G \in G$ *or* ${}^{q}_{p}\widetilde{G} \in \widetilde{G}$ *dependent on the value of* x_6 *and the numbers of connections and branches. There are four clusters of one state, two clusters of two states, ten clusters of six states, four clusters of nine states and two clusters of 12 states in the fundamental structure. The average number of states in one cluster is* $128/22 \approx 6$.

Proof. There are 128 states in the system. In four $q = 0$ clusters, each cluster has one state. In two $p = 3, q = 3$ clusters, each cluster has two states. In ten $q = 1$ clusters, each one contains six states. Four clusters of $q = 2$ and $p = 2$ or 4 have eight representatives of which four representatives map to three state sets and the other four representatives map to six state sets. In two clusters of $q = 2, p = 3$, each cluster has 12 states. Summing up all numbers, $4 \times 1 + 2 \times 2 + 10 \times 6 + 4 \times 9 + 2 \times 12 = 4 + 4 + 60 + 36 + 24 = 128$. For a total of 128 states in 22 clusters, the average number of states in one cluster is 128/22. □

Theorem 3.4.2 *It is necessary and sufficient to represent the fundamental structure of the kernel form of the hexagonal grid by three variables in six bits.*

Proof: The geometric distribution of Y in the fundamental structure (See Figure 5), is two conjugate triangles on a 3-D lattice. Because it is a 3-D geometric object, it is necessary to use three variables for description of this geometric shape: two to specify the position in the triangle, and one to select which triangle. The two conjugate sets need 1 bit for distinction, and 11 points on 2-D lattice can be specified relative to a rectangle of 2 by 6 or 3 by 4 requiring $\log_2 2 + \log_2 6$ or $\log_2 3 + \log_2 4$ i.e. $1 + 3$ or $2 + 2 = 4$ bits. When rearranging the triangle into a rectangle at least one extra bit is necessary to distinguish which part of the triangle is mapped to the current position in the rectangle. So in total six bits are required for any optimal description. In the fundamental structure, using one bit for conjugation, three bits for connections and two bits for branches, it is sufficient to use six bits for the description. □

Corollary 3.4.3 *The fundamental structure of the kernel form of the hexagonal grid is an optimal structure of geometric representation for the kernel form of the hexagonal grid in that reaches the minimum representation length to describe the information needed.*

Theorem 3.4.4 *The conjugate classification is a quintet integer system using 'conjugate', 'connection', 'branch', 'spin' and 'rotation' numbers as parameters. From any state of Y, it is possible to specify a unique quintet identifying that state. It is thus a complete classification for the kernel form on the hexagonal grid.*

Proof. By theorem 3.4.1, it is sufficient to investigate the extensions of the fundamental structure by spin and rotation. The spin number can separate the six $q = 2$ clusters in the fundamental structure to be 12 classes. Four of these classes are of three states and eight are of six states. Four variables divide the state set into 28 classes in which at most six states belong to any one class. All classes only have rotation invariant property. Finally, the rotation variable using the integers (0-5) describes different orientational directions and the integer (6) describes a non-orientational direction. Thus each state is represented by a collection of five integers and so has a specific position, i.e. it is a complete classification. □

Theorem 3.4.5 *It is necessary and sufficient to use a ten bit quantity for representing the conjugate classification for the kernel form of the hexagonal grid.*

Proof. For any representation for the kernel form of the hexagonal grid, two joined systems are required. One is the seven Boolean variable system to describe the state set with N states and the other one is the connectivity system to identify geometric forms with M instances. One system contains value information and the other system contains connectivity information, so the two systems are independent. By information theory [Hamming 1980], it is necessary and sufficient to use $\lceil \log_2 N \times M \rceil$ bits to give an order number for each state of a joined system. For an n Boolean variable system, $N = 2^n$. For any non-trivial connectivity system, it is necessary to have an essential set of forms to identify p_X connections on each form. If M is greater or equal to the number of values in $\{p_X\}$ then in our case, $N = 2^7$ and $M = 7$. Using these values, we have

$$\begin{aligned} \lceil \log_2 N \times M \rceil &= \lceil \log_2 N + \log_2 M \rceil \\ &= \lceil 7 + \log_2 7 \rceil \\ &= 10 bits. \end{aligned}$$

For counting the state set in the system, it is thus necessary to use a 10 bit unit for any representation. In the conjugate classification, we use six bits for the fundamental structure, one bit for spin and three bits for rotations, so 6 + 1 + 3 = 10 bits are sufficient. □

Theorem 3.4.6 *The conjugate classification divides the state set of the kernel form of the hexagonal grid into 2 conjugate sets, 14 groups, 22 clusters, 28 classes and 128 states by means of the five variables conjugate, connection, branch, spin and rotation.*

Proof. G and $\tilde{G}$ are two conjugate sets, $\{{}_pG\}$ and $\{{}_p\tilde{G}\}$ make up 14 groups, $\{{}^q_pG\}$ and $\{{}^q_p\tilde{G}\}$ contain a total of 22 clusters, $\{{}^q_pG^s\}$ and $\{{}^q_p\tilde{G}^s\}$ include 28 classes and $\{{}^q_pG^s_r\}$ and $\{{}^q_p\tilde{G}^s_r\}$ represent 128 states. □

Corollary 3.4.7 *For any state on the hexagonal grid, its fundamental structure can be represented as a vector of three variables in six bits attached to the center position of the state.*

Corollary 3.4.8 *For a binary image on the hexagonal grid, there is a pseudo-image of the same size with at most a ten bit vector of five variables for representing any subclass of the conjugate classification.*

4 COMPARISON AND REPRESENTATION

As mentioned in the introduction, cellular automata is an active branch for research in computational techniques. Many transformations and classifications have been proposed in the past four decades. We make a comparison to determine the relationship between our results and classical solutions. In this section, we show how to represent different schemes uniformly by our proposed structure. Given these equivalent relationships, it would be natural to use the new structure in all classical applications to replace those existing specific structures.

4.1 Bit Logic Scheme

The Bit logic scheme is the simplest scheme for specifying an instance of the kernel form. Only the center element needs to be involved in the representation. All simple Boolean operations can be performed on this single element. This is an incomplete scheme on the hexagonal grid. For any bit logic function $BL(x)$,

$$BL(x) = x_6 \text{ or } \overline{x}_6. \tag{10}$$

One Boolean variable x_6 is sufficient for implementing the scheme.

4.2 The Conway Transform

Counting the number of active elements as a parameter is a fundamental step, when constructing a transformation scheme in which the new value of an element is related to input value of the element and all values of its nearest neighbours. In a hexagonal grid, the transform can be generated by counting the number of 1-elements in the kernel form of the hexagonal grid. This number can divide the state set to be $n+1$ groups, and the p-th group contains $\binom{n+1}{p}$ states.

Let C_p^n be the l-th group of n elements in the kernel form, then

$$C_p^7 = {}_{p-1}G \cup_{6-p} \widetilde{G}, p \in \{0, \cdots, 7\}. \tag{11}$$

The p-th group of the Conway transform can be thus generated by a $p-1$ and a $6-p$ group from both conjugate sets. Two parameters, x_6 and p, are required for the transform.

4.3 The Crossing Number

The branch number has a direct relation with the crossing number of Deutsch [Deutsch 1970, Deutsch 1972], since the branch number is equal to half of the crossing number. Preston [Preston and Duff 1984, pp43-44] found relations between numbers of 1-elements plus crossings and the Golay transform. However, the concept of using only the center element with conjugate relation plus the alphabet arrangement (in a lookup table or logic transformation) restricted his further extension of those ideas. Let P_p^{2q} be a Preston group with p number of 1-elements and $2q$ number of crossings.

$$P_p^{2q} = {}_p^qG \cup_{6-p}^q \widetilde{G} = {}_p^q G \cup_{\overline{p}}^q \widetilde{G}; \tag{12}$$

$$\overline{p} = 6-p; p \in \{0, \cdots, 6\}, q \in \{0, \cdots, 3\}. \tag{13}$$

Each Preston group is composed of one cluster and its complement cluster from both conjugate sets. There is a skew symmetry between the two clusters. Three parameters, x_6, p and q, are required for the arrangement.

4.4 The Golay Transform

The Golay transform is the best known of the hexagonal parallel pattern transformation proposed by Golay [Golay 1969]. In this transform 14 neighbourhood patterns are grouped. These patterns comprise all orientation-independent cyclic binary codes of length six. Let $GT(n)$ be the n-th group of the Golay transform.

$$\begin{aligned} GT(n) &= {}^{q}_{p}G^{s} \cup^{q}_{6-p} \tilde{G}^{s} =^{q}_{p} G^{s} \cup^{q}_{\overline{p}} \tilde{G}^{s}; \\ \overline{p} &= 6-p; (n \in \{0,\cdots,13\}, p \in \{0,\cdots,6\}, q \in \{0,\cdots,3\}, s \in \{0,1\}). \end{aligned} \tag{14}$$

One Golay group makes up one class and its complement class with a skew symmetry. Four parameters, x_6, p, q and s, are required for the Golay transformation.

4.5 Look-up Table and Matrix Logic Programming

The simplest logic scheme, bit logic scheme, is not enough to describe the possible variations of the kernel form of the hexagonal grid. For a more complete analysis, look-up tables and matrix logic programming have been developed. The look-up table method uses an order number as the parameter to access a specific function in a table. It is convenient to fix the table facility in hardware and change its values by software for different applications. Since each entry of a table maps to a individual state, let $T(N)$ be the N-th entry of the table and we have

$$\begin{aligned} T(N) &= {}^{q}_{p}G^{s}_{r} \text{ or } {}^{q}_{p}\tilde{G}^{s}_{r}; \\ & 0 \leq N < 128, n \in \{0,\cdots,13\}, p \in \{0,\cdots,6\}, \\ & q \in \{0,\cdots,3\}, s \in \{0,1\}, r \in \{0,\cdots,6\}. \end{aligned} \tag{15}$$

It is necessary to use five parameters, x_6, p, q, s and r, describing an individual state for the new scheme.

Matrix Logic Programming is developed from the bit logic scheme. For describing the kernel form, it is natural to use a seven variable scheme to describe one state or any subset of states into logic equations. Let $L(x_0, x_1, \cdots, x_6)$ be a function of the kernel form, then we have

$$L(x_0, x_1, \cdots, x_6) = \bigcup \{{}^{q}_{p}G^{s}_{r}\} \text{ or } \bigcap \{{}^{q}_{p}\tilde{G}^{s}_{r}\}. \tag{16}$$

Because one ${}^{q}_{p}G^{s}_{r}$ is a 1-state and one ${}^{q}_{p}\tilde{G}^{s}_{r}$ is a 0-state, it is easy to see the equivalent relationship between two systems. For the logic equations, the matrix scheme uses seven Boolean variables as the parameters.

4.6 Comparison

By previous discussions, it is obvious that the main difference between the conjugate classification and other transforms is the conjugate condition. In our structure, the conjugate operation must be performed on the whole state, which other schemes are only concerned with the conjugate of the center element. The two policies thus have different symmetry properties: our structure has conjugate symmetry and the Golay transform has skew symmetry. To emphasize the importance of orientation-independence hides the important property of global conjugation of the kernel form. Consider the case of foreground and background identification on any binary grid. They play an equivalent role and complement each other in a balanced way. In any situation involving two complementary parts, processing emphasizing one part will weaken the opposite part.

We list the conjugate classification and other classical schemes in Figure 6 for comparison. From the ratio part of the table, it is obvious that the first two levels of the conjugate classification are linear relations, but it changes to be non-linear relations from the third level. The occupancy

Level	1	2	3	4	5
Symbols	$G, \tilde{G}$	${}_pG, {}_p\tilde{G}$	${}_p^qG, {}_p^q\tilde{G}$	${}_p^qG^s, {}_p^q\tilde{G}^s$	${}_p^qG_r^s, {}_p^q\tilde{G}_r^s$
Vector	$< x >$	$< x, p >$	$< x, p, q >$	$< x, p, q, s >$	$< x, p, q, s, r >$
Length	1 bit	4 bits	6 bits	7 bits	10 bits
Ranges	2	2×7	$2 \times 7 \times 4$	$2 \times 7 \times 4 \times 2$	$2 \times 7 \times 4 \times 2 \times 7$
Total	2	14	56	112	784
Group	2 sets	14 groups	22 clusters	28 classes	128 states
Ratio	1	1	0.39	0.25	0.16
Average	64	$64/7 \approx 9$	$64/11 \approx 6$	$32/7 \approx 4.5$	1
Dimension	1	2	3	4	5
New	center	connection	branch	spin	rotation
Approx.	Bit Logic	Conway(1971)	Deutsch(1972)	Golay(1969)	Table-Logic
Vector	$< x >$	$< p >$	$< p, 2q >$	$< n >$	$< N > \mid < x_0 - x_6 >$
Length	1 bit	3 bits	6 bits	4 bits	7 bits
Group	2 states	8 groups	11 groups	14 groups	128 states
Average	1	16	$128/11 \approx 12$	$128/14 \approx 9$	1
Dimension	1	1	2	1	1|7

'Level' indicates number of variables in the classification, 'Symbols' denotes each representative, 'Vector' is a variable unit and 'Length' is vector's length, 'Ranges' denotes whole variable ranges, 'Total' is total number of points in the ranges, 'Group' is number of representatives in the i-th level of classification and 'Ratio' is equal to *Group/Total*. 'Average' is the average number of states in each representative of the specific level. 'Dimension' indicates the variable dimensions of different levels. 'New' gives new variable, adding in the $i-1$ level to i level. 'Approx.' gives relevant classifications and their 'Vector', 'Length', 'Group', 'Average' and 'Dimension' are listed for comparison.

Figure 6: Table of the Conjugate Classification and Other Schemes on Each Level

ratio declines fast in the last three levels because branch, spin and rotation are all non-linear parameters. This fact means that the first two levels plus any one of last three levels would be highly efficient (but incomplete) for representations, however specific calculations are required if more than two non-linear factors are involved.

5 CONCLUSION

A new approach of using conjugation and connectivity classification on the hexagonal grid has been proposed. The intrinsically multi-symmetric properties of the kernel form makes possible an optimal representation for the conjugate classification. Compared with previous schemes, the conjugate classification is superior if only because it is more general. Moreover, the conjugate classification is a complete classification with minimum representation length, so it might be preferred for use on array cellular automata machines in matrix form as simple arithmetic plus logic operations are sufficient for using it in analytical operations.

ACKNOWLEDGEMENTS

The financial support of ADCSS Awards and Monash University Dep. of Computer Science Scholarship for the first author towards the undertaking of this work is gratefully acknowledged.

REFERENCES

E. S. Deutsch (1970). "On Parallel Operations on Hexagonal Arrays" *IEEE Trans. Comput.* C-19, pp982-983.

E. S. Deutsch (1972). "Thinning Algorithms on Rectangular, Hexagonal and Triangular Arrays" *CACM* Vol. 15 No. 9, pp827-837.

E. Dubois (1985). "The Sampling and Reconstruction of Time-Varying Imagery with Application in Video System" *Proceedings of the IEEE* Vol. 73, No. 4, pp502-522.

M. Gardner (1971). "On Cellular Automata, Self-reproduction, the Garden of Eden and the Game 'life'," *Scientific American* 224(2), pp112-117.

M. J. E. Golay (1969). "Hexagonal Parallel Pattern Transformations" *IEEE Trans. Comput.* Vol. 18, pp733-740.

S. B. Gray (1971). " Local Properties of Binary Images in Two Dimensions." *IEEE Trans. Comput.* C-20, 551-561.

R. W. Hamming (1980). "Coding and Information Theory" Prentice-Hall.

B. K. P. Horn (1986). "Robot Vision" Chapter 4: 'Binary Images: Topological Properties' The MIT Press.

M. Ingram and K. Preston, Jr. (1970). "Automatic Analysis of Blood Cells" *Scientific American* Vol. 223, No. 11, pp72-82.

T. Y. Kong and A. Rosenfeld (1989). " Digital topology: introduction and survey" *Computer Vision, Graphics and Image Processing* 48, 357-393.

T. L. Kunii and Y. Takai (1989). "Cellular Self-Reproducing Automata As a Parallel Processing Model for Botanical Colony Growth Pattern Simulation" *New Advances in Computer Graphics: Proceedings of CG International'89*, R. A. Earnshaw and B. Wyvill (Eds.), pp7-22, Springer-Verlag Tokyo.

E. Luczak and A. Rosenfeld (1976). "Distance on a Hexagonal Grid" *IEEE Trans. Comput.* C-25, pp532-533.

A. L. Loeb (1971). "Color and Symmetry" John Wiley & Sons, Inc.

R. M. Mersereau (1979). "The Processing of Hexagonally Sampled Two-Dimensional Signals" *Proceedings of IEEE* Vol. 67, No. 6, pp930-949.

K. Preston, Jr. (1971). "Feature Extraction By Golay Hexagonal Pattern Transform" *IEEE Trans. Comput.* C-20, pp1007-1014.

K. Preston, Jr. and M. J. B. Duff (1984). "Modern Cellular Automata: Theory and Application" Plenum Press, New York.

J. Serra (1982). "Image Analysis and Mathematical Morphology" Academic Press London.

H. Steinhaus (1960). "Mathematical Snapshots" New York Oxford University Press.

R. L. Stevenson and G. R. Arce (1985). "Binary Display of Hexagonally Sampled Binary Images" *Journal of the Optical Society of America* A, Vol. 2 No.6, pp1009-1013.

D. K. W. Walters (1986). "A Computer Vision Model Based on Psychophysical Experiments" *Pattern Recognition By Humans and Machines* Vol. 2, Visual Perception, E. C. Schwab and H. C. Nusbaum(eds), Academic Press, pp87-120.

A. F. Wells (1977). "Three-dimensional Nets and Polyhedra" John Wiley and Sons, New York.

H. Weyl (1952). "Symmetry" Princeton University Press.

AUTHORS BIOGRAPHIES

Zhijie Zheng is a PhD student in the Department of Computer Science, Monash University. He graduated with B.Sc (Physics) and M.Sc (Computer Science) from Yunnan University and Graduate School of Chinese Science and Technology University, P. R. China, in 1978 and 1981 respectively. He joined the Institute of Computing Technology(ICT), Academia Sinica as a researcher in 1981. Since 1983, he was a lecturer of ICT. From 1987-1990, he was a visiting scientist at the Institute of Systems Science(ISS), National University of Singapore. He worked in the fields of parallel algorithms, architecture, combinatorics, interconnection network topology, Chinese output processing, image processing, antialiasing, graphics, parallel and VLSI architecture, convexity, pattern recognition, visualization and computer vision. He is researching topologic and geometrical representations of 3-D digital images for his PhD degree.

Address: Victorian Centre for Image Processing and Graphics
Department of Computer Science
Monash University
Clayton Vic. 3168
Australia

Anthony Maeder is a senior lecturer in the Department of Computer Science at Monash University, where he has been a faculty member since 1983. He received the MSc (Computer Science) degree from University of Natal in Parallel Computing and has recently completed a PhD on Software Engineering for numerical applications at Monash. He is a member of ACM, IEEE and IREE and is President of the Australian Pattern Recognition Society. His research interests include many aspects of computer graphics and image processing/analysis, as well as data compression, parallelism and numerical methods. He is currently Acting Director of the Victorian Centre for Image Processing and Graphics in Melbourne.

Address: Victorian Centre for Image Processing and Graphics
Department of Computer Science
Monash University
Clayton Vic. 3168
Australia

Motions of Flexible Objects

Dennis Roseman

ABSTRACT

We have a flexible object in space. The object may be intrinsically simple, but the placement (knotting) in space complex. We are given the position of the object at two different times, but not given the motion (isotopy) between these two positions. The problem is to describe a motion (any motion) which goes between these positions.

Mathematical answers to versions of this problem are expressed in terms of "knot moves". However no useful general algorithms are known.

We describe the design of a system which expresses placements of objects (in terms of projections) in such a way that the symbolic manipulations known as "knot moves" and other calculations in geometric topology can be realized. This program is motivated by the problems of motions of surfaces in four dimensional space as well as knots and graphs in three dimensional space.

Key words: topology, knots, isotopy, graphs, motion, object-oriented

INTRODUCTION

Our basic problem is to determine a motion of a flexible object, given two positions. The flexibility of the object precludes simple geometric matching techniques. It is not assumed that these positions are close to each other, so it is not an interpolation problem. Our focus is on relatively simple objects with relatively complex placements. Methods of topology are relevant to analysis of this problem. We discuss the computational implementations of these methods.

These methods are part of a larger program for computation in geometric topology. Thus an important aspect is flexibility and extendibility. This need is found even if we are considering one geometric object since we may wish to extract information in several different forms and relate these views to each other.

Sections a), b) c) and d) give basic mathematical definitions for describing one-dimensional objects in space. Section e) discusses motions of these objects; relevant theoretical results as well as need for computational tools. Sections f) and g) describe our computational approach in terms of a collection of basic objects and methods. Sections g) and i) discuss mathematical concepts and results in some analogous problems in four and five dimensional space. Since most issues and methods are most easily introduced in the more accessible three-dimensional situation, these last sections are less detailed than in the first sections. Section k) discusses other calculational situations in geometric topology for which our design is applicable.

Contents:

In the literature, the terms "topology" and "geometry" are used in a variety of ways. To avoid confusion, we will use the topology and topological equivalence to refer to the usual mathematical terminology in the piecewise linear category (Hudson (1969), for example). When we refer to analytic geometry, we will refer to geometric objects and calculations involving points with fixed coordinates in some coordinate system.

a) A BEGINNING EXAMPLE

We are interested in motions of flexible objects in space. The simplest interesting example would be a motion of a flexible circle in space. The focus is on placement. One can place a circle in space so that it is knotted. Although the circle is intrinsically simple, its placement (knotting) may be very complex. Suppose we are given two positions of this circle in space corresponding to two different time frames of a motion, but we are not given the motion. The first placement is denoted X, the second Y. The general problem is to construct some motion which begins with placement X and ends with placement Y. In the language of topology, we wish to find an isotopy which takes X to Y.

To define the problem more precisely, we need to consider the form of the data. Is the circle represented by a smooth curve or by a polygonal path? For computation, it is best to represent knotted circles as closed polygonal paths. This causes no serious problems practically or theoretically since smooth curves can be approximated by arbitrarily close polygonal paths and vice versa. Mathematically, the notion of placement of an object corresponds to the concept of embedding. A motion of an object corresponds to an isotopy. For those unfamiliar with these concepts, we offer the following which will be adequate for the study of knotted circles or graphs in space.

We first define a standard closed polygonal path in space, Q , to be the the four edges of the unit square in first two coordinates. The verticies of this square are (0,0,0), (1,0,0), (1,1,0) and (0,1,0), see Figure 1 d). Now suppose we are given a closed polygonal path such as X in Figure 1 a). This is an "unknotted polygonal path". By definition, this means there is a motion in space of this closed polygonal path that begins at position X and ends at position Q. The three-dimensional complexity of the path X is indicated by the number of crossings in the figure. Figure 1a) shows a path with two crossing points.

The following steps describe how a topologist would describe this motion.

1) Topologically Figure 1a) can be simplified as in Figure 1e).
2) In the diagram of Figure 1e), there is a region shown as shaded in Figure 1f).

a) a polygonal space path X

b) a deformation disk in the diagram for a)

c) polygonal path X'

d) the "unknotted path" Q

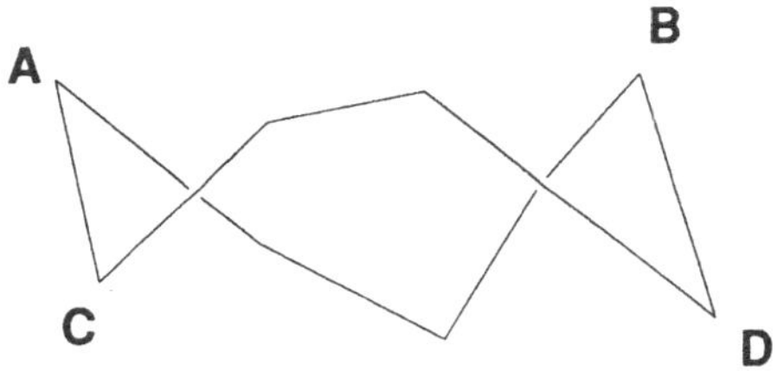

e) a diagram equivalent to that of X

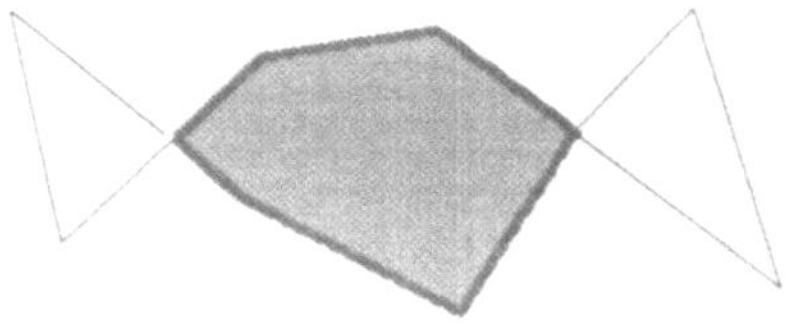

f) a deformation disk

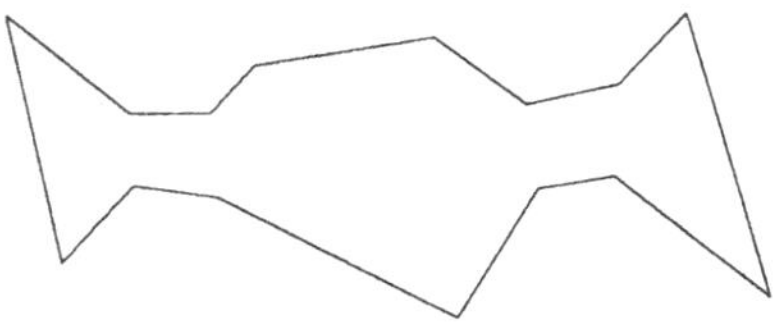

g) a diagram equivalent to that of X'

Figure 1

We call it a deformation disk.. The two crossings of the path are corners of this region.

3) We will get a motion of Figure 1e) which will have the effect of eliminating these crossings. We note that the "overs and unders" at the crossings are such that we may move the portion of the path from A to B across this disk, under the path from C to D. We can then move the path from C to D the other way across this disk and the result will be as in Figure 1g).

4) Note X' is a simple closed path in the plane. It is intuitively clear that we can find a motion in the plane which will take X' to U. Mathematically this is a non-trivial result known as the Schoenflies Theorem, see Rolfsen (1976).

5) Topologically, the deformation disk of 1f) corresponds to the shaded region of Figure 1b). We can use this disk to move the path, obtaining Figure 1c). The computation of this motion is not a trivial problem, but for many purposes may not be of great interest in the sense that it is a purely two-dimensional problem rather than a three dimensional one.

We would like to separate the computational from the theoretical aspects to make clear what mathematics is used and how it is used. The topologist is using three theorems.

Theorem A. If two knots have the same diagram, they are isotopic. In particular, they are topologically equivalent

Theorem B. An abstract knot move corresponds to an isotopy.

Theorem C. Any isotopy can be expressed as a sequence of moves on a diagram for the knot.

Step 1) and 4) use Theorem A. Theorem C assures the existence of moves as in Step 2). Step 3) and Step 5) use Theorem B.

For computation, we will see that we can abstractly express a diagram as a graph, so our computational techniques are of two kinds: combinatorial and analytic geometric. The coding of the drawing to obtain the diagram, and applications of Theorem B involve analytic geometry, the other techniques are combinatorial. We should mention that the design of our system is object-oriented, Roseman (1992).

b) GENERAL NOTIONS

In the above section we mentioned two possible points of view for knots--as a smooth simple closed curve or as a simple closed polygonal path. These two viewpoints correspond to two of the basic methods of geometric topology--differentiable topology and piecewise linear topology. In the first category all maps and objects are smooth (or piecewise smooth); in the second category objects and maps are piecewise linear. In high dimensional settings the mathematics of these two categories diverge. However in the problems we consider in this paper the differences are largely in the realm of different mathematical proof techniques. Basic concepts and results in one category have counterparts in the other. The proofs of our mathematical results are done on the smooth category using techniques such as Morse theory and similar specialized studies of singularities. However, for computational purposes it is far better to place everything in the piecewise linear category .

Objects we will consider are called **simplicial complexes.** These are "nice" unions of pieces such as line segments, triangles, etc. These "pieces" are called **simplexes**. An **embedding** of a simplicial complex X in a simplicial complex R, is a placement of X in R that is piecewise linear. That is an embedding of X into a space R is a continuous function, f, from X to R which is a homeomorphism of X onto the image f(X) such that f maps each simplex of X in a linear manner.

For those not familiar with the piecewise linear category we will give details here sufficient to describe knotted circles. Let Q be the edges of the unit square as above and let k be a function from Q into three-dimensional space. Suppose there is a subdivision of the edges of Q so that the restriction of k to each subinterval is a linear map, then we say that k is **piecewise linear**. If, in addition, k is a one-to-one function into space, we say that f is a **piecewise linear embedding**, and we will call k a **knotting of a circle**.

In this paper, R will be Euclidian space of some dimension. To consider R as a simplicial complex, we need to subdivide R into appropriate simplexes. On the theoretical side, we note that for most topological theorems and constructions, it is assumed that embeddings **are** described in terms of a simplicial structure of the target space R. For example, to consider a square path in the plane as an embedded complex, we are (conceptually) required to consider a triangulation of the entire plane so that each edge of the path is an edge of one of these triangles. We want to avoid such computationally expensive considerations whenever possible. The point here is that we don't always need triangulations but we do need to design a system that **allows** us to easily find triangulations (of at least certain portions of R) when needed.

In the various dimensions the basic equivalence notion of knots is isotopy. An isotopy may be thought of as a non-rigid motion of the knot in the ambient space between two given placements. We define an **isotopy** of X to be continuous map F from X x I to R such that for all t, the restriction of F to X x {t} is an embedding. (The remarks of the above paragraph on triangulations of R applies to isotopies as well.) If we are concerned with knotted circles, we may identify Q x I as the subset of all (x,y,z) such that $(x,y,0) \in Q$ and $0 \le z \le 1$. A map F from Q x I to space is called **piecewise linear homotopy** if there is a triangulation of Q x I such that the restriction of F to any triangle is a linear map. If F is a piecewise linear homotopy , let F_t be the restriction of F to the set of all $(x,y,z) \in Q$ x I such that z = t. If F_t is a piecewise linear embedding for all t, $0 \le t \le 1$, then we say that F is a **piecewise linear isotopy**. We say that two knottings k and k' are equivalent if there is a piecewise linear isotopy such that $F_0 = k$ and $F_1 = k'$. Such an equivalence class of a knotting is called a **knotted circle**. Much of the time we will be interested in the image of a knotting (a polygonal path in space) rather than the function itself. In this case we will say that a **knot** is the image of a knotting, and that two knots are equivalent if they can be represented by equivalent knottings. A union of disjoint knotted circles is called a **link**.

c) CLASSICAL KNOT DIAGRAMS

The **projection from three-dimensional space to two-dimensional dimensional space**, denoted by π , is defined by $\pi(x, y, z) = (x, y)$; the function $h(x, y, z) = z$ is called the **height function**. The **projection from four-dimensional space to three-dimensional space**, denoted by Π, is $\Pi(x, y, z, w) = (x, y, z)$; and $H(x, y, z, w) = w$ is the corresponding **height function**.

Classical knot theory is the topological study of knotted circles and links. A knot or link, M, is represented by a drawing of the planar projection $\pi(M)$, called the **projection of the knot (or link)**.

We will assume that M is in generic position with respect to projection. Term "generic" or its equivalent "general position" is often used in geometric topology. The definitions vary for different situations. For each notion of generic, there is a theorem which says that non-generic situations are, in some well defined sense, "avoidable". In the case of a planar projection of a knot, a the generic situation is one which satisfies the following two conditions. (1) If v is a

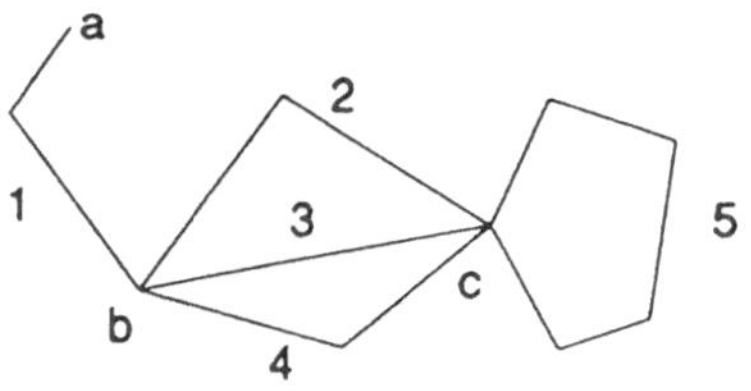

Figure 2, example of cell complex

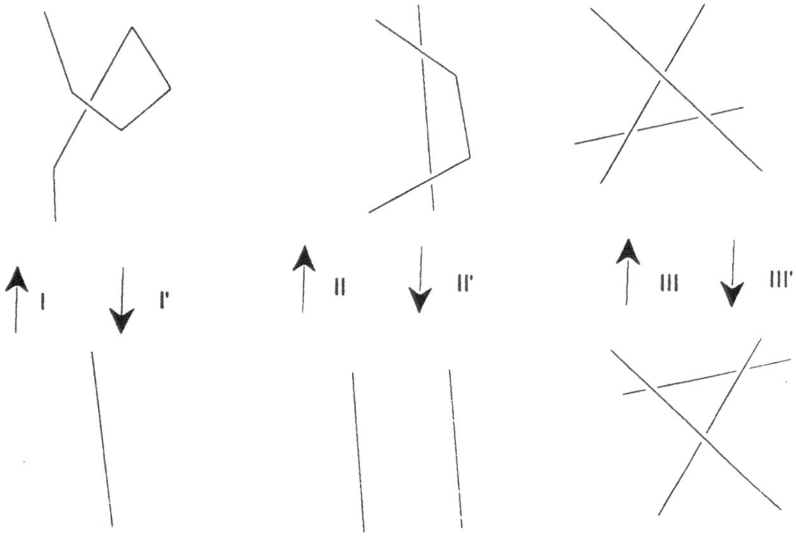

Figure 3, the classical Reidemeister moves I, I', II, II', III, and III'

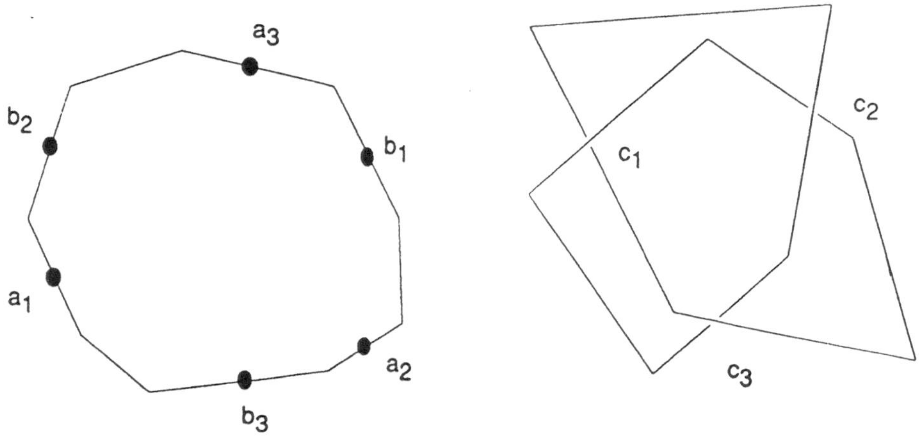

Figure 4, example of a Gauss code; string is $a_1b_2a_3b_1a_2b_3$

vertex of the knot then there is no other point of the knot, x, with $\pi(v) = \pi(v)$. (Note: this rules out the possibility of vertical edges projecting to points. It also rules out two disjoint edges projecting in such a way that the union of the projections of these edges is a line segment.) (2) The projection of three different edges cannot have a common point. There is a theorem which says that "most knottings are generic with respect to projection and furthermore any knotting is equivalent to a knotting which is generic with respect to projection".

Suppose now that M is in generic position. A point, c, of $\pi(M)$ is called a **crossing point** if $\pi^{-1}(c) \cap M$ consists of more than one point. In this case $\pi^{-1}(c) \cap M$ will consist to two points: a, and b. If $h(a) > h(b)$, we say that a is an **over point** and b is an **under point.** The set of crossing points is the **crossing set**; the set of over and under points is called the **double point set.** This projection with over/under labeling of double points at each crossing point is called a **knot diagram**

There are several common very useful ways to code a knot diagram which are variations of the Gauss code. Suppose we have a knotted circle with n crossing points, $c_1, c_2, ..., c_n$. Each crossing point, c_i, corresponds, via the knotting, to two points on the circle, a_i and b_i, where "the point a_i lies over the point b_i, and both project to c_i". We say that a_i is an **over point** and b_i is an **under point**. The union of these points is called the **double point set of the knot projection**. This labeling of the double point set is called the **Gauss code for the knot**. We can express this as circular list of the symbols $\{a_i\}$ and $\{b_i\}$, see Figure 4. There are several variations on this notation, the most well known is Dowker-Thistlethwaite (1983)

Although we make use of our own variations of this kind of code, it will not be, in itself, a good basis for our data structures. These codes are very efficient, but they have three drawbacks. First, the code determines the diagram only for "prime" knot diagrams; secondly it assumes that the projection of the knot is a connected subset. For most uses in classical knot theory these pose no problem. However, diagrams we must consider (see discussion of "projection links" below) cannot be reduced so as to have these properties. These problems can be taken care of by augmenting the notation. Thirdly, it is very difficult to extract certain kinds of information from such a code--especially the possible Reidemeister moves of type III discussed in Section e). A knot diagram is not simply a "picture of a knot"--it is a powerful symbolic representation of the knot , useful for symbolic calculations Kauffman (1983). One can use the knot diagram directly to calculate many algebraic invariants of the knot. The same will be true for diagrams for knotted surfaces which we will later describe. Manipulations on a given diagram can yield a collection of related knots (the so-called knot skeins) and these may be used to calculate the newer knot polynomials Kauffman (1988). Colorings of the knot diagrams can give representations of the knot groups Crowell-Fox (1977) and Kinoshita (1990). In addition, knots with special diagrams have special properties, (see for example Burde-Zieschang (1985))--bridge number, alternating knots, etc.

d) GRAPHS AND KNOTTED GRAPHS

One can view a graph as a topological space or as a combinatorial object. We will have need for both points of view

A **one dimensional cell complex**, topologically, is a finite one dimensional CW complex or cell complex. One general reference is Cooke-Finney (1967). It consists of points, called **zero cells**, and other subsets, called **one cells** (by which we mean, here, closed one cells) . A one cell may be homeomorphic to a closed interval with endpoints corresponding to zero cells. Otherwise it is homeomorphic to a circle and contains a single zero cell; in this case we call this cell a **loop**. Figure 2 shows a complex with three zero cells, a, b, and c and five numbered edges; edge 5 is a loop.

A **graph** consists of a finite set, called verticies together with a finite set of pairs of verticies called **edges**. In particular it is possible for two different edges to have the same set of verticies. (In some terminologies, this is called a multi-graph.) As a topological space, it corresponds to a one dimensional cell complex, however most of the time when we speak of a graph we will be emphasizing the combinatorial structure. Frequently, we will want to consider graphs with additional structure such as labeled and 'colored' verticies and edges and possibly directed edges.

A **knotted graph** will refer to the image, in three-dimensional space, of an piecewise-linear embedding of a one dimensional cell complex. Thus we may say that a knotted graph is a realization of a graph in space so that the image of each edge of the graph is a polygonal path in three-dimensional space. This terminology is a common, but a source of some confusion. Note that the term **edge** has two uses here. Suppose G is a graph and e an edge of the graph, let g be a piecewise-linear embedding of (the corresponding cell complex) of G into three-dimensional space. Since g(e) is a polygonal path with be a union of edges, but these edges do not correspond to edges of G, but rather edges of a subdivision of g(e).

e) CLASSICAL KNOT MOVES

As is well known, if two knots are equivalent, this equivalence may be represented as a finite sequence of changes (known as Reidemeister moves) of the knot diagram Reidemeister (1932), Burde-Zieschang (1985). To show that two knots given by distinct projections are equivalent, one exhibits a sequence of drawings which realize a sequence of Reidemeister moves. In Figure 3 we list show these moves; the diagrams are to be taken to be a small isolated portion of the knot diagram, outside of which the diagram is unchanged. The methods are ad hoc and interactive--one makes some changes on a diagram, looks at the result and tries to make a decision on reasonable moves to try next.

We remark that there are algorithms to do some of this. For example, by methods of Haken (1961), one can, in principle, write down an algorithm to untie a trivial knot. This algorithm has never been implemented since it is believed to be of little real calculational value. One begins with a triangulation of all of space so that the given knot is a sub-complex. One then proceeds to analyze all surfaces which are sub-complexes and have the given knot as bounding curve. The arguments is that one can reduce one's search to a finite number of possibilities, one of which will be an embedded disk. Another standard topological theorem then says that this disk will allow us to find an unknotting isotopy. Another method Homma-Ochiai-Takahashi (1980) has been implemented Ochiai, it works well but doesn't always succeed.

We now have a central problem. (This basic problem also occurs in other similar problems such as surfaces in four dimensional space, etc). We have a theorem which gives us a method for which there is no effective algorithm. On the other hand, this method of knot moves has been used very effectively to carry out hand calculations throughout the history of knot theory, as well as being a powerful theoretical tool.

Our conclusion is that a program designed to solve such problems must be in part interactive. We want to design a program to have the computer be able to furnish maximal calculational power in an interactive way. For example, we want the user to be able to define and program special sequences of moves and have the program able to search for possible applications of these sequences and then apply them.

In spirit such a situation is similar to designing a program to do symbolic algebra. We don't expect algorithms to "solve all algebraic equations" (in fact this is known to be mathematically impossible). But one can design a powerful calculational environment with built-in rules which are user-extendible and programmable. One thing that makes our problem different from a symbolic algebra program is that the symbolic inputs and outputs are graphical in nature.

Having to interactively use graphical inputs and outputs creates certain demands on the most basic structures of our system. The user needs the ability to input examples easily by drawing on a screen. One problem is that we only allow inputs that are in generic position. Mathematically, most knottings in space will be generic. However human users tend to do things non-generically. Sometimes non-generic situations arise because the data is entered interactively using a mouse in a drawing program. The fact that there are only finitely many pixels on the screen may force non-generic values for coordinates. Also, mathematically generated examples tend to have simplicity and symmetry which can result in non-generic situations. In addition, in practice, we may want to expand a strict mathematical notion of "non-generic" to include situations which are close to being non-generic.

For example, we may not want the user to be able to draw a new line segment which contains a previously drawn crossing point, since it would create an undesirable triple crossing point-- this will be our non-generic situation. In addition, we will want to avoid a situation where the three line segments come close to having a mutual intersection (where closeness here is measured by some predetermined numerical tolerance).

We need to have methods to warn the user in real time if they are trying to place an object in a non-generic position. Often this does not just depend on the region of the screen near the cursor, but depends on the how the position of the cursor relates to the abstract structure of the entire drawing.

f) REPRESENTING GRAPHS

At the early stages of development of our design, it became clear that we had need for a a basic underlying structure that was not easily derived from common existing ones. As we will see most of our methods can be described in graph theoretical terms, but the standard structures were not powerful enough or flexible enough for our needs. Foundational to our design is a generalization of a linked list.

The fundamental class is a **Link**. Most geometric and topological objects are sub-classes of Link, lists of Links, etc. Link is a generalization of the standard concept of a link in a (doubly linked, circular) linked list. In a standard link, there is a concept of a next link and a previous link. In Link each object may have several different pairs of next links and previous links. Each instance of Link will have implemented a subset of these directions, defined at run-time. In each of these directions, "nextLink" and "previousLink" will be defined (and will be instances of Link).

Think of a link object as a vertex, v, of an abstract graph. If n and p are verticies corresponding to the next and previous links from v in direction, d, then we will construct edges between v and n and v and p. We may think of a named direction as giving a "color" of an edge. At a vertex there are either no edges of a given color, or there are exactly two. If we begin at a vertex and choose a color of edge we can, consecutively, follow the next link in that direction thus generating a (circular) list. Furthermore, we may represent distinct subclasses of Link by distinct colors of the verticies of this graph as well.

The basic structure that uses link is called a **Loom**. Roughly, a Loom allows us to "weave together" different linked lists. An object of class, **Navigator**, can be used to facilitate complex searches in a loom. The navigator maintains a collection of partial logs of calls made to it that pertain to changes of direction as well as user-defined important points along some search path.

On a higher level the basic class is **ObjectGrid**, a subclass of Loom. An ObjectGrid is a virtual graphics interface. It is an abstract graph where the verticies correspond to most recognizable regions of the drawing. There are methods to relate a cursor position to any of these objects. We describe now an implementation of objectGrid which is two-dimensional (actually "two and one half dimensional"). This extends easily to a three-dimensional (even "three and a half dimensional") setting.

An objectGrid allows placement of objects into a coordinate system and provides for searches for objects so placed. Conceptually, the ObjectGrid allows a coordinate grid to be constructed by objects as they are placed in the plane. Points that are verticies in a drawing will be called **dPoints** (for drawn points, or data points). If we place a dPoint P, at position (a, b) in the plane, we create an ordered list, called a **tine**, of P together with all objects already placed in the plane which intersect the vertical line L_a containing P. We will let t_a denote the tine corresponding the the x-value a. If a tine has already been constructed corresponding to L_a, then P is simply placed, in order, on the tine. The order on the tine is based primarily on the second coordinate of the object. Furthermore, if a crossing point is produced from two drawn edges, a tine will be constructed for the x-value of this crossing. An ordered list, called a **back**, is maintained of the tines; the order corresponds to the x-value of objects on the tine. The back together with the tines form a structure we call a comb; this structure enables very fast searches for objects. See Roseman (1992) for more details.

Suppose we place an edge, E between two points already entered into the objectGrid. If we have two consecutive tines, t_x and $t_{x'}$ such that the corresponding vertical lines, L_x and $L_{x'}$, meet E, then we will add a node called a **gridEdgeNode** to the tine t_x at where the y-value used for insertion onto the tine is the second coordinate of the intersection of L_x and E. The name gridEdgeNode is refers to the use of this object as a node in an abstract graph which corresponds to an point on an edge with respect to a grid. An edge may have many gridEdgeNodes. A list of thee, ordered by increasing x-coordinate is constructed and becomes "woven into" the objectGrid. These objects allow us to divide up the diagram into computationally nice regions so that the bounded regions are either quadrilaterals with two sides parallel to the y-axis or a triangle with one side parallel to the y-axis. (We will not use gridEdgeNodes for vertical edges.) The unbounded regions are similarly "nice" There are two computational benefits. First this allows easy triangulations of regions if necessary. Secondly, it gives a way to quickly relate a cursor position to geometric objects.

Consider the drawing of a knotted graph as in Figure 5 a) . There will be ten tines in the corresponding objectGrid, These are indicated in figure 5 b) , where we label these tines from left to right. There will be four verticies on tine number 1. We will examine the tines "from bottom to top". The first vertex of this graph is called the base of the tine and is simply a header for this list. Next we have the two edges AB and AE which go from A towards the right. Each

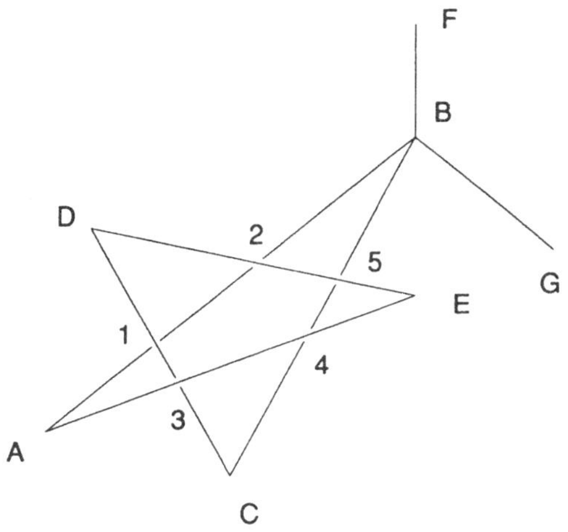

a) a drawing with 7 dPoints, 5 cPoints and 7 edges

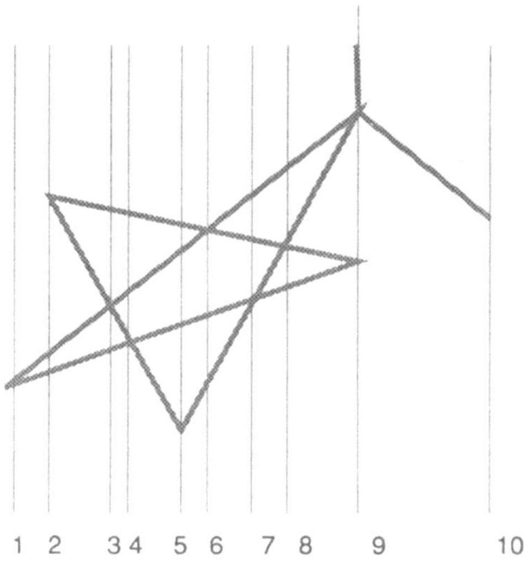

b) ten tines superimposed

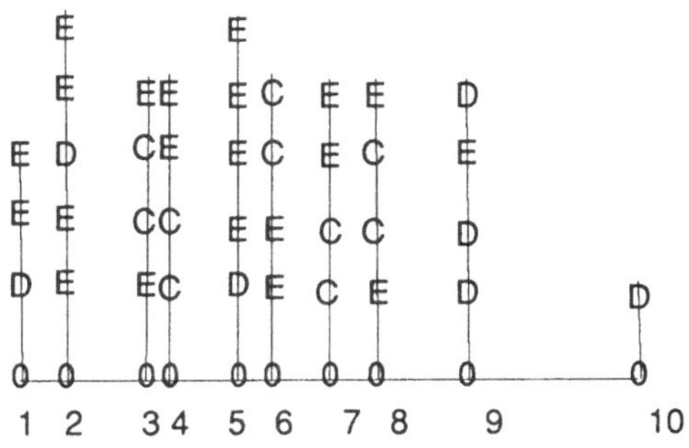

c) a depiction of a portion of the coressponding objectGrid
0 = base of tine, D = a dPoint, E = a gridEdgeNode,
C = cPointNode. The back corresponds to horizonal line segment containing bases of tines

Figure 5, example of an objectGrid

of these edges will give rise to a gridEdgeNode whose y-value is the same as the y-coordinate of A. In this case we need to augment our rules for placement of nodes on a tine. The rule will be that the point is placed first then the gridEdgeNodes are added next in order of increasing slope. The second tine begins with a base node then then a gridEdgeNode for edge AE and then one for edge AB. The third tine is created due to a crossing point where edge AE passes over edge DC.

Crossing points are very special. In the projection, they look like verticies of order 4. Yet in another way, a crossing point does not correspond to a point on the knot, but rather to two points--the "over point" and the "under point". Adding a vertex of order 4 would mean adding four directed edges--these are called **cPointNodes.** For each crossing point, two of these cPointNodes will be added to the objectGrid. The order in which these are added depends on the slope of the edges to which they correspond. (For technical reasons we allow such cPointNodes to correspond to vertical edges.) Thus on tine three the we find the following as we go up: a base node for the tine, a gridEdgeNode corresponding to the edge AE, a cPointNode corresponding to edge DC, a cPointNode corresponding to edge AB, and finally a gridEdgeNode corresponding to the edge DE.

On a higher level, we also represent higher level geometric objects such as paths, zero-cells, one-cells, and shards as verticies in a graph. This has been discussed in Roseman(1992). Each zero-cell is connected directly, or indirectly to a vertex of the objectGrid. These connections are given by directions in the underlying Link structure. Thus one can navigate back and forth between the abstract geometric level and the points and line segments which appear on the screen.

g) DESCRIBING A KNOTTED SURFACE, MATHEMATICALLY

By **surface**, we mean a two-dimensional manifold. Most interest lies in the case where the surface in question is compact, usually with empty boundary, and has low total genus. Examples are: a sphere, a projective plane, a torus, a Klein bottle, or a union of a small number of these manifolds. Most often, these manifolds will have empty boundary. By a **knotted surface** we will mean the image of a piecewise linear embedding of that surface into four-dimensional space. In computer graphics terminology, this means the surface is represented as a union of (triangular) polygons.

There two well known very general ways to describe a knotted surface; the method of slices and the method of projection. Each of these two methods have advantages and disadvantages. We use both, and have methods to go from one to the other. A third general method, projection links, is described below.

The method of slices is well known. The first published examples are found in Fox (1961) . For fixed t, let $H_t = \{(x, y, z, w) : w = t\}$ .There is a notion of generic position for a knotted surface. For a surface, S, in such generic position, $H_t \cap S$ (if non-empty) will be a link of circles in the hyperplane H_t for all but a finite number of such hyperplanes.The justification for this is most easily done in the smooth category. The idea is to show that, without loss of generality, we may assume that the fourth coordinate function describing the surface in 4-dimensional space is a Morse function with the property that each critical value, t, corresponds to exactly one critical point. For each such critical value, t, we will have a non-generic hyperplane. A basic source for Morse theory is Milnor (1963) or Guillemin-Pollack (1974). If the given surface is a two-dimensional sphere, then the knots and links we obtain in this way are called **slice knots** and **slice links**. As we cross a non-generic value of t there are two basic situations. The change between slices as we cross this value can be described as a "birth" or "death" of a circle if the value of t is, respectively, a local minimum or local maximum. The other possibility is that the non-generic point is a saddle point. The effect is to change the number of component circles as one crosses the slice; this change is called a "fission" or a "fusion", see Figure 6 b) and c) . If $t_0 < t_1$, with t_0 and t_1 regular values for slicing, then the subset of S which lies between H_{t_0} and H_{t_1} is called a **cobordism of** the slice links. If $t_0 < t_1$, such that for all t, with $t_0 \le t \le t_1$ t is a regular values for slicing, then this cobordism is topologically a product and can be considered to be the trace of an isotopy.

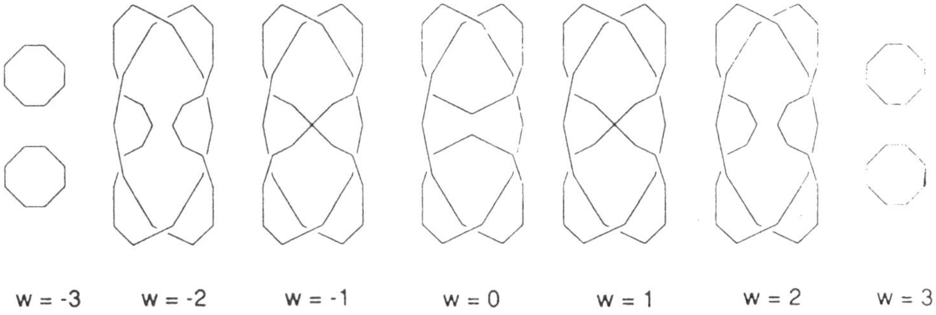

a) slices of a knotted 2-sphere at seven values of w

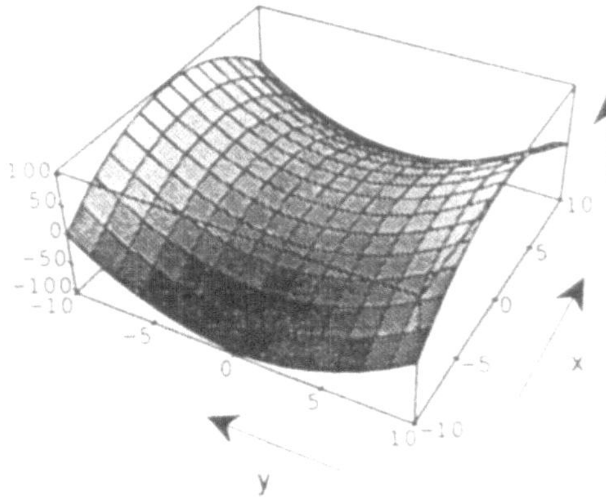

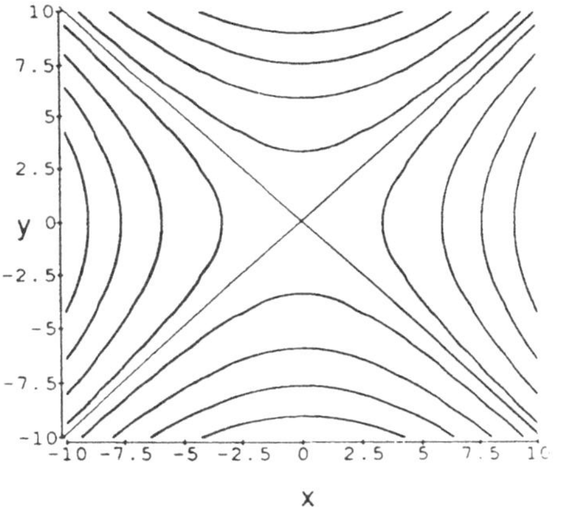

b) a saddle point

c) corresponding level curves for fixed w

Figure 6, slice pictures of a sphere in four-space, after Fox [FX1]

The method of projection, is analogous to the method used in classical knot theory. We put the surface, S, in general position with respect to Π, see Roseman (1992). Then $\Pi(S)$ is called the **projection of the knotted surface**. The set $\Pi(S)$ together with height relation information on the set of double points is called the **diagram for the knotted surface**. Examples may be seen in Roseman (1974, 1979, 1989).

Here is one way to input a knotted surface by describing its projection. Recall the usual way to draw a picture of a knotted circle is to draw an immersed curve in the plane and then describe height relations at the crossing points (i.e. "over" or "under"). Similarly, a knotted surface can be obtained as follows. One might begin with a previously obtained projection (even an unknotted sphere, for example). One then performs some changes on this projection (for example a regular isotopy if the projection was an immersion). Such changes can be described by a sequence of moves as has been studied in the PL case by Homma and Nagase (1987). When we are done, we will see if there is as height function definable on the crossing point set that will allow us to define our embedding; if so, we have now defined a knot Giller (1982). (The existence of such a height function can be determined by an examination of only the triple points of the image we are considering.)

There is a third general method of representing a knotted surface which we call the "projection link". One problem with a projection of a knotted surface is that it is an object in three-dimensional space We have developed a way of reducing the three dimensional information to a two dimensional diagram of which we call the **projection link.** This is discussed in the paper: Roseman (1989). It is in some sense, a higher dimensional analog of the Gauss code for knotted circles. For simplicity, we describe it here only for the case of a knotted sphere.

Suppose that S is a two-dimensional sphere in four-dimensional space. We will assume that S is generic with respect to Π. (We omit the technical definition of this notion of generic, but the following description spells out the important features.) A **crossing point** is a point of $\Pi(S)$ which corresponds to more than one point of the surface. The **crossing set** is the closure, in $\Pi(S)$, of the crossing points. If C is the crossing set, let $D = (\Pi)^{-1}(C) \cap S$. We will call D the **double point set**. Our general position requirement implies that only two situations can occur in a neighborhood of a crossing point. Either the crossing point corresponds to two points of the surface and locally the picture looks like Figure 7a), or it is a **triple point**, see Figure 7c). There is one other notable situation in which we have a point of the projection which is not a double point, but is a limit of double points, see Figure 7b) . We call these **branch points**, also called "pinch points" Francis (1987). (Thus the crossing set consists of crossing points and branch points.) If C is a crossing set, T is the set of triple points, and B is the set of branch points, a component of C-T-B will be called a **pure double point set** Knots which have a projection with no triple points can be shown to form a small subclass of all knotted surfaces, called **simply knotted spheres** Yajima (1962). We see that D is the union of immersed curves in S so that the crossings and self crossings are transverse. Crossing points of these curves are exactly the points that are mapped to triple points of the knot diagram. A crossing point, c, if it is not a triple point corresponds to exactly two points, a and b, in the double point set. If $H(a) > H(b)$ we will say a is an **over point**, otherwise we will say a is an **under point**, as in the Gauss code. For points in the triple point set, we speak of **over points, middle points** and **under points**.

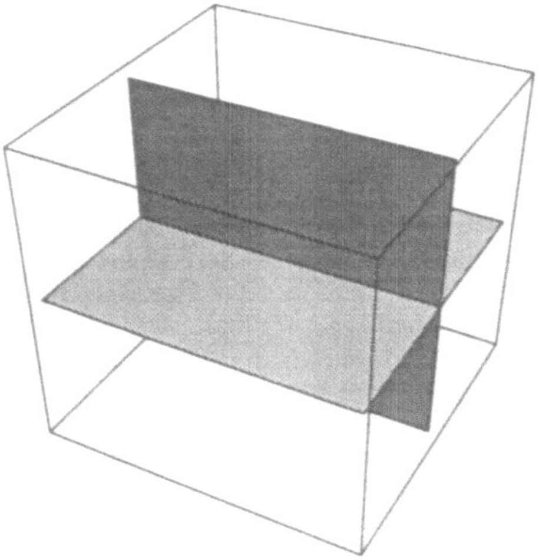

a) an arc of crossing points

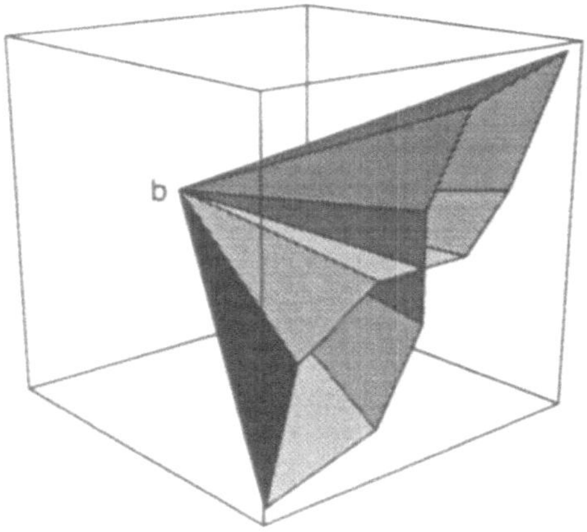

b) Local picture of a branch point, b

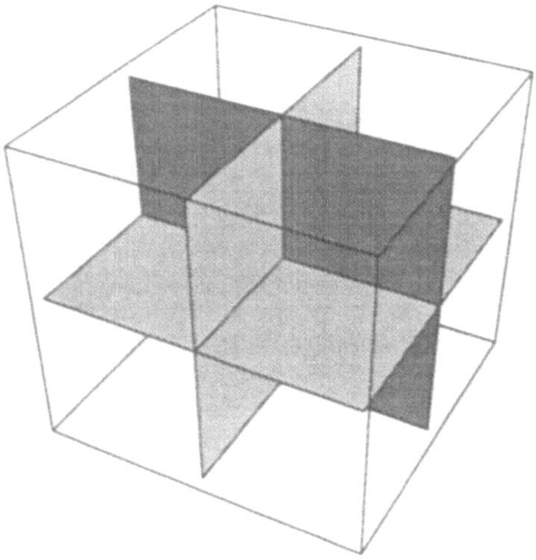

c) a triple point

Figure 7, local pictures of projection of surface

To keep track of height relations at a triple point, we can make this union of curves look like a projection of a link. We illustrate this with an example. Figure 8(b) shows a projection of a sphere with two triple points. The crossing point set, partly visible, consists of three circles A^*, B^*, and C^* which intersect at the triple points, p^* and q^* (q^* is hidden from view). Figure 8(a) shows the corresponding double point set--six circles. Note that $\Pi(p) = \Pi(p') = \Pi(p'') = p^*$; also $\Pi(A) = \Pi(A') = A^*$, etc. The point p is on two circles A and B. The p′ belongs to A′ (paired to A) and p″ belongs to B′ (paired to B). If the height of p′ is greater than that of p″, then we will determine that the curve A should pass over B at p, otherwise we will say that B passes over A. Continuing in this way we could determine over-under relations at the six crossing points. If we take the inverse image of this via the knotting for the surface, we obtain a diagram, the projection of a link as drawn on a standard sphere, Figure 8(c). This process can be defined for any knotted surface. This is now seen to be an analog of the Gauss code which describes the knot in terms of pairs of points in a standard circle.

Just as the Gauss code does not completely determine the knot diagram for classical knots, a given projection link does not completely determine the knot diagram, but it comes close to determining the knotted surface. Figure 9a) and Figure 9b) show two diagrams of knotted spheres with the same projection link. These two knots are in fact equivalent in four-dimensional space, even though their projections are not equivalent subsets of three-dimensional space. However, there is a minor augmentation of the code similar to that for the classical Gauss code, which will incorporate the needed extra information.

h) FROM DIAGRAMS TO GRAPHS

For knotted surfaces, it is not enough to reduce our data to three-dimensional data or even two-dimensional data. For computation, we need to reduce it further to one-dimensional data--namely graphs. An isotopy then can be described as a finite sequence of "different" knot diagrams. In the generic case, two diagrams will differ either by a single knot move, by a "birth/death" move, or a "fission/fusion" move. Thus we obtain a sequence of related graphs, G(i). Each of these graphs will have a distinguished vertex, a "root" vertex. One can use such a sequence to build a larger graph, Γ, by by joining each of the successive graphs G(i) and G(i+1) by an edge between their "root" verticies. It is usually desirable to have additional edges between G(i) and G(i+1) relating which express important relations between verticies these two graphs. The Loom structure allows us to weave together such interconnected data as needed. Topologically, Γ corresponds to a projection of the cobordism associated to the isotopy.

Suppose that S is a surface and X is a piecewise linear subset which is a one dimensional cell complex. A **shard** is the closure, in S, of a component of S-X. In other words, X breaks up the surface into pieces and these pieces correspond to the shards. Topologically, a shard is a surface with possible identifications made of finite subsets on the boundary of this surface.

We first show how to obtain a graph from a classical knot or link. The graphs we will want will be elaboration of this construction. This basic graph we call the "shard graph" . It is the dual graph of knot (or link) projection, where we view this projection as a one dimensional CW complex in the plane. Let X be the projection of a knot or link. Then X has the structure of a CW complex where the 0-cells correspond to the crossing points. This dual graph will have one vertex for every shard. Each one cell of X will give rise to an edge between two shards if the edge meets each shard. See Figure 10. We note that the shard graph naturally embeds in the plane. We use a natural canonical ordering of the edges about a vertex by ordering in a

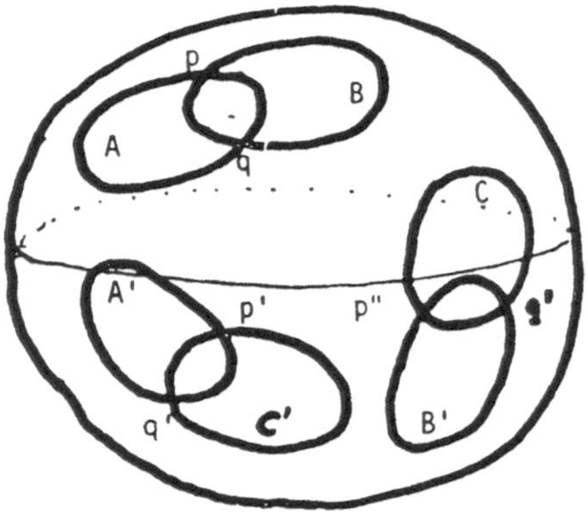

a)

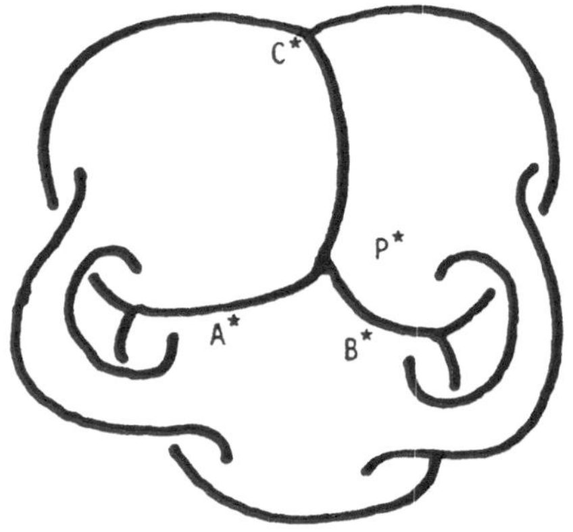

b)

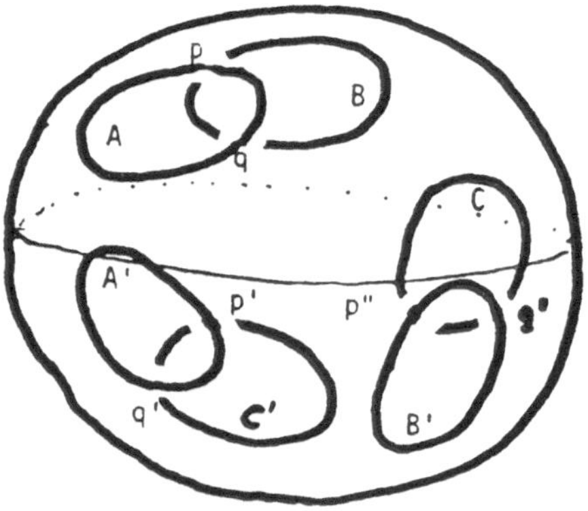

c)

Figure 8, example of projection link

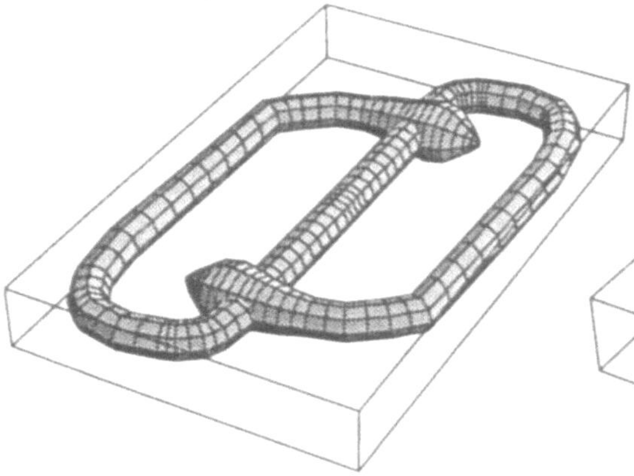

a) projection of one embedding

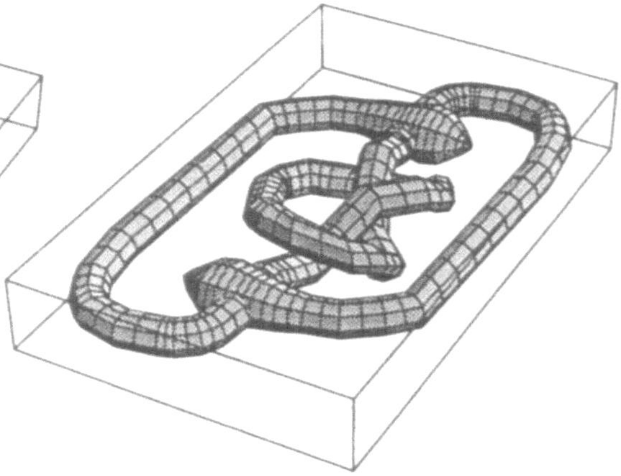

b) projection of second embedding

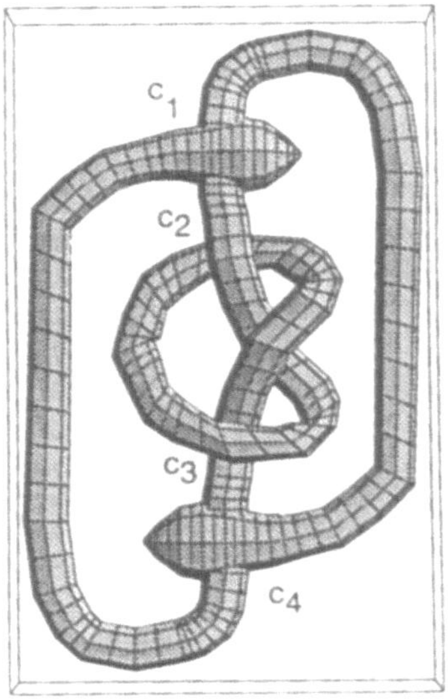

c) second view of example in b). The crossing set are the four circles of self intersection

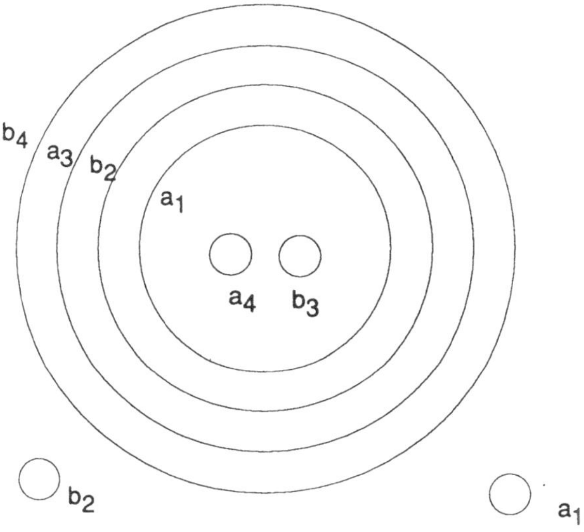

d) projection link drawn as subset of plane. Here circles a_1 and b_1 project to c_1, etc.

Figure 9, projections of two knotted spheres with the same projection link

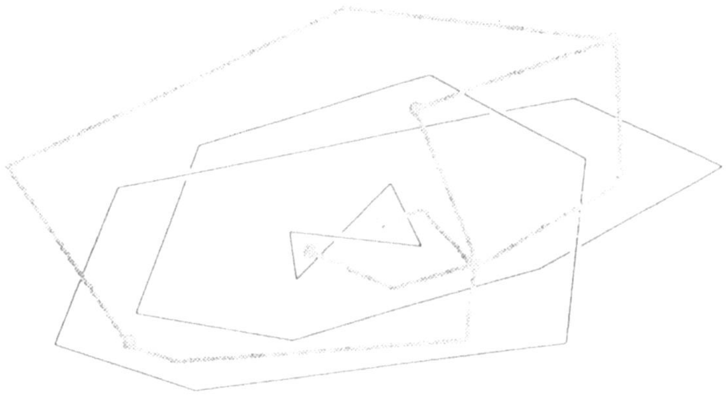

Figure 10, the graph of shards and oneCells

"clockwise" direction. This ordering of the edges about a vertex is an important part of the shard graph since, if we are given the graph and the ordering of the verticies. we can almost reconstruct X .

Note however that a figure eight curve and two disjoint circles have the same shard graph. See Figure 11 a). This and similar problems can be remedied by adding more verticies to the shard graph, corresponding to the crossing points. Locally, it looks like each crossing point lies on four portions of shards. (It is possible that two of these shards, diagonally opposite, are in fact the same as in the figure eight curve.) So to each crossing point we add four edges: one for each of these shards. Also, given a shard, we may wish to extract a list of one cells which give the oriented boundary of the shard. For this and similar reasons, we also add verticies to our graph, one for each one-cell of X ; we add an edge between such a one-cell vertex and a shard vertex if that one-cell lies on the boundary of that shard, see Figure 11 b). As before, there is a natural embedding of this graph into the plane. This graph, called the **graph of the diagram** now combines the information of the dual graph and also contains the information of the "graph of the knot" (for reference see Burde-Zieschang (1985)).

For a diagram of a knotted surface, S, we proceed analogously. A **region** will be the closure, in three-dimensional space of a component of the complement of the projection of the surface, $\Pi(S)$. In this situation, a **shard** will be the closure, in $\Pi(S)$, of a component of $\Pi(S)$ - C, where C is the crossing set. Thus the boundary of a region is a union of shards; two shards which intersect, do so along a subset of C. We construct a graph whose verticies are the regions, shards, pure double point sets, branch points and triple points of the diagram. We join region-vertex to a shard-vertex if the shard lies in the boundary of that region, join a shard-vertex to a pure-double-point-set-vertex if the pure double point set lies on the boundary of the shard, etc.

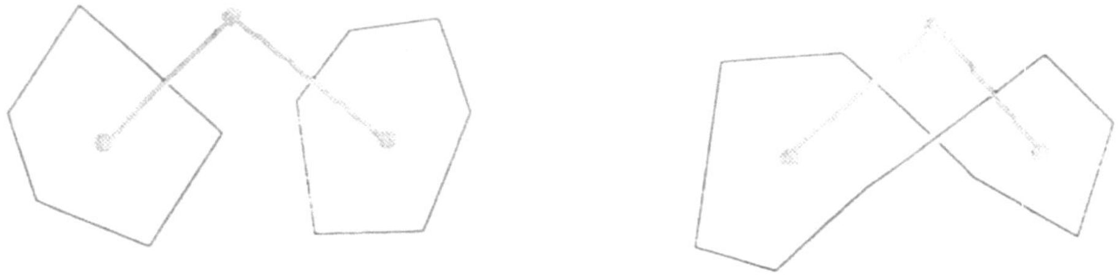

a) different diagrams with same graph of shards and oneCells

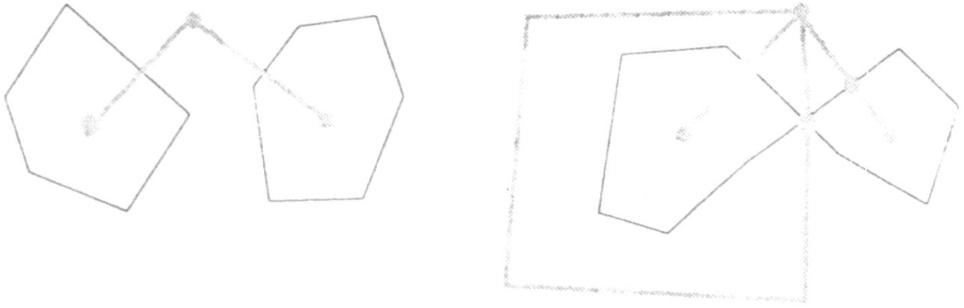

b) diagrams extended by adding verticies and edges at the crossing point and oneCells

Figure 11, extending the shard graph

i) KNOT MOVES IN DIMENSION FOUR

In a series of papers we have given techniques for finding and exhibiting isotopies between given embeddings Roseman (1974, 1979, 1989). Furthermore, there are other techniques and examples found in the literature.

We have discussed above three methods for describing a knotted surface in four-dimensional space. With each of these one has associated "knot moves" for describing isotopies. These move sets are very different from each other. By using moves from all three groups one has the best chance of finding an isotopy.

For knots described in the slice presentation, isotopies are found in several papers--the most complete reference on this is Suzuki (1976). For projections of knots we have defined an analog of Reidemeister-type moves for surfaces, see Roseman (1989), these are pictured in Figure 12. For projection links, one has a different set of moves. Each of these moves is obtained from the projection link by doing something associated with a classical Reidemeister move, see Figure 13. The local change in the knot diagram is shown in parts a) and b) of the figure; in part c) one sees the corresponding portions of the projection link. Using such moves we have been able to explicitly show the isotopy to show that the one-spun trefoil knot is unknotted Roseman (1989), a fact first proved in Zeeman (1965).

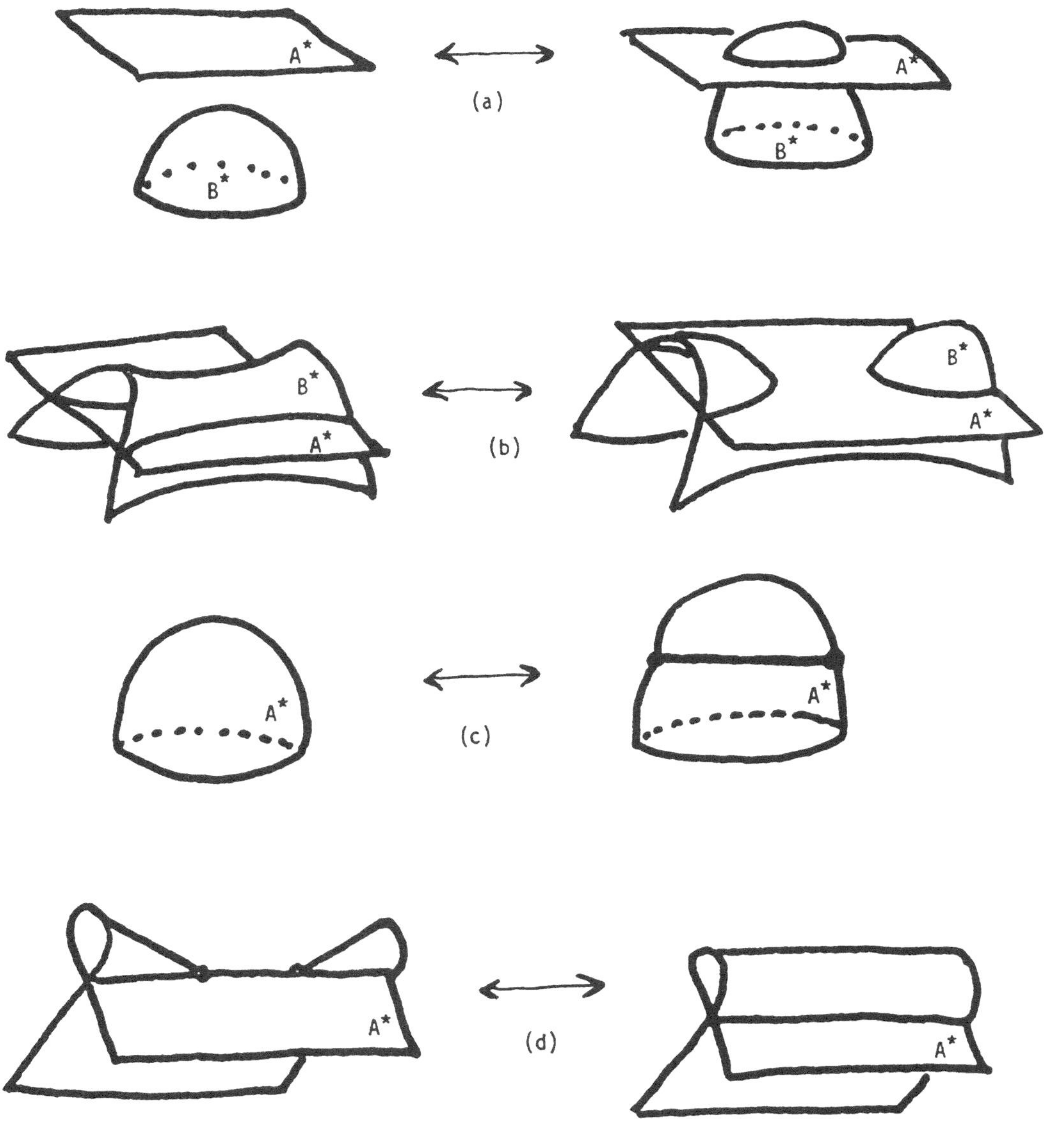

Figure 12, local pictures of knot moves for a surface in four-dimensional space [RS7]

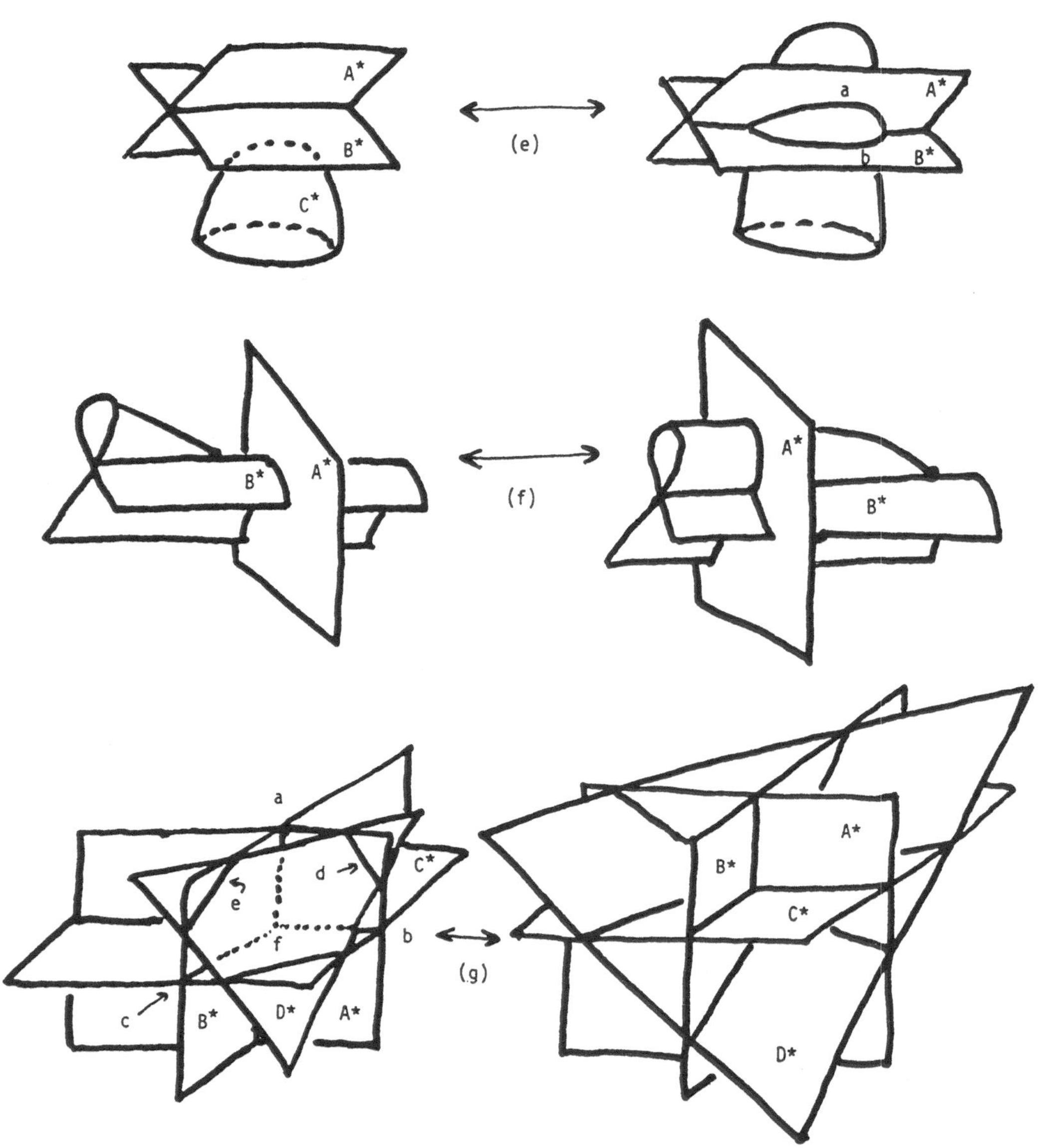

Figure 12 (continued)

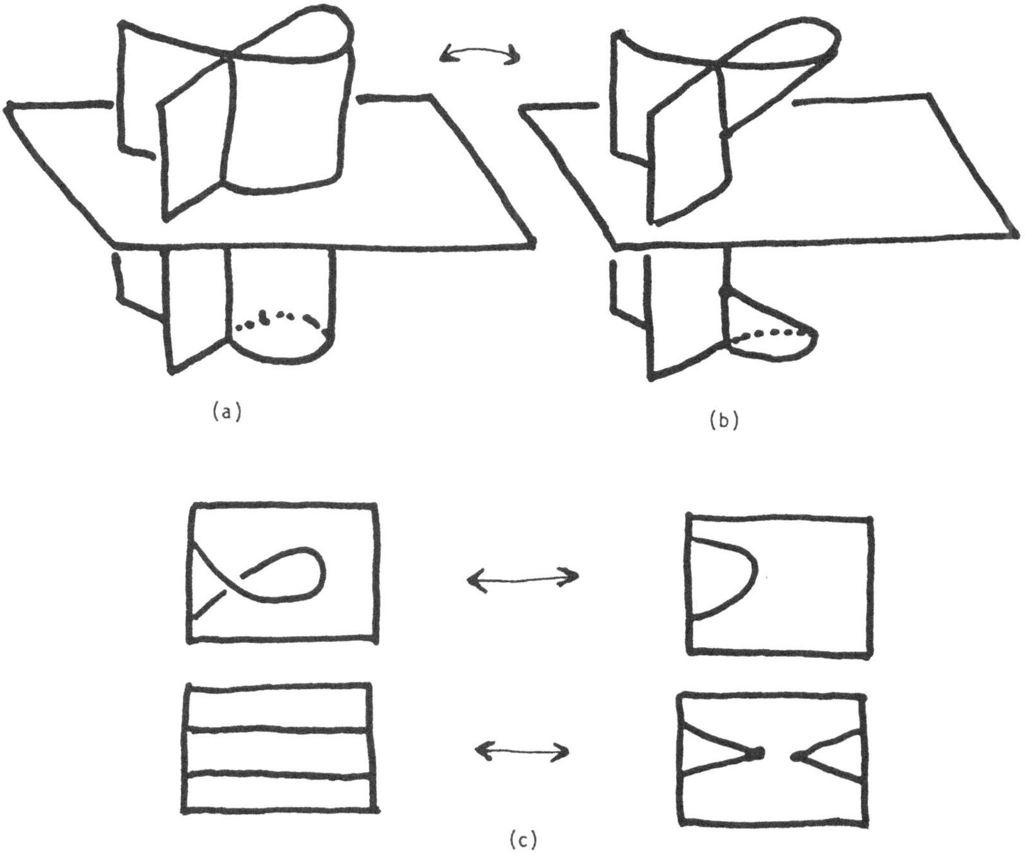

Figure 13, other knot moves associated with projection links [RS7]

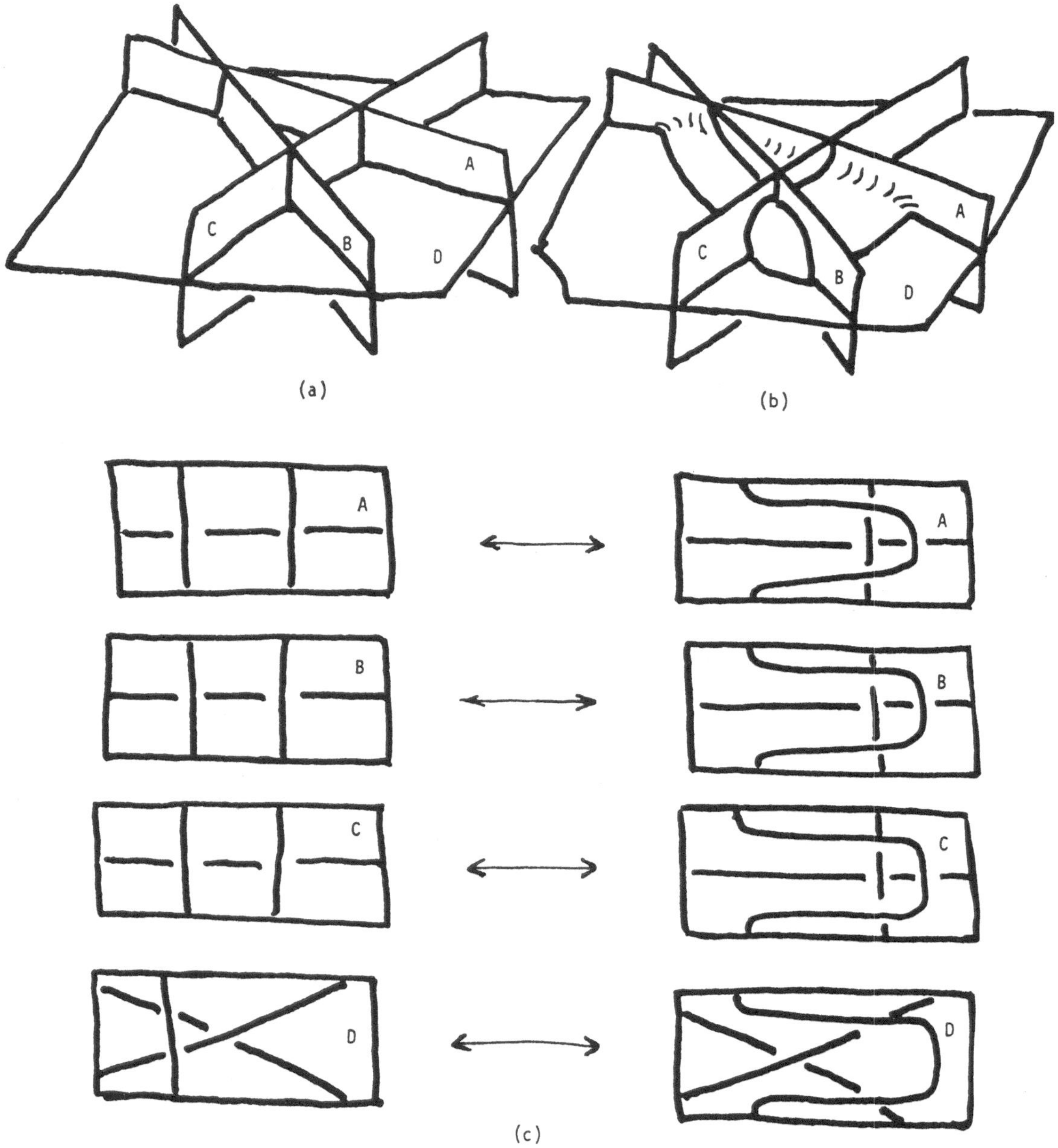

Figure 13 (continued)

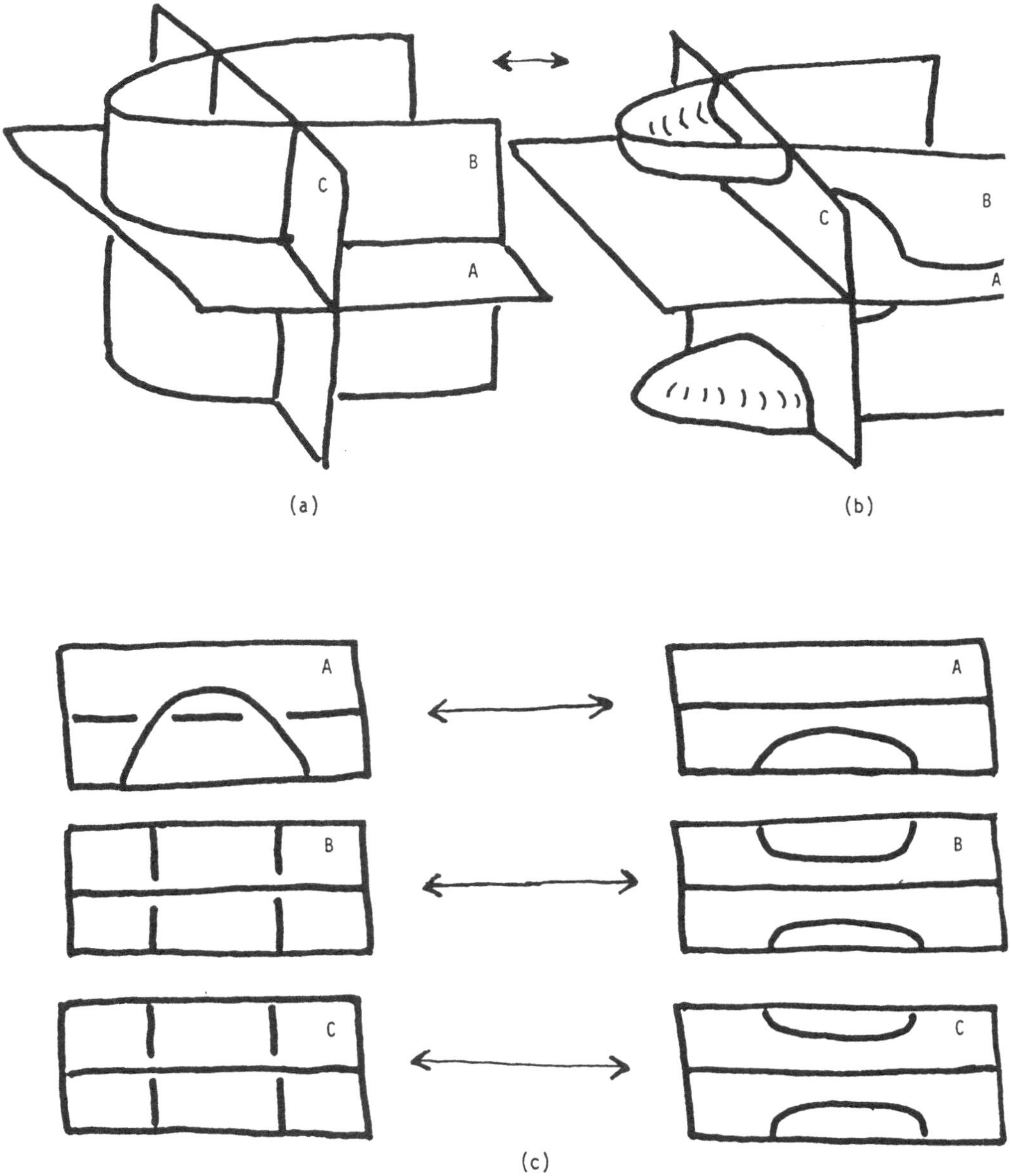

Figure 13 (contnued)

Once we have encoded a diagram for a knotted surface and reduced it to a graph, we see that the knot moves can be expressed as in the case of classical knots in terms of changing from one graph to another.

j) A PEEK AT FIVE DIMENSIONAL SPACE

We should also speak briefly about knotted three-dimensional spheres in five-dimensional space. As with knotted surfaces, we have two different approaches--the slice method and the projection method.

One could slice by four-dimensional hyperplanes. In Lomonoco (1983) we see one method of extending the slicing technique by using "slices of slices".

In terms of projection,we can extend the ideas of projection, crossing set double points set in the obvious way. The projection of a three-dimensional sphere in five-dimensional space would be a three-dimensional subset of four-dimensional space. A presentation of the knot group can be computed from this knot diagram Roseman (1974). We similarly define the **projection link** associated with such a knot. This projection link will be a subset of a three-dimensional sphere which we can visualize by depicting a corresponding subset of three-dimensional space. The double point set would, generically, look like the union of images of intersecting and self-intersecting surfaces in the three-dimensional sphere. As for surfaces, we can define height relations to give the double point set the structure of a knotted surface diagram.

Even simple cases where there are no triple (or quadruple) points is of interest. For example we could look at the projection link of a 2-spun trefoil knot. The trefoil knot has three crossings; thus six points in the double point set. Using the "obvious" knot diagram, the projection link will look like six parallel (i.e. concentric) two-dimensional spheres. We could also spin a spun trefoil; if so we get a different knot Cappell (1970). The projection link of this knot looks like six parallel copies of a standardly embedded torus. We could take a standard two-holed torus in the three-dimensional sphere and define a knotted three sphere by spinning a trefoil knot about this surface defined in Roseman (1989). The projection link of this will correspond to six parallel copies of the standard two-holed torus. One could perform similar constructions for the n-holed torus and obtain a sequence of knots. These knotted three-spheres are distinct Roseman (1989). Recently, Suciu (1990) has found some interesting non-reflexive knotted three spheres using a construction of Roseman (1989).

k) OTHER APPLICATIONS

Our goal is to implement a program that will do many calculations in geometric topology. Our name for this topological drawing program is TopDrawer. We have considered several problems in geometric topology. We have noted we need a program that will deal with projections of knots, links and graphs in three dimensional space, sequences of slices of knotted surfaces, projections of knotted surfaces. Once we have a program that will handle this complexity, it is a small step in terms of design to represent other things such as projection links for knotted three-dimensional spheres in five-dimensional space. This is only a sample of the situations we wish to handle. We briefly list some other problems to further understand our motivation for such flexible design.

The program would be useful for classical knot theory. There are several programs for classical knots but none allows interactive knot moves and other geometric manipulations. For example, we would like to implement a method for, getting braids from knots as in Morton(1986) , Vogel (1990). In addition, draw cables and doubles of given knots, etc. Another method of coding a knot diagram is the method of "tangles", Conway (1967); our graph based system can easily adapt to incorporate this notational system. In addition, the are a number of papers that deal with changes of knot diagrams different than the Riedemiester moves or the "crossing smoothing" changes such as in Nakanishi (1990), Murakami-Nakanishi (1989), and Hoste-Nakanishi- Taniyama (1987). These could all easily be incorporated into the TopDrawer program. In addition, there would be no difficulties in studying projections of links onto surfaces and related invariants as introduced in Turaev (1991).

One can enter a knotted graph into TopDrawer. There are "knot moves" for such graphs Kauffman (1989), Yetter (1989). Thus one could use our program to help make a table of knotted graphs. Tables of knots and links up to a certain complexity are well established, but tables for knotted graphs are still in a very early stage, Simon (1987). If two graphs are equivalently knotted, one could find and record a sequence of moves which would take one to the other. If the knotted graphs are different, there are a number of invariants we could try Kauffman (1989) and Reshetikhin-Turaev (1990) . Also, one invariant of a knotted graph is the set of knots and links one obtains from subsets of the graph. Our program could easily find these knots and links and it knows how to encode these for use in the SNAPPEA of Weeks(1990). This program is a very efficient one for distinguishing most knots and links.

Knot diagrams could also be used to describe four dimensional constructions. By adding framing information to a link diagram, the program could be used to do the diagram manipulations known as "Kirby calculus". This provides a way of describing four-dimensional manifolds and explicitly showing equivalences between two given manifolds (Kirby (1978, 1989), Mandelbaum (1980) and Fenn-Rourke (1982)). Such calculations have been used extensively in the study of four-dimensional manifolds, Akbulut (1984), Akbulut-Kirby (1985) Aitcheson-Rubinstein (1984). Freedman (1982) has remarked that this technique was instrumental in understanding of the basic structure of Casson handles.

One could also input a drawing which would describe a generic map of a surface into the plane by drawing the image of the critical points of the map (the fold set and the cusp points). In Kergosien (1991), there is a description of this terminology and an application to medical imaging. A similar approach can be used to study immersions of three-dimensional manifolds into four-space Levine (1985).

Also there is no difficulty to extending to piecewise-linear immersions, homotopies or regular homotopies of surfaces in three-dimension and four-dimensional space as in used in Kirk (1988) , Morin-Petit (1979), Francis (1987), Max (1977) and Carter (1988). For example, one could enter a link in three-dimensional space and in addition to the usual knot moves and surgeries, allow a move which passes one edge through another. A sequence of links connected by these moves will give rise to (generically immersed) surface in four-dimensional space. More generally, a sequence of knotted graphs related by such moves corresponds to a knotted two-dimensional complex in four-dimensional space.

The ideas involved with slicing to describe embedded or immersed surfaces in four dimensional space have obvious counterparts for embedded or immersed surfaces in three-dimensional space. This slicing point of view for embedded surfaces is discussed in Shinagawa-Kunii-Kergosien (1991). In this case a generic slice is a union of contours and the parent-child contour graph of this slice is the same as the shard graph of this diagram as in this paper.

BIBLIOGRAPHY

Adams C, (1990) SNAPPEA, the Weeks Hyperbolic 3-Manifolds Program,*Notices A. M. S.* (**37**) No. 3

Akbulut S, (1984) A fake 4-manifold, *Four-manifold theory*, A. M. S. Contemp. Math (**35**) pp. 75-141

Akbulut S, Kirby R, (1985) A potential smooth counterexample in dimension 4 to the Poincare conjecture, the Shoenflies conjecture, and the Andrews-Curtis conjecture, *Topology* (**24**) pp. 375-390

Aitcheson IR., Rubinstein JH, (1984), Fibered knots and involutions on homotopy spheres, *A. M. S. Contemp. Math* (35), pp.1-74

Burde G, Zieschang H, (1985) *Knots*, Walter de Gruyter,

Cappell SE,(1970) Superspinning and knot complements, *Topology of Manifolds, Proc. Univ. Georgia Inst.*, Ed. Cantrell and Edwards, Markham, pp. 358-385

Carter JS, (1988) Surguring the Equatorial Immersion in Low Dimensions, *Differentiable Topology, Lecture Notes in Mathematics* # 1350, Springer-Verlag

Crowell RH, Fox RH, (1977) *Introduction to knot theory*, Grad. Text Math. #57, Springer-Verlag,

Cooke G, Finney R, (1967) *Homology of Cell Complexes*, Mathematical Notes, Princeton University Press,.

Conway JH, (1967) An enumeration of knots and links and some of their related properties, *Computational problems in Abstract Algebra, Proc. Conf. Oxford*, Pergamon Press, 329-358.

Dowker C H, Thistlethwaite, MB, (1983) Classification of Knot Projections, *Topology and its Applications*, (**16**) pp. 19-31.

Fenn R, Rourke C, (1982) On Kirby's calculus of links, *Topology* (**18**) pp. 1-15.

Freedman MH, (1982) The topology of 4-manifolds, *J. Diff. Geom.* (**17**) 357-453.

Francis GK, (1987), *A Toplological Picturebook*, Springer-Verlag

Fox RH, (1961) A quick trip through knot theory, *Topology of 3-manifolds and related topics*, Prentice Hall pp. 120-167.

Guillemin V, Pollack A,(1974) *Differential Topology*, Prentice-Hall

Giller C, (1982) Towards a classical knot theory for surfaces in R^4,?*Ill. J. Math* . (**26**) 4 591-631

Hudson J FP, (1969), *Piecewise Linear Topology*, W. A. Benjamin,

Haken W, (1961) Theorie der Normalflachen , *Acta. Math.* (**105**) 245-375.

Homma, Tatsuo , Nagase, Teruo, (1987) On Elementary Deformations of Maps of Surfaces into 3-Manifolds II, *Topology and Computer Science* Ed. by S. Suzuki, Kinokuniya Company Ltd. Tokyo

Hoste J, Nakanishi Y, Taniyama K, (1990) Unknotting Operations Involving Trivial Tangles, *Osaka J. Math* (**27**), pp.555-566

Homma T, Ochiai M, and Takahashi M, (1980) An algorithm for recognizing S3 in 3-manifolds with Heegaard splittings of genus two, *Osaka J. Math.* 17 pp. 625-648

Kauffman LH, (1983) *Formal Knot Theory, Mathematical Notes* 30, Princeton University Press

Kauffman LH, (1988) New invariants in knot theory, *Amer. Math. Monthly* (**95**) 195-242.

Kauffman LH, (1989) Invariants of Graphs in Three-space, *Trans. AMS* (**311**) 2 , 697-710

Kinoshita S, (1990) Talk on knotted graphs, University of Iowa,.

Kirby R, (1978) A calculus for framed links in S3, *Inv. Math* **45** pp. 36-56

Kirby R, (1989) *The Topology of 4-Manifolds, Lecture Notes in Mathematics* #1374, Springer-Verlag

Kirk P, (1988) Link maps in the four sphere, *Differential Topology Lecture Notes in Mathematics* # 1350,, Ed. U. Koschorke, Springer-Verlag pp. 31-43,

Kergosien Y, (1991) Generic Sign Systems in Medical Imaging, *IEEE Computer Graphics and Applications*, Vol. 11 No. 5,pp. 46-65

Lomonoco SJ Jr, (1983) Five dimensional knot theory, *Low Dimensional Topology*, A. M. S. Contemp. Math (20)
Levine H, (1985) Classifying Immersions into R^4 over Stable Maps of 3-manifolds into R^2, *Lecture Notes in Math.* #1157, Springer-Verlag
Milnor J, (1963) Morse Theory, *Annals of Math. Studies*, No. 51, Princeton Universilty Press
Mandelbaum R, (1980) Four-dimensional topology: an introduction, *Bull. A. M. S* (**2**) pp. 1-159
Morin B, Petit, JP, (1979) Le retournement de la sphere, *Pour la Science,* (15), pp. 34-41.
Morton H, (1986) Threading knot diagrams, *Math. Proc. Camb. Phil. Soc.* (99) pp. 247-260
Murakami H, Nakanishi Y, (1989) On a certain move generating link-homology, *Math Ann.* (284) pp. 75-89
Max N, (1977) *Turning a Sphere Inside Out* International Film Bureau, Chicago
Nakanishi Y, (1990) On Fox's Congruence Classes of Knots II, *Osaka J. Math.* (27) 207-215
Ochiai M, *Knot Theory by Computer,* program in development for Macintosh system.
Reidemeister K, (1932) , *Knotentheorie*, Ergebn.Math. Grenzgeb., Bd 1, Springer-Verlag
Rolfsen D, (1976) *Knots and Links*, Publish or Perish Press,
Reshetikhin NY., Turaev VG, (1990) Ribbon Graphs and Their Invariants Derived from Quantum Groups, Preprint
Roseman D, (1974) Projection of knots, *Fund. Math.* (**89)** , pp. 307-312.
Roseman D, (1974) Woven knots are spun knots, *Osaka J. Math* (**11**), pp. 307-312
Roseman D, (1975) The spun square knot is the spun granny knot, *Bull. Soc. Math. Mex.* (**20**) .
Roseman D,(1989) Projections of Codimension Two Embeddings, Preprint .
Roseman D, (1989) Reidemeister-type Moves for Surfaces in Four Dimensional Space, Preprint
Roseman D, (1989) Spinning knots about submanifolds; spinning knots about projections of knots, *Topology and its Applications.* (**31**) pp. 225-241
Roseman D (1992) Design of a Mathematicians' Drawing Program, *Computer Graphics Using Object-Oriented Programming*, Ed. S. Cunningham, J. Brown, N. Craghill and M. Fong, John Wiley & Sons, 279-296.
Shinagawa Y , Kunii T, and Kergosien Y, (1991) Surface Coding Based on Morse Theory, *Computer Graphics and Applications*, Vol. 11 No. 5 pp 66-78.
Simon J, (1987)Graph Theory and Topology in Chemistry, *Studies in physics and theoretical chemistry* #51, Ed King & Rouverg pp. 43-75.
Suciu A, (1990) Inequivalent frame-spun knots with the same complement, Preprint
Suzuki S, (1976)Knotting Problems of 2-spheres in the 4-sphere, *Math.Sem. Notes Kobe Univ* . (**4**) , pp. 241-371.
Turaev V, (1991) Shadow Links and the IRF-Models of Statistical Mechanics, Preprint, Univ. Louis Pastuer, Inst. Rech. Math. Avancee
Vogel P, (1990) Representation of links by braids: a new algorithm, *Comm. Math. Helv* 65 pp. 104-113
Yajima T, (1962) On simply knotted spheres in four-dimensional space, *Osaka Math. J.* (**13**), pp. 63-71
Yetter D, (1989) Category Theoretic Representation of Knotted Graphs in S^3, *Advances in Mathematics* (77) 137-155
Zeeman EC, (1965) Twisting spun knots, *Trans. AMS*, (**115**) pp. 471-495

AUTHORS BIOGRAPHIES

Dennis Roseman is an Associate Professor of Mathematics at the University of Iowa. His research interests are in topology, particularly the topology of knotted surfaces in four-dimensional space. He has written several papers on these topics as well as papers on higher dimensional knottings. He is currently developing a software system, called TopDrawer for computation in geometric topology. Roseman received his B. S. (1961) and M. S. (1962) in mathematics from the University of Wisconsin; Ph. D. in mathematics from the University of Michigan.(1968). He is a member of AMS and ACM.

Address:
University of Iowa, Iowa City, Iowa, USA (52242)
E-mail: roseman@dimension4.math.uiowa.edu
Tel: (319) 335-0779
Fax: (319) 335-0627

Shape Description and Classification Based on Extremal Points and Their Relations

Yu Nakajima, Hirobumi Nishida, and Shunji Mori

ABSTRACT.

Humans classify shapes naturally. However, nobody knows this classification mechanism which is known as a very profouned problem. Here shapes on 2-Dimension are treated. Mathematics is essential to approach this open problem, but it seems that topology is too rough and differential geometry is too precise. In this sense, this paper proposes a new description of binary images, based on the fundamentals of topology and differential geometry, and gives a natural classification of shapes according to the description. A contour of shape is described by concatenation of four symbols which correspond to four kinds of extremal points where we assume that the contour of shape is a simple closed curve. Some properties of the strings/words consisting of these symbols are shown. Operations on the string, named horn making and horn removing are introduced. A set of such strings is closed under these operations. The positional relations of extremal points are investigated and it is shown that there exist positional orders of them which are invariants for continuous mapping under the condition of keeping the symbol representation. Based on the relations, a more detailed, but not so precise classification of shapes which meets our intuition is given.

Keywords: topology, contour description, extremal point, dp code, height relation, horn operation, switching pair, rotation value, curl value,

1. INTRODUCTION.

To describe the contour of a binary images, many methods have been developed in the field of optical character recognition (OCR).

An extensive review paper is available, which alludes very recent works (Mori 1992). The objective of describing a binary image in some ways is to recognize it by a machine. Such an approach is called structure analysis approach (Pavlidis 1977). A structure of a binary image is described as simply as possible under the condition that essential features of a given shape are not lost. In this sense, topology of a shape was noticed together with the singular points of the shape. Therefore, the number of connected components, the number of holes, end points and singular points (intersection points, for example) and their relations are typical features of the shape. Geometric features such as curvature and line length are also important features. In this connection, concavity and convexity are very effective features of a shape. Such features are called quasi-topological features in the field of OCR.

In particular, some of the authors have developed an algebraic description of shape based on a quasi-topological approach (Nishida 1990, 1991, 1992a, 1992b). That is, the algebraic method describes curves by a combination of clockwise curves, each partially lies on another. And each of clockwise curves (primitive sequences) is made by integrating lines (primitives) digitized in four directions. In this method, the primitive is made by very rough conditions, so it should not be classified as a geometric feature, but can be considered to be close to topology.

On the other hands, in the field of computer graphics, it becomes more important to describe shape, 3-D objects in particular. But, in general, descriptions of a 3-D object are based on parametric descriptions and are exact in the sense that the original shape is preserved in the description. Nowadays, to obtain descriptions of objects by extracting some essential features, called "coding", are researched on. Recently, a method of surface coding based on Morse theory was proposed (Shinagawa 1991). It focuses on critical points which are topological features of objects. On the other hand, an interesting method of coding a contour was proposed (Kergosien 1991). Plotting a contour against the angle of projection so-called contour diagram is obtained, in which the order and orientations of cusps and crossings on it provide a precise description for shape.

We propose a new description of a contour in the sense that it is very simple from both theoretical and practical points of view compared with any other methods describing concavities and convexities of a contour as far as we know. It should be classified as a quasi-topological method. It makes the structure of shape clear and gives us the perspective to the complexity of shape. It is also useful for the first step classification of our character recognition system. We believe that the description can be the first step to get simple mathematical description between topology and parametric curve description.

In section 2, we describe the new description named the **dp code**, which is made by focusing extremal points of y-coordinates of a contour. And some properties of the codes are described. In section 3, we define transform operations on a contour, named **horn operations**. It makes us easier to understand dp codes. Somewhat a related work was done (Kergosien 1991), but again our operation is very simple. In section 4, we describe height relations implied by the dp code. When a dp code is settled, some extremal points must be higher than others. A method to find these relations are described. In section 5, we define **switching pairs** and **curl values**. Distinguishing some contours which have the same dp codes is sometimes useful and interesting, and curl values are good for this purpose. In section 6, we mention an application of the description to the recognition of handprinted numerals. Section 7 is the discussion and section 8 is the conclusion.

2. THE DP CODES.

In this section, we propose a description of a contour called **dp code** , which can distinguish Fig.1(a) and Fig.1(b). First, we describe some premises, then, we classify them into four classes and the dp code is defined. And some basic properties about the code are shown.

2.1. Basic concepts.

Premises.

- The term **contour** is defined as "A Jordan curve with a domain called **interior** on the inside or the outside."
- In this paper, we only consider contours which have a finite number of extremal points of y-coordinates.
- The description introduced here strongly depends on the direction of the coordinate system. We use the standard coordinate system such that x-axis goes from left to right and y-axis goes from bottom to top.

A Contour.
A contour which has the interior on the inside is called an **outer contour**, and a contour which has the interior on the outside is called an **inner contour**.

Directions of contours are defined as follows : The direction looking at the interior on the left side is called **positive**, and the reverse direction is called **negative**.

Notations.
In this paper, extremal points of y-coordinates on a contour are called extremal points in short. For a contour C and a point $P \in C$, x-coordinate and y-coordinate of P are written as $x(P)$ and $y(P)$, respectively.

2.2. A Classification of Extremal Points.

In this subsection, we classify extremal points into four types, such as "d", "p", "∩", and "∪", respectively. Definitions are as follows (cf. Fig.2(a)) :

(a)

(b)

Fig.1 : Two contours and their dp codes.

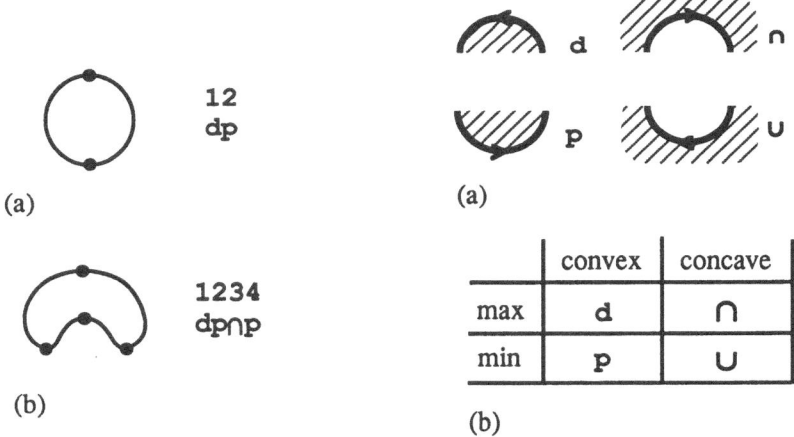

(a)

	convex	concave
max	d	∩
min	p	∪

(b)

Fig.2 : The classification of extremal points.
(a) : Arrows show the positive direction.
(b) : Attributes of classified extremal points.

A maximal point which has the interior beneath it:	d
A maximal point which has the interior on it:	∩
A minimal point which has the interior beneath it:	∪
A minimal point which has the interior on it:	p

Points d and p are called **convex extremal points**, or being convex in short, and ∩ and ∪ are called **concave extremal points** or being concave. We also call maximal points d and ∩ as **max** and p and ∪ as **min**. (cf. Fig.2(b)). We write these relations as, for a point a, $type(a)=d$, and so on.

2.3. The Dp Code of a Contour.

We define **dp code** as an ordered and cyclic sequence of types of extremal points along the positive direction of a contour starting from any point. For a code s = $a_0a_1 \cdots a_{n-1}$, and a code t = $b_0b_1 \cdots b_{m-1}$, we write as "s = t" when,

$$n = m \text{ and } \exists_k , \forall_{i\in[0,n-1]} \; a_i = b_{i+k} \quad \text{(the additions of suffixes are under module n.)}$$

For example, for a dp code s of a contour in Fig.1(b),

$$s = \mathrm{dp{\cap}p} = \mathrm{p{\cap}pd} = \mathrm{{\cap}pdp} = \mathrm{pdp{\cap}} .$$

For a dp code $a_0a_1 \cdots a_{n-1}$, we say a_i and a_{i+1} are next to each other. (But the addition of the suffixes of a is under module n).

For a dp code of a contour, we write the numbers of characters of d, p, ∩, and ∪ in the code as N_d, N_p, $N_\cap$, and $N_\cup$, respectively.

2.4. Basic Properties of the Dp Code.

After removing all extremal points from a contour, we get some arcs, and for each arc, y-coordinate is monotone increasing or monotone decreasing when tracing the arc along positive direction. We call the former **upward arc** and call the latter **downward arc**. Upward arcs and downward arcs appear alternately along a contour. So,

Lemma 1:

(1) The dp code is an alternate sequence of characters of type of max and type of min.

(2) The length of the dp code is even number. So, (by (1))

$$N_d + N_\cap = N_p + N_\cup .$$

(end of lemma 1.)

Proposition 1: On a dp code of a contour, for $\lambda = N_d + N_p - N_\cap - N_\cup$,

$\lambda = 2 \quad \Leftrightarrow$ the contour is an outer contour,
$\lambda = -2 \quad \Leftrightarrow$ the contour is an inner contour.

(end of Proposition 1.)

We mention that, the sum of all λ of contours that form a image, is twice as many as the Euler number of the image. The union of two conditions of lemma 1 and a condition of $\lambda=2$, is called **the contour conditions of dp codes**. Since a dp code of an inner contour can be transformed into that of the outer contour easily and vice versa. From now on, we focus only on an outer contour, not an inner contour.

Remark : The model of the dp code can be regarded as cell-division with fixing height function in Morse theory. Our aim is to classify and examine the reconstructed structures from divided pieces systematically. We also aim to apply such mathematical idea to real problems by simple descriptions for computers.

3. HORN OPERATIONS.

In the last section, we described properties of dp codes of contours. On the contrary, when given a some string, it is an interesting question whether there is a contour whose dp code is the given string. In this section, we define an operation on a contour, and give an answer to this question.

We will define a transformation on a contour, named **horn removing** and **horn making**. These are called **horn operations**. Along these transformations, the dp code of the contour changes. We call these changes, **horn operations on the dp code**. As described later, horn operations are always possible on only a dp code as symbolic operations. But it seems to require more study to describe whether these all operations on the code have corresponding transformations on a contour. We will only show possibility of horn makings on a contour.

3.1. Horns.

On a dp code, if the types of points next to each other are "d" and "$\cup$", or "p" and "$\cap$" (convex and concave), we call the pair a **horn** on the code. On a contour, a horn is defined as a union of two extremal points and three arcs : Extremal points corresponding to a horn on its dp code, an arc between the points, and two monotonic arcs connecting to the points.

Horns "d$\cup$", and "$\cap$p" contain upward arcs at both ends. They are called **upward horns**. Horns "$\cup$d" and "p$\cap$" contain downward arcs at both ends. They are called **downward horns**.

3.2. Horn Removings on Dp Codes.

We call the operation to remove a horn from a dp code and reduce the code by two characters, **horn removing on the code**. This term is used as a symbolic operation on a code. If there is any horn on the code, this operation is possible. (but existence of corresponding transformation on a contour is another problem.)

Lemma 2: When an dp code satisfies ***the contour conditions of dp codes*** (described in the last section), even if one horn removing on the code is done, the conditions are still satisfied.
(end of lemma 2.)

Theorem 2: If a string *s* with length n satisfies ***the contour conditions of dp code***, it can be transformed into the code "dp" by $\frac{n}{2} - 1$ times of horn removings on the code.
(end of Th 2.)

An outline of the proof is the following : One horn removing on the code is always possible under the conditions except for a code "dp". Then, lemma 2 is used recursively.

3.3. Horn Making.

As the following, horn makings are always possible on both contours and dp codes if symbolic operations are possible.

Theorem 3: For any contour, it can be transformed as follows :

(1) Changing any upward arc into an upward horn. Both "d∪" and "∩p" are possible.

(2) Changing any downward arc into an downward horn. Both "∪d" and "p∩" are possible.

And these transformations can be done without changing other parts of the contour.
(end of Th 3.)

The proof uses a close neighborhood of a point on the arc. Its intersection to the contour must be a simple arc, and y-coordinates of the end points of the arc must differ. Then, transformation of the arc in the neighborhood is possible.

3.4. Existence of Contours of Some Dp Code.

Now, the above-mentioned problem is solved.

Theorem 4: For any string *s* that is a concatenation of characters of "d", "p", "∩", and "∪", satisfying ***the contour conditions of dp codes***, there exists a contour whose dp code is *s*.
(end of Th 4.)

This is an outline of the proof. cf. Fig.3 :

1. Transform given code *s* into "dp" by horn removings on the code.
2. Start from the code "dp" with one contour of circle.
3. Transform the code and the contour together in reverse order of step 1 by one-by-one horn making.
4. When the code returns to the first one, the contour has the given code.

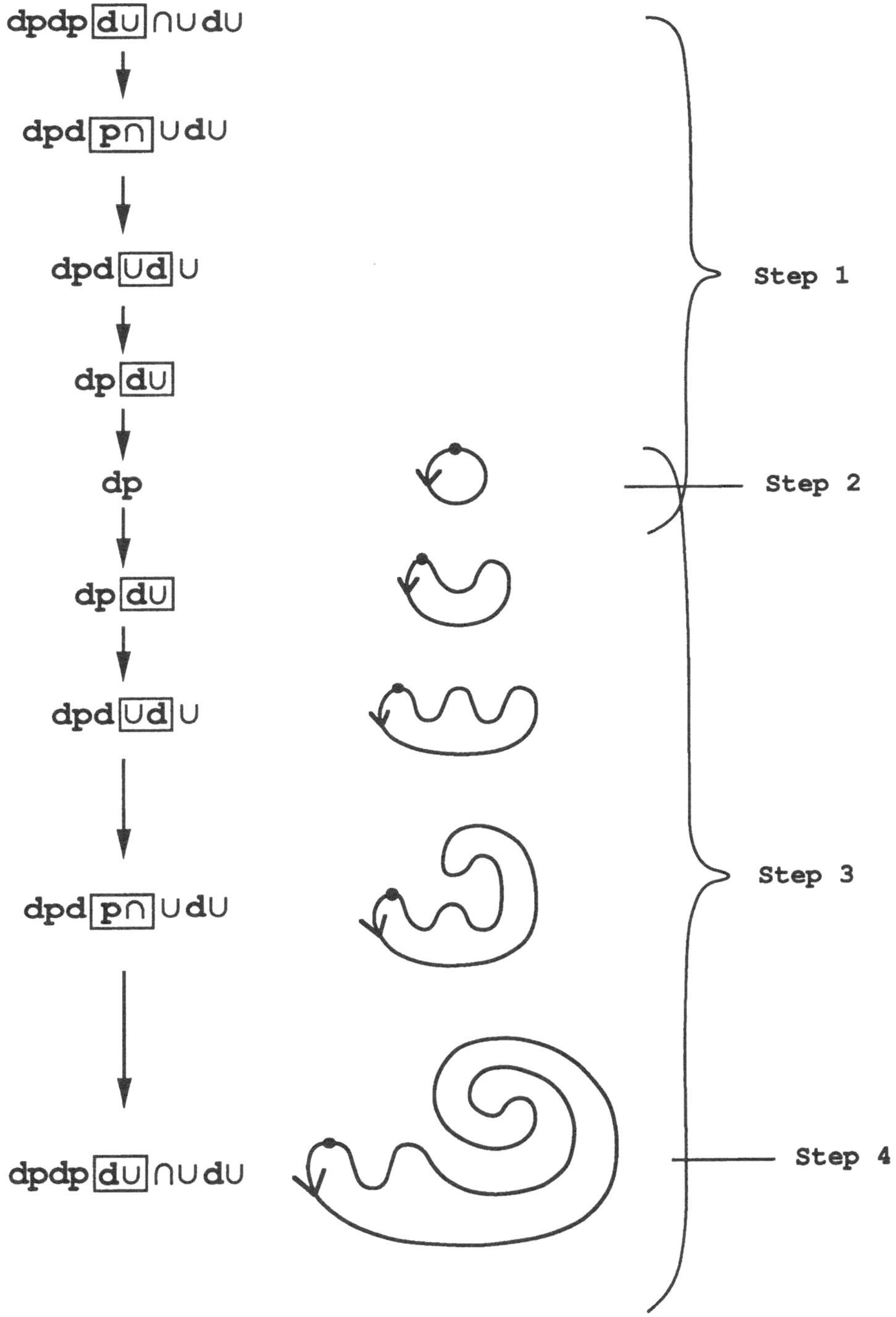

Fig.3 : An example of the proof of theorem 4.
A dot on each contour means the first extremal point on the corresponding dp code.

4. HEIGHT RELATIONS ON DP CODES.

In this section, we describe height relations depending on dp codes. When a dp code is settled, some extremal points must be higher than others. We call the relations **first height relations** and **second height relations**. The first one is trivial and the second one is interesting. We also define some terms such as **a path**, and so on. These are not only necessary for defining the second height relations, but also important themselves.

4.1. First Height Relation.

For y-coordinates $y(a)$, $y(b)$ of extremal points a, b which are next to each other :

a *is max* $\Leftrightarrow y(a)>y(b)$ and a *is min* $\Leftrightarrow y(a)<y(b)$.

Because the arc between a and b is an upward arc or a downward arc.
We define this relation as the **first height relation**.

4.2. Terms.

The following terms are indispensable to define second height relations.

○ **Sequences.**
In this subsection and later, we write a **sequence** as values separated by comma, and surrounded by brackets, such as

$$[a_1,\ a_2,\ .\ .\ .\ ,a_n]$$

Sequences of numbers, sequences of extremal points, and so on will be used.

○ **Paths.**
For a contour and two extremal points a and b on it, we call a subcontour from a to b with positive or negative direction, a **path**, and it is written as $P_+[a;b]$ *or* $P_-[a;b]$ respectively. For any pair of a and b of a contour, the union of $P_+[a;b]$ and $P_-[a;b]$ covers the whole contour.

A path can also be written as a sequence of extremal points or its types. For example, some paths p_1 and p_2 are written as :

$$p_1 = P_-[a_1;a_n] = [a_1,\ a_2,\ .\ .\ .\ ,a_n]\ ,$$
$$p_2 = [d,p,\cap,p,\cap]\ .$$

Remark: In the description by a sequence, the order of the extremal points (or its type) indicates the direction of the path. So, in the example of p_1 , $a_1 \rightarrow a_2 \rightarrow a_3$ implies the negative direction.

○ **The inner rotation number.**
For a set of extremal points S, let $N_{dp}(S)$ be the number of convex extremal points of S, and $N_{\cap\cup}(S)$ be the number of concave extremal points of S.

For a path $p = P_{\pm}[a_1;a_n] = [a_1, a_2, \ldots, a_n]$, and for two sets $S_1=\{a_i|1\le i\le n\}$ and $S_2=\{a_i|1<i<n\}$, the following values are called **inner rotation number of path** p, and are written as the following (double signs of P and N are in same order) :

$N_{dp}(S_1)-N_{\cap\cup}(S_1)$: $N[p]$ *or* $N_{\pm}[a_1;a_n]$,
$N_{dp}(S_2)-N_{\cap\cup}(S_2)$: $N(p)$ *or* $N_{\pm}(a_1;a_n)$

Example: When $p=[d,p,\cap,p]$, $N[p]=3-1=2$ and $N(p)=1-1=0$.

○ **The sequence of inner rotation numbers.**
For a path $p = P_{\pm}[a_1;a_n] = [a_1, a_2, \ldots, a_n]$, we define **the sequence of inner rotation numbers of** p as a sequence of $N_{\pm}[a_2;a_i]$ $(2\le i\le n-1)$ and write it as $NN(p)$ or $NN_{\pm}(a_1;a_n)$. (double signs of P, N, and NN are in same order). When $n\le 2$, the sequence is defined as [ ] (null sequence).

Example : When $p=[d,p,d,p,\cap,\cup]$, $N[a_2;a_2]=1$, $N[a_2;a_3]=2$, and so on. (The direction of p has no influence on this example, so omitted.) Thus, $NN(p)$ = [1,2,3,2] .

4.3. Second Height Relations.

Let points 1 and 3 be extremal points of type d and ∩ of a contour which has a dp code of "dp∩p" illustrated in Fig.1(b). It seems that $y(1)>y(3)$ for all contours which have the same dp codes. We call such relations second height relations. We describe the definition in this subsection.

Proposition 5: For two extremal points a and b of any contour,

A. (1) and (2) and (3) $\Longrightarrow y(a)>y(b)$ holds, for the following conditions (1),(2), and (3) :
   (1) ; $type(a)=d$ and $type(b)=\cap$,
   (2) ; $N_{+}(a;b) = N_{-}(a;b) = 1$,
   (3) ; Both $NN_{+}(a;b)$ and $NN_{-}(a;b)$ have no negative numbers.

B. (1) and (2) and (3) $\Longrightarrow y(a)<y(b)$ holds, for the following conditions (1),(2), and (3) :
   (1) ; $type(a)=p$ and $type(b)=\cup$,
   (2) ; The same as A ,
   (3) ; The same as A.

(end of Proposition 5.)

Remark: A and B in Proposition 5 are up-down symmetric.
Under the condition (1), $N_{+}(a;b)=1 \Leftrightarrow N_{-}(a;b)=1$ because of Proposition 1.

An outline of the proof is illustrated in Fig.4.

We call these relations, **second height relations**.

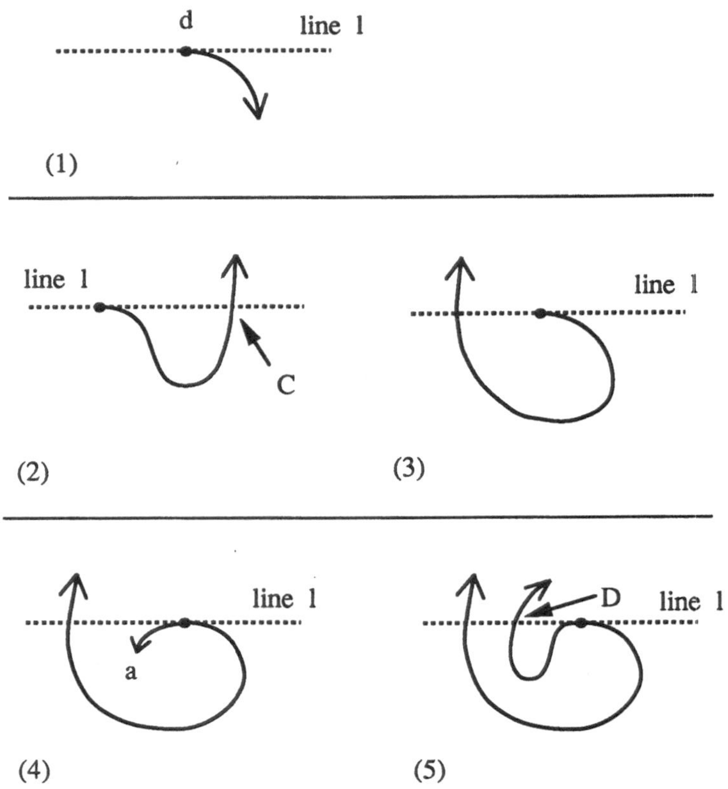

Fig.4 : An outline of proof of proposition 5. (Under the condition A.)
We use reduction to absurdity. First, we assume that an extremal point of type ∪ is above an extremal point of type d:
(1) : To go to above l, (2) or (3) are all cases.
(2) : If (2), $N_{dp}-N_{\cap\cup}$ becomes negative at C. So, (2) is impossible.
(3),(4) : Then, the other end a in (4) must go to above l as (5).
(5) : $N_{dp}-N_{\cap\cup}$ becomes negative at D. So, $y(d)\leq y(\cap)$ is impossible.

4.4. Examples.

For a dp code $\overset{1\,2\,3\,4}{\mathbf{dp\cap p}}$ illustrated in Fig.1(b), among all the pairs only 1-3 pair satisfies condition(1) . Condition(2) : $N_+(1;3) = 1-0 = 1$, so $N_-(1;3)$ is also 1. Condition(3) : $NN_+(1;3) = [1]$ and $NN_-(1;3) = [1]$; there are no negative numbers in both sequences of $NN_\pm(1;3)$, so condition (3) is satisfied. So, all the second height relations of this code are $y(1)>y(3)$.

Figure 5(a) is the example of " $\overset{1\,2\,3\,4\,5\,6}{\mathbf{dp\cap\cup dp}}$ ". The pairs 1-3, 5-3, 2-4, and 6-4 satisfy condition (1) . The pairs satisfy condition (2) of these four are 1-3 and 6-4. Both these two pairs satisfy condition (3). So, the second height relations $y(1)>y(3)$ and $y(6)<y(4)$ hold.

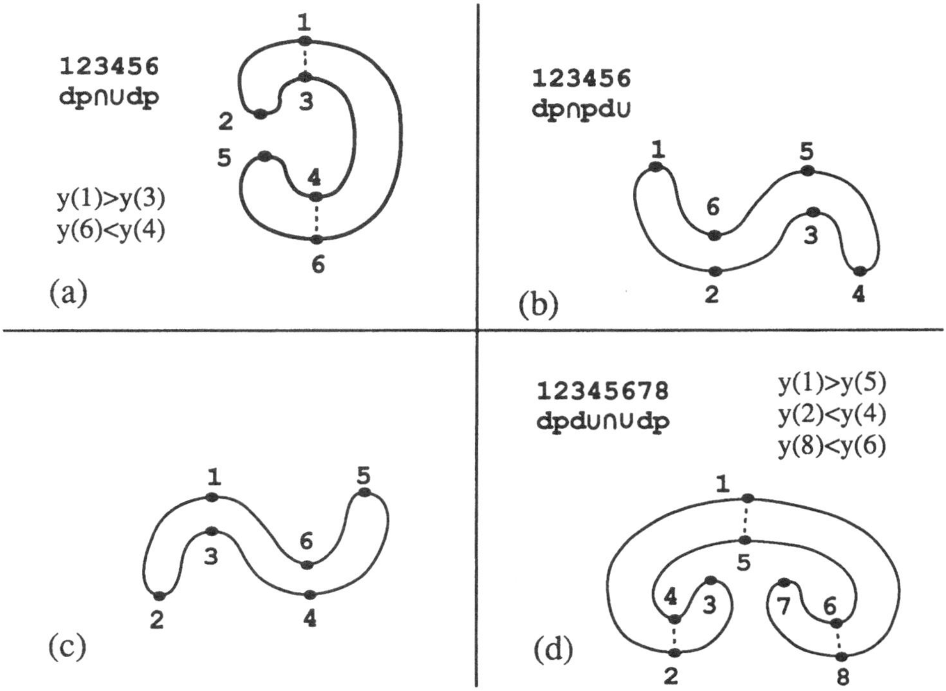

Fig.5 : Examples of second height relations.
Second height relation are shown by doted lines and inequalities.
(b) : There is no second height relations on this dp code.
(c) : This contour has the same dp code as (b). So, the result of (b) is reasonable.

Figure 5(b) is the example of " $\overset{123456}{\text{dp}\cap\text{pd}\cup}$ ". Four pairs satisfy conditions (1) and (2), but no pairs satisfy condition (3). So, there are no second height relations in this code. The contour illustrated in Fig.5(c) also has the same dp code. So, this result is reasonable.

Figure 5(d) is another example. It illustrates the second height relations by doted lines and inequalities.

5. SWITCHING PAIRS AND CURL VALUES.

Three contours illustrated in Fig.8(a) have the same dp code " dp∩pd∪ ". In this section, we describe a attribute of a contour which can distinguish these three. To define this new attribute, a characteristic number of paths and its properties are described.

5.1. Switching Path.

On the path.
For a path $p=P_{\pm}[a;b]$, "$-p$" is defined as $P_{\mp}[b;a]$ (double signs in same order), and is called the reverse path of p. The following definition of a dp code of a path is intended to be irrespective of its direction. **The dp code of a path** is defined as a string consisting of characters of types of extremal points on the path along the ***positive direction*** and is written as $code[p]$. For example, consider a path $p=[d,p,\cap,p,\cap]$ whose direction is negative, the $code[p]$ is given as follows: $code[p]=\cap p\cap pd$. For any path p, $code[p]=code[-p]$ holds. For a path p, a string excluding the first and the last characters from $code[p]$ is called **the open dp code of a path**, and written as $code(p)$.

The switching path.
For an extremal point a of type min and an extremal point b of type max on a contour, and for a path p from a to b, if the inner rotation number of p, $N(p)=\pm 2$, then the path p is called the **switching path**. Remark that for any path q of $N(q)=\pm 2$, the length of the $code(q)$ is an even number, so, q or $-q$ is the switching path. (cf. lemma 1.)

5.2. The Rotation Value.

For a switching path $p=P[s;e]$, let q be an oriented curve excluding the point s from p. Let l_1 and l_2 be half-lines from the point s, excluding the point s itself, extending horizontally to right and left respectively. And let l_3 and l_4 be similarly on point e. (l_3 : right, l_4 : left.)

An **upward crossing count** $U(l)$, of a half-line l and an oriented curve q, is defined as follows: Let u be the number of crossings of l and upward segments of q, and let d be the number of crossings of l and downward segments of q,

$$U(l) = u-d$$

When the end point e of q is on l, it contributes to one count of u. (Even if s is on l, it is not counted. We defined that s is not on q because of this reason.) Some examples are shown in Fig.6.

The **rotation value** $r(p)$ **of the switching path** p, is defined as

$$r(p) = U(l_1)+U(l_4)-U(l_2)-U(l_3)$$

Figure 6 illustrates examples of paths whose rotation values are -1 to 4.

Approximately speaking, negative rotation values correspond to the right-hand rotation, and positive ones correspond to the left-hand rotation, when ignoring the directions of the paths and focusing only on the shapes of them.

Proposition 6: For a switching path $p=P[s;e]$, and its rotation value r, let c be the remainder of division of r by 4 $(0 \le c \le 3)$. Then, the following relations hold :

$$c=0 \Leftrightarrow y(s)>y(e) ,$$
$$c=1 \Leftrightarrow y(s)=y(e) \text{ and } x(s)<x(e) ,$$
$$c=2 \Leftrightarrow y(s)<y(e) ,$$
$$c=3 \Leftrightarrow y(s)=y(e) \text{ and } x(s)>x(e) .$$

(end of Proposition 6.)

q	U(l1) (s, r)	U(l2) (s, l)	U(l3) (e, r)	U(l4) (e, l)	r(p)	code(p)
	0	0	0	-1	-1	dp or un
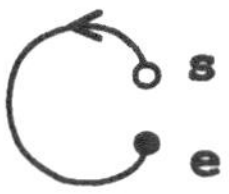	0	-1	0	-1	0	dp or un
	1	-1	0	-1	1	dp or un
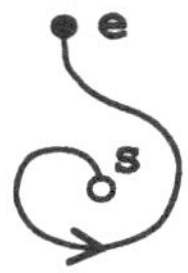	1	-1	0	0	2	dp or un
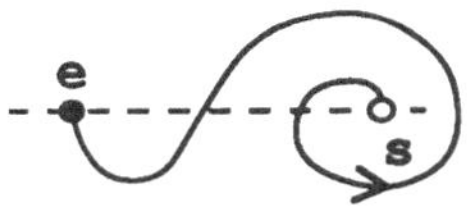	1	-1	-1	0	3	dpdu or pnun
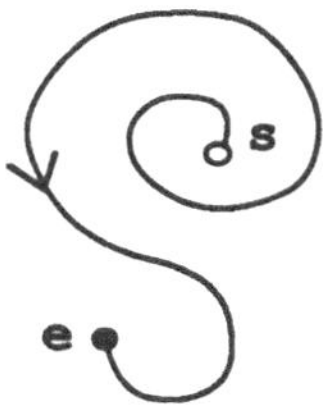	1	-2	-1	0	4	dpdu or pnun

Fig.6 : Examples of rotation numbers of switching arcs.
Arrows show the direction of q (same as p).
p, q, $U(l)$, $r(p)$, and $code(p)$ are described in the text.

5.3. The Curl Value.

For a switching path p and its rotation value r, **the curl value** m **of** p is defined as:

$$m = sgn(r)\left\lceil \frac{|r|}{2} \right\rceil ,$$

where $\lceil k \rceil$is the smallest integer that is equal to or greater than k, and on the cases where $k<0$, $k=0$, and $k>0$, $sgn(k)$ is defined to -1, 0, and 1, respectively.

Proposition 7:
(1) For a switching path p, and its curl value m, and for the length n of $code(p)$, $2|m| \leq n$.
(2) For any non zero integer m, we can make a switching path q, whose curl value is m and whose length of $code(q)$ of $n=2|m|$.
(end of Proposition 7.)

For example, Fig.7 illustrates a transformation of a switching path p, of $code(p)$ = *pd or* ∩∪. The transformations are done by rotating end points counterclockwise without changing its dp code. By these transformations, the rotation value changes from -2 to 2, and the curl value changes from -1 to 1. It seems impossible to rotate the points counterclockwise beyond the last figure of Fig.7. If we rotate them further, the shape is deformed and the dp code changes.

5.4. Switching Pairs.

When the path $P_+[a;b]$ and $P_-[a;b]$ of a contour are both switching paths, an ordered pair of a-b is defined as **the switching pair**. This definition is equivalent to the following A or B conditions:

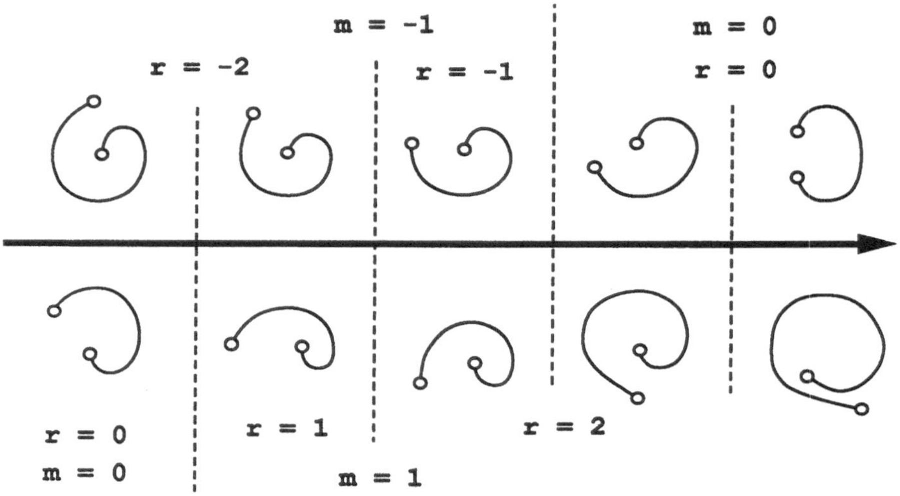

Fig.7 : An example of proposition 7.
Some transformations which do not change the dp code are shown.

A. (1) $type(a)=\cup$ and $type(b)=\cap$,
(2) $N_+(a;b)=N_-(a;b)=2$;

B. (1) $type(a)=p$ and $type(b)=d$,
(2) $N_+(a;b)=\pm 2$ and $N_-(a;b)=\mp 2$ (double signs in same order).

Remark that for the pairs p-∩ and ∪-d, $N_+(a;b)+N_-(a;b) = 2$ by Proposition 1, so, it is impossible for both $P_\pm[a;b]$ to be switching paths, and the pairs cannot be the switching pairs.

Proposition 8: For any switching pair a-b of a contour, two switching paths $P_+[a;b]$ and $P_-[a;b]$ have the same rotation values. *(end of Proposition 8.)*

By this proposition, **the rotation value of a switching pair** and **the curl value of a switching pair** are defined as ones of any of corresponding switching paths of $P_\pm[a;b]$.

5.5. Examples of Classifications of Contours by Curl Values.

Now, we show some examples of classifications of contours which have the same dp codes, by curl values of switching pairs. (Classification by rotation values is also possible.)

Example 1.
For the dp code " $\overset{1\,2\,3\,4\,5\,6}{\text{dp}\cap\text{pd}\cup}$ ", switching pair is 6-3 and nothing else. The range of the curl value of 6-3 is $[-1,1]$. Figure 8(a) illustrates the examples of contours which have the curl values -1, 0, 1 of the pair respectively.

Example 2.
4-1 and 2-5 are the switching pairs of the example illustrated in Fig.8(b). In this figure, (1, -1) means that the curl value of 4-1 is 1 and the curl value of 2-5 is -1. (the former is of 4-1 and the latter is of 2-5.) Possible combinations of this two curl values are shown in a table in the figure.

6. APPLICATIONS.

We made a handprinted numeral recognition system in which a decision tree is used. On the program, we used a description finer than this dp code, called **extended dp code** such as shown in Fig.9. It preserves the order of heights of extremal points of all contours of a given image. This is made as follows: First, given image is cut by horizontal lines at positions of all extremal points. Then, along each horizontal lines, contours are examined from left to right, and the codes of l, r, d, p, ∩, and ∪ are gotten. "l" and "r" means the edge left of inside and the edge right of inside, respectively. Others are the same as those of dp code. Finally, these codes of each lines are concatenated with characters of ",".

The algorithm works as follows: First, a given image is described by runlength data and extended dp code is made from it. Secondly, noise removing is done on this extended dp code and corresponding runlength data. Finally, the classification is done by decision tree as the following steps. (1): Images are classified by the extended dp code. (2): These are classified finer by simple formulas of positions of extremal points and thresholds. (3): Moreover these are classified finer by the shape of some parts of the contours of the image.

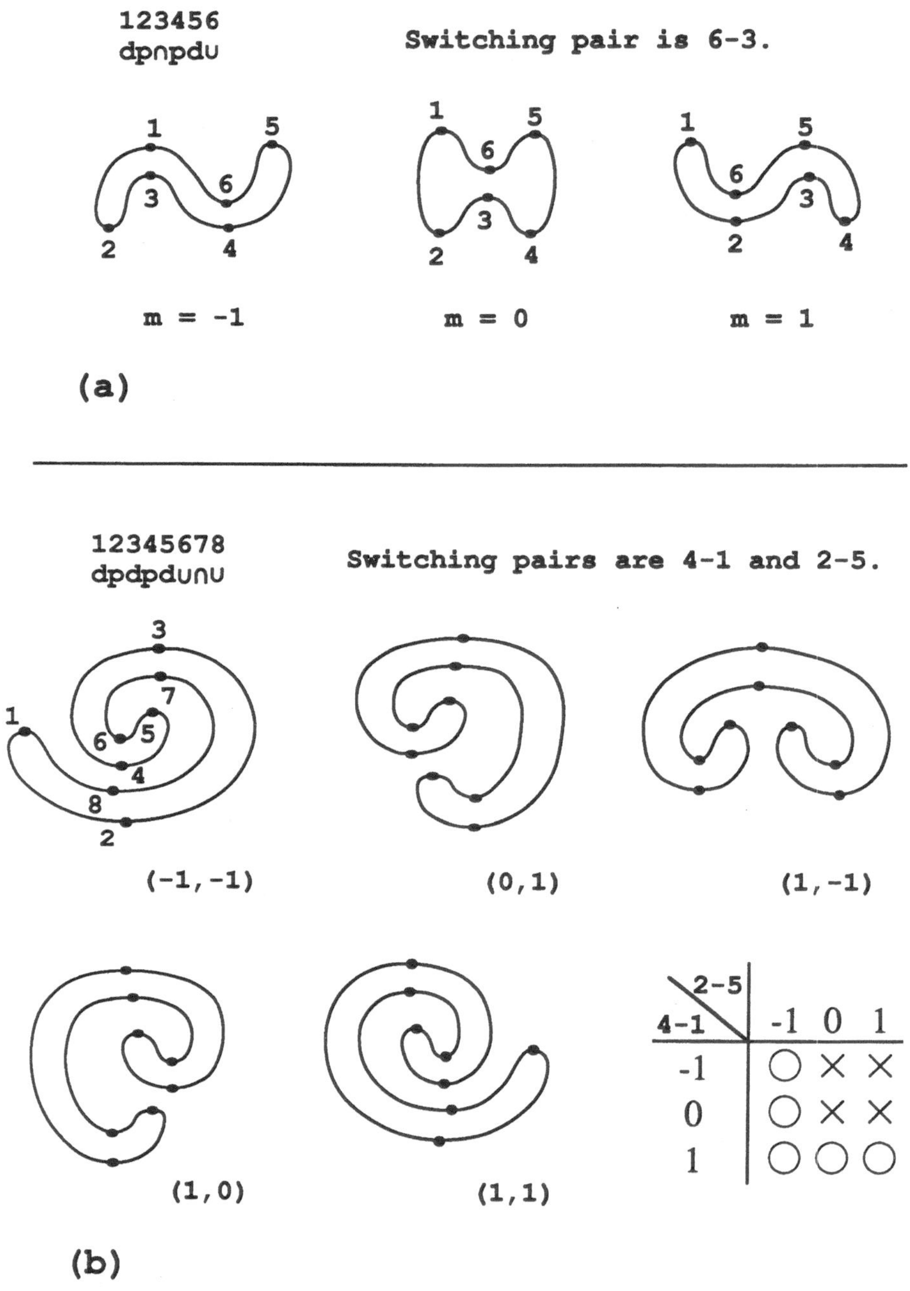

Fig.8 : Examples of classifications of contours by curl values.
(a) : m is the curl value of the switching pair 6-3.
(b) : This example has two switching pairs. Tables in the figures show all the possible combinations of curl values. ○ is possible, and × is impossible.

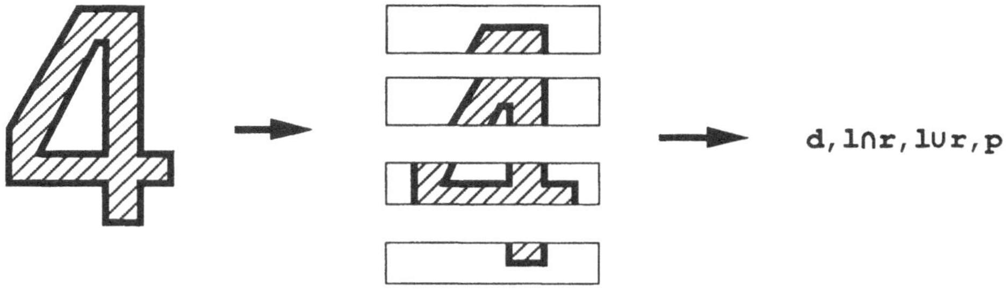

Fig.9 : The extended dp code.
It is finer than dp code description, and used in our OCR algorithm.

The noise removing operation consists of two parts of smoothing low horns and removing small connected components. This operation is very fast compared to traditional pixelwise noise removing methods, because the place where considered to be noise is searched through compact extended dp code, neither through huge pixel data nor runlength data.

The decision tree is made manually with about 13000 of loosely constrained handprinted numeral data. At the first step, about 92 % of the data fall into 20 kinds of extended dp codes. These data go down the tree. Other 55 kinds of extended dp codes have no overlap for numeral and seems to safe to decide this time, and recognition results of that data are decided at this time (3.2% of all data). Other data are rejected. At the second step, formulas and thresholds are decided manually for each extended dp code, respectively. At the last step, some path on the image is described by fixed numbered sequence of digitized directions of the shape of it. (Figure 10). The shape of the path is gotten from runlength data indexed by extended dp code. Then, these sequences are classified by automatons. Each automaton means one result of numerals ('0'-'9'). What parts of contours are used to get sequences, the length of the sequence (= precision to look at the shape), and the structures of the automatons are decided manually for each branch of the decision tree. The number of all the automatons of the whole decision tree is about 150.

The recognition time is very fast, about 25 m sec per one character on PC-9801RA, with 80386, 20MHz. The recognition rate of this algorithm is about 95% and it has no substitution errors for that numeral data of about 13000. Figure 11 shows randomly picked up data from correct data (12802), rejected data out of the 75 kinds of extended dp codes (648), and rejected data within the 20 kinds of extended dp codes (90), respectively.

7. DISCUSSION.

Open problems and fu'ure works are shown :

- Propositions of 1, 5, 6, 7, and 8 are inducted from many examples and there are no counter examples until now. Proposition 1 looks right, and for the others, we found models to explain them and believe their right. But, we have not precise proofs of them yet.
- How to find possible combinations of rotation values of a contour, is an interesting problem.

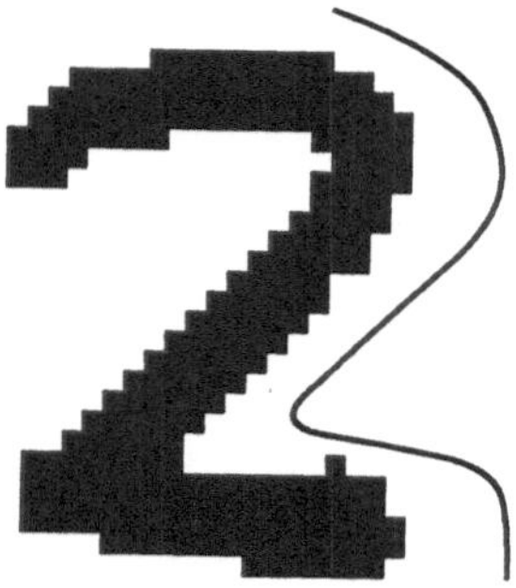

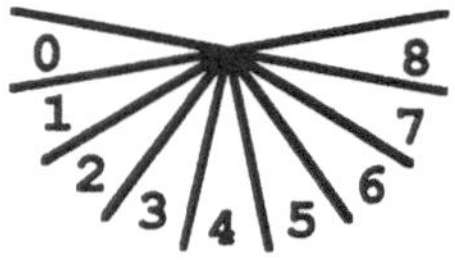

(b) Digitized directions.

7533227874

(a) A path on an image.

(c) A sequence of digitized directions of the path of (a).

Fig.10 : A description of some parts of contours.

Fig.11 : Example data from results of our OCR algorithm.
(a): Randomly picked up data from 12802 of correct data.
(b): From 648 of rejected data whose dp codes were out of the 75 kinds.
(c): From 90 of rejected data whose dp codes were within the 20 kinds.

- ○ Using dp codes to group extended dp codes seems the possibility of making decision tree of OCR algorithm semi-automatically.

8. CONCLUSION.

We proposed a new description of dp code of a contour. It can describe convexity and concavity of the contour roughly depending on a coordinate system, but is more precise than topology, and meets to human's intuition. The description also implies some height relations of extremal points, and we found the method to find these relations and found some theoretical properties. We also proposed attributes of the description. By curl values, the description becomes richer. This is compact and has great effect to distinguish shapes. And another attribute of rotation value is suitable to theoretical study. Then, we mentioned an application of this description to an OCR algorithm. Finally, we showed interesting future works.

ACKNOWLEDGEMENT.

We want to thank Prof. T.L.Kunii for encouraging us to write this paper and Dr. Y.Shinagawa for giving useful information. We also thank the refrees for the useful comments, and Motoko Nakamura for caring about a comfortable and concentratable atmosphere of the library of R&D Center.

REFERENCES

Kergosien YL (1991) Generic Sign Systems in Medical Imaging. *IEEE Computer Graphics & Applications,* 11(5):46-65

Mori S, Suen CY, and Yamamoto K (1992) Historical Review of OCR Research and Development. *IEEE Proceedings,* (In press.)

Nishida H and Mori S (1990) A structural description of curves by quasi-topological features and singular points. *Proc. IAPR Workshop on Syntactic & Structural Pattern Recognition,* Murray Hill, NJ, pp 310-334.

Nishida H and Mori S (1991) An approach to automatic construction of structural models for character recognition. *Proc. First International Conference on Document Analysis and Recognition,* Saint Malo, France, pp 231-241

Nishida H and Mori S (1992a) Algebraic description of curve structure. *IEEE Transactions on Pattern Analysis and Machine Intelligence,* (to appear).

Nishida H and Mori S (1992b) Structural analysis and description of curves by quasi-topological features and singular points. In: Baird HS, Bunke H, and Yamamoto K (eds) *Structured Document Image Analysis.* Springer-Verlag, Heidelberg, (to appear).

Pavlidis T (1977) *Structural Pattern Recognition.* Springer-Verlag, Berlin

Shinagawa Y, Kunii TL, and Kergosien YL (1991) Surface Coding Based on Morse Theory. *IEEE Computer Graphics & Applications,* 11(5):66-78

AUTHORS BIOGRAPHIES

Yu Nakajima was born in Kashiwa, Chiba, Japan, on November 5, 1965. He received the B. Eng. degree in precision machine engineering from the University of Tokyo, Tokyo, Japan, in 1988.

From 1988, he has been with Ricoh Research and Development Center, Yokohama, Kanagawa, Japan. His current research interests are in the design and analysis of algorithms for machine recognition with emphasis on character recognition and in Artificial Intelligence.

Address: 612RG AI Tech. Department,
Ricoh research and development center, 16–1 Shin-ei-cho Kohoku-ku Yokohama, Kanagawa, 223 Japan.

Hirobumi Nishida was born in Morioka, Iwate, Japan, on July 13, 1962. He received the B. Eng. degree in mathematical engineering from the University of Tokyo, Tokyo, Japan, in 1985.

From 1985 to 1987, he was with Nippon Schlumberger, Sagamihara, Kanagawa, Japan, and worked on interactive systems for seismic data interpretation and object-oriented data base systems for the reservoir modeling workstation. Since then, he has been with Ricoh Research and Development Center, Yokohama, Kanagawa, Japan. His current research interests are in the design and analysis of algorithms for machine vision with emphasis on character and document recognition.

Mr. Nishida is a member of the IEEE Computer Society and the Institute for Electronics, Information, and Communication Engineers of Japan.

Address: 612RG AI Tech. Department, Ricoh research and development center, 16–1 Shin-ei-cho Kohoku-ku Yokohama, Kanagawa, 223 Japan.

Shunji Mori was born in Sapporo, Hokkaido, Japan, on February 25, 1934. He received the B. Eng. and Dr. Eng. degrees in electrical engineering from Hokkaido University, Sapporo, Hokkaido, Japan, in 1956 and 1978, respectively.

From 1957 to 1983, he was with the Electrotechnical Laboratory of the Ministry of International Trade and Industry of Japan, where he served as Head of the Pattern Processing Section from 1969 to 1981, and was a supervisor of PIPS (Pattern Information Processing System) Project of National Project of Japan from 1971 to 1973. In 1975, he was a visiting researcher in the Computer Vision Laboratory, University of Maryland, for half a year, and from 1981 to 1982, he was a visiting professor in the Department of Computer Science, Concordia University, Montreal, Quebec, Canada. From 1983 to 1987, he worked for Nippon Schlumberger, Sagamihara, Kanagawa, Japan, as Head of the Modeling Department of the System Engineering. Currently, he is Head of Artificial Intelligence Research Department of Ricoh Research and Development Center. His research interests are in pattern recognition, image processing, and knowledge engineering.

Dr. Mori is a Guest Co-Editor of Special Issue on Optical Character Recognition of the Proceeding of the IEEE, and will serve as a Program Co-Chairman of Second International Conference on Document Analysis and Recognition to be held in Japan in 1993. He is a member of IEEE, IEEE Computer Society, AAAI, the Institute for Electronics, Information, and Communication Engineers of Japan, the Information Processing Society of Japan, and the Chinese Language Computer Society.

Address: 612RG AI Tech. Department, Ricoh research and development center, 16–1 Shin-ei-cho Kohoku-ku Yokohama, Kanagawa, 223 Japan.

Visualisation of Hyperobjects in Hgram-Space by Computers

Yang Ming Pok and Yeong Kong Huen

ABSTRACT

This paper describes a novel method of using CAD-workstation to visualise the rotational symmetries of hyperobjects using the Hgram-graphs which are based on the multi-dimensional Hgram system of coordinates [4]. The visualisation technique will be demonstrated by examples of the 3-cube and the 4-cube on a CAD-workstation. Point geometry is a new geometry based on this system of coordinates which will enable the bijective mapping of points from the E^n-space to the nD-Hgram-space. In this geometry, the meanings of bijection and graphical origin have to be modified. Whereas points in E^n-space cannot be visualised beyond 3-dimensions, they can be visualised uniquely in the Hgram-space to any finite dimensions [4-13]. Conventional methods of visualising a hyperobject in the n-dimensional space by its successive perspective or parallel projections down to 2-space do not give insight on such objects as the projections do not preserve the coordinate values of vertices [3]. In Hgram projection, the mapping does not represent the shadow of the hyperobject even though the visualisation medium is 2-dimensional. The Hgram projection gives correctly the coordinates of the vertices of the hyperobject under multiple-axial rotations. The computer technique can be extended to the visualisation of hyperspheres and other regular polytopes.

Keyword: Visual Computing, Point Geometry, Hgram Graphs, Hgram System Of Coordinates, Multi-Dimensional Graph

1. INTRODUCTION

Hgram is the acronym for Huen's diagram, which is a multi-axial graphical format based on the Hgram system of coordinates. The Hgram system of coordinates and point geometry based on this system were reported in previous papers [4 to 13]. These were the results of a research program dubbed "Supervisualisation" initiated by the author in 1988 in the Department Of Chemical Engineering, N.U.S. The original objective was to make use of CAD-workstations to visualise multi-dimensional mathematical functions in Hgram graphical format. Point geometry and the visualisation of hyperobjects were recent developments. Points from Euclidean n-space, E^n, can be bijectively mapped into this graph without any loss of coordinate information.

A full understanding of the geometrical properties of the Hgram-space is important for Hgram geometers. This is done by the mappings of points between the E^n-source-space and the nD-Hgram-target-space. Although we cannot visualise hyperobjects in the E-space beyond 3-dimensions, the axiomatic extension of regular objects to hyperspace can be formulated either algebraically or purely by intuitions. Once these equations or the coordinates of a set of vertices are known, they can be easily mapped into the Hgram-space for visualisation. To Hgram geometers, it is sometimes easier to build hyperobjects intuitively in the Hgram-space rather than in the abstract E^n-space. This paper describes the computer technique of the visualisation of hypercubes in Hgram-format and the study of their rotational symmetries. The technique could be extended to other regular hyper-polytopes.

2. THE THEORY OF POINT GEOMETRY

Point geometry (PG for short) is an extremely simple geometry which is only concerned with the bijective mappings of points from the E^n-source-space to the nD-HGRAM-target-space. Computer visualisation of hyperobjects in the E-space do not yield much insight due to our lack of understanding of the physical limitations of display media such as the printed page and the CRT-screen.

The axiom of point geometry is stated as follows:

*Axiom Of Point Geometry (PG -axiom): n:m mapping from the n-dimensional Euclidean space, E^n, to the target Hgram space, $H^{p(m)}$,can only be bijective if the number of graphical reference points (called suborigins) in the target-space is increased according to p=float(n/m) corrected upward to the nearest positive integer. The dimensionality of the primitve space m can take on any value from 1 to a large countable positive finite integer. p *m will either be equal to n or greater than n depending on whether upward correction is needed on not.*

This axiom has three special cases described as follows:

- Case (1) n = m: This is the case of self-mapping or identity mapping. Float(n/m) = 1 specifies that the number of graphical suborigins needs not be increased beyond unity.
- Case (2) n < m: This is the case of mapping a point from a lower dimensional space to a higher dimensional space. Float(n/m) < 1 which is corrected upward to 1. This specifies that the number of graphical suborigins remains at unity.
- Case (3) n > m: This is the case with the most utility. For the specific case of m = 2, this is defined as the n:2 mappings of points from the E^n-space to the nD-Hgram-space built up from the primitive E^2-space. In general, float(n/m) > 1, and, the number of graphical suborigins of the target-space must be increased to ensure the bijective mapping of points from one space to another.

Conventionally, a mapping f:X -> Y is said to be 'one-to-one and onto' (or bijective) if f is both injective and surjective as shown in figure 1a. Since points are not single-points in the Hgram-space, the meaning of bijection has to be redefined as follows:

Definition 1: n:m Mapping - This is defined for the mapping of points from the E^n*-space to the* $H^{p(m)}$ *space where* E^n *stands for the n-dimensional Euclidean space and* $H^{p(m)}$ *stands for the (p*m)D-Hgram-space built upon the* E^m*-space as the primitives. Due to the use of superfices,* $H^{p(m)}$ *is unlikely to be confused with Hilbert's space.*

Definition 2: Bijection - In n:2 mapping, if every point in E^n*-space is mapped to the (p*m)D-Hgram-space on a 'one-to-one and onto' basis, then the mapping is bijective. In this mapping, 'one-to-one' means the correspondence between a single point in the* E^n*-space with a group of p-subpoints in the Hgram-space but this definition excludes that for the graphical origin (see theorem 13 immediately following).*

Theorem 13: Every point $P' = [(x_1,x_2),\ldots,(x_{n-1},x_n)]$ *in the Hgram-space has its own graphical origin given by* $P_o' = [(0,0),(x_1,x_2),\ldots(x_{n-4},x_{n-3})]$*. If P' is a trajecotry, so also is* P_o'*.*

Figure 1a shows the conventional '1-1 and onto'mapping (a bijection) and figure 1b shows the modified definition of bijection used in n:2 mapping. In figure 1b, it can be seen that the graphical origin can be mapped to any point within the Hgram-space and is therefore non-unique in the conventional sense.

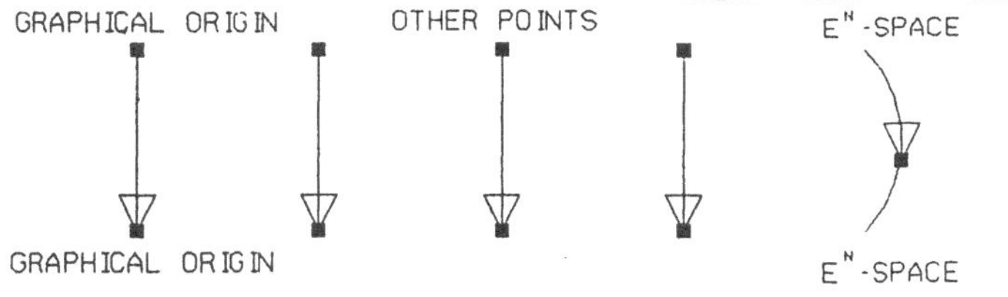

Fig.1a - '1-1 & Onto' Mapping In Euclidean Space (Bijection)

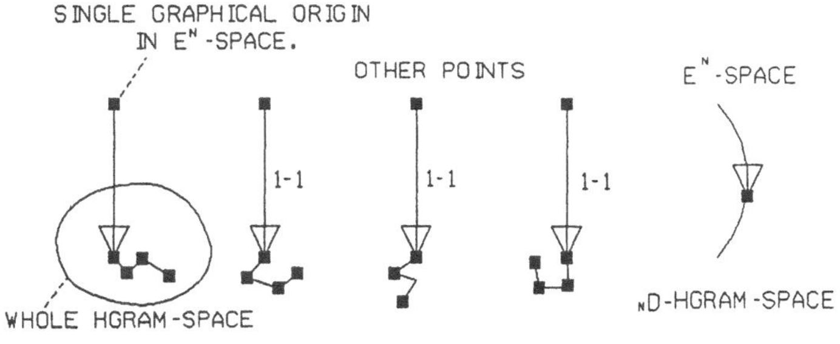

Fig.1b - '1-1 & Onto' In N:2 Mapping To The Target Hgram-Space (Bijection)

3. THE HGRAM SYSTEM OF COORDINATES

In n:2 mappings, the Hgram system of coordinates is based on the use of the Cartesian 2-space or E^2-space as its primitives. In Hgram-space, this is called the 2D-subplane or 2D-subspace. By HgraM convention, an nD-point is denoted by $P' = [(x_1,x_2),(x_3,x_4),...,(x_{n-1},x_n)]$ where it is understood that all variables with odd suffices will be plotted along the principal abscissa or X-axis and all those with even suffices along the principal ordinate or Y-axis. It is also understood that each pair of variables within round brackets is to be plotted in one graphical level or subspace. The alignment of axes into two principal directions will mean a loss of angular information. This explains why the space is non-metric for distances between points. In this paper, P stands for the point in the E^n-space and P' its bijective mapping into the (p*m)D-Hgram-space.

To plot P', the pair (x_1,x_2) is plotted in the first subspace called the reference plane or level 1. The next pair (x_3,x_4) will be plotted in the next 2D-subspace called level 2 using the point (x_1,x_2) as its graphical origin (or suborigin) and this procedure is repeated until all ordered pairs are plotted. The nD-point will look like a pattern of points in the Hgram graphical space. We reserve nD- to describe the dimensionality of the Hgram space and n-dimensional for the Euclidean space. A point in the nD-space is called the nD-point. Since the Hgram space is built up from the primitive Cartesian 2-space, one should expect that plane Euclid's geometry is a subset of point geometry within each 2D- subspace. This also means that some geometrical limitations of the E^2-space are automatically inherited by the Hgram-space. A prominent case is the inability to do vector multiplications by geometrical constructions.

In Euclid's geometry, a point is defined as having no extent and it remains zero-dimensional irrespective of the dimensionality of the space in which it is located. In point geometry, the axiom requires that the dimensionality of the point must match the dimensionality of the space in which it is located. Thus a point in the nD-Hgram space is an nD-point. Furthermore all geometrical objects are described by their vertices and the dimensionality of the object must match the dimensionality of the vertices [5]. Thus an nD-line must be bounded by two nD-points, an nD-surface must be bounded by nD-lines and an nD-volume by nD-surfaces.

4. GRAPHS AND MANIFOLDS

From the point of view of point geometry, graphs may be classified into two type viz., *true graphs* and *pseudo-graphs* [11] and these are defined as follows:

Definition 3: A true graph is point-visualisable and can have any number of axes and if a point is drawn on its space, the coordinate values of the point can be read correctly by X-Y coordinations without further geometrical aid. Any graph which cannot satisfy the above criterion is a pseudo-graph.

Comment: The plane Cartesian graph is a true graph. There is no possibility of establishing a true graph using the Cartesian 3-space on writing paper or the CRT-screen without introducing ambiguity on the coordinate values of a point drawn in this space. A well-known example of a pseudo-graph is the isometric projection. This ambiguity is exploited to good effects by the graphical illusionist Escher [14]. The reason why the Hgram system of coordinates generates true graph is because of its compliance with the PG-axiom. On the other hand if you use multiple layers of plane Cartesian graphs with coincident graphical origins, it still remains a pseudo-graph. For example the point P' = [1,1,1,1] will appear as a single point on this graph and will give rise to ambiguity. No ambiguity is encountered when this is plotted in a Hgram graph as the point is identified by the linkline pattern of subpoints.

Ask an engineer what manifolds are and the immediate association is with pipeline manifolds. Control engineers customarily view the state space of a system as a vector space. But when a state space is not a vector it may still be a space known as a manifold. Examples of manifolds include hypersurfaces in R^n. For example, the surface of the unit 3-sphere is described by the parametric equation $x_1^2 + x_2^2 + x_3^2 = 1$ and may be called a 2-dimensional manifold in R^3 usually denoted S^2 [2].

The Hgram-graphs are suitable for the display of multi-dimensional functions in manifold format. For example to display the unit n-sphere, one could partition pairwise the variables in the parametric equation $x_1^2 + x_2^2 + ... + x_{n-1}^2 + x_n^2 = 1$ and plot in n/2 levels of submanifolds described as follows:

Level 1 submanifold: $(x_1, x_2) = (r_1 \sin(\alpha 1), r_1 \cos(\alpha 1))$,

Level 2 submanifold: $(x_3, x_4) = (r_2 \sin(\alpha 2), r_2 \cos(\alpha 2))$,

....

Level n/2 submanifold: $(x_{n-1}, x_n) = (r_{n/2} \sin(\alpha_{n/2} - 1), r_{n/2} \cos(\alpha_{n/2})$,

where $r_1^2 + r_2^2 + ... + r_{n/2}^2 = 1$.

Regular polytopes such as hypercubes are not describable by analytical expressions in which case the concept of manifolds may not be immediately obvious. However the vertices of a square can be considered as the samplings at 90^0 angular displacements around a circle i.e. a 1D-manifold or S^1 and by axoimatic extension the vertices of a cube as the samplings on the surface of a sphere i.e. S^2. By viewing in this manner, an n-cube can be considered as a form of samplings on the manifolds of an n-sphere.

5. THE HGRAM DISPLAY TECHNIQUES

There are two display modes used in Point geometry one called the *continuous display mode* and the other the *discrete display mode* all coming under the generic name of "*multi-dimensional walk*". In plane Cartesian graph where we plot $y = f(x)$, the stepping of x to compute the values of y is straightforward. In a multi-parameter function such as $y = f(x_1, x_2, ..., x_n)$, multi-dimensional steppings are carried out by the technique of "multi-dimensional walk" [7]. Such walks can be classified as the spiral walk, the circular walk and the linear walk but for the displays of n-dimensional manifolds, the most convenient one is the circular walk. To handle the display of the above function as manifolds, we express this in the Hgram-format as $P' = [(x_1,x_2),...(x_{n-1},x_n),(y,0)]$ and step the independent and dependent variables using the circular walk strategy with axial assignments listed as follows:

Level 1: $(x_1,x_2) = (\cos(\omega 1 * T), \sin(\omega 1 * T))$;Circular walk in the reference plane or first subspace. T is either a time-variable or simply a dummy stepping variable.

Level 2: $(x_3,x_4) = (\cos(\omega 2 * T), \sin(\omega 2 * T))$;Circular walk in the second subspace.

Level 3: ....

Level n/2: $(x_{n-1},x_n) = (\cos(\omega_{n/2} * T), \sin(\omega_{n/2} * T))$; $n/2^{th}$ subspace.

Level $\overline{n/2 + 1}$: $(x_{n+1},x_{n+2}) = (y,0)$;$(n/2 + 1)^{th}$ subspace.

where ω_i for $i = 1$ to $n/2$ are the frequency multiplying factors subject to the condition that $\omega_i > \omega_{i-1}$. For example, if we choose $\omega_1 = 1$ radian per second, (x_1,x_2) will trace a circle for T from 0 to 2π. In the continuous display mode, (x_3,x_4) must rotate faster than (x_1,x_2) and ideally ω_2 should equal infinity so that for each discrete pair of values of (x_1,x_2), (x_3,x_4) will take on an infinite number of pairs of values for T from 0 to 2π. According to sampling theory, the frequency of sampling should be at least twice that of the highest frequency of the process to be sampled. In multi-dimensional walk, every higher subtrajectory is in fact sampling the lower subtrajectory. As a rule of thumb, choose ω_i equal to 5 to 10 times the value of ω_{i-1}. For high dimensional manifolds, one must narrow the range of computation in order to save on CPU-time.

In the discrete display mode we really follow the ideal case in which (x_1,x_2) is fixed constant whilst (x_3,x_4) is varied for T from 0 to 2π. There are pros and cons between the two modes of display. In the continuous mode, we save CPU-time but the sampling is coarser whilst in the discrete display mode, it is CPU-intensive but it gives a more representative display of the manifolds. The choice depends upon applications, for examples, we prefer to use the continuous display mode in graphical optimisation and the display of system stability [5 - 7] whilst in the study of the n-spheres and isometries, we prefer the discrete display mode [10].

6. HGRAM MATRIX TRANSFORMATION

The forward and reverse mappings from the E^n-space to the (p*m)D-HGRAM-space are governed by the Hgram-matrices given as follows:

Forward-mappings: Let the point in E^n-space be given by $P = [x_1, x_2, .., x_{n-1}, x_n]$ and the corresponding mapped point in the (p*m)D-Hgram-space be given by $P' = [(x_1, x_2), ...(x_{p*m-1}, x_{p*m})]$. It is understood that each ordered pair is assigned to one level of 2D-subspace. The transformation is given by $P' = A*P$ where A is a $n \times n$ matrix given by:

A =MAT((1,0,..0,0),(0,1,0, ..0,0),(1,0,1,..0,0),(0,1,0,1,0..0,0),.....,(0,1,0,1,0,1,..,0,1,0,1)) ....(1).

Reverse-mappings: For reverse mappings, the transformation is given by $P = A^{-1}*P$ where A^{-1} is an $n \times n$ matrix given by:

A^{-1} =MAT((1,0,..0,0),(0,1,0, ..0,0),(-1,0,1,..0,0),(0,-1,0,1,0..0,0),.....,(0,0,0,..,0,-1,0,1)) ....(2).

Furthermore $\det(A) = \det(A^{-1}) = 1$ and is nonsingular.

The geometrical properties of the Hgram-space can be studied using the above transformations in both directions. This is because although we have visual experience within the physical limitation of our 3-space, beyond this, we either have to rely on intuitions or algebraic manipulations. Sometimes, it is easier to draw unfamiliar hyperobjects in the Hgram-space and apply reverse transformation in order to gain some insight in the abstract E^n-space, if that is at all possible.

From the Hgram transformation matrices A and A^{-1} of equations (1) and (2) respectively, one geometrical property is immediately apparent. The first two rows of the matrices contain only unity diagonal elements. This implies that the E^2-space is identity mapped to the 2D-Hgram-space and vice versa. This means that Euclid's plane geometry is perfectly compatible with point geometry in 2D-Hgram-space. From row 3 onward, each row of matrix A contains more than one element showing that the axial variable along either the principal X- and Y-direction is the sum of the current variable plus all previous variables assigned in the same axial direction in the lower levels.

7. ISOMETRIES

Isometries consist of translational, rotational and reflectional symmetries. In this paper, we focus only on rotational symmetries which are more tractable. The meanings of n-dimensional reflection still awaits geometrical interpretation as the conventional definition of reflectional symmetries is confined to the plane only. For the purpose of this paper rotational symmetry will be defined as follows:

Definition 4: For a rigid regular polytope in nD-Hgram-space undergoing successive plane rotations, if the spatial coordinates of the vertices at the beginning of the trajectories remain invariant by the end of the rotation, then this polytope is said to possess rotational symmetries for the specified sequence of angular rotations in the planes. (The spatial coordinates are viewed as detached from the labelled mobile vertices which may not take the same spatial positions after the rotations.)

Pure translational symmetries can be defined explicitly for a rigid polytope in n-dimensional space in accordance with defintion 5. If translation is combined with rotations about one or more planes, no general definition about symmetries can be defined. However these can still be visually investigated using the Hgram graphical format on the computer screens.

Definition 5: If a rigid polytope is translated without any rotational motion in the n-dimensional space in such a way that all vertices describe straightlines, then by necessity these straightlines must be parallel and the hyperobject will have continuous tranlsational symmetries.

The study of symmetries so far have been confined to algebraic analysis. It is more intuitive to be able to visualise such symmetries from the locii of points traced by these vertices in Hgram-space although the method does not give general solutions to such problems. In the study of symmetries of hyperobjects, the advantage of the visual method is obvious and could supplement algebraic methods the expressions of which may be difficult to interprete.

8. VISUALISATION OF HYPERCUBES

Since Hgram-graph is based on the E^2-space as its primitive, 3-dimensional objects are not represented in the conventional way in this space since each vertex of 3D-object is split into 2 x 2D-subpoints so that for a 3D-cube, the total number of vertices in Hgram space is 16 (same as that for the 4-cube) instead of 8. The reason why the 3D-cube has to be represented in the 4D-Hgram-space is because according to theorem 15 (see appendix 2), it is impossible to coordinate a point with two axes of different dimensionality. The conventional method of viewing the 4-cube is to visualise its 2-dimensional shadow either by parallel or perspective projection. The difficulty with this method of representation is that the coordinates of the vertices cannot be directly read from the graph. The other problem is that the representation becomes extremely complicated for higher cubes. Those who try to count the number of 3-cubes in a 6-cubes will realise the visual complexity.

The graphical display of a hypercube with sides of 2 units of length can be developed intuitively as shown in figure 2. Here one starts with a square plane parallel to the x1-x2-plane with its centroid coinciding with the 4D-origin P_o'[0,0,0,0] so that the object matrix of the four vertices A,B,C and D are given by P'_a=[(1,1)], P'_b=[(-1,1)], P'_c=[(-1,-1)]and P'_d=[(1,-1)] or written in

REDUCE syntax the object matrix is given by H_2=MAT((1,-1,-1,1),(1,1,-1,-1)].

Note that H_2 's cyclic sequence of A,B,C and D is preserved by choosing all odd numbered rows in the object matrix in the (1,-1,-1,1) order. By keeping the hypercube body-centred, one could write down the $n \times 2^n$ object matrix of the n-cube entirely by rote. For example the object matrix of the 4-cube will be a 4

x 16 matrix given by H_4 = MAT((*1,-1,-1,1,1,-1,-1,1,1,-1,-1,1,1,-1,-1,1*),(1,1,-1,-1,1,1,-1,-1,1,1,-1,-1,1,1,-1,-1),(*1,1,1,1,-1,-1, -1,-1,-1,-1,-1,-1,1,1,1,1*),(1,1,1,1,1,1,1,1,-1,-1,-1,-1,-1,-1,-1,-1)) where the odd-numbered rows are in italics.

To derive the algebraic matrix equations of the rotation of the n-cube in hyperspace, we need to know the object-matrix H_n of the n-cube and the rotational matrix associated with the particular plane of rotation [3]. A square has one plane of rotation, a cube three and in general an n-cube has (1/2)*n*(n-1)- planes of rotation. We use the notation R_{ab} to designate the rotation about the plane defined by the axes x_a and x_b. For the 3-cube, R_{12} means the rotation abut the axis normal to the plane x_1-x_2 i.e. around the x_3-axis. However for hypercubes, the rotation about multi-axes is hard to perceive. We can compute such composite rotations as the product of several plane rotations.

We give below the formulations for the rotation of the 3-cube and the 4-cube for equal angular displacement in each plane of rotation. If the angular displacement is to be different in each plane of rotation, all that is required is to introduce a multiplying factor to the angle of rotation in the particular level. There is little difference between the 3-cube and the 4-cube in Hgram-representation except that the linklines for the former are horizontal (or vertical) and the latter are inclined at $+45^o$. In other words we equate the fourth axis to zero for the 3-cube. We start with the 3-cube since we have visual experience with it and thus could pick out any discrepancy from the graphical display. The extension to higher cubes entails more computational effort but otherwise the procedure is the same.

9. ROTATIONS OF HYPERCUBES

(i) The Rotation Of The 3-cube

We define $Y_{jk,lm}$ as the rotation of the plane l-m from axis l to axis m followed by the rotation of the plane j-k from axis j to axis k. The angle of rotation is

positive (anti-clockwise) about the axis normal to the plane. Care must be taken to adopt a consistent convention in the rotation of planes in hyperobjects. For example in the 3-cube, Y_{12}, Y_{23} and Y_{31} entail positive angles of rotation in each

plane whereas Y_{21}, Y_{32} and Y_{13} will entail negative angles of rotation in each plane.

Using the REDUCE syntax, A_{3x3} = MAT((a_{11},a_{12},a_{13}),(a_{21},a_{22},a_{23}),(a_{31},a_{32},a_{33})) where the inner round brackets represent rows and each element a_{ij} within a round bracket represents the element in the ith row and j^{th} column. In conventional matrix notation, this could be expressed as A_{3x3} = ((a_{11},a_{12},a_{13}), (a_{21},a_{22},a_{23}), (a_{31},a_{32},a_{33}))^t where t represents the transpose of this matrix.

For the 3-cube, there are three planes of rotations given by:

R_{12}=MAT((cos(α12),-sin(α12),0),(sin(α12),cos(α12),0),(0,0,1))

R_{31}=MAT((cos(α31),0,-sin(α31)),(0,1,0),(sin(α31),0,cos(α31)))

R_{23}=MAT((1,0,0),(0,cos(α23),-sin(α23)),(0,sin(α23),cos(α23))) .... (3)

where R_{pq} represents the rotation through angle α_{pq} in the plane bounded by axes x_p and x_q. The matrix element a_{pq} = 1 when p=q except a_{pp} = a_{qq} = cos(α) and a_{pq} = 0 except a_{pq} = - a_{qp} = - sin(α_{ij}). The expressions for R_{21}, R_{13} and R_{32} are similar to the aboves except that α_{ij} is replaced by - α_{ij}.

The object-matrix for the body-centred 3-cube with 2 units of length for each side is given as follows:

H_3 = MAT((1,-1,-1,1,1,-1,-1,1),(1,1,-1,-1,1,1,-1,-1),(1,1,1,1,-1,-1,-1,-1)) ....(4)

For an n-cube, the number of vertices will be 2^n. The general expression for composite rotations of the 3-cube is given as follows:

$Y_{ij,...,pq}$ = R_{ik} *...* R_{pq}* H_3 ....(5)

In conventional methods, this is subjected to a further projection (either perspective or parallel) onto the 2-space which represents the shadow of the skeletal cube. In the Hgram-method, the eight vertices of the 3-cube are mapped bijectively onto the Hgram-space and the projection is not equivalent to the shadow of the 3-cube in 2-space.

As the Hgram-space is viewed through a combination of 1D- and 2D-windows. One must get used to viewing planes spanning axes across levels. If one insists on viewing all planes in their plan views, then multiple assignments of axes will have to be adopted to give the number of 2D-windows. For example the point

P'=[(x1,x2),(x3,x4)] is in the unique axial assignment mode whereas P'=[(x1,x2),(x1,x3),(x1,x4),(x2,x3),(x2,x4),(x3,x4)] is in the multiple axial assignment mode which will give six 2D-windows. The latter mode of representation is cumbersome and is best avoided if possible.

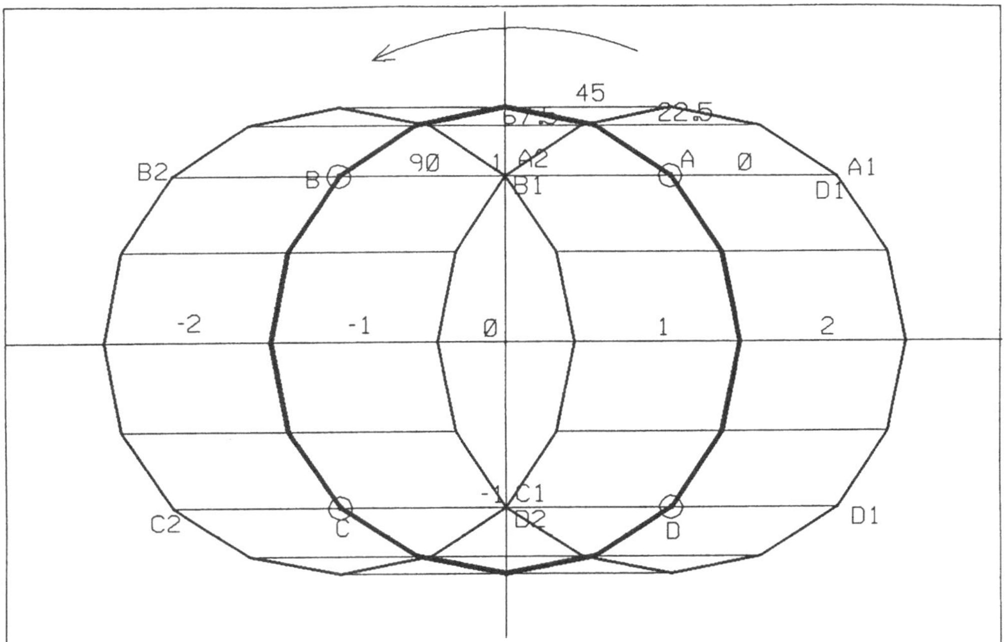

Fig. 2 - Rotation Of 3-cube In Y12 Mode

RANGE: Ø - 9Ø°; STEPSIZE = 22.5°.

AA1-BB1-CC1-DD1 SYMMETRIES AA2-BB2-CC2-DD2 SYMMETRIES

Figures 2 and 3 show the rotation of the 3-cube in Y_{12} and $Y_{12,13}$ mode for angular displacements from 0 to 90° in equal increment of 22.5°. Figure 3 shows that for the $Y_{12,13}$ mode, vertices B and D are stationary points. Figures 4 and 5 shows the rotational symmetries for the $Y_{12,13}$ mode for the six non-stationary vertices divided into two groups. In addition to giving unique displays of the 3- and 4-cube, the half-turn symmetries of the vertices are also displayed. If a full 360° rotation is made, then all four modes of symmetries will be visualised. If it is confined to positive angles of rotation, then each plane rotation gives 4 modes of symmetries and since there are three planes, we expect $4^3 = 64$ variations of symmetries.

Figure 4 and 5 show two half-turn symmetrical groups in the 3-cube in $Y_{12,13}$ mode. The labelling convention of the vertices adopted is to label the subvertices of the square in level 1 as A,B,C and D. Then in level 2 for the 3-cubes the eight subvertices are labelled in two groups of four as A1,B1,C1,D1 and A2,B2,C2,D2. For the 4-cube, the square in level 1 is also labelled as ABCD and in level 2, the 16 subvertices are labelled in four groups of four as A1,B1,C1,D1, A2,B2,C2,D2,A3,B3,C3,D3,and A4,B4,C4,D4 in anticlockwise sequence. The trajectories of each 4D-vertex consists of two subtrajectories. For example point A-A1 is the beginning of the trajectory for vertex A. Angles of increment are labelled against the trajectory for vertex A only. The subtrajectory in level 1 is drawn thicker for ease of identification compared to those in level 2.

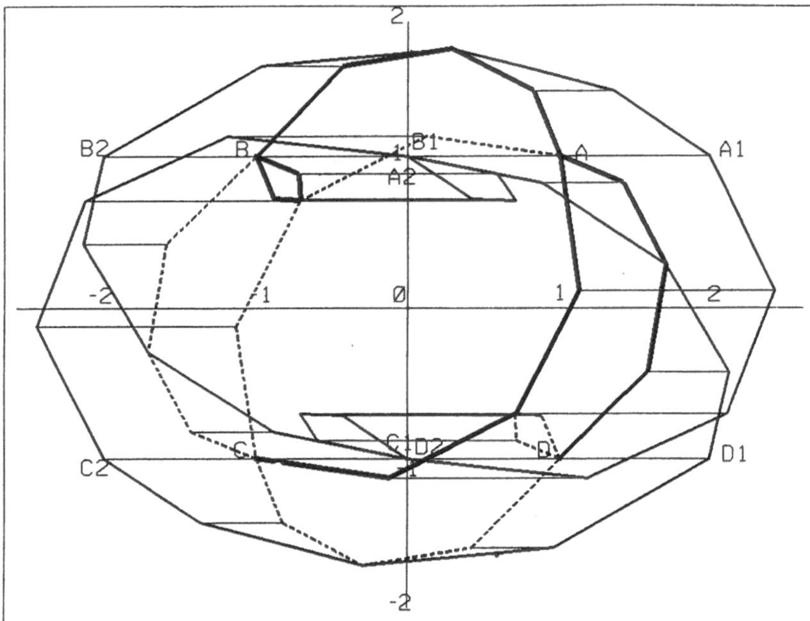

Fig.3 - Rotation Of 3-cube In Y12,13 Mode

RANGE: 0 - 90° ; STEPSIZE 22.5°.

For the detection of symmetries, one could try various angles of increments interactively and to detect the intersection of two trajectories at a time. For a rigid polytope it is not possible for these trajectories to intersect the same spatial point at the same angles of rotation. Only when intersections are found at the same angular displacement for all the trajectories (including self-mappings) can one conclude that symmetries exist for the chosen angles of rotation. For the hypercube, by intuition we know that symmetries could only occur at multiples of half-turns no matter how many planes of rotations are considered. In general the task is easier for regular polytopes than for irregular ones.

(ii) The Rotation Of The 4-cube

In the 4-cube, there are 6 planes of rotation. By axiomatic extension using the same procedure as outlined for the 3-cube (see §(i)), the object matrix is written as follows:

H_4 = MAT((1,-1,-1,1,1,-1,-1,1,1,-1,-1,1,1,-1,-1,1),(1,1,-1,-1,1,1,-1,-1,1,1,-1,-1,1,1,-1,-1),(1,1,1,1,-1-1-1-1,-1,-1,-1,-1,1,1,1,1),(1,1,1,1,1,1,1,1,-1,-1,-1,-1,-1,-1,-1,-1)) ...(5)

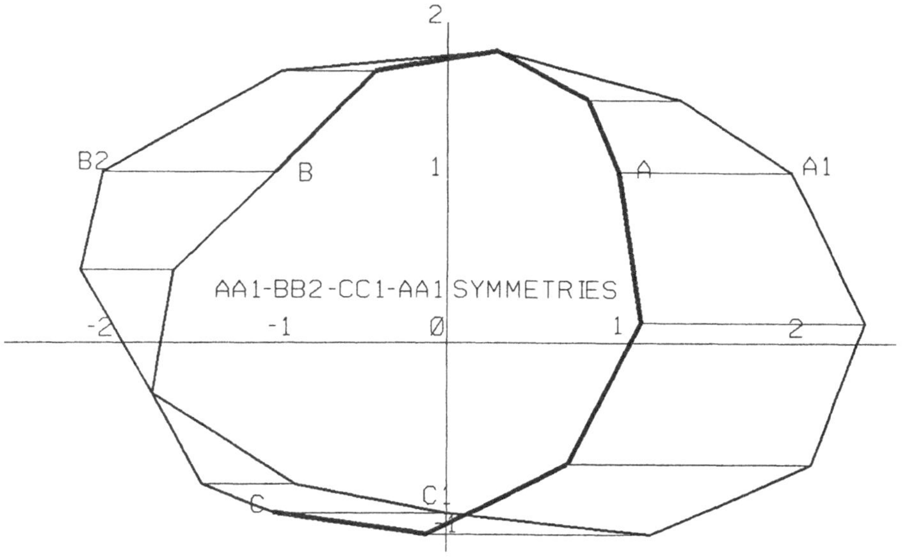

Fig.4 - AA1-BB2-CC1-AA1 Rotational Symmetries In Y12,13 Mode
RANGE:Ø-9Ø°; STEPSIZE:22.5°.

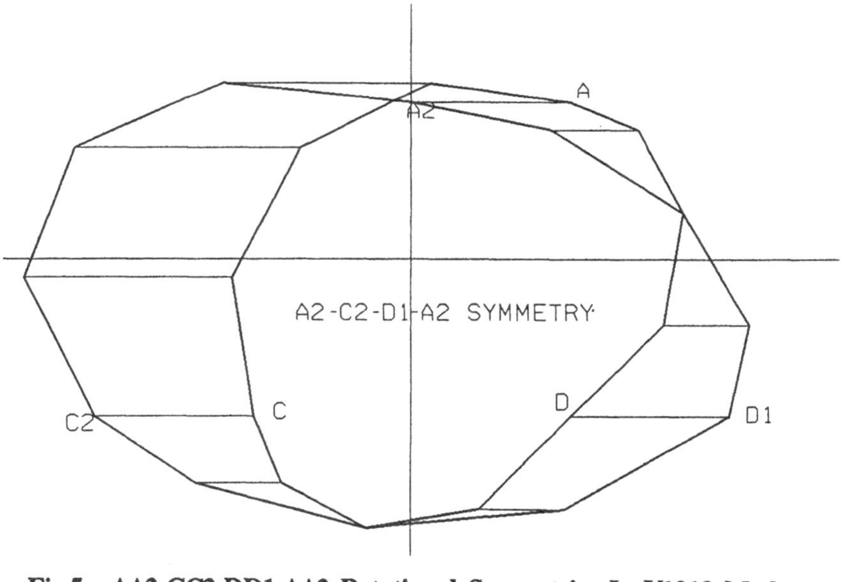

Fig.5 - AA2-CC2-DD1-AA2 Rotational Symmetries In Y1213 Mode

and the six rotation matrices for equal angles of anticlockwise rotations are written as follows:

R_{12} = MAT((cos(a),-sin(a),0,0),(sin(a),cos(a),0,0),(0,0,1,0),(0,0,0,1))

R_{31} = MAT((cos(a),0,-sin(a),0),(0,1,0,0),(sin(a),0,cos(a),0),(0,0,0,1))

R_{41} = MAT((cos(a),0,0,-sin(a)),(0,1,0,0),(0,0,1,0),(sin(a),0,0,cos(a)))

R_{23} = MAT((1,0,0,0),(0,cos(a),-sin(a),0),(0,sin(a),cos(a),0),(0,0,0,1))

R_{24} = MAT((1,0,0,0),(0,cos(a),0,-sin(a)),(0,0,1,0),(0,sin(a),0,cos(a)))

R_{34} = MAT((1,0,0,0),(0,1,0,0),(0,0,cos(a),-sin(a)),(0,0,sin(a),cos(a))) ....(6).

We give here the visualisation of two rotational modes i.e. Y_{12} and $Y_{12,13}$. Figure 6 displays Y_{12} and figure 5 displays $Y_{12,13}$ over the same angular displacement range from 0 to 90° in equal steps of 22.5°. In addition to the unique displays of the 4-cubes, the half-turn symmetries can be recognised for this special case. For positive angular rotations with 6 distinct planes, we expect 4^{6} = 2904 variations of symmetries. All these could be individually studied on the computer screen.

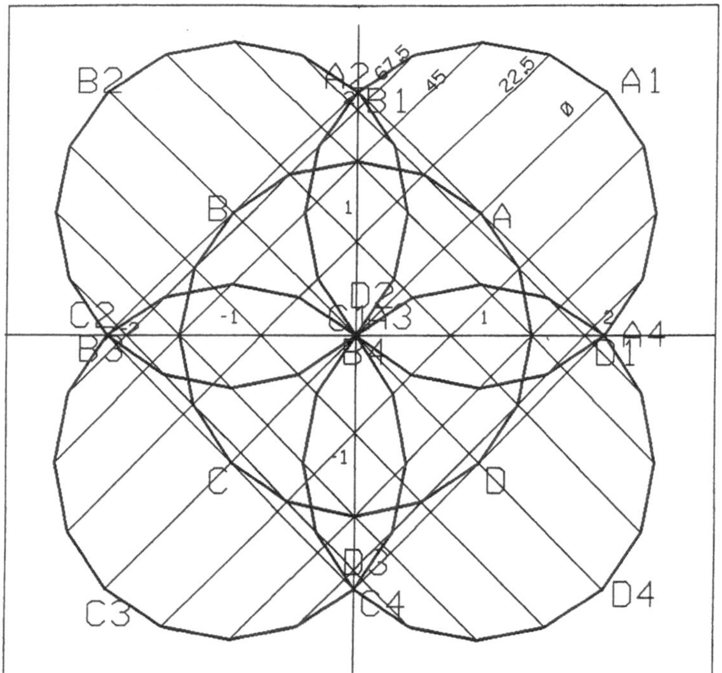

Fig. 6 - Rotation Of 4-Cube In Y12 Mode

Figure 7 shows the rotation of the 4-cube in $Y_{12,13}$ mode. The figure looks rather complicated on paper but on the computer screen each vertex is assigned to one level and it can be studied by switching on selectively particular levels. Also the figures will be in colours. The visual study of rotational symmetries can be carried out interactively on the computer screen. This will reveal the translation of each vertex to the spatial position of another vertex. If the vertices can be interchanged without changing the shape of the hypercube, then symmetries exist for the specified sequence of plane rotation. There is no need to further elaborate on this as the procedure has been demonstrated for the $Y_{12,13}$ mode for the 3-cube. Figure 8 and 9 shows two samples of rotational symmetries for

paths AA1-BB2-CA3-AA1 and AB1-CB3-DA4-AB1 respectively. One observes that these are closed paths in the 4D-HGRAM space. LV's indicate the numbering of the levels in which the vertice are assigned to.

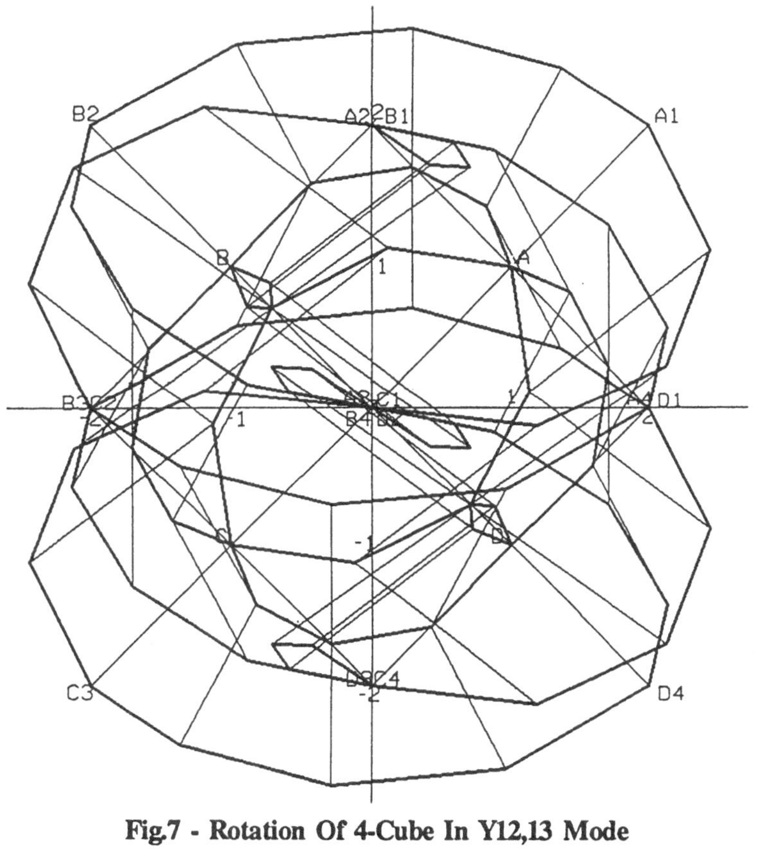

Fig.7 - Rotation Of 4-Cube In Y12,13 Mode

RANGE: 0 - 90° ; STEPSIZE - 22.5°.

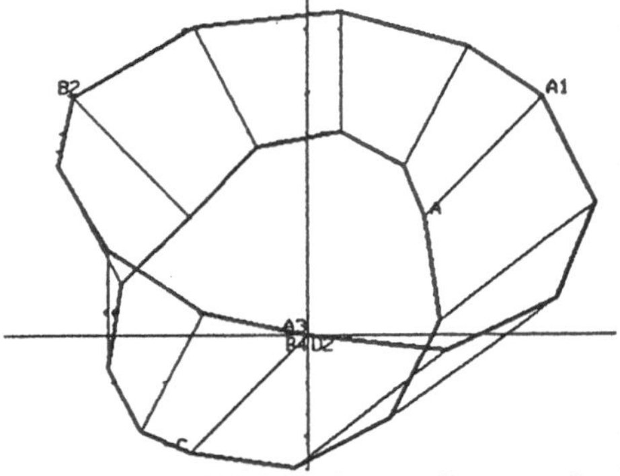

Fig.8 - AA1-BB2-CA3-AA1 Symmetries In Y12,13 Mode
LV1-LV16-LV7-LV1

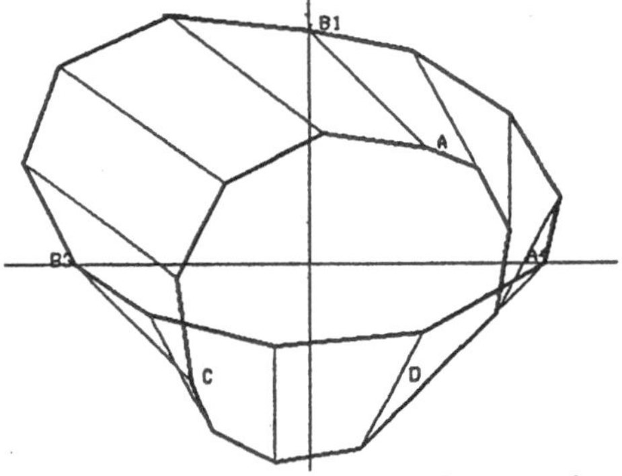

Fig.9 - AB1-CB3-DA4-AB1 Symmetries In Y12,13 Mode
LV13-LV19-LV10-LV13

10. REAL WORLD APPLICATIONS

Hgram geometers consider point geometry as the natural extension of plane Euclid's geometry, so that, most real world applications in the latter can be extended to the former. A typical case is that of graphical optimisation. Up to the present, optimisation has been solely developed along analytical line due to the limitation of graphical visualisation beyond 2-dimensions. This situation is now rapidly changing due to the introduction of Hgram graph. In the department of chemical engineering, Wawan [ref 8 to 10] has carried out research over the past two years on graphical optimisation. It has been found that the method is particularly suitable for global optimisation since the user can visualise globally the presence of local extrema on the computer screen. Such display is not affected by the presence of discontinuities which presents difficulties in algebraic methods of analysis. The finding gathered so far is that for graphical optimisation of problems with up to 6 independent variables, the accuracy is almost as good as analytical methods. One great advantage of this method is that the operator needs not be a good mathematicians. Almost any school leavers with good visual faculties could be trained to handle linear and nonlinear optimisation on the computer screens. The other advantage is that one gains a much deeper insight into the interplays of parameters in a complicated algebraic expression by graphical visualisation than by abstract algebraic analysis.

Another potential area of real world applications which could affect engineering and architectural professions is in the unambiguous representation of solid objects such as mechanical components and buildings. To illustrate this point, figure 10 shows the conventional engineering orthogonal projection of a solid cube. Suppose this drawing is used for calling tenders to manufacture a million copies. There is ambiguity in the conventional representation as one is not sure whether the cube has six sides or three sides in spite of the provision

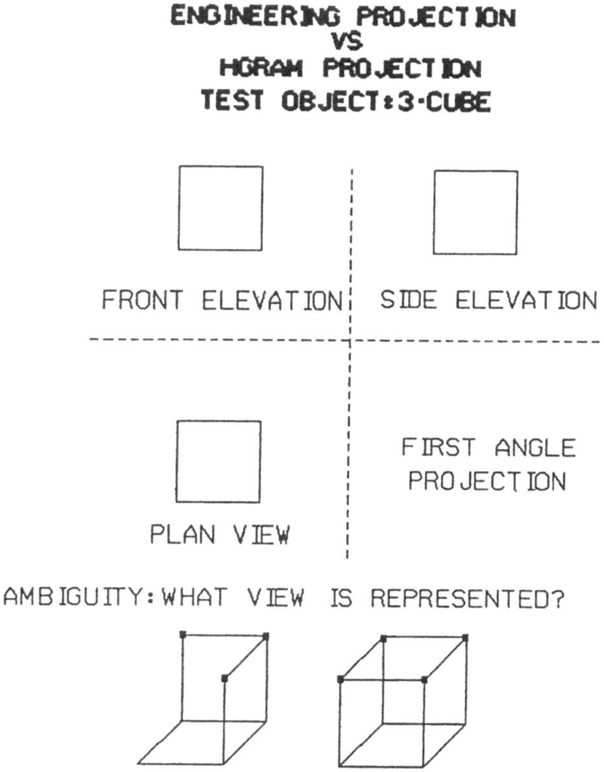

Fig.10 - Ambiguities In Orthogonal Projection Of A Cube

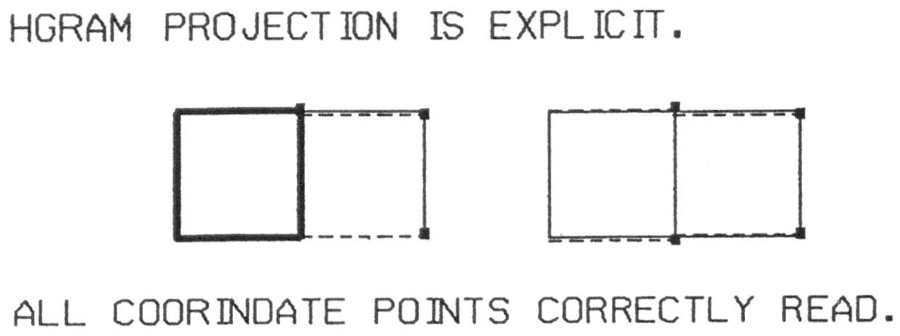
HGRAM PROJECTION IS EXPLICIT.
ALL COORINDATE POINTS CORRECTLY READ.

Fig. 11 - 3D-Hgram Representation Of The 3D-Cube

of three orthogonal projective views. If the cube is represented by the Hgram graphical format, there will be no ambiguity whatsoever, as the coordinates of the eight vertices can be read accurately from the drawing as showning in figure 11. Furthermore, only one drawing is shown instead of three as are needed in engineering projection!

Another important area of visualisation is the display of 3-dimensional trajectories of ballistic missiles which is simply the application of technique already described in this paper. There are many other real world applications which could be cited but restriction in printed space do not allow further elaboration [3-14]. It must be pointed out that as far as the 2-dimensional display media is concerned, a 3-dimensional object is already a hyperobject. The failure to grasp this important point is the source of ambiguities found in all types of 3:2 projections such as isometric, parallel, perspective and othorgonal projections.

11. CONCLUSIONS

The vertices and trajectories of rotational symmetry of 3D- and 4D-cube can be visualised using the Hgram-system of coordinates. This technique can be applied to hyperobjects of any number of dimensions, although in this real world, most of the examples of applications are 3-dimensional. However, multi-dimensional state-space trajectories are of real importance to control system engineers.

The Hgram-graph will be more suitable for work on CAD-workstations than in manual mode. This is because a hyperobject is represented by a multiple of levels of 2D-representations and these are conveniently manipulated by the switiching on or off of various levels in a CAD-workstation. One may state that the age of electronic papyrus has finally arrived with the use of Hgram graphs.

The Hgram-graph is only suitable for point representations although within each 2D-level, Euclid's geometry is valid. This is because the primitive 2D-space in Hgram graph is the Cartesian 2-space. In order to interprete the Hgram-graphical representations correctly, one has to get used to the new graphical language.

It is realised that the trend in modern geometry is to go abstract and algebraic. The main source of difficulty is Euclid's definition of a point. A point cannot be subdivided in a Cartesian graph because of the adoption of this definition. Point geometry has departed from Euclid's definition of the point. The dimensional limitation of Cartesian graph is thus overcome.

Many advanced physical problems face analytical difficulty due to a lack of visual geometrical models to work from. A glaring example is superstring theory. Einstein's general theory of relativity was based on geometrical considerations, and the elegant mathematics came afterward. Will multi-dimensional visualisation help these superstring theorists? Or has the pendulum swung too far to abstract analysis to allow the revival of visualisable geometrical models? Only time will tell.

12. ACKNOWLEDGEMENTS

We express our thanks to many past graduates who have contributed to progress in this research project which started in 1988.

APPENDIX 1 - GLOSSARY OF HGRAM- & PG-TERMS

PG: Abbreviation for "point geometry".

Point Geometry: A geometry based on the Hgram system of coordinates and is in general only valid for point information. However within each 2D-subspace, Euclid's plane geometry is valid provided the space has been metricised in accordance with PG theorem 4 (see appendix 2) by the shifts of graphical suborigins to share one common reference point.

Stationary nD-Points: All graphical origins are considered stationary even if they appear in a trajectory (see Theorem 13).

APPENDIX 2 - SHORT LIST OF PG-THEOREMS

Most of these theorems are self-evident. No proofs will be included here.

Theorem 1: n:m mapping is always point bijective.

Theorem 2: In n:m mapping, if a geometrical object can be uniquely represented in the E^n-space by its vertices, it can be uniquely represented by the vertices mapped into the target Hgram-space built from the E^m-space as the primitives.

Theorem 3: In the n:m mapping of two nD-trajectories, full intersection between the two trajectories is only possible if the two points are exactly identical.

Theorem 4: The true metric shape of a 2D-figure in a given level can be found by geometrical constructions by shifting all the linklines of the vertices to share one common vertex.

Theorem 5: In n:m mapping, the actual geometrical shape of the object can be interpreted from any one of the permutated display modes but the spatial orientation may be altered.

Theorem 6: Irrespective of the dimensionality of the Hgram-space, the only point which has an absolute reference location is the zero point P' = [0,0,..,0,0].

Theorem 7: In n:2 mapping, whether by unique axial asignments or multiple axial assignments, the elements of an nD-point may be expressed in the absolute displacement format as recursive nested functions of x1 or in the relative displacement format as the difference between two recursive nested functions of x1.

Theorem 8: In n:m mapping, the absolute position of a subpoint is non-unique but its relative position to its own suborigin is unique.

Theorem 9: When three collinear points A,B and C where C is between A and B are mapped into the Hgram-space, then both the betweenness of C and its segment-ratio with respect to AB are preserved.

Theorem 10: In n:2 mapping, the linkline in each level can be resolved into components in the principal X- and the principal Y-direction.

Theorem 11: The geometrical properties of linearity, betweenness and collinearity are transitive through the levels if the nested functions are all linearly related.

Theorem 12: An nD-Hgram graph can be replaced b y a 2D-Hgram graph if only the subline in the top-level is of interest.

Theorem 13: Every point in Hgram-space given by **P'** = [(x1,x2),..(xn-1,xn)] has it own graphical origin $\mathbf{P_0}$' = [(0,0),(x1,x2),....,(xn-4),xn-3)]. Graphical origins in HGRAM-space are non-stationary w.r.t. the absolute origin $\mathbf{P_{abs}}$' = [(0,0),...,(0,0)] but are considered stationary since readings of coordinate values are by relative displacement mode.

Theorem 14: The dimensionality of the Hgram-space is always even. (This means that in n:m mapping, m is always even and is either numerically equal to n or greater than n).

Theorem 15: It is impossible to coordinate a point if the two principal axes are of different dimensionality. (This echoes theorem 14 in that Hgram-space must have even dimensionality).

APPENDIX 3 - REFERENCES

(1) **Toth Fejes L. (1964)** "Regular Figures", Pergamon Press, page 129-130.

(2) **Bell D.J. (1990)** "Mathematics of Linear and Nonlinear Systems - An Introduction For Engineers and Applied Scientists", Oxford Science Publications, pages 236-260.

(3) **Brisson D.W. (1978)** "Hypergraphics - Visualizing Complex Relationships in Art, Science and Technology", American Association for the Advancement of Science (AAAS) Selected Symposium 24, Westview Press, Inc., Colorado, pages 147 to 158.

(4) **Huen Y.K. (1988)** "An Introduction To The Hgram (an n-Dimensional Graph Paper). Copyright Application Document". (USA Library Of Congress Copyright Registration No.TXU 354026).

(5) **Huen Y.K. (1991)** "The Hgram graphical format - its geometrical interpretation and its applications", Int. J. Math. Educ. Sci. Technol., Vol.,22, No.3,pages 403-418.

(6) **Huen Y.K. ,Wawan S.,Ang L.E., & Ho B.T. (1990)** "Visualisation Of System Stability Using The Hgram Graphical Display Format", Proceedings of CHEMICA '90, 27-30th August, 1990, Auckland, New Zealand, Vol.2, pages 517-524.

(7) **Huen Y.K. & Chow H.S. (1990)** "Microcomputer Assisted Visualisation Of Multi-dimensional Space-Walk Using The Hgram Graphical Method", Institution Of Engineers Singapore Journal (Special Issue On Chemical Engineering), Vol.30, No.2, pages 40-46.

(8) Wawan S. & Huen Y.K. (1991) "Novel Concepts In Data Displays For Computer Screens", Proceedings Of International Conference On Instrumentation, Measurement & Control, 1991, Singapore, pages 177-193.

(9) Wawan S., Huen Y.K. & Loi S.H. (1991) "Multi-Dimensional Visualisation Of Information On Computer Screens", Proceedings Of The Second IES Information Technology Conference - Advances and Development in Information Automation, Singaore. Volume 2, pages 99-108.

(10) Wawan S. , Huen Y.K.,Rangaiah G.P.,& Sim S.L. (1992) "The Technique Of Graphical Optimisation", Conference paper accepted for International Conference On Optimisation: Techniques and Applications, ICOTA '92, Singapore. (To be presented).

(11) Huen Y.K. (1992) "Classification And Design Criteria Of Vector-Codes For The Visual Representation Of Biological Sequences Using Point Geometry Analysis", Paper accepted for the book entitled : "Visual Display Of Information", Edited by C.J.Pickover, I.B.M. Research Centre, N.Y.,U.S.A. To be published in 1992.

(12) Huen Y.K., Wawan S., Loi K.S. & Allen R.M.: (1991) "How Will Hgram Graphs Affect Teaching And Research Methodology In Engineering Education?", Proceedings Of The Third Triennial Conference Of The Association For Engineering Education In South-East And The Pacific, (AEESEAP), 1991, Christchurch, N.Z., page 498-503.

(13) Pok Y.M. & Huen Y.K. (1992) " Visual Analysis Of Lyapunov Stability Of A Linear Time-Invariant System Using The Hgram Graph", Conference paper to be presented in the Second International Conference On Automation, Robotics And Computer Vision, (ICARCV '92). Paper accepted.

(14) Escher M.C.: (1971) "The Graphics Work Of M.C.Escher", A Hawthorne/Ballantine Book, 1971.

AUTHORS BIOGRAPHIES

Pok Yang Ming is currently a Principal Lecturer of electrical engineering in Ngee Ann Polytechnic of Singapore. Pok received his B.Eng in electrical engineering from the University of Malaya in 1972 and is currently a part-time research fellow in the Department of Chemical Engineering of the University of Singapore, pursuing his M Eng and PhD. He is a Professional Engineer with working experience in the fields of electrical engineering design and process control instrumentation in oil refineries, steel mills and water utilities. He is a corporate member of the Institution of Engineers in Singapore. His research interests include computer graphics, control engineering, process control and instrumentation, software engineering including software for control, machine automation, medical and health rehabilitation.

Address: Electrical Engineering Department, Ngee Ann Polytechnic, 535, Clementi Road, Singapore 2159.

Dr. Huen Yeong Kong is at present a senior lecturer in the Department of Chemical Engineering where he has been lecturing in process control and instrumentation for the past 20 years. He is M.Eng. supervisor to Mr. Y.M.Pok who will present this paper. Previous to that, he worked as instrumentation engineer in an international oil company. He shall be retiring from academic teaching from the end of June, 1992. Thenceafter he intends to spend most of his time in fine art rather than engineering. However, he plans to go into business as a publisher of a journal called the CAH-journal. CAH is abbreviation for Computer-Aided Hypervisualisation.

Chapter 3
Applications of Modern Geometry

Computation of Singularities for Engineering Design

Nicholas M. Patrikalakis, Takashi Maekawa, Evan C. Sherbrooke, and Jingfang Zhou

ABSTRACT

The computation of singularities or critical points of polynomial and other more complex vector fields in a finite subdomain of the n-dimensional Euclidean space is the underlying fundamental process behind several important engineering and scientific problems. These include, for example, design, analysis, scientific visualization, and manufacture of complex objects in a computer environment. This paper starts with a review of extant solution techniques and focuses on recent research by the Design Laboratory in this general area. Specifically, we summarize the algorithmic techniques we have developed on computation of solutions of systems of non-linear polynomial equations and other more complex equations involving irrational functions. Such equations arise in shape interrogation problems including intersections of sculptured objects, symmetry transforms, distance function computations, visualization of rational and offset or parallel surfaces, stationary point computations of maps of physical properties, and in detailed analysis of differential geometry properties of complex free-form surfaces. Examples illustrate our techniques and their applications.

Keywords: CAD, CAGD, CAM, interrogation, geometric modeling, intersection, distance computation, symmetry transforms, offsets.

1 INTRODUCTION

A fundamental problem behind several important engineering and scientific applications is the computation of singularities or critical points of vector fields within a subdomain of the n-dimensional Euclidean space. For example, in geometric modeling of complex objects, it is often necessary to compute all characteristic points of the intersection set between two objects in order to identify and trace all branches of the intersection set in a topologically reliable manner [35]. Intersection is a basic process in geometry needed in building and interrogating models of complex shapes in a computer environment. By building geometric models we mean computer encoding in terms of Boundary Representations, while interrogation includes visualization such as ray tracing, contouring, mesh generation etc. If the geometries involved are described by polynomial functions we can typically derive a polynomial vector field $\mathbf{V} = [V_1, V_2, \ldots, V_m]$ where $V_i = V_i(\mathbf{u}), \mathbf{u} = [u_1, u_2, \ldots u_n]$, and the u_i are parameters within a subdomain S of the n-dimensional Euclidean space. The singular points of the field [1], i.e. the set of points $\mathbf{u} \in S$ at which $\mathbf{V} = \mathbf{0}$, identify the relevant characteristic points. If the geometries involved are more complex, such as offset or parallel surfaces of polynomial patches, the resulting vector fields are irrational, typically involving radicals of high degree polynomials.

Similarly, in computer-based engineering, it is often necessary to compute the stationary points of distance functions between point sets [48]. Such computations are needed, for example, in problems of shape comparison and symmetry detection, in geometric and solid modeling (particularly Boolean operations [21] [23]), in inspection of manufactured objects against a toleranced design model, in robotic motion planning and localization and navigation problems [37] [33]. The solution of these problems when the point sets in question are described by polynomial functions can be similarly formulated in terms of singular point computation of polynomial vector fields.

In addition, in the area of feature recognition, the computation of medial axis and of the more general symmetry set requires determination of branch points. If the equations describing the geometries involved are polynomial, the computation of branch points can be recast in terms of singularities of polynomial and sometimes more general vector fields involving irrational functions [34]. The symmetry and medial axis sets have important applications in shape analysis and description, idealization and discretization in terms, for example, of finite elements [15] [43] [16].

Further, in the area of interrogation of differential geometry properties, such as the computation of free-form surface degeneracies and curvature contouring, we can similarly recast the problem in terms of singular point computation of polynomial and other more complex (irrational) vector fields [27]. Surface degeneracies such as cusps and ridges have important applications in animation, simulation, geometric design and feature recognition [25]. Curvature contouring is useful in design evaluation and fairing of free-form surfaces such as propeller and turbine blades and in their manufacture by milling machines [29] [28] [18].

Finally, in the area of visualization, interrogation and abstraction of maps of physical properties, it is frequently advantageous to compute the stationary point set of such representations [30] [25]. In ocean engineering, for example, such maps may include the ocean bottom topography and the distribution of physical properties within the ocean column. Such properties may include scalar and vector quantities such as temperature and magnetic field intensities. To reduce the data necessary for map encoding, it is frequently advantageous to employ piecewise parametric polynomial representations. The stationary point set for such maps can be formulated in terms of singular points of polynomial vector fields.

The objective of this paper is to summarize some of our recent research in the Design Laboratory at MIT on the underlying mathematical and numerical problem involved (namely the computation of singular points of polynomial and some more complex vector fields), and on its application in several engineering and scientific problems. The paper is structured as follows: Section 2 gives a brief literature review on vector field singular point computation. Section 3 summarizes two algorithms, the Projected-Polyhedron (PP) and Linear Programming (LP) techniques, which we have developed for computing singular points of polynomial vector fields within a rectangular subdomain of n-dimensional Euclidean space; in this section also we state their convergence and asymptotic complexity properties. Section 4 focuses on interrogation of differential geometry properties of polynomial surfaces and summarizes some of our research in this area. Section 5 provides illustrative examples of the methods developed in earlier sections in the areas of intersection, distance computation, and curvature contouring. Finally, Section 6 provides some conclusions and recommendations for further research.

2 LITERATURE REVIEW

The determination of singular points of polynomial vector fields is equivalent to finding the solutions of a system of simultaneous, nonlinear polynomial equations. In recent CAD-related research, three classes of methods for the computation of solutions of nonlinear polynomial systems have been favored: algebraic techniques, homotopy, and subdivision [41]. These methods may be classified as *global* because they are designed to compute all roots in some area of interest. There also exist a number of *local* numerical techniques which employ some variation of Newton-Raphson iteration or numerical optimization [7]. These methods are used in CAD applications requiring high accuracy because they are efficient (usually exhibiting quadratic convergence rates close to simple roots) and are straightforward to program. However, they typically require good initial approximations to roots; such approximations are usually obtained through some sort of global search like sampling, a process which cannot provide full assurance that all roots have been found. This lack of robustness makes the development of efficient and stable global techniques desirable; in what follows, we briefly review three classes of global methods.

The computation of all complex roots of nonlinear polynomial systems has typically been approached with *algebraic geometry techniques* like elimination or Groebner basis methods [4] [5]. These methods have many advantages; they are theoretically elegant, guaranteed to find all complex roots of a system irrespective of the dimensionality of the solution set, and well-suited for implementation in symbolic mathematical systems [44]. However, they suffer from numerical instability, making implementation in floating point arithmetic difficult. Furthermore, they are inefficient in memory and processing time requirements and therefore unattractive for systems only moderate in degree or dimensionality.

The second category of methods is the class of *homotopy techniques* [14] [47]. These methods may be used to find all complex solutions of a nonlinear polynomial system if the number of roots is finite. Unfortunately, investigation of such methods indicates that they also tend to be numerically ill-conditioned. If we try to get around this problem by implementing the algorithm in exact rational arithmetic, we end up with enormous memory requirements because we have to solve large systems of complex initial value problems. Furthermore, such techniques are excessive in many problems we encounter where we only need real roots within a bounded set.

The third class, the category of *subdivision-based techniques*, is the class to which both the Projected-Polyhedron and Linear Programming methods described in this paper belong. Lane and Riesenfeld [26] investigated the application of binary subdivision and the variation diminishing property of polynomials in the Bernstein basis to eliciting the real roots and extrema of a polynomial. Boehm [3] and Cohen et al. [6] extended this idea to general nonuniform subdivision of B-splines. Formulation of a class of geometric problems in more than one dimension, requiring the solution of nonlinear piecewise polynomial systems expressed in terms of B-splines, was made by Dokken[9], who suggested a solution approach based on [6]. Subdivision techniques have also been used in a wide variety of intersection problems for geometric modeling. Sederberg [38] developed an adaptive subdivision algorithm to intersect planar algebraic curves expressed in the barycentric Bernstein basis within triangles. Patrikalakis, Prakash, and Kriezis [35] [24] investigated the use of subdivision of algebraic curves in intersecting an implicit algebraic surface with a rational polynomial surface. Their method relies on the computation of real characteristic points of an algebraic curve represented in the tensor-product Bernstein basis within a rectangle, which typically involves intersecting two or three algebraic curves by repeated adaptive subdivision and minimization. Minimization is used to increase the precision of the root quadratically. Nishita et al. [31] developed an adaptive subdivision technique to intersect rays with trimmed rational polynomial surface patches, also recasting the problem as the intersection of two algebraic curves expressed in the Bernstein basis. Sederberg and Nishita [40] extended this method to intersect parametric curves with parametric surfaces. Vafiadou and Patrikalakis [45] employed an early two-dimensional form of the Projected-Polyhedron algorithm coupled with minimization to ray-trace offset surfaces. Topological methods based on Poincaré index theory and rotation number concepts were developed by Kriezis, Patrikalakis, and Wolter [21] [23] for the derivation of necessary conditions facilitating the computation of singular points of two-dimensional vector fields arising in parametric surface intersections. Sufficient conditions for the detection of such points based on bounds for rational B-spline surfaces and their partial derivatives can be found in [42] [39] [21] [22] [17]. In this paper, we outline the n-dimensional extension of the Projected-Polyhedron algorithm, along with the related Linear Programming approach. It should be noted that subdivision techniques themselves have a number of disadvantages. They are not as general as algebraic methods, since they are only capable of isolating zero-dimensional solutions. Furthermore, although the chances that all roots have been found increase as the resolution tolerance is lowered, there is no certainty that each root has been extracted. Lastly, subdivision techniques provide no explicit information about root multiplicities without additional computation. However, despite these drawbacks, their speed and stability make them attractive as root-finding schemes.

3 COMPUTATION OF SINGULAR POINTS OF POLYNOMIAL VECTOR FIELDS

3.1 Formulation

Because the vector fields we consider typically arise from problems involving bounded geometries, the singular point sets that we require are themselves bounded, within some subset of $\mathbf{R}^n$. Although the two techniques we now outline for determining these singular points (described fully in [41]) may also be applied to find complex or unbounded roots, they are especially well-suited to the problem at hand. Both techniques require an initial n-dimensional box of search; subsequent steps consist of creating smaller, more accurate boxes by geometric considerations and discarding domains containing no roots. Once any box has become sufficiently small, a root is assumed to lie within. Before we introduce the two algorithms, we must reformulate the problem into a geometric problem involving the intersection of hypersurfaces in $\mathbf{R}^{n+1}$; this restatement will allow us to use geometric properties of the hypersurfaces in order to generate better bounding boxes.

Suppose we seek the singular points of a vector field $\mathbf{f} = (f_1, f_2, \ldots, f_n)$ over the box $S \in \mathbf{R}^n$ where S is defined by

$$S = [a_1, b_1] \times [a_2, b_2] \times \ldots \times [a_n, b_n]. \tag{1}$$

That is, we wish to find all $\mathbf{u} \in S$ such that

$$f_1(\mathbf{u}) = f_2(\mathbf{u}) = \ldots = f_n(\mathbf{u}) = \mathbf{0}. \tag{2}$$

By making the *affine parameter transformation* [10] $u_i = a_i + x_i(b_i - a_i)$ for each i between 1 and n inclusive, we simplify the problem to one of determining all $\mathbf{x} \in [0,1]^n$ such that

$$f_1(\mathbf{x}) = f_2(\mathbf{x}) = \ldots = f_n(\mathbf{x}) = \mathbf{0}. \tag{3}$$

Now furthermore suppose that each of the f_k is polynomial in the independent parameters $x_1, x_2, \ldots, x_n$. Let $m_i^{(k)}$ denote the degree of f_k in the variable x_i; then f_k can be written as

$$f_k(\mathbf{x}) = \sum_{i_1=0}^{m_1^{(k)}} \sum_{i_2=0}^{m_2^{(k)}} \cdots \sum_{i_n=0}^{m_n^{(k)}} c_{i_1 i_2 \ldots i_n}^{(k)} x_1^{i_1} x_2^{i_2} \ldots x_n^{i_n}. \tag{4}$$

Now by a simple *change of basis* [10], (4) can be expressed in the multivariate Bernstein basis:

$$f_k(\mathbf{x}) = \sum_{i_1=0}^{m_1^{(k)}} \sum_{i_2=0}^{m_2^{(k)}} \cdots \sum_{i_n=0}^{m_n^{(k)}} w_{i_1 i_2 \ldots i_n}^{(k)} b_{i_1, m_1^{(k)}}(x_1) b_{i_2, m_2^{(k)}}(x_2) \ldots b_{i_n, m_n^{(k)}}(x_n). \tag{5}$$

where

$$b_{i,m}(u) = \binom{m}{i} u^i (1-u)^{m-i} \tag{6}$$

is the ith Bernstein polynomial of order m. The notation in (5) may simplified by letting $I = (i_1, i_2, \ldots i_n)$, $M^{(k)} = (m_1^{(k)}, m_2^{(k)}, \ldots, m_n^{(k)})$, and writing (5) in the equivalent form

$$f_k(\mathbf{x}) = \sum_{I}^{M^{(k)}} w_I^{(k)} B_{I,M^{(k)}}(\mathbf{x}). \tag{7}$$

Here we have merely rewritten the product of Bernstein polynomials as a single *Bernstein multinomial* $B_{I,M^{(k)}}(\mathbf{x})$.

Based on this new expression of the f_k, we will create the *graphs* of these functions $\mathbf{F}_k : \mathbf{R}^n \to \mathbf{R}^{n+1}$:

$$\begin{aligned} \mathbf{F}_k(\mathbf{x}) &= (x_1, x_2, \ldots, x_n, f_k(\mathbf{x})) \\ &= (\mathbf{x}, f_k(\mathbf{x})). \end{aligned} \tag{8}$$

Note that the graph defined here is simply an extension to n dimensions of the familiar one-dimensional notion of graphing a curve.

Clearly, (3) is satisfied by a point $\mathbf{x}$ if and only if

$$\mathbf{F}_1(\mathbf{x}) = \mathbf{F}_2(\mathbf{x}) = \ldots = \mathbf{F}_n(\mathbf{x}) = (\mathbf{x}, 0). \tag{9}$$

Now because, as shown in [10], the *linear precision* identity

$$\sum_{i=0}^{m} \frac{i}{m} b_{i,m}(u) = u; \tag{10}$$

holds, it can be easily shown that [41]

$$\mathbf{F}_k(\mathbf{x}) = \sum_{I}^{M^{(k)}} \mathbf{v}_I^{(k)} B_{I,M^{(k)}}(\mathbf{x}) \tag{11}$$

where

$$\mathbf{v}_I^{(k)} = (\frac{i_1}{m_1^{(k)}}, \frac{i_2}{m_2^{(k)}}, \ldots, \frac{i_n}{m_n^{(k)}}, w_I^{(k)}). \tag{12}$$

These $\mathbf{v}_I^{(k)}$ are called the *control points* of $\mathbf{F}_k$.

The preceding development has transformed the determination of singular points from an algebraic problem to a geometric one. Because the problem is now phrased geometrically, we can use the *convex hull property* of the multivariate Bernstein basis to bound the set of roots.

For a fixed k, the convex hull C_k of the $\mathbf{v}_I^{(k)}$ is the set of points $p \in \mathbf{R}^{n+1}$ which can be expressed in the form

$$p = \sum_I^{M^{(k)}} c_I \mathbf{v}_I^{(k)} \tag{13}$$

for some c_I which must be nonnegative and which sum to 1.

Referring to (11) and noting that Bernstein multinomials are nonnegative for $\mathbf{x} \in [0,1]^n$ and sum to 1 (and therefore satisfy the restrictions on the c_I) leads immediately to

$$\mathbf{F}_k(\mathbf{x}) \in C_k \tag{14}$$

for $\mathbf{x} \in [0,1]^n$ and for each k between 1 and n inclusive.

It is apparent, then, that if $\mathbf{x}$ is a root of (3), then because $\mathbf{F}_k(\mathbf{x}) = (\mathbf{x}, 0)$ for each k, $(\mathbf{x}, 0)$ lies within each C_k. Thus if we were able to intersect the C_k with one another and with the hyperplane $x_{n+1} = 0$, the point $(\mathbf{x}, 0)$ would belong to the intersection set.

In practice, this intersection is a tedious task if more than one variable is involved. Fortunately, all we need out of this somewhat complicated intersection set is an n-dimensional rectangular box bounding the set of roots of (3), because the simple multivariate De Casteljau subdivision we will perform as a recursive step needs to work on a rectangular box. If we could find such a box, we could structure a root-finding algorithm as follows:

1. Start with an initial box of search.
2. Scale the box and, as we did in converting between equations (2) and (3), perform an appropriate affine parameter transformation to the functions f_k, so that the box becomes $[0,1]^n$. However, keep track of the scaling relationship between this box and the initial box of search. This transformation can be performed with multivariate De Casteljau subdivision.
3. Using the convex hull property, find a sub-box of $[0,1]^n$ which contains all the roots.
4. Using the scaling relationship between our current box and the initial box of search, see if the new sub-box represents a sufficiently small box in $\mathbf{R}^n$. If it does, conclude that there is a root inside, and return it.
5. If any dimensions of this sub-box are not much smaller than 1 unit in length (i.e., the box has not decreased much in size along one or more sides), split the box evenly along each dimension which is causing trouble. Continue on the next iteration with several independent sub-problems.
6. Go back to step 2, once for each new box.

Both the Projected-Polyhedron and Linear Programming algorithms execute with this sort of recursive logic; however, they differ in their method of generating bounding boxes.

3.2 The Projected-Polyhedron Algorithm

The essential idea behind the box generation scheme in this algorithm is to transform a complicated $n+1$-dimensional problem into a series of n two-dimensional problems. Suppose $\mathbf{R}^{n+1}$ can be coordinatized with the $x_1, x_2, \ldots, x_{n+1}$ axes; we can then employ these steps:

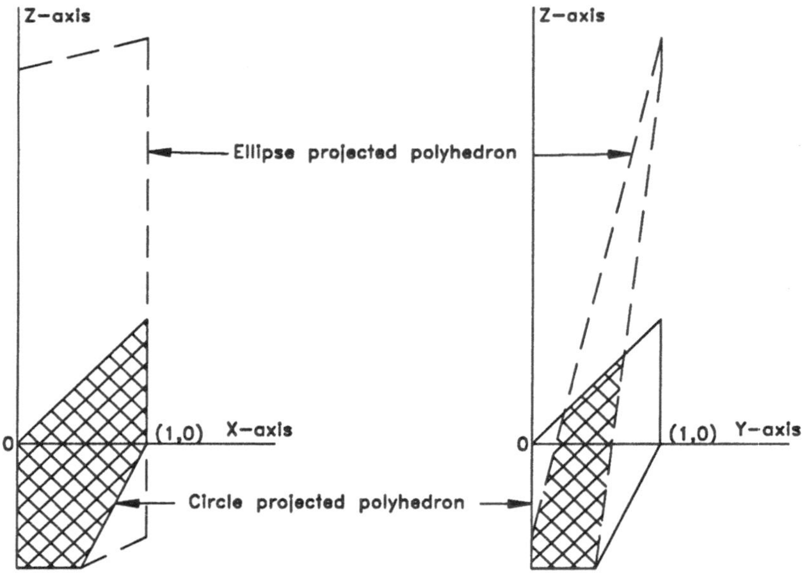

Figure 1: Projecting the polyhedra of $(x, y, x^2 + y^2 - 1)$ and $(x, y, \frac{x^2}{4} + 4y^2 - 1)$

1. Project the $\mathbf{v}_I^{(k)}$ of all of the $\mathbf{F}_k$ into n different coordinate planes; specifically, the (x_1, x_{n+1})-plane, the (x_2, x_{n+1})-plane, and so on, up to the (x_n, x_{n+1}) plane.
2. In each one of these planes,
   (a) Construct n two-dimensional convex hulls. The first is the convex hull of the projected control points of $\mathbf{F}_1$, the second is from $\mathbf{F}_2$ and so on.
   (b) Intersect each convex hull with the horizontal axis (that is, $x_{n+1} = 0$). Because the polygon is convex, the intersection may be either a closed interval (which may degenerate to a point) or empty. If it is empty, then no root of the system exists within the given search box.
   (c) Intersect the intervals with one another. Again, if the result is empty, no root exists within the given search box.
3. Construct an n-dimensional box by taking the Cartesian product of each one of these intervals in order. In other words, the x_1 side of the box is the interval resulting from the intersection in the (x_1, x_{n+1})-plane, and so forth.

It can be shown [41] that this box does in fact contain all the roots within the given box of search. In [41] it is also shown that this algorithm gives rise to an algorithm which is quadratically convergent in one dimension but only linearly convergent for higher dimensional problems. This lowered rate of convergence arises from the "loss of information" involved in projecting these hypersurfaces. However, the cost per step involved in generating these boxes is sufficiently low [41] to mitigate this problem. We have developed an experimental version of this algorithm which performs especially well in high-dimension, low-degree problems.

Figure 1 shows the computation of a bounding box in the case of a circular arc intersecting with an elliptical arc in the (x, y)-plane. Notice that the projection of the convex hulls into the (x, z)-plane covers the entire $[0, 1]$ interval of the x-axis, giving no useful information; however parts of the y-axis may be eliminated immediately. One can see from the figure that there is no root of the system whose y-coordinate is less that 0.1875 or greater than 0.625.

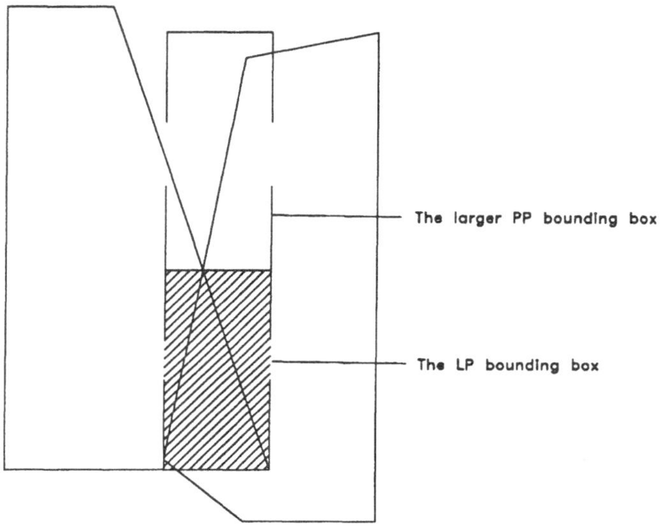

Figure 2: A comparison between an LP box and a PP box

3.3 The Linear Programming Algorithm

Although the boxes generated by the Projected-Polyhedron algorithm are fairly good, they are not as tight as they could be. In the Linear Programming algorithm we in fact seek the tightest possible box we can achieve based on the convex hull property alone. As a result, we obtain an algorithm whose cost per step is higher than the Projected-Polyhedron algorithm (particularly, for high-dimensional problems) but which nevertheless is quadratically convergent irrespective of the dimension of the problem as shown in [41].

In order to generate a box using this algorithm, we describe the complicated intersection set of the convex hulls and the hyperplane $x_{n+1} = 0$ which we described in section 3.1 in terms of a set of *linear constraint equations.* Then, using the powerful techniques of linear programming, we find the smallest and largest values of x_1 in this set, the smallest and largest values of x_2, and so forth, and create a box from these resulting intervals. Of course, if we are unable to find a minimum or maximum of any of these variables according to the constraints, then our given search box contains no roots.

The constraints themselves arise simply from the convex hull property. We note that if $\mathbf{x}$ lies within the convex hull C_k then there exist unknown, nonnegative coefficients $c_I^{(k)}$ such that

$$\mathbf{x} = \sum_{I}^{M^{(k)}} c_I^{(k)} \mathbf{v}_I^{(k)} \tag{15}$$

by direct application of the convex hull property. Added to this is the constraint that

$$\sum_{I}^{M^{(k)}} c_I^{(k)} = 1 \tag{16}$$

for each k. Now $\mathbf{x}$ is unknown, but notice that the left hand side of (15) is the same for each k. Therefore it is straightforward to eliminate the left hand side, and the resulting constraint equations interrelating the $c_I^{(k)}$ are linear [41].

The n *objective functions* to maximize and minimize according to these constraints, which will simply be $x_1, x_2, \ldots, x_n$, are also linear in the $c_I^{(k)}$ and may be obtained from (15).

Figure 2 demonstrates that Linear Programming boxes are generally smaller than Projected-Polyhedron boxes. The two polygons represent the intersection of the convex hulls of two surfaces with the (x, y)-plane.

4 INTERROGATION OF DIFFERENTIAL GEOMETRY PROPERTIES

4.1 Motivation

Free-form surfaces, also called sculptured surfaces, are widely used in scientific and engineering applications. For example, the hydrodynamic shape of propeller blades has an important role in marine applications, and the aerodynamic shape of turbine blades determines the performance of an aircraft engine. Free-form surfaces arise in the bodies of ships, automobiles and aircraft, which have both functionality and attractive shape requirements.

Propeller blades are manufactured by numerically controlled (NC) milling machines. When a ball end-mill cutter is used, the cutter radius must be smaller than the smallest concave radius of curvature of the surface to be machined to avoid local overcut (gouging). Gouging is the one of the most critical problems in NC machining of free-form surfaces [2] [11] [19]. Therefore, we must determine the distribution of the principal curvatures of the surface, which are upper and lower bounds on the curvature at a given point, to select the cutter size [13].

Developable surfaces are the surfaces which can be unfolded or developed onto a plane without stretching or tearing. They are of considerable importance to plate-metal-based industries as shipbuilding. For a developable surface the Gaussian curvature is zero everywhere [8]. Thus the manufacturer would profit from prior knowledge of the distribution of the Gaussian curvature of the metal plate.

Fairing is the process of eliminating shape irregularities in order to produce a smoother shape. The Gaussian, mean and principal curvatures are used for the detection of surface irregularities [29] [28] [18]. The set of curvature extrema of a fair surface should coincide with the designer's intention. Therefore, computation of all extrema of curvatures is desirable.

The variation of curvature can be displayed using a color coded map. Color coded maps provide a rough idea of the differential properties of surface but are not sufficient to provide detailed machining information nor permit automation of the process. Contour lines of constant curvature can also be used to display and visualize the variation of curvature, and are commonly evaluated using lattice methods. Discrete color coded maps and lattice methods do not guarantee to locate all the stationary points of curvature (local maxima, minima and saddle points), and hence may fail to provide the correct topological decomposition of the surface on the basis of curvature to the manufacturer.

This section presents a procedure for contouring curvature of a free-form surface and subdividing the surface into regions of similar order of magnitude curvature which can be used for surface tessellation and manufacturing automation. This section is structured as follows. Section 4.2 outlines a method for computing the stationary points of curvature of a free-form surface. Section 4.3 describes how to contour constant curvature lines and polygonize the area between the contour lines.

4.2 The Stationary Points of Curvature of Free-Form Surfaces

4.2.1 Surface Curvature Stationary Points

To subdivide the surface into regions of similar order of magnitude curvature, we need to determine the following.

1. Locations of all the stationary points of the curvature and the associated values of curvature to provide a correct topological decomposition of the surface on the basis of curvature.
2. Global maximum and minimum of the curvature to find the range of curvature.

For simplicity, the underlying surface is assumed to be an integral Bézier patch as follows.

$$\mathbf{R}(u,v) = \sum_{i=0}^{m}\sum_{j=0}^{n} \mathbf{P}_{ij} B_{i,m}(u) B_{j,n}(v) \tag{17}$$

where m, n are the the degrees of the patch in u, v parametric directions, and $\mathbf{P}_{ij}$ are the control points, $0 \le u, v \le 1$ and $B_{i,m}(u)$, $B_{j,n}(v)$ are the Bernstein basis functions [10]. Extension to rational Bézier and rational B-spline patches, although tedious does not present conceptual difficulties. We also assume that the surface is regular, i.e. $\mathbf{R}_u \times \mathbf{R}_v \neq \mathbf{0}$. Points where $\mathbf{R}_u \times \mathbf{R}_v = \mathbf{0}$ correspond to either singularities of the parametrizations or intrinsic degeneracies of the surface like ridges and cusps.

Gaussian, mean, maximum and minimum principal curvatures can be evaluated in terms of parametric derivatives of $\mathbf{R}(u,v)$ [8]. Let the curvature in question be denoted by $C(u,v)$, then the following need to be evaluated to locate all the stationary points of curvature and to find the global maximum and minimum values of the curvature.

1. The 4 values of curvature at the parameter domain corners

$$C(0,0),\ C(0,1),\ C(1,0),\ C(1,1) \tag{18}$$

2. Stationary points along parameter domain boundaries (roots of the 4 equations)

$$\begin{aligned} C_u(u,0) = 0,\ C_u(u,1) = 0,\ 0 \le u \le 1 \\ C_v(0,v) = 0,\ C_v(1,v) = 0,\ 0 \le v \le 1 \end{aligned} \tag{19}$$

3. Stationary points within the parameter domain (roots of the 2 simultaneous equations)

$$C_u(u,v) = 0,\ C_v(u,v) = 0,\ 0 \le u,\ v \le 1 \tag{20}$$

where subscripts denote partial derivatives.

4.2.2 Stationary Points along Domain Boundary

For the computation of stationary points along the boundary, we need to find all the real roots of equations (19). For Gaussian and mean curvatures they can be expressed in terms of univariate polynomials and are easier to process, but the maximum and minimum principal curvature functions involve irrational expressions containing polynomials and square roots of polynomials which are more difficult to process.

A. Polynomial Functions: For the Gaussian curvature K and the mean curvature H, equations (19) reduce to

$$K_t(t) = \frac{A(t)}{S^6} = 0 \tag{21}$$

$$H_t(t) = \frac{B(t)}{2S^5} = 0 \tag{22}$$

where t or subscript t is u or v, $S = |\mathbf{R}_u \times \mathbf{R}_v|$, A is an univariate polynomial of degree $M = 10m - 7$ $(t = u)$ and $M = 10n - 7$ $(t = v)$ and B is an univariate polynomial of degree $M = 9m - 6$ $(t = u)$ and $M = 9n - 6$ $(t = v)$. For detailed formulations see [27]. Since we are assuming a regular surface, $S \neq 0$, we need only set the numerator of the above equations to zero. The resulting equations can be expressed in terms of univariate Bernstein polynomials by using Bernstein polynomial arithmetic operations including addition, subtraction and multiplication [12]. To avoid cancellation and round-off errors, in the above and follow up formulations, rational arithmetic may be employed.

Using the linear precision property of Bernstein polynomials, we can rewrite the Bézier function as an explicit Bézier curve. Now the problem of finding roots of the univariate polynomial has been transformed into a problem of finding the intersection of the Bézier curve with the parameter axis which can be solved using the techniques described in section 3. Such a recursive subdivision using the convex hull property process can be continued until the interval width becomes as small as required, but the convergence rate may be slow and accuracy could be lost for high degree polynomials, if floating point arithmetic is employed. Using rational arithmetic, this would not present a problem but computation time would rise. To acquire high accuracy and quick convergence, a minimization technique may be employed, once the initial interval is determined by a coarse subdivision process.

B. Non-Polynomial Functions: When the curvature functions are the principal curvatures κ, equations (19) are given by

$$\kappa_t(t) = \frac{h_1(t) \pm h_2(t)\sqrt{h_3(t)}}{4(\kappa - H)S^8} = 0 \tag{23}$$

where t or subscript t is u or v, h_1, h_2 and h_3 are polynomials of degree $14m-9$ $(14n-9)$, $9m-6$ $(9n-6)$, $10m-6$ $(10n-6)$ when $t = u$ $(t = v)$. Equation (23) is singular when $\kappa = H$. The plus and minus signs correspond to the maximum and minimum principal curvatures. First we assume that $\kappa \neq H$, then we need only set the numerator of equation (23) equal to zero. Since h_3 is inside the square root, we cannot in general use Bernstein polynomial arithmetic to do the multiplication of $h_2\sqrt{h_3}$. Therefore it is necessary to bound $\sqrt{h_3}$ as $h_3^{low}(t) \leq \sqrt{h_3(t)} \leq h_3^{upp}(t)$, where $h_3^{low}(t)$ and $h_3^{upp}(t)$ are constants or polynomials. Then we can construct lower and upper Bézier functions that bound the numerator of function (23). In the case of maximum principal curvature with constant bounds, h_3^{low} and h_3^{upp}, the lower and upper bounding Bézier functions are given by

$$F^{low}(t) = \sum_{i=0}^{M} f_i^{low} B_{i,M}(t) = 0 \tag{24}$$

$$F^{upp}(t) = \sum_{i=0}^{M} f_i^{upp} B_{i,M}(t) = 0 \tag{25}$$

where M is the same degree as the degree of polynomial h_1 and Bézier ordinates are separated in cases:

$$a) \quad \bar{h}_{2i} \geq 0 \quad f_i^{low} = h_{1i} + \bar{h}_{2i}h_3^{low}, \quad f_i^{upp} = h_{1i} + \bar{h}_{2i}h_3^{upp} \tag{26}$$

$$b) \quad \bar{h}_{2i} < 0 \quad f_i^{low} = h_{1i} + \bar{h}_{2i}h_3^{upp}, \quad f_i^{upp} = h_{1i} + \bar{h}_{2i}h_3^{low} \tag{27}$$

where h_{1i} and $\bar{h}_{2i}$ are the Bézier ordinates of Bézier functions h_1 and $\bar{h}_2$ which is the polynomial resulting from degree elevation [10] of h_2 to the degree of h_1.

We can rewrite the lower and upper Bézier functions into explicit Bézier curves, as we did in section 4.2.2 A. Taking the union of the two convex hull of the lower and upper Bézier curves, we can form a large convex hull which bounds the numerator of the non-polynomial function (23) as shown in Figure 3. Then we can apply the same recursive de Casteljau subdivision process to this large convex hull followed by the same minimization technique we used for the polynomial case. This large convex hull should shrink as the interval of the parameter goes to zero. Therefore we need to recompute the equations (24), (25) each time we apply the de Casteljau subdivision to the original Bézier patch, however for the polynomial case we compute the explicit Bézier curve once. If the bounds for $\sqrt{h_3}$ are loose, we need to subdivide the patch many times, therefore computation time depends largely on the tightness of the bounds. We are therefore developing general methods for determining tight bounds for functions involving square roots of polynomials.

An alternative method we are investigating involves a transformation leading to a polynomial problem of higher dimensionality. To this purpose let $s^2 = h_3(t)$ and substitute into numerator of equation (23), to obtain a system of polynomial equations with two variables t and s.

$$h_1(t) \pm h_2(t)s = 0 \tag{28}$$

$$s^2 - h_3(t) = 0 \tag{29}$$

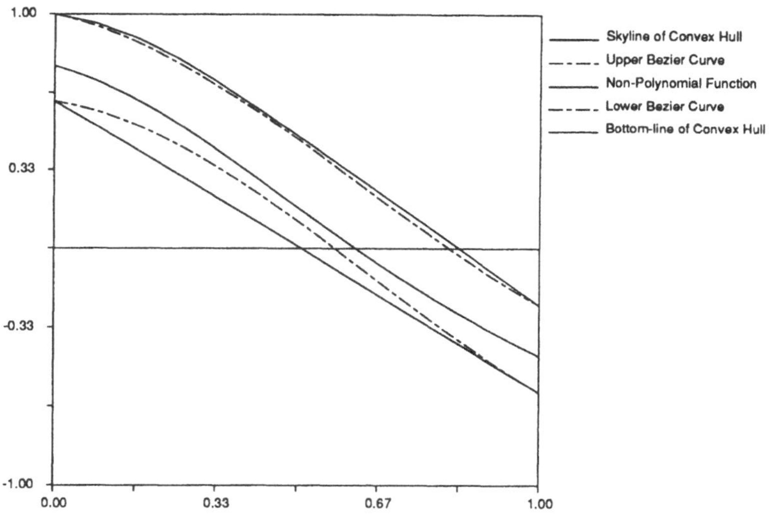

Figure 3: Lower and upper bounding Bézier curves

where $L \le s \le U$ and L, U are appropriate lower and upper bounds of $h_3(t)$ which can be easily obtained. This system of polynomial equations can be converted from the power basis to the bivariate Bernstein basis and can be solved by the technique described in section 3.

When $\kappa = H$, equation (23) becomes singular. This condition is equivalent to the point where the two principal curvatures are identical. This point approximates a sphere and is called an *umbilical point* [8]. In the special case, when the identical principal curvatures vanish, the surface becomes locally *flat*. If the umbilical point coincides with a local maximum or minimum of the curvature, we cannot use equation (23) to locate such a point. In such case we need to locate the umbilical or flat point first by finding the roots of

$$H^2 - K = \frac{h_3(t)}{4S^6} = 0 \tag{30}$$

As $S \neq 0$, equation (30) is satisfied if

$$h_3(t) = 0 \tag{31}$$

Equation (31) can be solved by the technique we described for polynomial functions. Then we compute the principal curvatures at the umbilical point and compare their values to their small neighborhood to check if the umbilical point corresponds to a local extremum.

4.2.3 Stationary Points within Domain

Stationary points within the parameter domain are the roots of the two simultaneous bivariate equations (20). We can apply a similar procedure to that used to compute stationary points along the domain boundary. When the curvature is Gaussian or mean, equations (20) can be expressed in terms of two simultaneous bivariate Bernstein polynomials. However for the principal curvatures, the equations become two simultaneous bivariate functions involving polynomials and square roots of polynomials.

A. Polynomial Functions: As in the univariate case, the numerators of equations (20) for the Gaussian and mean curvature can be expressed in terms of bivariate Bernstein polynomials. These bivariate Bézier functions can be represented as explicit Bézier patches in a (u,v,w) coordinate system using the linear precision property of the Bernstein basis. From a geometric point of view, solving all the roots of two simultaneous bivariate polynomial equations has been replaced by finding the intersections of two Bézier patches with the plane w=0. This problem can be solved by the methods we described in section 3. The recursive process can be continued until the resulting rectangles potentially containing roots are as small as required. For manufacturing purposes, high accuracy is required. In such a case a minimization technique may be employed following coarse subdivision to accelerate the computation and obtain high accuracy.

B. Non-Polynomial Functions: In the case of maximum and minimum principal curvatures, equations (20) become

$$\kappa_u(u,v) = \frac{f_1(u,v) \pm f_2(u,v)\sqrt{f_3(u,v)}}{4(\kappa - H)S^8} = 0 \tag{32}$$

$$\kappa_v(u,v) = \frac{g_1(u,v) \pm g_2(u,v)\sqrt{f_3(u,v)}}{4(\kappa - H)S^8} = 0 \tag{33}$$

where f_1, f_2, f_3, g_1, g_2 are polynomials of degree $(14m-9, 14n-8)$, $(9m-6, 9n-5)$, $(10m-6, 10n-6)$, $(14m-8, 14n-9)$, $(9m-5, 9n-6)$ in u and v parameters. The plus and minus sign correspond to maximum and minimum principal curvatures. Assuming $\kappa \neq H$, we can find lower and upper bounds for $\sqrt{f_3(u,v)}$ which can be constants or bivariate polynomials similarly to the one-dimensional case. Then we can bound the numerator of equation (32) using bivariate Bézier functions as follows.

$$F^{low}(u,v) = \sum_{i=0}^{M}\sum_{j=0}^{N} f_{ij}^{low} B_{i,M}(u)B_{j,N}(v) = 0 \tag{34}$$

$$F^{upp}(u,v) = \sum_{i=0}^{M}\sum_{j=0}^{N} f_{ij}^{upp} B_{i,M}(u)B_{j,N}(v) = 0 \tag{35}$$

and similarly for equation (33) using $G^{low}(u,v)$ and $G^{upp}(u,v)$ with degree M' and N', where $M = 14m-9$, $N = 14n-8$, $M' = 14m-8$ and $N' = 14n-9$. These four bivariate Bézier functions can be transformed into four explicit Bézier patches using the linear precision property of Bernstein basis. Taking the union of two convex hulls of the lower and upper Bézier patches of equations (34) and (35), we can construct a larger convex hull which bounds numerator of equation (32). We can similarly construct a convex hull for the numerator of equation (33). Then we can apply the same technique which we described in section 4.2.3 A to these two larger convex hulls.

An alternate method we are studying is to introduce a new variable $\tau^2 = f_3(u,v)$ and rewrite the numerator of equations (32), (33) into a system of three trivariate polynomial equations.

$$H_1(u,v,\tau) = f_1(u,v) \pm f_2(u,v)\tau = 0 \tag{36}$$

$$H_2(u,v,\tau) = g_1(u,v) \pm g_2(u,v)\tau = 0 \tag{37}$$

$$H_3(u,v,\tau) = \tau^2 - f_3(u,v) = 0 \tag{38}$$

where $L^* \leq \tau \leq U^*$ and L^*, U^* are appropriate lower and upper bounds for $f_3(u,v)$ which can be easily obtained. This system of polynomial equations can be converted into three trivariate Bernstein polynomial equations and then into a triple product Bézier hyperpatch using the linear precision property of the Bernstein basis, and solved as in section 3.

At the umbilical point, equations (32), (33) become singular and similarly to the one-dimensional case, we need to locate the umbilical points first by finding the roots of $f_3(u,v) = 0$. This equation represents an algebraic curve which can be traced as in [35] [24] [21]. More analysis is necessary to compute the extrema of curvature in this case.

4.3 Constant Curvature Contouring

The constant curvature lines divide the surface into regions of similar order of magnitude of curvature. The contouring levels should be determined to faithfully represent the curvature distribution. To do this, the following should be used:

1. Maximum and minimum curvature values in the entire domain to find the range of curvature values.
2. Locations of all the local maxima and minima of curvature inside the domain around which loops may be formed.
3. Locations of all the saddle points of the curvature where the contour lines cross or exhibit more complex behavior [20].

Contour lines in the parameter space of a bivariate function can be separated into three categories:

1. Local maxima and minima of the function are encircled by closed contour lines.
2. At the precise level of a saddle point, contour line cross or exhibit more complex behavior.
3. Contour lines start from a domain boundary point and end at a distinct domain boundary point.

If the surface is subdivided along the iso-parametric lines which contain the local maxima and minima of curvature inside the domain and the contouring levels of curvature are chosen such that the contour lines avoid saddle points, each sub-patch will contain simple contour branches without loops or singularities. Therefore we can find all the starting points of the various levels of contour lines along the parameter domain boundary of each sub-patch by finding the roots of

$$C(t) = \alpha \tag{39}$$

where $C(t)$ is a univariate curvature function consisting of a numerator and denominator which are polynomial functions or irrational functions involving square roots and α is a constant taking various appropriate curvature values. Multiplying the denominator on both sides of equation (39), we obtain

$$C^{num}(t) - \alpha C^{den}(t) = 0 \tag{40}$$

where $C^{num}(t)$ and $C^{den}(t)$ denote the numerator and denominator of $C(t)$. $C^{num}(t)$ is polynomial for Gaussian and mean curvatures and an irrational function for the two principal curvatures, while $C^{den}(t)$ is polynomial only for the Gaussian and an irrational function for the mean and two principal curvatures. We can apply the same method that we used in section 4.2.2 to find all the roots. Note that for maximum and minimum principal curvatures, there are two square roots in the equation (40) and this fact will loosen the bounds. These starting points occur in pairs, since non-loop contour lines must start from the domain boundary and must end at the distinct domain boundary point.

We used the Trip Algorithm introduced by Preusser [36] to polygonize the area between contour lines. The points of the contour lines are computed successively by integrating an initial value problem for a system of coupled nonlinear differential equations (41) using variable step size and variable order Adams method [32].

$$\dot{u} = \beta C_v, \quad \dot{v} = -\beta C_u \tag{41}$$

where dot denotes first derivative with respect to t, $(\dot{u}, \dot{v})$ gives the direction of the contour line, C_u, C_v are the first partial derivatives with respect u and v direction of the curvature C and β is an arbitrary non-zero factor that can be chosen to provide arc-length parametrization.

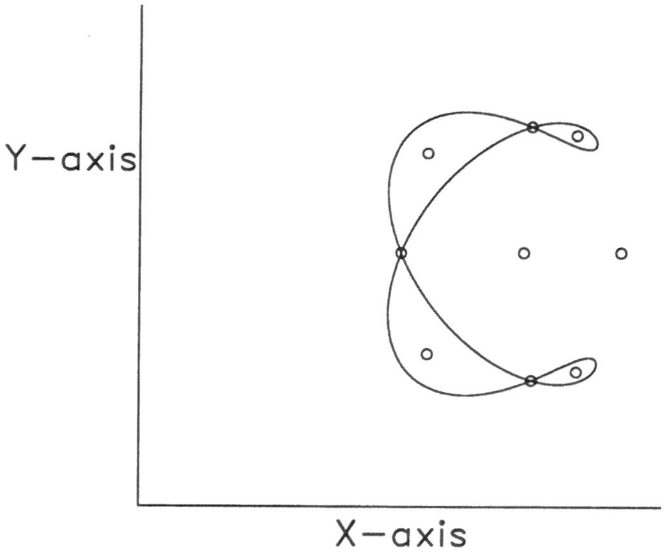

Figure 4: The curve $f(x, y) = 0$ of section 5

5 EXAMPLES AND APPLICATIONS

A well known problem in computer-aided design is the discovery and subsequent tracing of all branches of an implicit algebraic curve $f(x, y) = 0$. Such curves arise from surface intersection problems. The computation of *turning points* (where $f = \frac{\partial f}{\partial x} = 0$ or $f = \frac{\partial f}{\partial y} = 0$) or *critical points* (where $\frac{\partial f}{\partial x} = \frac{\partial f}{\partial y} = 0$) is important in solving this problem [35] [24]. As an example, let us find the critical points of the curve $f(x, y) = 0$ illustrated in figure 4, which is defined by [41]

$$f(x,y) = -64y^4 + 128y^3 - 96x^2y^2 + 140xy - 139y^2 + 96x^2y - 140xy + 75y \qquad (42)$$
$$-96x^4 + 276x^3 - 313x^2 + 165x - 36 = 0$$

Taking the two partial derivatives and setting them equal to 0 gives us two simultaneous equations which we can use either the PP or the LP method to solve. With a tolerance of 10^{-8}, the LP method computes the following nine roots:

Critical points of f to 8 digits		
Root number	x	y
1	0.92143996	0.50000000
2	0.83640890	0.73280861
3	0.75000000	0.75000000
4	0.73481004	0.50000000
5	0.55109110	0.69759134
6	0.50000000	0.50000000
7	0.83640890	0.26719139
8	0.75000000	0.25000000
9	0.55109110	0.30240866

As mentioned in Section 1, the computation of distance functions between point sets is a basic problem in computational geometry and geometric modeling. It is useful in numerical control machining, in tolerance region and access space representation in solid modelling, robotics, inspection of manufactured objects, and in feature recognition through the construction of medial axis transforms. These applications need reliable, accurate, and efficient algorithms. Various inspection problems and problems of shape comparison are based on computing maximal and minimal distance deviations between points in the Euclidean space. For this purpose, it is important to have computational methods which are efficient and reliable to compute extrema for the distance between two variable points where each of those variable points assumes all possible positions in a given set. In practical situations, this set can be a surface, a curve, or a single point. Therefore, we are interested in the computation of the distances between: a fixed space point and a variable point on a 3D space curve (P-C); a space point and a variable point on a surface (P-S); two variable points located on two given 3D space curves (C-C); two variable points, one of which is located on a space curve and the other is located on a surface (C-S); two variable points, each of which is contained on a given surface (S-S). Curves and surfaces are represented here as rational B-splines. The first process is to subdivide the curve or surface patch into a number of rational Bezier curves or rational Bezier patches. So the problem is then reformulated to the computation of the distances between the point sets which are space points, rational Bezier curves and Bezier surface patches. The squared distance functions expressed in the Bernstein form are then developed for the various point sets. This development is based on direct addition or multiplication of two Bernstein forms. The method of section 3 coupled with minimization is used to reach accurate numerical results.

The squared distance function between two point sets $D(\mathbf{u}) = |\mathbf{R}_1(\mathbf{u}^{(1)}) - \mathbf{R}_2(\mathbf{u}^{(2)})|^2$ (where $\mathbf{R}_1$ and $\mathbf{R}_2$ are functions representing the two point sets involved and $\mathbf{u} = [\mathbf{u}^{(1)}, \mathbf{u}^{(2)}]$) can be represented by

$$D(\mathbf{u}) = \frac{P(\mathbf{u})}{Q(\mathbf{u})} \tag{43}$$

where $P(\mathbf{u})$ and $Q(\mathbf{u})$ are non-negative polynomials in $\mathbf{u}$ expressed in the multivariate Bernstein basis of section 3 within an n-dimensional box in Euclidean space; and $\mathbf{u} = [u_1, u_2, ..., u_n], n \in (1,2,3,4)$ is the parameter set. For example, for the distance between a point and a curve, $n = 1$ and $\mathbf{u} = [u_1]$. For more detailed derivation, see [48].

The derivatives of $D(\mathbf{u})$ are:

$$D_{\mathbf{u}}(\mathbf{u}) = \frac{P_{\mathbf{u}}(\mathbf{u})Q(\mathbf{u}) - P(\mathbf{u})Q_{\mathbf{u}}(\mathbf{u})}{Q^2(\mathbf{u})} \tag{44}$$

If $D_{\mathbf{u}}(\mathbf{u}) = 0$, the numerator of the above expression should be zero which leads to n implicit nonlinear polynomial equations. The computation of the stationary point set of the squared distance function can be performed by expressing $D_{\mathbf{u}}(\mathbf{u})=0$ in the Bernstein basis and then finding the zeros of these equations as in section 3. When a box size tolerance preset by the user is reached after subdivision, minimization may be invoked for higher accuracy if necessary. The equation $D_{\mathbf{u}}(\mathbf{u}) = 0$ has an interesting geometric interpretation involving orthogonality concepts useful in surface intersection problems [21] [23].

The major steps of the algorithm, described in more detail in [48], are

1. Find and characterize the stationary points of the squared distance in the interior domain of the point sets.
2. Find and characterize the stationary points of the squared distance along the four edges of surface if one point set is a surface.
3. Find and characterize the stationary points of the squared distance at end points if one point set is a curve.
4. Compare the distances to get the distribution of local extrema and saddle points and global extrema.

Sample distance computations are shown in figures 5–9 for the five cases listed above. For clarity, some of the figures do not include all four types of solutions identified above.

To illustrate interrogation of differential geometry properties, we used a saddle-like bicubic integral Bézier patch surface (see Figure 10). Figure 11 shows a non-degenerate offset or parallel surface of the surface patch of Figure 10 at offset distance d=0.5. Figure 12 shows a self-intersecting offset surface of the same patch at offset distance d=1. This behavior can be explained from the range of values of the principal curvatures and

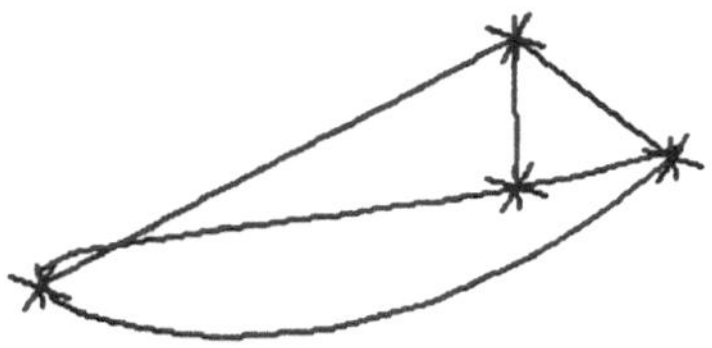

Figure 5: Distances of a point and a rational cubic B-spline curve

the resulting principal radii of curvature illustrated below (see also [46] for a related discussion). To display the curvature of the subdivided surface clearly, we assigned discrete color to each closed polygon based on curvature level. The level was determined by taking the average value of the curvature values of the contour lines excluding the boundary lines which form the polygon. We assigned R (red), G (green) and B (blue) to the minimum, zero and maximum curvature values of the whole domain. Curvature values in between are linearly interpolated. Figure 13 shows a color map of the Gaussian curvature K. Since the shape of the surface is hyperbolic, the Gaussian curvature is negative everywhere, and has a minimum value of K=-1.265 at (0.5, 0.5). The mid points of the domain boundaries have a local minimum of K reaching a value of K=-0.498. The four corners of the domain have the same maximum value for K=-0.365. Figure 14 shows a color map of the mean curvature H. Because of symmetry at point (0.5, 0.5), we have a saddle point of H with value H=0.0. There are no stationary points along the domain boundaries. We have the same maximum 0.326 at two corners (0, 0), (1, 1) and the same minimum H=-0.326 at the other two corners. Figure 15 shows a color coded map of the maximum principal curvature κ_{max}. Since the Gaussian curvature is negative everywhere, the maximum principal curvature κ_{max} is positive everywhere. There are three stationary points of κ_{max} within the domain, a maximum at (0.5, 0.5) with the value κ_{max}=1.125 and two saddle points at (0.041, 0.041) and (0.959, 0.959) with the value κ_{max}=1.010. There are no stationary points along the boundaries. We have the same minimum at the corners (1, 0) and (0, 1) of the value κ_{max}=0.360. Figure 16 shows a color map of the minimum principal curvature κ_{min}. As expected, the minimum principal curvature is negative everywhere. Similarly to the maximum principal curvature, there are three stationary points inside the domain. A minimum at (0.5, 0.5) with value κ_{min}=-1.125 and two saddle points at (0.041, 0.959), (0.959, 0.041) with value κ_{min} =-1.010. There are no stationary points along the boundaries. The maximum κ_{min} is located at (0, 0) and (1, 1) having the value κ_{min}=-0.360.

6 CONCLUDING REMARKS

Both the Linear Programming and Projected-Polyhedron algorithms were implemented in exact rational arithmetic as well as in double-precision floating point. The decision to write versions in rational arithmetic as well as floating point was based on several considerations. First, we noticed that floating point implementations tend to perturb roots unpleasantly or miss them altogether in ill-conditioned problems. With arbitrary-precision rational arithmetic, of course, this problem would not exist; any accuracy can theoretically be achieved as long as the time and memory requirements are reasonable. Secondly, we wished to see under what conditions rational arithmetic could efficiently achieve accurate results. We discovered that rational arithmetic was extremely useful (as well as fast) in the preprocessing necessary to obtain the governing equations in the Bernstein basis. However, in the solution phase rational arithmetic was frequently inefficient except for low-degree, low-dimensional problems. The subdivision phase in particular was inefficient, because the numerators and denominators of the rationals involved often grew large. We were able to mitigate this problem by expanding bounding boxes slightly in order to reduce the number of digits involved in the representation of the rationals.

A few modifications to the algorithms could improve performance. One possibility is to develop a hybrid algorithm which would employ the fast Projected-Polyhedron iterations in the early stages and then use

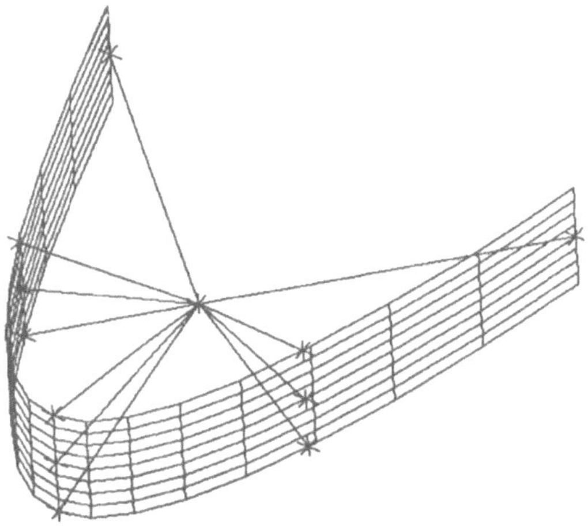

Figure 6: Distances of a point and a linear-quadratic Bezier surface

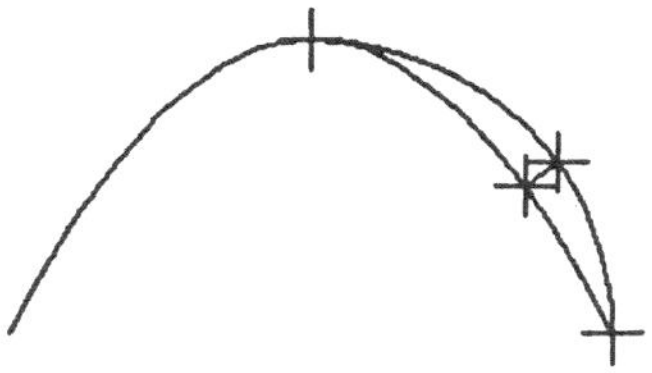

Figure 7: Distances of two rational quadratic Bezier curves

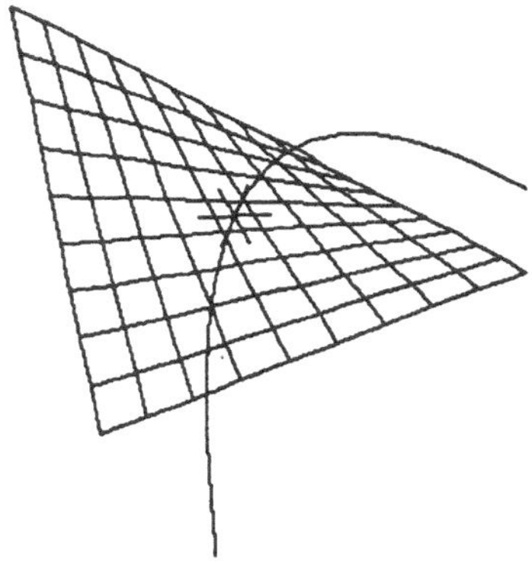

Figure 8: Distances of a quadratic Bezier curve and a bicubic Bezier patch

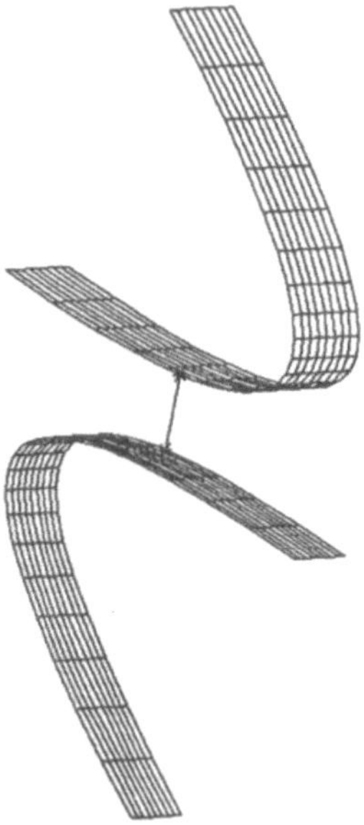

Figure 9: **Distances of two linear-quadratic Bezier patches**

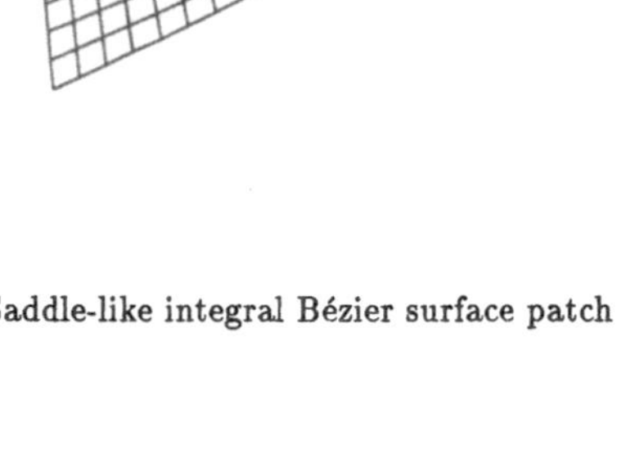

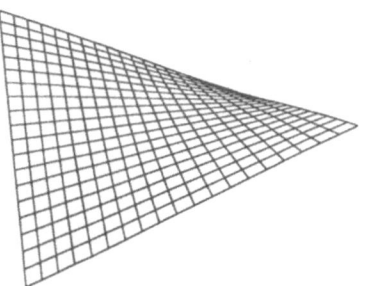

Figure 10: Saddle-like integral Bézier surface patch

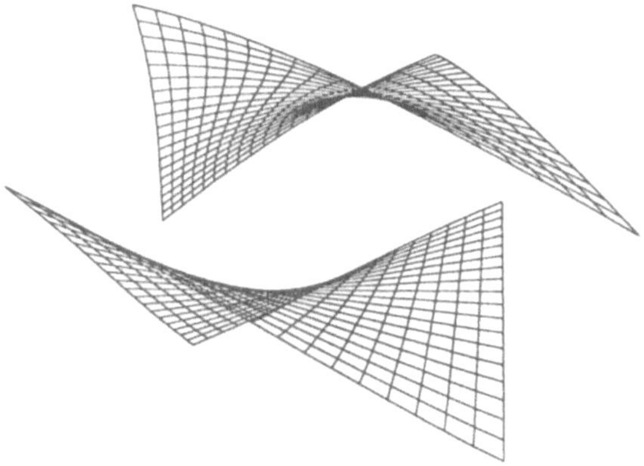

Figure 11: Non-degenerate offset surface with d=0.5

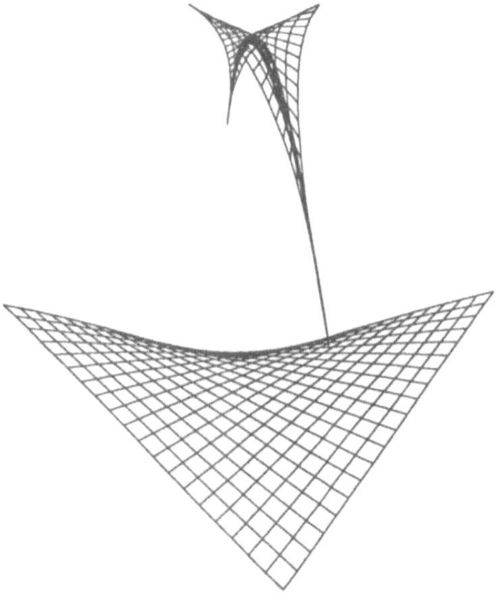

Figure 12: Degenerate offset surface with d=1.0

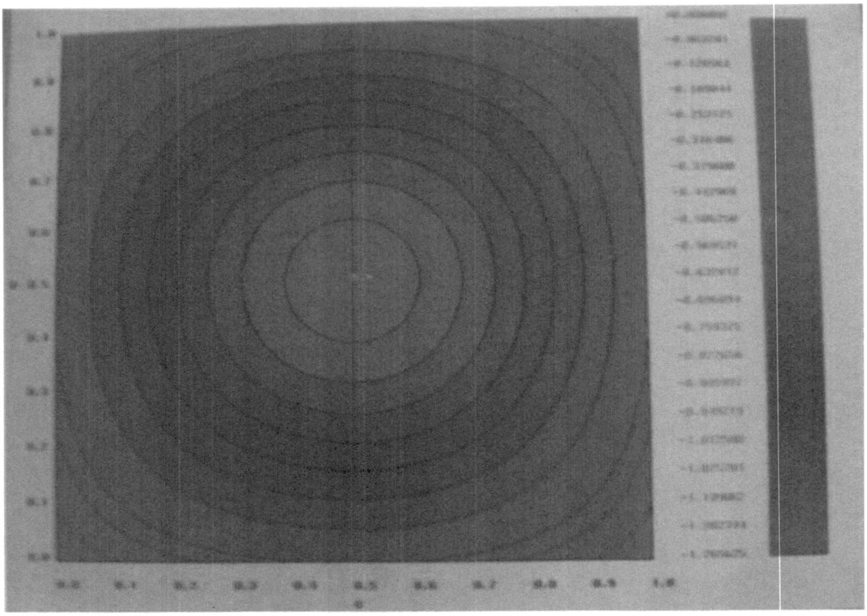

Figure 13: Gaussian curvature color map

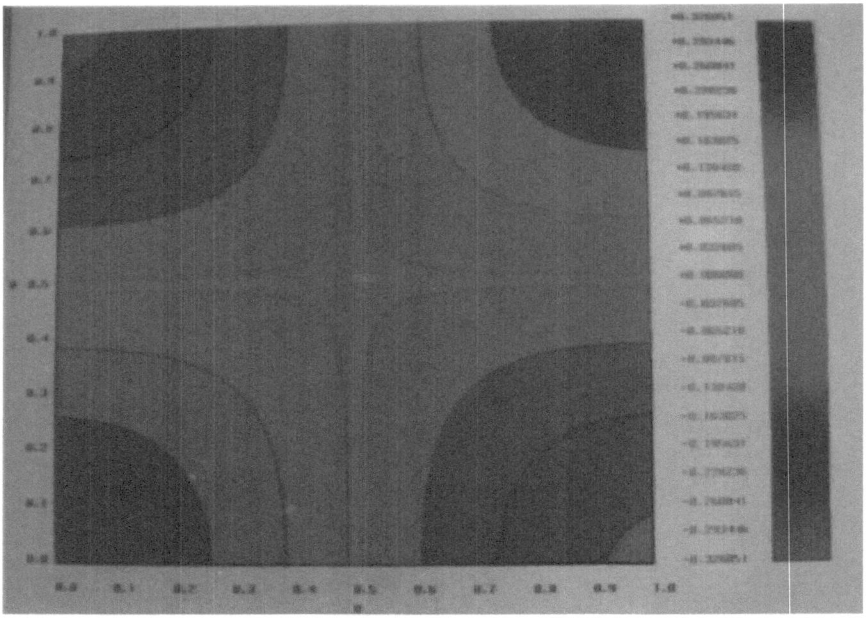

Figure 14: Mean curvature color map

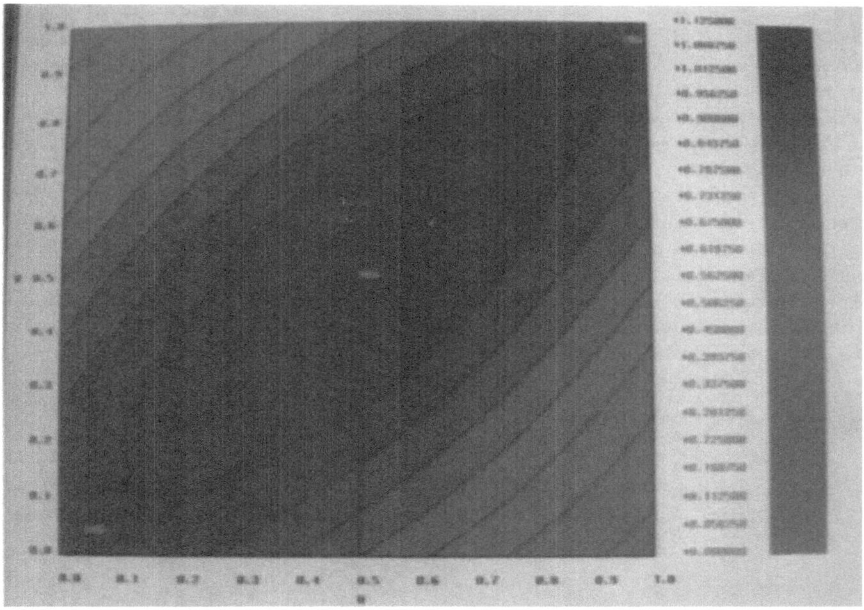

Figure 15: Maximun principal curvature color map

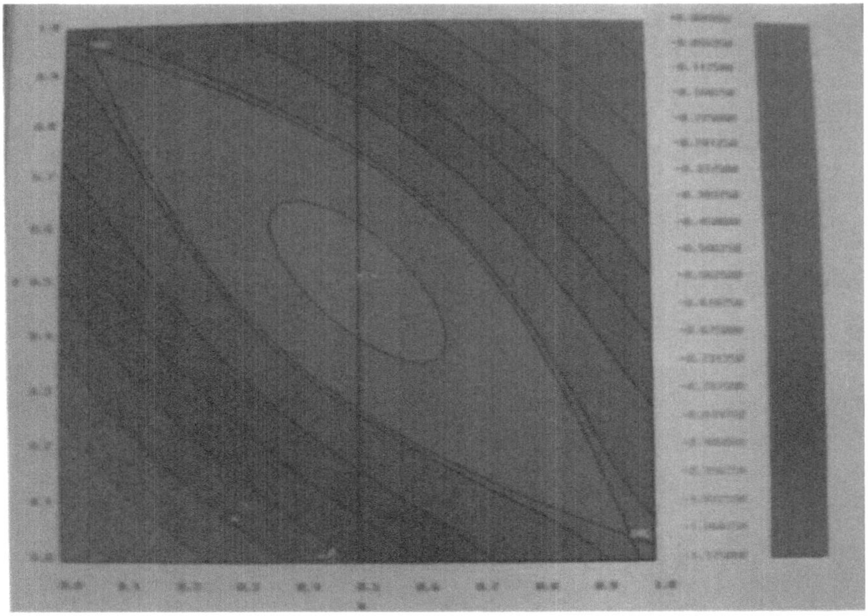

Figure 16: Minimum principal curvature color map

Linear Programming iterations to take advantage of quadratic convergence. Another improvement would be to select a better place than the midpoint to split a box when convergence slows; one might make such a selection by analyzing the pattern of the reduction in box size. Lastly, if finite precision arithmetic is employed, stability analysis should be performed on these algorithms in order to anticipate and control numerical inaccuracies. In the area of intersections, distance computations, and interrogation of differential geometry properties, as well as in other applications, it is frequently necessary to deal with solution sets that are not zero-dimensional. Our algorithms are designed to compute isolated solutions, and therefore methods to identify, characterize, and parameterize higher-dimensional solution sets need to be developed. For problems involving irrational functions, such as ray-tracing of offset surfaces [45] and differential geometry property interrogation, comparison of alternate solution methods to allow the development of efficient algorithms is recommended. Such methods could rely on tighter polynomial bounds for irrational functions or the higher-dimensional solution procedures introduced in this paper. Finally, much remains to be done in order to apply our techniques fully to specific problems in computer aided design, visualization, analysis, simulation, and manufacturing.

ACKNOWLEDGEMENTS

This work was supported, in part, by the MIT Sea Grant College Program and the Office of Naval Research in the USA under grant numbers NA90AA-D-SG-424 and N00014-91-J-1014. Mr. S. L. Abrams, Mr. H. S. Nam, and Mr. S. T. Tuohy provided valued assistance.

References

[1] V. I. Arnold. *Ordinary Differential Equations.* MIT Press, Cambridge, MA, 1981.

[2] J. M. Beck, R. T. Farouki, and J. K. Hinds. Surface analysis methods. *IEEE Computer Graphics and Applications*, 6(12):18–36, December 1986.

[3] W. Boehm. Inserting new knots into B-spline curves. *Computer Aided Design*, 12(4):199–201, 1980.

[4] B. Buchberger. Gröbner bases: An algorithmic method in polynomial ideal theory. In N. K. Bose, editor, *Multidimensional Systems Theory: Progress, Directions and Open Problems in Multidimensional Systems*, pages 184–232. D. Reidel Publishing Company, Dordrecht, Holland, 1985.

[5] J. Canny. Generalised characteristic polynomials. *Journal of Symbolic Computation*, 9:241–250, 1990.

[6] E. Cohen, T. Lyche, and R. F. Riesenfeld. Discrete B-splines and subdivision techniques in computer-aided geometric design and computer graphics. *Computer Graphics and Image Processing*, 14:87–111, 1980.

[7] G. Dahlquist and A. Björck. *Numerical Methods.* Prentice-Hall, Inc., Englewood Cliffs, NJ, 1974.

[8] P. M. do Carmo. *Differential Geometry of Curves and Surfaces.* Prentice-Hall, Inc., Englewood Cliffs, New Jersey, 1976.

[9] T. Dokken. Finding intersections of B-spline represented geometries using recursive subdivision techniques. *Computer Aided Geometric Design*, 2:189–195, 1985.

[10] G. Farin. *Curves and Surfaces for Computer Aided Geometric Design, A Practical Guide.* Academic Press, New York, 1990.

[11] R. T. Farouki. The approximation of non-degenerate offset surfaces. *Computer Aided Geometric Design*, 3(1):15–43, 1986.

[12] R. T. Farouki and V. T. Rajan. Algorithms for polynomials in Bernstein form. *Computer Aided Geometric Design*, 5:1–26, 1988.

[13] I. D. Faux and M. J. Pratt. *Computational Geometry for Design and Manufacture*. Ellis Horwood, Chichester, England, 1981.

[14] C. B. Garcia and W. I. Zangwill. Global continuation methods for finding all solutions to polynomial systems of equations in n variables. In *Extremal Methods and Systems Analysis*, pages 481–497. Springer-Verlag, New York, NY, 1980.

[15] H. N. Gursoy. *Shape Interrogation by Medial Axis Transform for Automated Analysis*. PhD thesis, Massachusetts Institute of Technology, Cambridge, MA, November 1989.

[16] H. N. Gursoy and N. M. Patrikalakis. Automated interrogation and adaptive subdivision of shape using medial axis transform. *Advances in Engineering Software*, 1992. (To appear).

[17] M. E. Hohmeyer. A surface intersection algorithm based on loop detection. In J. Rossignac and J. Turner, editors, *Proceedings of the Symposium on Solid Modeling Foundations and CAD/CAM Applications*, pages 197–207, Austin, TX, June 1991. ACM SIGGRAPH. New York: ACM Press, 1991.

[18] G. R. Hottel, S. T. Tuohy, P. G. Alourdas, and N. M. Patrikalakis. Praxiteles: A geometric modeling and interrogation system. In *Marine Computers '91: Proceedings of the Second Symposium on Computer Applications in the Marine Industry*, Burlington, MA, September 1991. SNAME, New England Section. Paper CC5.

[19] R. B. Jerard, R. L. Drysdale, B. Schaudt, K. Hauck, and J. Magewick. Methods for detecting errors in sculptured surface machining. *IEEE Computer Graphics and Applications*, 9(1):26–39, January 1989.

[20] M. A. Krasnoselskiy, A. I. Perov, A. I. Povolotskiy, and P. P. Zabreiko. *Plane Vector Fields*. Academic Press, New York, 1966.

[21] G. A. Kriezis. *Algorithms for Rational Spline Surface Intersections*. PhD thesis, Massachusetts Institute of Technology, Cambridge, Massachusetts, March 1990.

[22] G. A. Kriezis and N. M. Patrikalakis. Rational polynomial surface intersections. In G. A. Gabriele, editor, *Proceedings of the 17th ASME Design Automation Conference, Vol. II*, pages 43–53, Miami, FL, September 1991. New York: ASME.

[23] G. A. Kriezis, N. M. Patrikalakis, and F. E. Wolter. Topological and differential equation methods for surface intersections. *Computer Aided Design*, 24(1):41–55, January 1992.

[24] G. A. Kriezis, P. V. Prakash, and N. M. Patrikalakis. A method for intersecting algebraic surfaces with rational polynomial patches. *Computer Aided Design*, 22(10):645–654, December 1990.

[25] T. L. Kunii and Y. Shinagawa. Visualization: New concepts and techniques to integrate diverse application areas. In N. M. Patrikalakis, editor, *Scientific Visualization of Physical Phenomena*, pages 3–25. Tokyo: Springer-Verlag, 1991.

[26] J. M. Lane and R. F. Riesenfeld. Bounds on a polynomial. *BIT: Nordisk Tidskrift for Informations-Behandling*, 21(1):112–117, 1981.

[27] T. Maekawa and N. M. Patrikalakis. Interrogation of differential geometry properties for design and manufacture. Memorandum 92-5, Cambridge MA: MIT Ocean Engineering Design Laboratory, 1992.

[28] F. Munchmeyer. On surface imperfections. In R. Martin, editor, *Mathematics of Surfaces II*, pages 459–474. Oxford University Press, 1987.

[29] F. Munchmeyer. Shape interrogation: A case study. In G. Farin, editor, *Geometric Modeling*, pages 291–301, Philadelphia, PA, 1987. SIAM.

[30] L. R. Nackman. Two-dimensional critical point configuration graphs. *IEEE Transactions on Pattern Analysis and Machine Intelligence*, 6(4):442–450, July 1984.

[31] T. Nishita, T. W. Sederberg, and M. Kakimoto. Ray tracing trimmed rational surface patches. *ACM Computer Graphics*, 24(4):337–345, August 1990.

[32] Numerical Algorithms Group, Oxford, England. *NAG Fortran Library Manual*, mark 14 edition, 1990.

[33] N. M. Patrikalakis and L. Bardis. Localization of rational B-spline surfaces. *Engineering with Computers*, 7(4):237–252, 1991.

[34] N. M. Patrikalakis and H. N. Gursoy. Shape interrogation by medial axis transform. In B. Ravani, editor, *Proceedings of the 16th ASME Design Automation Conference: Advances in Design Automation, Computer Aided and Computational Design, Vol. I*, pages 77–88, Chicago, IL, September 1990. New York: ASME.

[35] N. M. Patrikalakis and P. V. Prakash. Surface intersections for geometric modeling. *Journal of Mechanical Design, ASME Transactions*, 112:100–107, March 1990.

[36] A. Preusser. Computing area filling contours for surface defined by piecewise polynomials. *Computer Aided Geometric Design*, 3:267–279, 1986.

[37] J. R. Rossignac and A. G. Requicha. Offsetting operations in solid modelling. *Computer Aided Geometric Design*, 3(2):129–148, 1986.

[38] T. W. Sederberg. Algorithms for algebraic curve intersection. *Computer Aided Design*, 21(9):547–554, 1989.

[39] T. W. Sederberg and R. J. Meyers. Loop detection in surface patch intersections. *Computer Aided Geometric Design*, 5:161–171, 1988.

[40] T. W. Sederberg and T. Nishita. Geometric Hermite approximation of surface patch intersection curves. *Computer Aided Geometric Design*, 8:97–114, 1991.

[41] E. C. Sherbrooke and N. M. Patrikalakis. Computation of the real solutions of nonlinear polynomial systems. Memorandum 91-12, Cambridge MA: MIT Ocean Engineering Design Laboratory, 1991.

[42] P. Sinha, E. Klassen, and K. K. Wang. Exploiting topological and geometric properties for selective subdivision. In *Proceedings of the ACM Symposium on Computational Geometry*, pages 39–45. New York: ACM, 1985.

[43] V. Srinivasan, L. R. Nackman, J.-M. Tang, and S. N. Meshkat. Automatic mesh generation using the symmetric axis transformation of polygonal domains. Technical Report RC 16132, Yorktown Heights, NY: IBM, September 1990.

[44] Symbolics, Inc. *MACSYMA Reference Manual*, version 13 edition, November 1988.

[45] M. E. Vafiadou and N. M. Patrikalakis. Interrogation of offsets of polynomial surface patches. In F. H. Post and W. Barth, editors, *Eurographics '91, Proceedings of the 12th Annual European Association for Computer Graphics Conference and Exhibition*, pages 247–259 and 538, Vienna, Austria, September 1991. Amsterdam: North-Holland.

[46] F. E. Wolter. Cut locus and medial axis in global shape interrogation and representation. Memorandum 92-2, Cambridge MA: MIT Ocean Engineering Design Laboratory, 1992.

[47] W. I. Zangwill and C. B. Garcia. *Pathways to solutions, fixed points, and equilibria*. Prentice-Hall, Englewood Cliffs, NJ, 1981.

[48] J. Zhou, E. C. Sherbrooke, and N. M. Patrikalakis. Computation of stationary points of distance functions. Memorandum 92-4, Cambridge MA: MIT Ocean Engineering Design Laboratory, 1992.

Authors' Biographies

Nicholas M. Patrikalakis is Associate Professor of Ocean Engineering at the Massachusetts Institute of Technology, Department of Ocean Engineering. Professor Patrikalakis' research and teaching focus in the general area of applications of computational geometry in design, analysis, simulation and fabrication of complex systems. For his work in computer aided design, Dr. Patrikalakis was appointed Doherty Professor of Ocean Utilization. He has authored more than eighty technical papers and edited several books. He is a member of ACM, ASME, CGS, IEEE, ISOPE, SNAME and TCG. Dr. Patrikalakis has served as consultant to various organizations, has sat on committees of several professional societies, and is a member of the board of directors of the Computer Graphics Society. He is Associate Editor-in-Chief of IJOPE, and participates in the editorial boards of several journals. He has recently served as program chair of Computer Graphics International '91, as editor of its proceedings published by Springer, and as guest editor of The Visual Computer. Professor Patrikalakis received his Diploma in Naval Architecture and Mechanical Engineering in 1977 from the National Technical University of Athens, Greece, and his Ph.D. in Ocean Engineering in 1983 from MIT.

Address: MIT Room 5-428, 77 Massachusetts Avenue, Cambridge, MA 02139-9910, USA. **Electronic Mail:** nmp@deslab.mit.edu

Takashi Maekawa is a doctoral graduate student in the Design Laboratory of the Department of Ocean Engineering at the Massachusetts Institute of Technology. His reseach interests are in Computer Aided Design and Manufacturing. He received a B.S. and an M.S. in Mechanical Engineering from Waseda University, Tokyo in 1976 and 1978, respectively, and an Ocean Engineer's Degree from MIT in 1987. From 1978 to 1989 he worked for Bridgestone Corporation in Japan as a design and manufacturing engineer.

Address: MIT Room 5-424, 77 Massachusetts Avenue, Cambridge, MA 02139-9910, USA. **Electronic Mail:** tmaekawa@deslab.mit.edu

Evan C. Sherbrooke is a doctoral graduate student in the Design Laboratory of the Department of Ocean Engineering at the Massachusetts Institute of Technology. He graduated Phi Beta Kappa from MIT in 1990 with an S.B. in Mathematics. Mr. Sherbrooke's research interests include modeling and interrogation of complex objects and numerical stability issues in computational geometry.

Address: MIT Room 5-424, 77 Massachusetts Avenue, Cambridge, MA 02139-9910, USA. **Electronic Mail:** esher@athena.mit.edu

Jingfang Zhou is a doctoral graduate student in the Design Laboratory of the Department of Ocean Engineering at the Massachusetts Institute of Technology. She graduated from Huazhong University of Science and Technology in Wuhan, China with a B.S. and an M.S. in Naval Architecture in 1985 and 1988, respectively. Her research interests include computational geometry, computer aided design, and computer aided engineering.

Address: MIT Room 5-422, 77 Massachusetts Avenue, Cambridge, MA 02139-9910, USA. **Electronic Mail:** fzhou@athena.mit.edu

A Geographical Database System Based on the Homotopy Model

Tetsuya Ikeda, Tosiyasu L. Kunii, Yoshihisa Shinagawa, and Minoru Ueda

ABSTRACT

A new concept for a geographical database system based on the homotopy model is proposed. The homotopy model was developed for surface reconstruction using a series of contours from an object with a complex shape. In the case of geographical applications, an object is comparatively less complex in terms of topology. This model can be used for constructing a database. In the database, the data structure is extended to represent topological characteristics and the associated values contain geometrical characteristics.

This paper extends the toroidal graph that represents the relationship between two adjacent contours, to a new type of toroidal graph that represents the relationship between multiple contours including the branching and merging of contours at critical points.

Keywords: homotopy, Reeb graph, terrain visualization, multiple toroidal graph, critical point, surface network

1. INTRODUCTION

This paper proposes a new concept for a geographical database system based on the homotopy model. Many researchers have been interested in the development of terrain visualization systems for more than ten years now. For the large amounts of terrain data, efficient data structures are required. There are several ways to tackle this problem.

One way is to construct fractal-based data structures. This method identifies a fractal dimension D of the terrain data, and reconstructs the surfaces from less data using the fractal with fractal dimension D (Miller 1986; Agui, Miyata and Nakajima 1986; Musgrave, Kolb and Mace 1989; Brivio, Marini, Marotta and Righetti 1991) . It is well known that terrain data has fractal structures. Proper estimation of the fractal dimension will raise the quality of the reconstructed surfaces.

Other researchers introduce classification of the terrain data according to the topological structures (Pfaltz 1976; Peucker and Douglas 1975; Watson, Laffey and Haralick 1985; Falcidieno, Pienovi and Spagnuolo 1991) . The additional data provides simplicity for the topologically complicated data, though the data construction requires significant time.

The fractal-based data structures include no topological characteristics of the terrain data. Classified data structures cannot describe the precisely geometrical characteristics of the terrain data. If we describe topological characteristics and geometrical characteristics simultaneously, we will obtain other possible ways of treating the terrain data.

The terrain data can be obtained in the form of a series of contours as well as in the form of mesh structures. The homotopy model (Shinagawa, Kunii, Nomura, Okuno and Hara 1989; Shinagawa and Kunii 1991) was proposed for the surface reconstruction of an object with a complex shape from a series of contours. The homotopy model is applicable to widespread categories, and terrain visualization is not an exception. If we neglect the over-hang, the terrain data has comparatively less complexity and the Reeb graph forms a tree structure. This fact enables us to attend to the terrain data in another way.

In this paper, the continuous version of the toroidal graph (Shinagawa and Kunii 1991) is extended to a new type of toroidal graph (in this paper, it is called a multiple toroidal graph or MTG) that represents the relationship among multiple contours. The MTG composes the data structure (in this paper, an MTG-tree). The MTG-tree structure corresponds to the Reeb graph of the terrain. An MTG-tree represents topological characteristics with the structure and represents geometrical characteristics with the associated values.

In Section 2, the homotopy model overview is presented. Then we explain the MTG representation in Section 3. Handling of branching and merging of contours at the critical points are also described here. In Section 4, we describe the querying method on MTG-tree. Finally, Section 5 concludes with possible applications of the MTG-tree.

2. HOMOTOPY MODEL

The homotopy model is a generalized model to reconstruct surfaces from a series of contour lines using continuous deformation represented by homotopy. This model solved various problems of the triangulation method which is a traditional method, and the most popular. The problems arise from discontinuity in the triangular mesh.

The model includes three components: Reeb graph, surface reconstruction using homotopy, and toroidal graph representation.

2.1 Reeb Graph

The Reeb graph represents the topological structure of the 3-D object. It is defined as follows (Shinagawa, Kunii, Nomura, Okuno and Young 1990) :

Definition 1 Let $f : \mathrm{M} \rightarrow \mathrm{R}$ be a real value function on a manifold M. The Reeb graph of f is the quotient space of the graph of f in $\mathrm{M} \times \mathrm{R}$ by the equivalence relation $\sim$ given below:

$(X_1, y_1) \sim (X_2, y_2)$ holds if and only if $y_1 = y_2$ and $X_1 and X_2$ are in the same connected component of $f^{-1}(y_1)$ where $y_1 = f(X_1)$ and $y_2 = f(X_2)$. □

By considering the Reeb graph of the height function h which gives the height of the point on the manifold R^3, we can see that all the contour lines of each cross sectional plane are represented by a point on the Reeb graph. We also recognize that the nodes of the Reeb graph represent the cross sectional planes which include the critical points. Here, and throughout this paper, "Reeb graph" means the Reeb graph of the height function h.

2.2 Surface Reconstruction Using Homotopy

Once the Reeb graph of the object is obtained, one can reconstruct surfaces between adjacent contours which are represented by the same edge. In the homotopy model, each i-th contour line is parameterized by a variable $s \in [0,1]$ and represented by a function

$f_i : [0,1] \rightarrow \mathrm{R}^2$.
The surface reconstructed between f_i and f_{i+1} is represented by a homotopy:

$F : \mathrm{R} \times [0,1] \rightarrow \mathrm{R}^2$
such that $F(s,0) = f_i(s)$ and $F(s,1) = f_{i+1}(s)$ for all points , where $s \in [0,1]$.

If adjacent contour lines are not homeomorphic, branch handling is done by introducing a virtual contour line between the two contours such that the two loops are joined together at one point.

2.3 Toroidal Graph Representation

In reconstruction of the surface between complicated contour lines, proper correspondence is needed between the points on adjacent contours to avoid reconstructing folded or twisted surfaces. The toroidal graph represents these correspondences. If the toroidal graph between the contours is represented by a monotonically increasing function $U : [0,1] \rightarrow [0,1]$, the homotopy that represents the surface between the contours is $F(s,t)$ such that $F(s,0) = f_i(s)$ and $F(s,1) = f_{i+1}(U(s))$.

3. THE DATA STRUCTURE USING MULTIPLE TOROIDAL GRAPH REPRESENTATION

This section presents the definition of the MTG, then describes the construction of the MTG-tree and the handling of critical points in it. In this section, all the contours are parameterized as described above.

3.1 MTG

Let $f_0, f_1, \cdots, f_i$ be a sequence of contours which are homeomorphic, $h_j (j = 0, \cdots, i)$ be the height of f_j and $U_k (k = 0, \cdots, i-1)$ be the function which represents the toroidal graph between f_k and f_{k+1}. Then the MTG of the sequence of the contours is defined as follows:

Definition 2 Let there be a function $f : [0,1] \times \mathrm{R} \rightarrow \mathrm{R}^2$ such that $f(s, h_j) = f_j(s)$ and a function $U : [0,1] \times \mathrm{R} \rightarrow \mathrm{R}$ such that $U(s, h_0) = s$ and $U(s, h_j) = U_0^{-1}(U_1^{-1}(\cdots(U_{j-1}^{-1}(s))\cdots))(j = 1, \cdots, i)$, where $s \in [0,1]$. A pair of these functions (f, U) is called the *MTG* of the contours $f_0, \cdots, f_i$. The domain of the f and U functions, namely, the space $[0,1] \times [h_0, h_i]$, is called the *MTG sheet*. □

Figure 1 illustrates an example of a series of contour lines and its MTG sheet. f is hard to show in the sheet, but U can be illustrated by some locuses of points that have a value equal to some sampling value. Since each U_k is monotonically increasing, the locuses do not intersect each other.

Then, the reconstructed surface using MTG is represented by a series of homotopy: $F_k : \mathrm{R} \times [0,1] \rightarrow \mathrm{R}^2$ such that $F_k(s,0) = f(s, h_k)$ and $F_k(s,1) = f(s', h_{k+1})$ for all points $s \in [0,1]$ where $s' \in [0,1]$ is a number with which $U(s, h_k) = U(s', h_{k+1})$ holds.

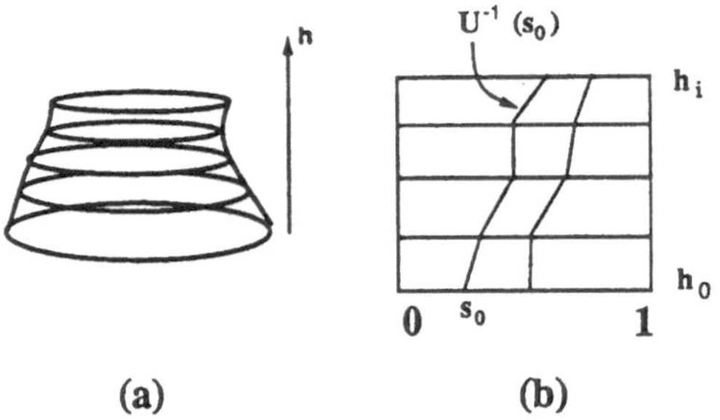

Fig. 1. (a) A series of contours (b) The corresponding multiple toroidal graph

The following proposition ensures that the reconstruction described above is meaningful.

Proposition 1 For each $k = 0, \cdots, i-1$, the homotopy F_k from $f(s, h_k)$ to $f(s, h_{k+1})$ can be defined as described above. F_k is also the homotopy from f_k to f_{k+1} such that $F_k(s, 0) = f_k(s)$ and $F_k(s, 1) = f_{k+1}(U_k(s))$.

Proof Obviously, $f(s, h_k) = f_k(s)$. Because f_k and $f_{k+1}(k = 0, \cdots, i-1)$ are homeomorphic, the homotopy F_k exists. We now only need to prove the equation $s' = U_k(s)$. By Definition 2, $U(s, h_k) = U_0^{-1}(U_1^{-1}(\cdots(U_{k-1}^{-1}(s))\cdots))$. On the other hand, $U(U_k(s), h_{k+1}) = U_0^{-1}(U_1^{-1}(\cdots(U_{(k+1)-1}^{-1}(U_k(s)))\cdots)) = U_0^{-1}(U_1^{-1}(\cdots(U_{k-1}^{-1}(s))\cdots))$. Therefore, $U(s, h_k) = U(U_k(s), h_{k+1})$. This implies that $s' = U_k(s)$. □

Proposition 1 can also hold with other definitions of f and U. For example, f can be defined such that $f(s, h_k) = f_k(U_{k-1}(U_{k-2}(\cdots(U_0(s))\cdots)))(k = 1, \cdots, j)$ and U can be defined such that $U(s, h_k) = s$. In this definition, U is meaningless and MTG can be constructed with f only. This suggests a possibility of reducing the amount of data in MTG-tree. The current method needs flexible behavior from U in the handling branching, so we define MTG as Definition 2.

Now, the second parameter of $fandU$ is not necessarily restricted to h_k. Namely, the contours can be non-planar curves, unless the following conditions are satisfied:

- The contours are closed curves.
- The contours are homeomorphic to each other.
- The contours do not intersect each other.
- $U(s, t)$ is monotonically increasing with respect to s. In other words, $\frac{\partial U}{\partial s} > 0$ holds for all $s \in [0, 1], t \in [h_0, h_i]$.

A series of homotopy F_k which represents surface reconstruction can be formulated in a way similar to the case of planar contours.

3.2 Handling of Critical Points

We have proposed the MTG. The MTG can be used only for surface reconstruction between contours homeomorphic to each other. In other words, we can reconstruct the surface between contours which are represented by points on the same edge of the Reeb graph.

It is often the case that the contour lines branch or merge at critical points. Given terrain data, we have many MTG sheets equal in number to the edges of the Reeb graph. Each MTG sheet is connected to another MTG sheet if the edges of the Reeb graph corresponding to the MTG sheets are connected. The Reeb graph of the terrain data forms a tree structure(Figure 3). So we call the complete set of the connected MTG sheets an MTG-tree.

Introducing a virtual pit under the whole contours (Figure 2), it can be said that the mountaineer's equation (e.g. Griffiths 1981) $\#pits + \#peaks - \#passes = 2$ holds[1].

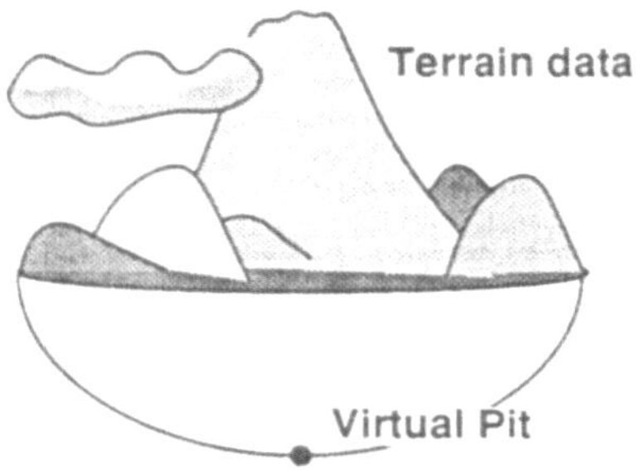

Fig. 2. Adding the virtual pit

To detect the relationships between MTG sheets and critical points, the surface network (Pfaltz 1976) is useful. Throughout the rest of this part, we use the words ridges and courses to mean the same as in Pfaltz 1976.

To simplify, some assumptions are made before going forward:

Assumption 1

- **1-1** All the critical points are non-degenerate[2].
- **1-2** The critical points, ridges, and courses were all obtained previously.
- **1-3** No two critical points are at the same height.
- **1-4** The terrain data has enough information such that it is possible to find contours between every pair of critical points.

[1] The right hand of the mountaineer's equation is in general $\chi(S)$. With a virtual pit, we can assume that the terrain is homeomorphic to sphere, and $\chi(Sphere) = 2$.

[2] For example, the detail description of non-degenerate can be found in Milnor 1963.

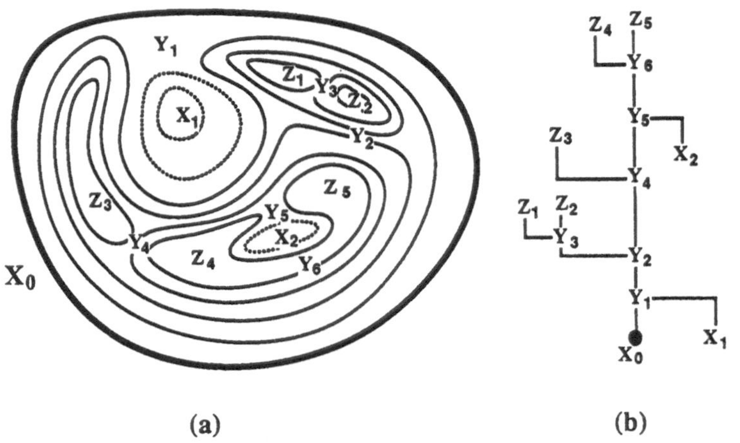

Fig. 3. An example: (a) is a set of contours and critical points. (b) is the Reeb graph of these points

3.2.1 Structural Limitation of Reeb Graph of Terrain Data

The Reeb graph puts some limitation on the structure, because the terrain data is usually defined in the form of $height = f(x, y)$. We start this discussion with a definition:

Definition 3 A contour line is called *normal* if the object exists in its interior and is called *reverse* if the object exists in its exterior. □

Roughly speaking, the reverse contour represents a contour around a basin. Because terrains are spatially limited, the outermost contour line must be a normal contour line. We must distinguish reverse contours from normal contours.

The above leads us to find a classification of the deformation of the contours in scanning the contours from lowest to highest. By assumptions 1-3 and 1-4, it can be generally shown that when a pass point exists, the two contour lines below it merge together into one contour line above it, or one contour line below it divides into two contour lines above it (Figure 4). There are two cases in merging or dividing contours. One is the case of merging two contour lines when one includes the other. The other case is the case of merging two contour lines when neither includes the other. So there are four deformation types of contour.

In the case of terrain data, these four types restrict the types of contour lines. For example, merging no-including contours into one contour line can be done with reverse contour lines. Figure 5 shows details of the classification and their corresponding Reeb graph. In each of (a)~(d), the picture to the left of the arrow represent the contours below a pass while that to the right represents the contours above a pass. Between both contours, there is no other critical point than the pass marked with a cross.

The rightmost pictures show the part of the Reeb graph corresponding to each deformation type. Edges drawn with a thick line correspond to normal contours. These drawn with a thin line correspond to reverse contours.

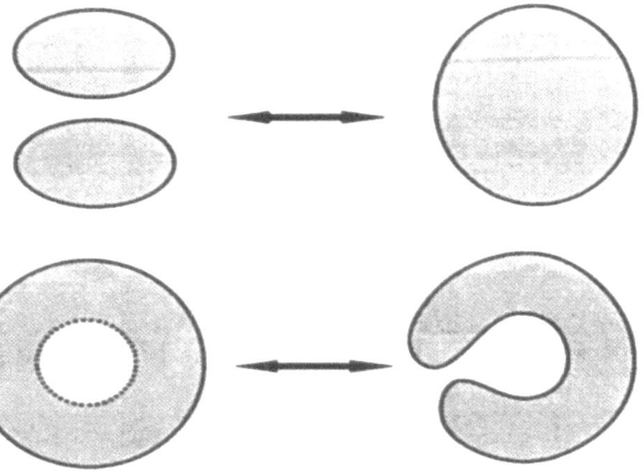

Fig. 4. Four deformation types of contours in the neighborhood of a pass (in general)

Now, we can describe the method to connect the MTG sheets. Let us start with a simple case, that is, a peak and a pit.

3.2.2 Peak and Pit

Construction of the MTG which includes a peak or pit is very simple. Scanning the contour lines from the bottom up, the contour lines are produced at the pits and vanish at the peaks. No MTG sheet is connected at the top of the MTG sheet which contains the peak or at the bottom of the MTG sheet which contains the pit.

In this case, the MTG $= (f, U)$ must satisfy the condition: $f(s,1) = P_{peak}$ or $f(s,0) = P_{pit}$ for all $s \in [0,1]$ where P_{peak} is the position of the peak and P_{pit} is the position of the pit. Figure 6 illustrates the case of the peak.

3.2.3 Pass

By the discussion in Section 3.2.1, it is sufficient that we show the connection corresponding to (a)~(d) in Figure 5. (a)~(d) can all be treated similarly. Like most other methods, we handle a branching or a merging by assuming a virtual contour line which includes the pass.

Figure 7 shows the outline of the case for (a) while Figure 8 shows that for (b). We can see that the virtual contour plays the role of an additional non-planar contour in MTG and that the function U is extended to be defined on three MTG sheets such that continuity is preserved. The connection of MTG sheets is topologically equivalent to the Reeb graph. In (c) and (d), branching and merging can be defined similarly.

Let us present a formal definition of branching in the case of (a)(see Figure 7). Other cases can be discussed in a similar way.

Let P_{pass} be the position of the pass. Let $MTG_l = (f_l, U_l)$ be the multiple toroidal graph of lower contour lines, and let $MTG_{h1} = (f_{h1}, U_{h1})$ and $MTG_{h2} = (f_{h2}, U_{h2})$ be these of higher contour lines. The sheet of MTG_l is $[0,1] \times [h_0, h_v]$ and the sheet of MTG_{h1} and MTG_{h2} is $[0,1] \times [h_v, h_n]$ where h_0 is the height of the bottom of the lower contours, h_v is the height of the pass, and h_n is the

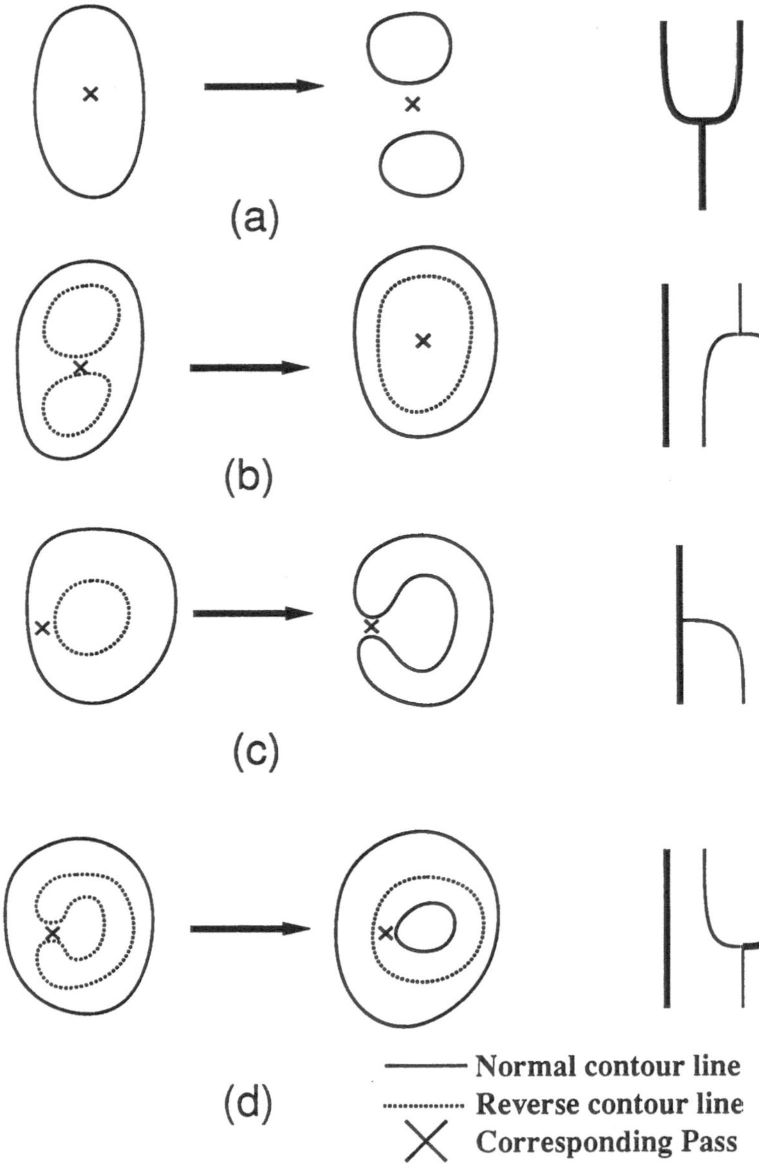

Fig. 5. Four deformation types of contours in the neighborhood of a pass (Terrain) and their corresponding Reeb graphs

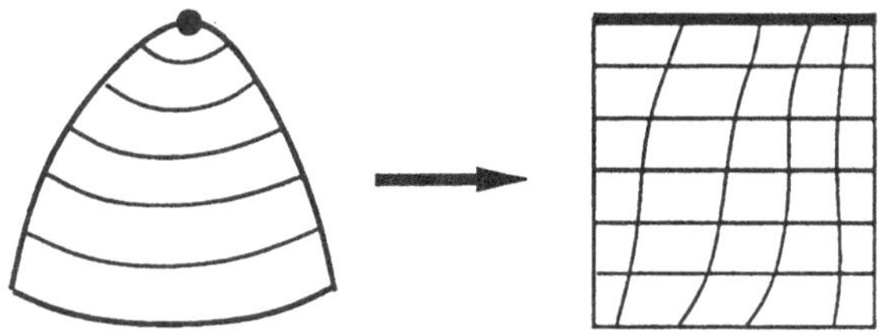

Fig. 6. MTG construction for the contours which include a peak.

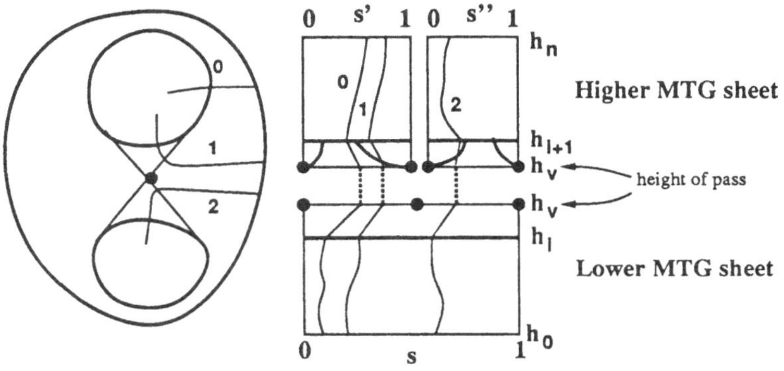

Fig. 7. Branching MTG sheet

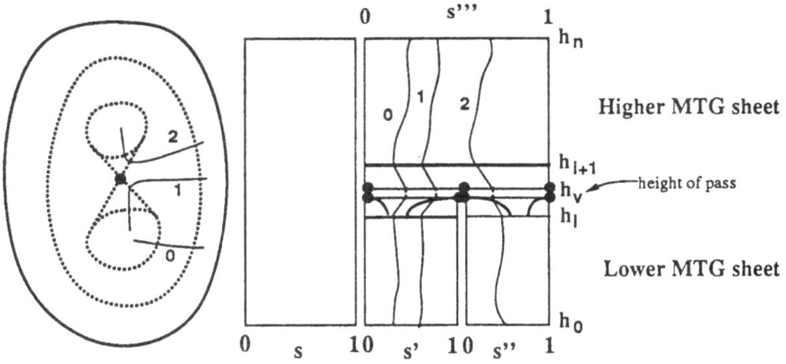

Fig. 8. Merging MTG sheet

height of the top of the higher contours. Let h_i be the height of the highest contour among the value attached contours in MTG_l and let h_{i+1} be the height of the lowest contour among the value attached contours in MTG_{h1} and MTG_{h2}.

To preserve the feature of U, i.e. $\frac{\partial U}{\partial s} > 0$, we must put P_{pass} on the $f(s, h_v)$ line in MTG sheets such that

$$\begin{array}{lllll} & f_l(0, h_v) & = & f_l(\frac{1}{2}, h_v) & = f_l(1, h_v) \\ = & f_{h1}(0, h_v) & = & f_{h1}(1, h_v) & \\ = & f_{h2}(0, h_v) & = & f_{h2}(1, h_v) & \\ = & P_{pass} & & & \end{array}$$

hold. In this constraint, we extend $U_l, U_{h1}, and U_{h2}$ on the regions $[0,1] \times [h_i, h_v], [0,1] \times [h_v, h_{i+1}], and [0,1] \times [h_v, h_{i+1}]$ respectively.

We make the virtual contour represented by a continuous function $c_{h1}(s')$ on the sheet of MTG_{h1} such that $c_{h1}(0) = c_{h1}(0) = P_{pass}$ and for all $s \in [s_s, s_e], c_{h1}(s) = f_{h1}(s)$ for $\exists s_s, \exists s_e \in [0, 1]$.

$U_l, U_{h1}, and U_{h2}$ is relate to each other by the following equations:

$$\begin{array}{lll} U_{h1}(s * 2, h_v) & = U_l(s, h_v) & \text{for all } s \in [0, \frac{1}{2}], \\ U_{h2}(s * 2 - 1, h_v) & = U_l(s, h_v) & \text{for all } s \in [\frac{1}{2}, 1]. \end{array}$$

From the above, MTG sheets are branched and U still allows us to trace the locuses of points which have equal value. So surfaces can be reconstructed under the branching while preserving the continuity and smoothness.

4. CONSTRUCTION OF GEOGRAPHICAL DATABASE

This section discusses the construction of an MTG-tree. The MTG-tree is homomorphical to a binary tree, so all the MTG sheets can be arranged in a 2-dimensional rectangular. Therefore, the whole MTG-tree is described on the rectangular as a set of scattered records. Each record consists of three real numbers, that is, $X_i, Y_i, and U_i$ which correspond to $f_x(s, h), f_y(s, h), and U(s, h)$ respectively.

Surface reconstruction is essentially equivalent to querying geometrical information (e.g. height, slope, and curvature.) for given position parameters x and y. The query is performed in MTG-tree as follows:

Algorithm 1

1 Search through the MTG-tree for the nearest point to (x, y), i.e. search for the parameter (s_m, h_m) that minimizes the norm $|(x, y) - f(s_m, h_m)|$.

2 Look around the (s_m, h_m) on the MTG and get four sets of points which exists in different directions. More formally, find the sets

$$\begin{array}{lll} Upper_{s_m,h_m} & = & \{f(s, h) \mid (|U(s, h) - U(s_m, h_m)| < \delta U) \wedge (h > h_m)\}, \\ Lower_{s_m,h_m} & = & \{f(s, h) \mid (|U(s, h) - U(s_m, h_m)| < \delta U) \wedge (h < h_m)\}, \\ Right_{s_m,h_m} & = & \{f(s, h) \mid (|h - h_m| < \delta h) \wedge (s > s_m)\}, \\ Left_{s_m,h_m} & = & \{f(s, h) \mid (|h - h_m| < \delta h) \wedge (s < s_m)\}, \end{array}$$

where δU and δh are the maximum interval of adjacent values of U and h respectively(Figure 9).

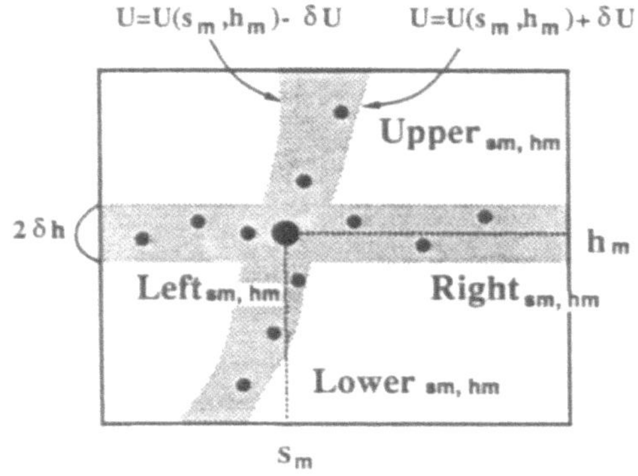

Fig. 9. Search a neighborhood in four directions

3 Find a certain number of the nearest points in the four directions. In other words, for a certain integer k, set $P_{upper,j}(j = 1, \cdots, k)$ such that $|(x,y) - P_{upper,1}| \leq |(x,y) - P_{upper,2}| \leq \cdots \leq |(x,y) - P_{upper,k}| \leq |(x,y) - P|$ where $P \in Upper_{s_m,h_m} - \{P_{upper,j}(j = 1, \cdots, k)\}$. Similarly, we can set $P_{lower,j}, P_{right,j}, and P_{left,j}$.

4 The geometric information can be interpolated using the set of points $\{P_{upper,j}, P_{lower,j}, P_{right,j}, P_{left,j}(j = 1, \cdots, k)\}$. □

Step 1 of Algorithm 1 requires a search for points on the MTG sheet with given x and y values. On the MTG sheet, $f(s,h)$ shows no monotonical characteristics with respect to s and h. This tells us that it seems that the search cannot be performed in time less than $O(n)$, where n denotes the number of data in the whole MTG-tree.

To introduce the monotonical characteristics of $f(s,h)$, we attach an additional data, i.e. a minimum rectangular that includes a contour. For a given h, let $Region_h(f)$ denote the minimum rectangular $[x_{min}, x_{max}] \times [y_{min}, y_{max}]$ where $x_{min} \leq f_x(s,h) \leq x_{max}$ and $y_{min} \leq f_y(s,h) \leq y_{max}$ for all $s \in [0,1]$.

As far as we go with the terrain data, it can be said that for all $h_0 < h_1$ such that $f(s,h_0)$ and $f(s,h_1)$ are both normal contours and are represented in the same MTG sheet, $Region_{h_0}(f) \supseteq Region_{h_1}(f)$ holds. For reverse contours, $Region_{h_0}(f) \subseteq Region_{h_1}(f)$ holds. Therefore, we can develop a more efficient search algorithm for Step 1 of Algorithm 1.

Algorithm 2

1 Find MTG sheets in which $(x,y) \notin Region_{h_{max}}(f)$ and $(x,y) \in Region_{h_{min}}(f)$ hold, where $h_{max} and h_{min}$ are the maximum and minimum values of h in the MTG respectively.

2 For each MTG sheet found in 1, search for the adjacent value of h_i and h_{i+1} with which $(x,y) \in Region_{h_i}(f)$ and $(x,y) \notin Region_{h_{i+1}}(f)$ hold.

3 Search the nearest point to (x,y) between contours $f(s,h_i)$ and $f(s,h_{i+1})$. □

With a binary search, Step 1 executes in time $O(\log N_e)$ where N_e denotes the number of edges in the MTG-tree. Step 2 needs execution time $O(\log N_h)$ where N_h denotes the number of contour lines in an MTG sheet. Step 3 cannot adopt a binary search or such an efficient searching algorithm and executes in time $O(N_s)$ where N_s denotes the number of data in a contour line. Therefore, the time complexity of Algorithm 2 is $O(\log N_e \log N_h + N_s)$. On the other hand, Step 1 of Algorithm 1 requires time $O(N_e \cdot N_h \cdot N_s)$ in the initial version.

The other steps in Algorithm 1 can be executed in time $O(k)$. We can see that Algorithm 1 is executed in time $O(\log N_e \log N_h + N_s + k)$.

5. CONCLUSION

We have presented a new concept for construction of a geographical database system, MTG-tree. The MTG-tree consists of a set of MTG sheets. MTG sheets are rectangular regions in R^2 and an MTG is defined for each of them. Surfaces are interpolated by the homotopy using MTG representations. The MTG-tree represents topological characteristics and geometrical characteristics simultaneously.

The MTG-tree is applicable in various use of the terrain data. The following are some examples we studying now.

MTG-tree can reduce amount of the terrain data while still preserving topological characteristics. A flat region is represented by four points on the MTG-tree. Unlike in the mesh structure, a flat region is not necessarily rectangular.

Deformation of the terrain data (e.g., erosion and the generation of folds.) may cause critical points to vanish or appear. The MTG-tree can handle this by merging MTG sheets or dividing a MTG sheet.

Because the terrain data has fractal structures, the MTG-tree has fractal structures. This fractal based approach is applicable for MTG-tree construction.

There is an important disadvantage to the MTG-tree: inefficiency. A point in the MTG-tree consists of three numbers, where the mesh structure requires one number at each mesh point. Moreover, in visualizing a region of the terrain data, one must get all the contours which include the region. This data can be excessive. Clustering points on contours according to Gaussian curvature solves the latter. Study on this is also being conducted.

ACKNOWLEDGMENT

The authors thank Mr. S. Nishimura, Mr. K. Maeda, Mr. H. Saji and Mr. T. Tsukioka for their constructive suggestions and comments.

REFERENCES

Agui T, Miyata K, Nakajima M (1986) "A Reconstructing Method of 3D Mountainous Shapes from Contours". *Transactions, IEICE*, J69-D(12):1905–1912. in Japanese.

Brivio PA, Marini D, Marotta M, Righetti M (1991) "Fractal Approaches to Digital Terrain Modeling". In: *Proceendings of the Eurographics Workshop on Computer Graphics and Mathematics*, Springer-Verlag. Genova - Italy, pp. 173–191.

Falcidieno B, Pienovi C, Spagnuolo M (1991) "Discrete Surface Models: Constraint-based Generation and Understanding". In: *Proceendings of the Eurographics Workshop on Computer Graphics and Mathematics*, Springer-Verlag. Genova - Italy, pp. 107–121.

Griffiths HB (1981) *Surfaces.* Cambridge University Press, Cambridge, 2nd edition.

Miller GSP (1986) "The Definition and Rendering of Terrain Maps". *Computer Graphics (SIGGRAPH '86 proc.)*, 20(4):39–48.

Milnor J (1963) *Morse Theory.* Princeton University Press, Princeton, New Jersey.

Musgrave FK, Kolb CE, Mace RS (1989) "The Synthesis and Rendering of Eroded Fractal Terrains". *Computer Graphics (SIGGRAPH '89 proc.)*, 23(3):41–50.

Nackman LR (1984) "Two-Dimensional Critical Point Configuration Graphs". *IEEE Transaction on Pattern Analysis and Machine Intelligence*, 6(4):442–450.

Peucker TK, Douglas DH (1975) "Detection of Surface-Specific Points by Local Parallel Processing of Discrete Terrain Elevation Data". *Computer Graphics and Image Processing*, 4:375–387.

Pfaltz JL (1976) "Surface Networks". *Geographical Analysis*, 8:77–93.

Shinagawa Y, Kunii TL (1991) "The Homotopy Model: A Generalized Model for Smooth Surface Generation from Cross Sectional Data". *The Visual Computer*, 7:72–86.

Shinagawa Y, Kunii TL, Kergosien YL (1991) "Surface Coding Based on Morse Theory". *IEEE Computer Graphics & Applications*, 11:66–78.

Shinagawa Y, Kunii TL, Nomura Y, Okuno T, Hara M (1989) "Reconstructing Smooth Surfaces from a Series of Contour Lines Using a Homotopy". In: Earnshaw RA, Wyvill B, editors, *New Advances in Computer Graphics*, Springer-Verlag. Tokyo, Berlin, Heiderberg, New York, London, Paris, Hong Kong, pp. 147-161.

Shinagawa Y, Kunii TL, Nomura Y, Okuno T, Young Y (1990) "Automating View Function Generation for Walk-through Animation Using a Reeb Graph". In: Thalmann NM, Thalmann D, editors, *Computer Animation '90*, Springer-Verlag. Tokyo, Berlin, Heiderberg, New York, London, Paris, Hong Kong, pp. 227–237.

Watson LT, Laffey TJ, Haralick RM (1985) "Topographic Classification of Digital Image Intensity Surfaces Using Generalized Splines and the Discrete Cosine Transformation". *Computer Vision, Graphics, and Image Processing*, 29:143–167.

AUTHOR'S BIOGRAPHIES

Tetsuya Ikeda is currently a master course graduate student of the University of Tokyo. His research interests include computer graphics, computational geometry and computer animation. He received the B.Sc. degrees in information science from the University of Tokyo in 1991. He is a student member of ACM and IPSJ. **Address:** Department of Information Science, Faculty of Science, the University of Tokyo, 7-3-1 Hongo, Bunkyo-Ku, Tokyo, 113 Japan

Tosiyasu L. Kunii is currently Professor of Information and Computer Science, the University of Tokyo. At the University of Tokyo, he started his work in raster computer graphics in 1968 which was let to the Tokyo Raster Technology Project. His research interests include computer graphics, database systems, and software engineering. He authored and edited over 32 computer science books, and published over 120 refereed academic/technical papers in computer science and applications areas.

Dr.Kunii is Founder of the Computer Graphics Society, Editor-in-Chief of *The Visual Computer: An International Journal of Computer Graphics* (Springer-Verlag), Associate Editor-in-Chief of *The Journal of Visualization and Computer Animation* (John Wiley & Sons) and on the Editorial Board of *IEEE Transactions on Knowledge and Data Engineering*, *VLDB Journal* and *IEEE Computer Graphics and Applications.* He is on the IFIP Modeling and Simulation Working Group, the IFIP Data Base Working Group and the IFIP Computer Graphics Working Group. He is on the board of directors of Japan Society of Sports Industry and also of Japan Society of Simulation and Gaming.

He received the B.Sc., M.Sc., and D.Sc. degrees in chemistry all from the University of Tokyo in 1962, 1964, and 1967, respectively. He is a fellow of IEEE and a member of ACM, BCS, IPSJ and IEICE.

Address: Department of Information Science, Faculty of Science, the University of Tokyo, 7-3-1 Hongo, Bunkyo-Ku, Tokyo, 113 Japan

Yoshihisa Shinagawa is currently a Pesearch Associate of the Department of Information Science of the University of Tokyo. His research interests include computer graphics and its applications. He received the B.Sc. and M.Sc. degrees in information science from the University of Tokyo in 1987 and 1990 respectively. He is a member of the IEEE Computer Society, ACM, IPSJ and IEICE. **Address:** Department of Information Science, Faculty of Science, the University of Tokyo, 7-3-1 Hongo, Bunkyo-Ku, Tokyo, 113 Japan

Minoru Ueda is currently a technical advisor to Wavefront Japan Ltd. and CSK Corp. He started his work in remote sensing and global climatic model projects at NASA Goddard Flight Center for Space Studies NY NY in 1975. Engaged in reservoir modelling workstation project at Nipon Schlumberger Co. Ltd.

Ueda received his BSc and MA in geoscience from Kyoto University in 1966 and 1972. Ph.D in regional science from Columbia University in 1983.

A Case Study for Building a Database and 3-D Visualization in Geomorphology

Minoru Ueda, Tetsuya Ikeda, Tosiyasu L. Kunii, and Yoshihisa Shinagawa

ABSTRACT

The study of global environmental problems poses two technical challenges to the graphic capabilities of today's workstation. The first is the construction of a more compact geographical information database to store complex land and marine geomorphologies (irregular but mathematically homeomorphic to a plane). The second is the development of better 3-D visualization tools to scan the area of interest. The most popular approach today is to represent topologies as 3-D polygonal surfaces consisting of triangular patches, and to store this topographic data in a simple uniform grid system.
With an ideal fractal structure, the entire image can be reconstructed through contraction mapping. The reproduced topography may then be graphically represented as a series of homotopic surfaces. The actual geomorphology of a given area is the result of interaction between crustal movements and local climate dependent erosion. The landscape patterns created by this selective erosional process are observed on a scale of 1000 square km. To measure the deviation from the ideal fractal structure, a trial measurement was taken for the island of Hokkaido, Japan.

Keywords: GIS (geographical information system), GTM (digital terrain model), selective erosional process, fractal, homotopy

INTRODUCTION

The intention of this paper is to summarize recent developments in Geographical Information Systems (GIS), and to propose a set of consistent guidelines for the storage and 3-D representation of geographical data, regardless of area size and mapping scale.

Classic geomorphology was established around the First World War, as major expeditions into the deep interior regions of Africa, the central Asia and the polar regions were successful.The explorers mostly recorded the locations of villages and outlines of their routes. Precise land surveys were carried out by army survey squads from developed countries: on a scale of 1:50,000 in their own countries and on a scale of about 1:500,000 in their overseas colonies. As for oceans,surveys and soundings only were done along the coastal zones and in shallow bays by coastal based military forces.

This geographical knowledge was presented as printed maps, using adequate projection methods such as Mercatol or multi-conic projections. Based upon these accumulated measurements, geoscientists classified landscapes. But they covered only a small part of the earth's surface and the measurements were done from mere morphological point of view, with very little understanding of the prevailing mechanisms of the earth.

The crucial weakpoint in classic geomorphology was that the concepts (e.g. basin and bay) reflect only topological features, ignoring the absolute size so that the small Kyoto Basin (10x20Km) and Silicon Valley CA. (100x500Km) were regarded as being in the same intermountain flat land category.

Even though it was still premature, A. Penck proposed a project to map the entire surface of the globe at a scale of 1 to 1 million, at the First International Geographic Conference held in 1905.

After World War II, echo sounding technology started supplying topographic data on deep ocean floors with an error of ten meters, for the sake of the US navy's global strategy establishment. As a byproduct, the data let geophysicists explore the theory of "global plate tectonics", which is regarded as integrated achievements of centuries of study on inner crustal movements. Worldwide oil and gas exploration efforts have accumulated enormous amounts of geographical and geological data on recent sediments and ancient sedimetary rocks. It resulted in establishment of modern sedimentology in the early 1970's.

By the mid 1980's, laser-beam triangulation from geodetic satellites begin to provide precise land topological with an error of ten meters. In addition, remote sensing satellites are providing meteorological data and geographical data such as surface vegetation cover and water quality information at 40 m resolution, on a worldwide and almost real-time basis. Since the late 1980's, the French satellite SPOT has provided stereoscopic data at 20 m resolution. Based upon this new knowledge, there has been the large scale topographic classification from the viewpoint of morphology in association with better understanding of the mechanisms of inner and outer processes (the selective erosional process). Figure 1 illustrates this.

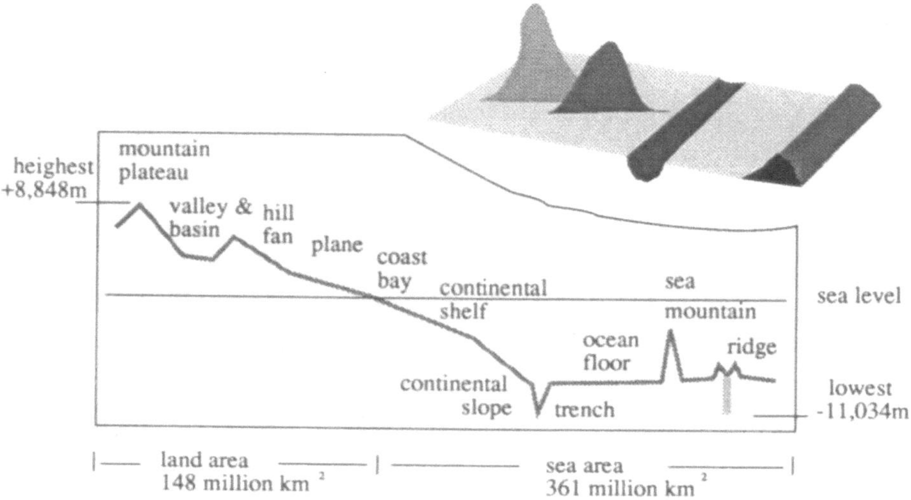

Fig. 1 Land and Ocean

Penck's dream was realized when the Operational Navigation Chart series mapping at a scale of 1:1,000,000 and prepared by the US Air Force, completed coverage of the entire globe. As an aside, note that world atlases have been traditionally prepared by superpowers of the time for their own global management needs.
For the first time in history, we are equipped to look at any area of the globe in the scale most relevant to our needs. As we approach the new millennium, we are faced with the task of perfecting geographical database technologies and polishing the graphic tools used to display the wealth of data collected in 3-D represen tations (TAble 1).

Table 1 Achievements and Tasks in Geomorphology

	1930	1990	1992	2001 ??
known area	30% of land little sea	all land & sea		
accuracy	1:50,000 surveyed area	10cm on land 10m on sea		
classification	done on land little sea	done on land & sea		
inner mechanism	little on land none sea	better understanding on land & sea		

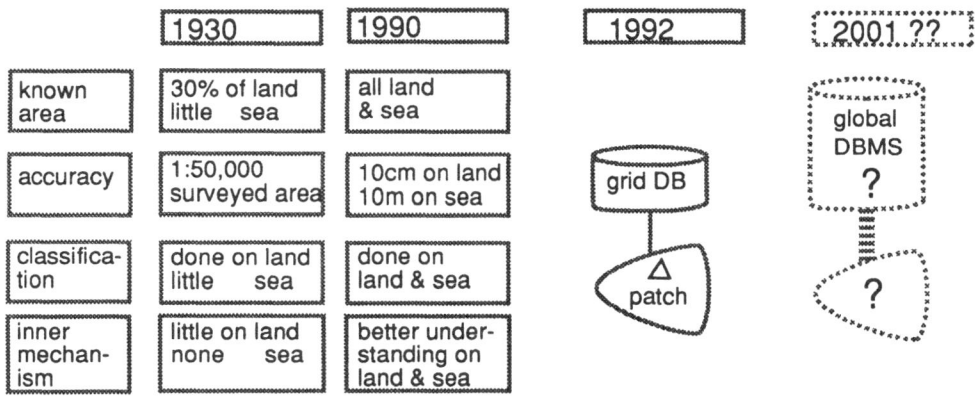

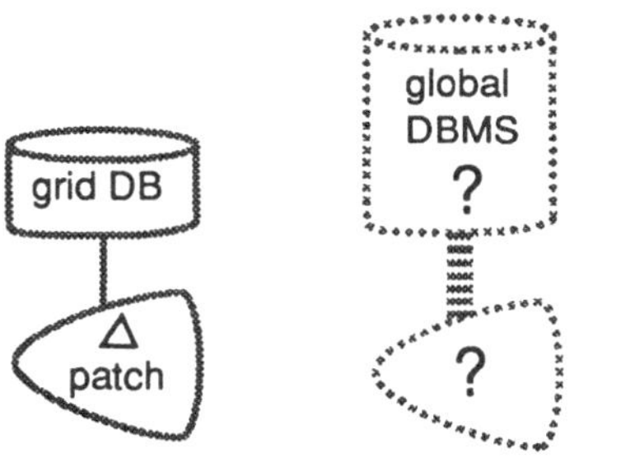

MODERN GEOGRAPHICAL INFORMATION SYSTEM AND DIGITAL TERAIN MODEL

As information technology advances, geoscientists are starting toAs information technology advances, geoscientists are starting to convert newly acquaired knowledge into digital data format and search for better visualization methods in computer graphics. This has been triggered by remote sensing data, which starts in digital form. The Japan Geographical Survey Institute started to build the National Numeric Database System in 1972 and completed it in 1985. It employed, literally, "human wave tactics". By drawing grid lines at 250 m intervals on 1:50,000 scale printed maps, many technicians manually calculated the average altitude of each mesh (Figure 2). (Automatic digitizing, which scans a printed map by CCD scanner and discriminates geographical items correctly, is still far from feasible, in spite of intensive research efforts.)

This is the same as using pixel (mesh) type data as remote sensing data (20-80m in resolution). Linear objects, such as roads and rivers are treated as sets of vector lines within each mesh. Thus, this GIS is a mixture of pixel type data and vector type data. The size of data volume (both physical and natural geography) is about 20 G byte.

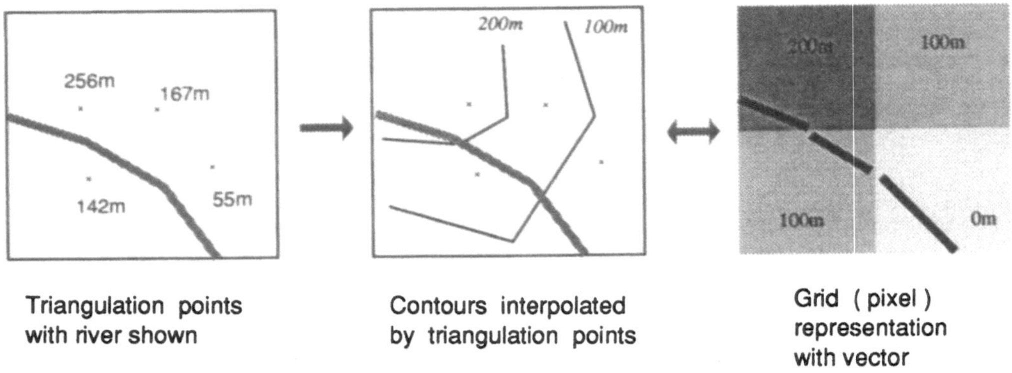

Fig . 2 Contour Representation and Grid Representation

Almost simultaneously, the US Geological Survey also completed their GIS, called TIGER, which covers all the states of the U.S.. It contains altitude data as mesh data, political boundaries, and major rivers as vector data, human settlements as point data. The total size is more than 19 G byte. Other developed countries are conducting similar projects.

The major characteristics of this database is its equal intervalled grid (mesh) system. Burrough (1986) states that this is just barely okey for today's DBMS capability, as long as it is limited to the national level.

Digital terrain models in the scales below may be considered empirically practical for the specific application listed:

A. Architectural & street planning : 1 Km
1:500 - 1:1,000 scale
B. City or town planning : 10 Km
1:5,000 - 1:10,000 scale
C. Agri-forest planning : 100 Km
1:50,000 - 1:100,000 scale
D. Global (& national) planning : 1000 Km
1:50 mil - 1:100 mil scale

For levels A,B, & C, we can assume the earth's surface to be flat. One image from a remote sensing satellite is 200 km x 200 km, which suits prefectural level regional planning. At level D, we must first assume that the earth is a sphere, then take a subset of it for planning of a national level. Texture mapping of the remotely sensed image of the earth taken by meteorological satellite is a good technique.

Special characteristics of GIS and its 3-D visualization

Database theory has been developed mostly for business applications. In CAD/CAM technology, searching for engineering database system is ongoing. The aim being to integrate both text data and graphics data. GIS can be regarded as a special case of the engineering database.

Unlike CAD/CAM applications, data in GIS consists of two major parts, because of user interests. One can be called "static data" and the other is "dynamic data".

A good example is a flight simulator, there the most important objective is to check the possible flight paths of movable objects (dynamic data). The user should play with dynamic data interactively represented by the same graphic primitives as in CAD/CAM. Landscape (static data) is mere background to help the user to understand the situation. The static data consists of natural geographical items (geomorphology, vegetation cover, drainage systems, etc) and human geographic items (cities, buildings, roads, railways, etc). In CAD/CAM, no matter how large the data volume, all data items are equally handled in an interactive way. In spite of the supportive role of static data, the volume is disproportionally large compared to the dynamic data in most of cases. A graphics workstation does not distinguish dynamic data from the total data volume. When the size of the static data is too large, the simulation program cannot run properly. Even with the best graphic workstation of 1992, the zoom and pan operation in 3-D mode for more than 2,000 patches becomes intolerably slow.

Recent Advances

3-D Graphic Representation

Modeling in computer graphics takes its origin from dealing with the shapes used in mechanical engineering. Starting from simple conic curves and surfaces in 3-D space, researchers have devised many highly sophisticated surfaces. Recently, all surfaces look like they will be integrated as family members of NURBS.

Compared to many graphic primitives used in CAD/CAM, graphic elements used in DTM (digital terrain model) are very simple.

A The largest volume of data is a polygon mesh consisting of triangular patches which show a 3-D geomorphological outlook of the area of interest.
B Lines for linear objects (roads, drainage systems, etc)
C Points for locations

B and C are generally smaller than type A data.

Thus, given identical hardware capabilities, better treatment of geomorphology is the key to improving the operational environment.

In spite of this, geoscientists and computer scientists who deal with DTM have become used to the triangular patch over the last 20 years.
In addition, there is no consistent guideline for when a researcher changes the scale of the 3-D display of an area (e.g. from 1:10,000 to 1:100,000 or vice versa).It is done arbitrarily.
Researchers devise specific temporal solutions.(e.g. study by Nakamae and Nishita (1989)).

Homotopy was first introduced into computer graphics to show complex human inner organs (Shinagawa et al(1991)). In 1991, Ikeda et al applied the homotopy concept to 3-D visualization of geomorphology, utilizing the concave and convex nature of valleys to the slope.

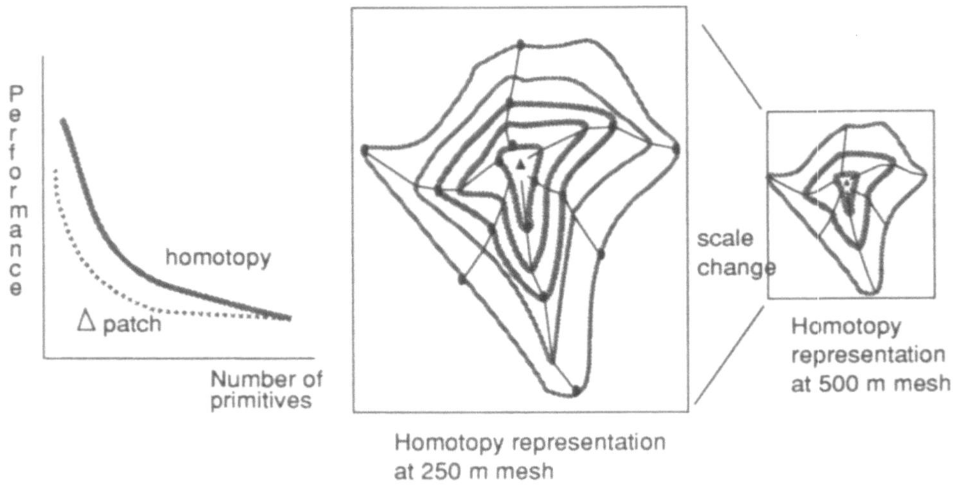

Fig. 3 Topological Features Preserved with Scale Change

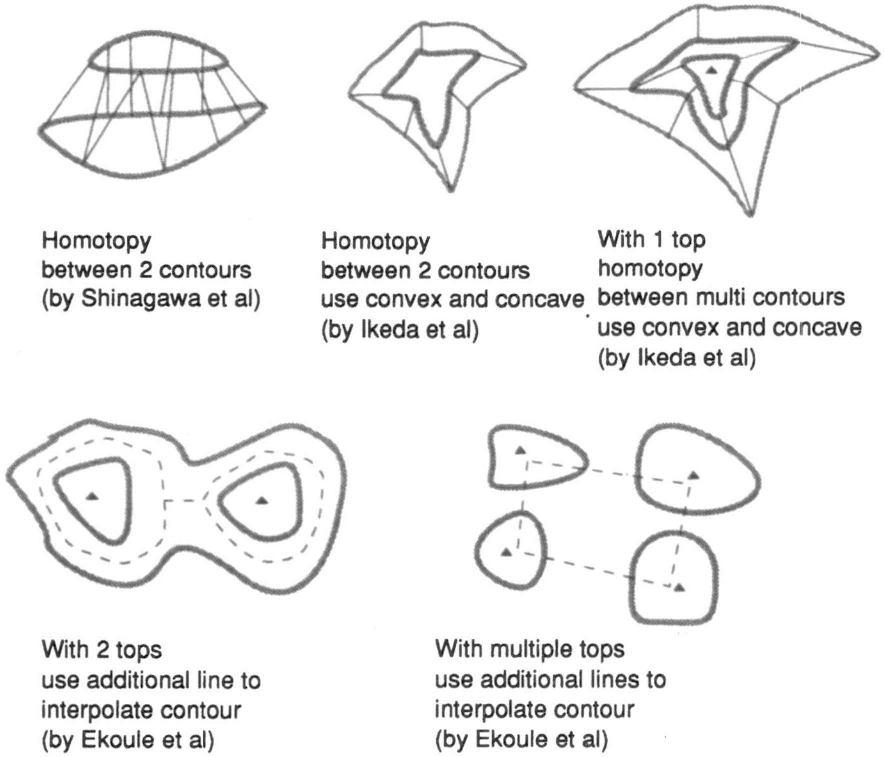

Fig. 4 Interpolation Contours and Patches

Ikeda tries to extend his approach to deal with multi-contours which have one common peak point. It is clear that homotopy approach gives far better 3-D visualization than triangular patches, when the same number of patches are given at a fixed map scale.

In addition, homotomy is the best at preserving the topological features of an area, when the display scale is change e.g. if the scale is changed from a 250 m mesh level via 500 m to 1 km level (Figure 4). *Thus, homotopy may provide a solution to the scale problem in classic geomorphology and GTM.*

For situations with multiple peaks, Ekoule et al (1991) presented a solution for a specific environment, even though, it uses triangular patches (Figure 4).

Other Data Storage Methods
Shinagawa and Kergosien (1991) have shown a way to represent 3-D structure as a set of singular points based on Morse Theory Tsukamoto (1991) speak of a possibility to store geomorphological data as a tree structure of singular points such as peak, bottom, saddle points in topology, as a special case of the multi-peaks surface problem

Fractal Approaches
A technique which has been in vogue recently is the measurement of various natural phenomena to isolate the statistically fractal structures within (8). Mountain (fractal dimension D = 2.1-2,3), drainage systems (D = 1.2 - 1.8), and rias-type coast (D = 1.2) have proved to be good examples, because they look similar even when we change the display scale.
This is the core of the scale problem in geomorphology. (In CAD/ CAM, depicted industrial products are not fractal in nature.)

We have several criteria to determine phenomena are fractal or not.

A Measure the total extension of a given 2-D geometry, using different unit lengths. D is given as follows.

$$\log(\text{Extension}) = \log(\text{Constant number}) - (-D+1)\log(\text{Unit})$$

B In 1972, K.Wilson applied the renormalization theory to percolation phenomena. If the ratio between the number of grids and their singular points stays statistically the same when the scale of observation is changed,the phenomena may be regarded as self-similar,and therefore fractal in nature.

If the ground material (soil and rocks) is homogeneous and active agents, such as rain or wind erosion, can be regarded as having an influence in a no-equilibrium open system, the resulting geomorphic appearance could become statistically fractal. But, such an ideal environment is limited in actual earth environments (Figure 5).

For example, rias type coast has been well studied as a good specimen with a statistical fractal structure (Agui et al (1990)). However, the classification of coastal zone have been well established on a worldwide basis for the last 20 years and the use of three stage classification based on the scale of geomorphic agents working *in situ*, has become the second nature to geoscientists. i.e.

endegenetic (inner) agents	interbedding of hard and soft rocks	soft sediments	completly homogeneous sediments
exogenetic (outer) agents	dry climate slow erosion	humid climate fast erosion	fast erosion

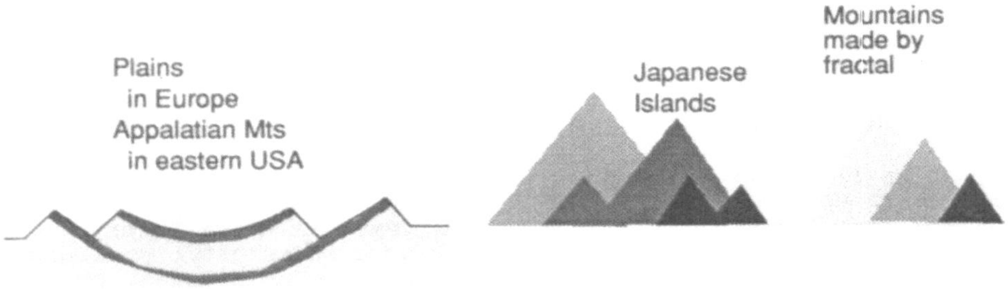

Fig. 5 Results of Selective Erosional Process and Fractal Nature

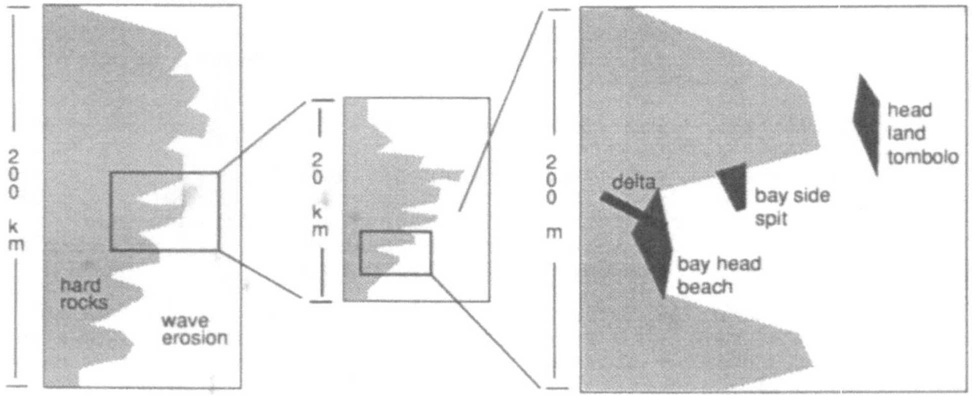

Fig . 6 Rias Type Coast at Various Scales

1000 km length order:	defined by tectonic movement	
100 km length order:	interaction between geologic structure and local erosion	
10 km length order:	micro local depositional process	

Table-3 Classification of Coast Geomorphology (after King 1959, Toyoshima 1990)

1000 km order	100 km order		10 km order
mid-plate area e.g Gulf of Mexico category (3) in Figure 8	estuary delta bar and dune reef and mangrove		
new mountain belt category (2)	volcanic slope fan delta		
old mountain belt category (1)	fjord morain		
	rias	bay head; bay side; headland;	beach,delta,barrier beach ,spit beach, sand spit tombolo, cuspate

Rias-type coasts occurs, when ancient hard rock area has been attacked by waves for more than 100,000 years.
If we take a look at them at a scale of less than 1 km, we can observe many micro geomorphological features (Figure 6).
Thus, the fractal nature of rias coast is valid as long as we confine our measurements to a length of around several tens kiro meter.

A common problem with prior mathematical studies on geomorphology is that *few authors justify their selection of the area to be studied.* (The same problem may be said to apply to topological studies in other fields.) Natural phenomena have their own inner structure and order.

PROPOSAL FOR GUIDELINES AND CASE STUDY

We begin with the widely accepted geoscientific premise that the classification of global geomorphology proceeds from the macro level through a mid-range and on to the micro level. Now, in 1992,it is possible for us to cover the entire globe with a 250 m mesh which shows location and altitude data with 10 m accuracy. The volume of data approaches 200 Gbyte. This data volume is not homogeneous in nature, so caution must be exercised if any subset is to be isolated for study.

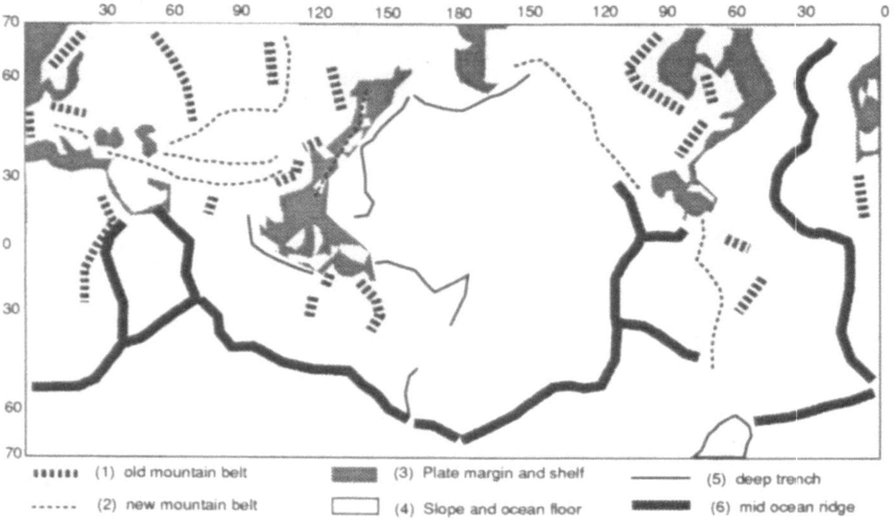

Fig. 7 World Tectonic Atlas at 1000 km Level

Large Scale Classification (1,000 km level) (Figure 7)

At a scale of 1000 km, the surface of the earth is classified into six major categories.

(1) Old mountain belt & plateau:
Europe,eastern USA, and southern India were all geomorphologically formed more than 200 million years ago. They consist of hard rocks so that topological features reflect their geological nature rather than any erosional process. e.g questa in the Paris basin

(2) New mountain building belt:
The formation of the Alps and circum-Pacific zone mountains first began during the Cenozoics era (60 million years ago), by the collision of two plates collide. These elongated belts are about 500 km wide and extend thousands of kilometers. Like the Japanese Arc Islands, the materials are soft and both the uprising crustal movement and the erosional process are faster than in any other areas in the world.

(3) Plate margin land and continental shelf:
There is little crustal movement and depositional processes is prevail. e.g. the Gulf of Mexico (oil and gas deposits are common).

(4) Continental slope and ocean floor:
Both crustal movement and depositional movement are minimal. They form the largest area on the globe (Figure 8)

	(1)	(2)	(3)	(4)	(5)	(4)	(6)
Ende-genetic (inner) agents	little move-ment	fast rise	small rise	little move-ment	large sink	little move-ment	large rise
Exo-genetic (outer) agents	mode-rate ero-sion	large ero-sion	large depo-sistion	small depo-sistion	small depo-sistion	small depo-sistion	small depo-sistion

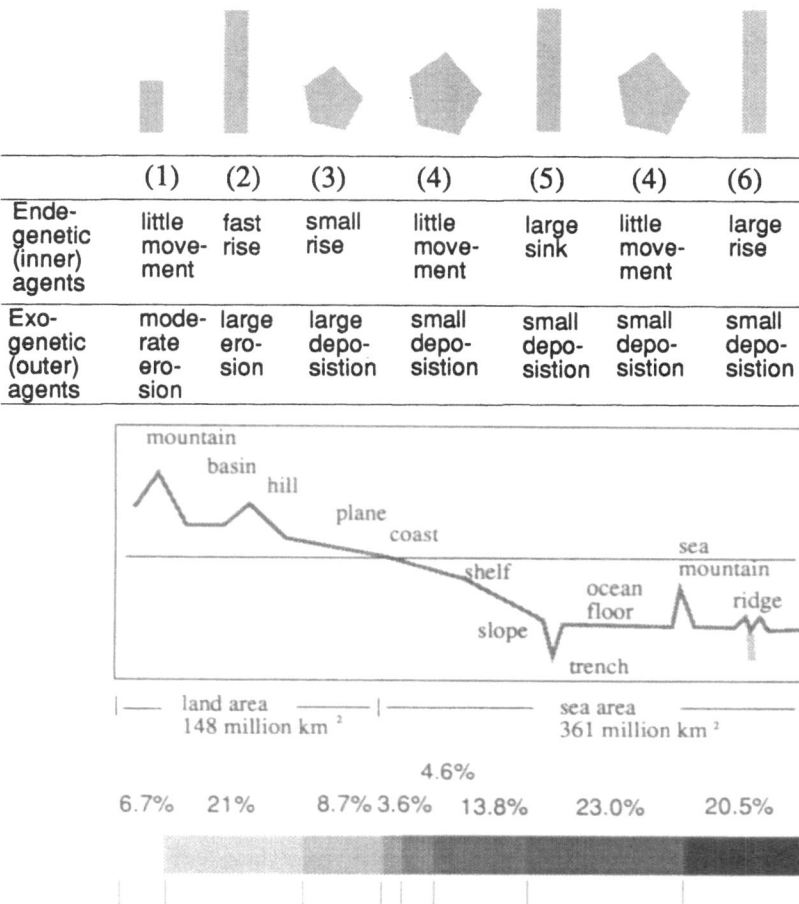

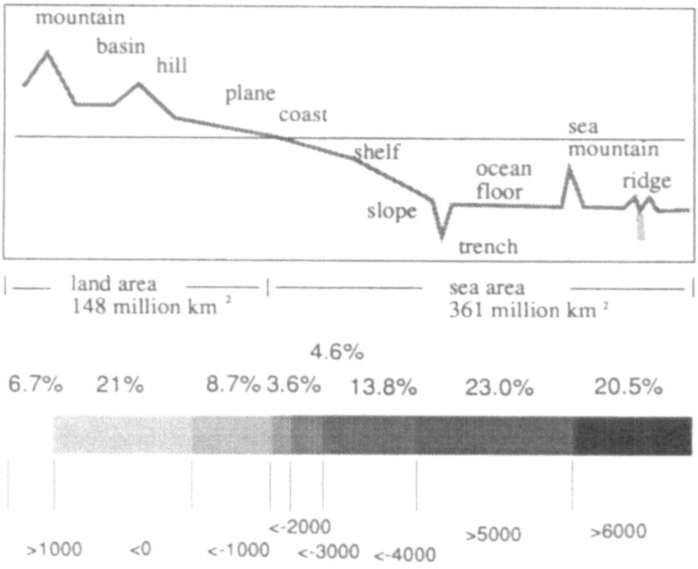

Fig. 8 Agents and Area Proportions at 1000 km Level

(5) Deep ocean trench:
Here, two plates collide and one plate slides underneath the other so that a very deep elongated trench valley is created, the depth of which exceeds that of the neighboring ocean floor.

(6) Mid ocean ridge:
A mid ocean ridge is a fracturing and aparting zone bewteen two plates. 500 km in width and extending more than 60,000 km, mid ocean ridges cover the bottom of the earth's oceans. Here, crustal movement is dominant.Rising up more than 3 km from the ocean floor, its topological appearance is somewhat similar to the new mountain building belt on land.

We selected Hokkaido Island, Japan, which belongs to category (2), as our specimen.

Hokkaido Island (at 100 km level)

Hokkaido Island is in the northernmost part of the Japanese Arc Islands system and belongs to the new mountain building belt. Here, earth materials are a mixture of Mesozoic and Cenozoic. Due to fast upward crustal movements (ca.1mm/yr), the material is not consolidated and fractured into pieces. Japan has a humid climate so that the erosion rate is fairly large (ca.0.4mm/yr) and rather uniform all over the area. This condition dominanted for the last 100,000 years (after Kaizuka 1969, Naruse 1980).

We used 250 m grid data from the Hokkaido subset (24 Mbyte) of the National Numerical Information System, prepared by the Geographical Survey Institute. The reason for selecting Hokkaido is because it is an island such that the topological features form a closed data set. i.e. arbitrarily-shaped multiple planar contours, which are homeomorphic to a plane mathematically. (If we artificially exclude any part of a large land mass as our specimen, we do not have the tools to analyze the phenomena that may occur along the artificial boundary zone) (Figure 9).

Select Mountainous Area (Figure 10)

On a global basis, land below 200 m is regarded as coastal plains on the 100 km level classification and their gradient is small. Areas above 200 m are regarded as mountains but their gradients vary from place to place. There exist valleys, basins, and plateaus depending on the local average gradient. Thus, taking 200 m in altitude as a threshold value, we separate areas from Hokkaido Island to get two regions: the central mountains and a southwest peninsula area. The Ishikari plain runs between the two. The southwest area is a massive intrude of volcanic rocks. The central area has two major axes of tectonic movements. One runs north-south and the other extends to Alaska Peninsula via Kamchatka Peninsula.

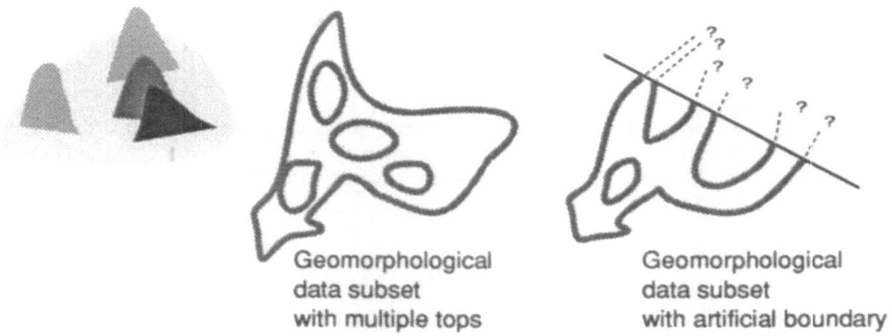

Fig. 9 Geomorphological Data Subset

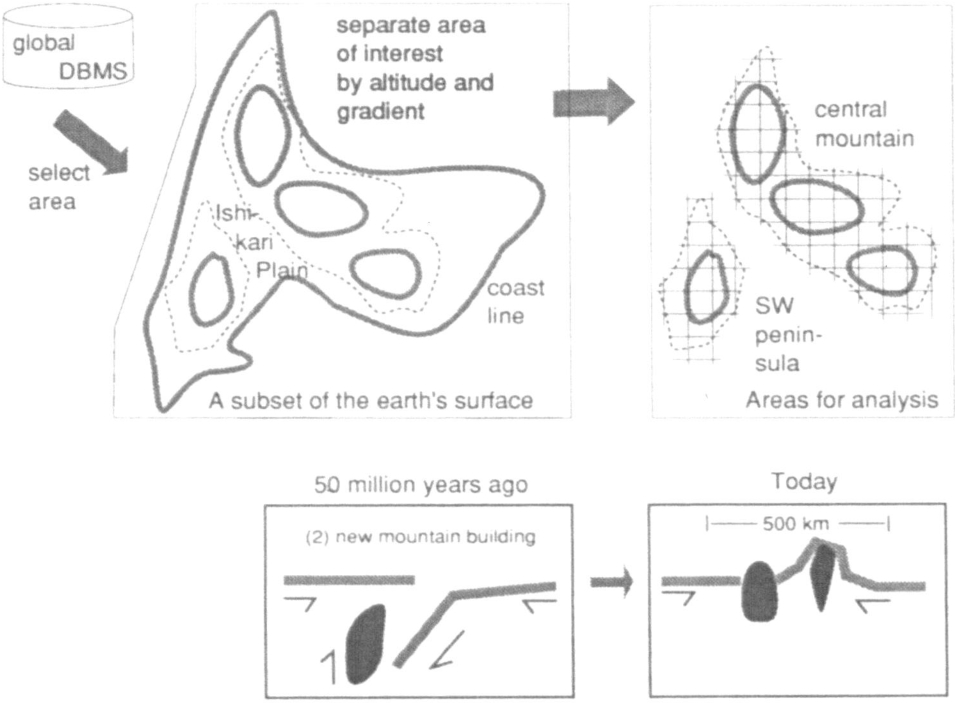

Fig. 10 Selection of Hokkaido for Analysis

Calculate Singular Points with Various Mesh Sizes

We calculate singular points (peak, saddle, and pit) with various scales.
The result are as follows:

stage

A mesh size more than 320 km :
selected area becomes flat.

B mesh size 160 km :
only 1 peak

C mesh size 80 km and 40 km : (Figure 11)
Shown in Figure 11, tendencies defined by 1000 km level tectonic movements appear.

D mesh size 20 km and 10 km :
It becomes rather difficult to recognize the characters mentioned at stage C.

E mesh size 5 km : (Figure 12 Photo)

F mesh size 1 km :
3-D visualization has to deal with these levels.

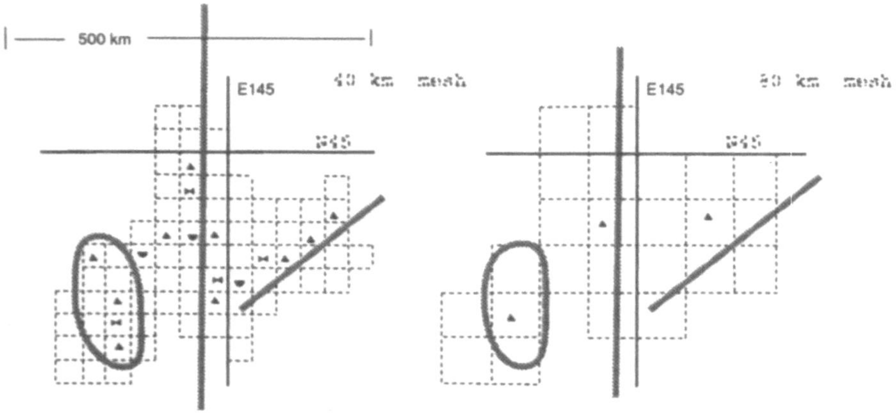

Fig. 11 Singular Points on 40 km Mesh
Follow 1000 km Level Tectonic Movement (2)

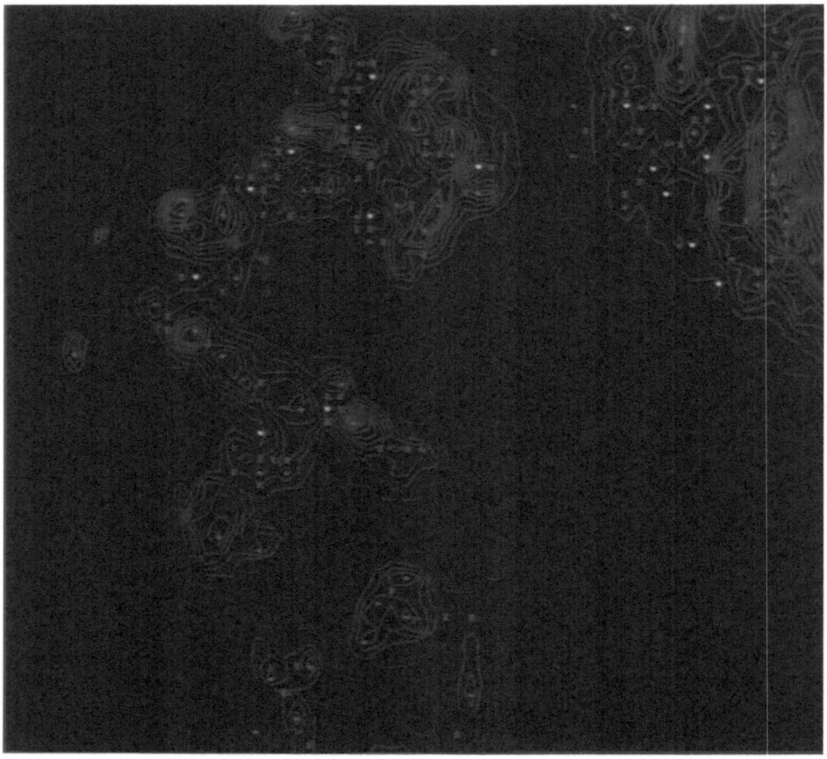

Fig. 12 Singular Points and Contours

Table-4 Singular Points and Mesh Size

mesh size (km)	number of singular points	number of non-sea level meshs
> 320	0	4
160	1	12
80	3	28
40	18	80
20	38	246
10	147	856
5	156	3338
1	1513	14186

Observation On The Relationship Between Singular Points And Contours

It would be of great help if we could reconstruct contours out of singular point data (on smaller database than mesh type database). As mentioned before, Ikeda has solved the case where the bounding area has only one peak devicing a multi-troidal graph method. Tukamoto provides only descriptive tree-structures to represent a given geomorphology. He selects sample areas which are limited to 10 x 10 km with one peak.

Our question is:
A Can we only store singular points in a descriptive way ?
B *Is the inner order controlled by the geographical nature of the area ?*
An issue to pursue is the relationship between peaks and saddles. The situation is schematized as shown in Figure 13.

Based upon the observations of our study on Hokkaido Island, we may be able to make some empirical suggestions.
(The levels are mesh size of 1 km, 5 km, and 10 km.)

Observation 1:
we should confine our mesh size to under 10 km.

Observation 2:
Pit points seem to be insignificant, even though we calculate them.

Observation 3:
When we check the relationship between singular points and contours, the interval of contours best simplifies the relationship between points and contours.
5 km mesh: 250 m interval
1 km mesh: 100 m interval
Thus, in case B (saddle between peaks), we should increase the mesh size, until we get the simplest diagram (two peaks and one saddle), then start analysis.

Observation 4:

In case A (no saddle between peaks), not more than 5 peaks are integrated along a straight axis whose width is about 20 km. This may be because of a geological structure*in situ*. e.g. a single valcano is abount 20 km in diameter at its base.

Observation 5:

When a group of integrated peaks merges the next peak, it selected is the next lowest peak with one saddle point. If there are more than two candidates, selection is based on *the waist of the new contour curve* (Figure 13).
Thus, the highest altitude peaks make their own hierarchy, integrating lower altitude peaks. i.e. if peak1 and peak2 are almost at the same altitude, they may be organized into the hierarchy below.

```
same altitude----------------- lower altitude
peak 1 ______ saddle 1-1 ______ lower peak 1-1
       ______ saddle 1-2 ______ lower peak 1-2
       ______ saddle 1-3 ______ lower peak 1-3
peak 2 ______ saddle 2-1 ______ lower peak 2-1
       ______ saddle 2-2 ______ lower peak 2-2
```

CONCLUSION AND FUTURE WORK

We can state our conclusions as follows;

A There are three feasible ways to build a global geomor phological database (Figure 14).

Case 1 Like today's GIS, use a uniform size mesh through-out.

Case 2 Use a smaller mesh where topology is rigid and a larger mesh where the area is flat (quad-tree approach). The cut-out area is visualized by a polygon mesh.

Case 3 Modify a quad-tree mesh for database. As for visualiza-tion, we use a proper polygonal mesh and homotopy, depend ing upon local irregularities.
Polygonal meshs is good for areas with rather simple topography or areas such as questa created by selective erosion.
On the other hand, homotopy may have a large future, if we can develop a method for smaller size data storage. Today, a data set for homotopy expression tends to be larger than its polygonal mesh counterpart.Thus, the tests on areas need to be fairly statistically fractal in nature.
As, Barnsley (1988) found, if the phenomena is fractal to some extent, it is possible to reconstruct the original situation from a very small data base by means of contrac tion mapping.

B To explore the possibility of case 3, we should strictly confine the mesh size of the study area to *between 500 m and 10 km*.

C Find out whether the hierarchy of singular points could be searched by an expert system such as method based upon the local geographical characteristics*in situ*, as we accumulate observations.

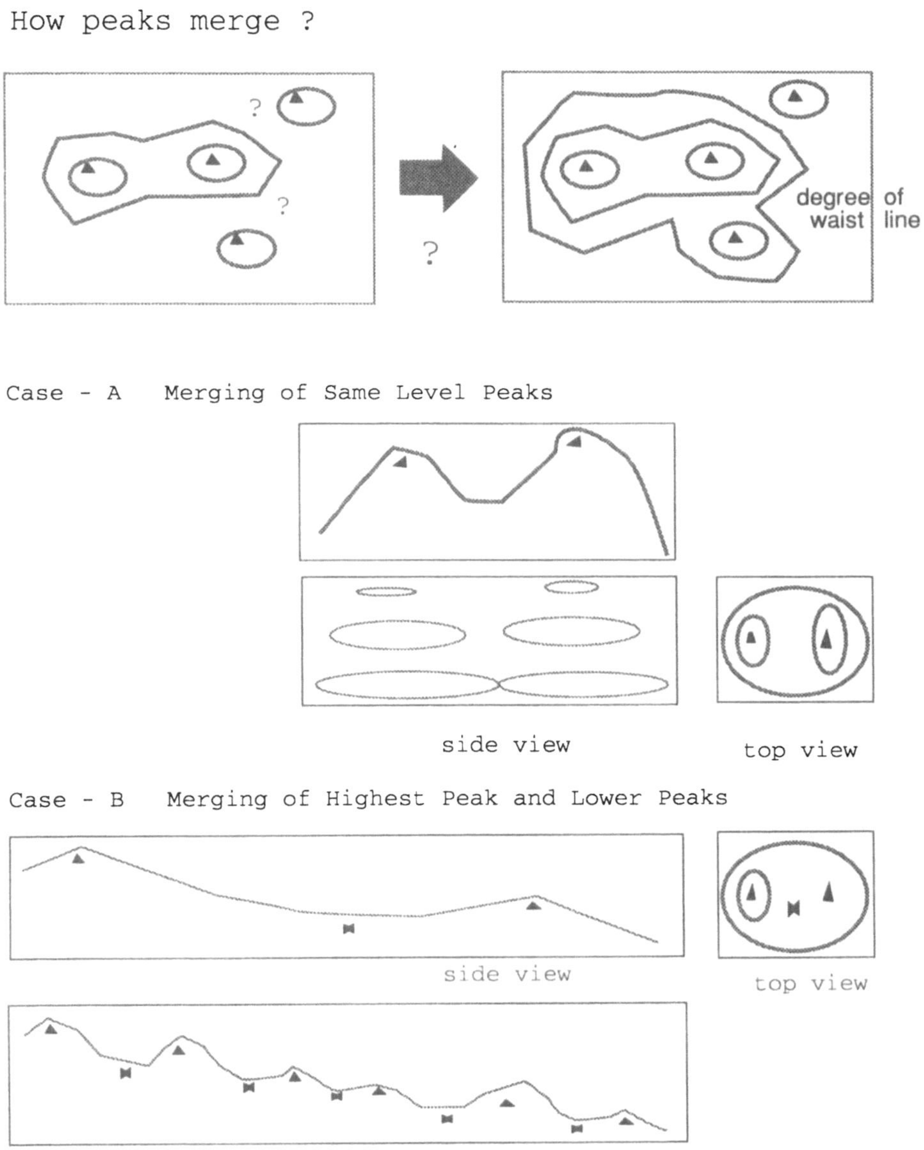

Fig. 13 Peak Merging

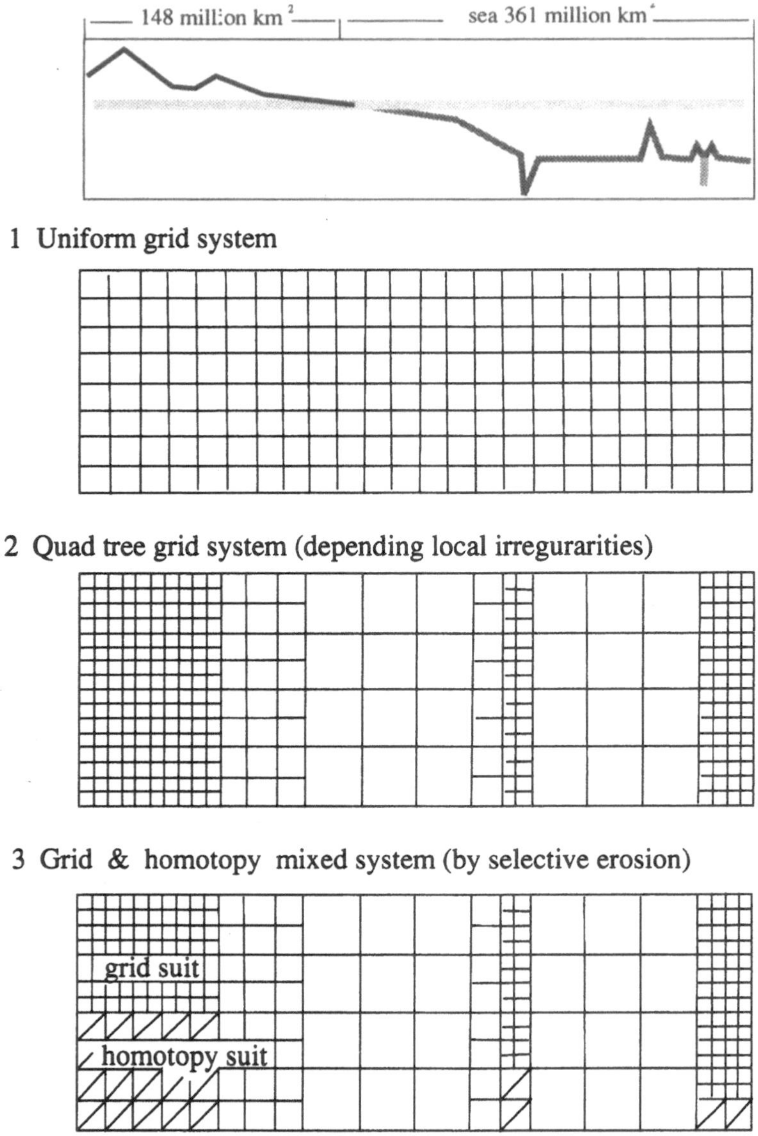

Fig. 14 Proposing Global DBMS in Geomorphology

This time, we have looked to see whether Hokkaido is statistically fractal to some extent. However, the Hokkaido data volume was too large for a personal IRIS workstation to handle. Even at the 5 km mesh level, it was not possible to handle and display the entire island in a single window. Thus, pursuing a feasible hierarchy of singular points is left for future study. The direction could follow the sequence below.

homotopy model -- a set of singular points -- a very compact DB

ACKNOWLEGMENT

We wish to express our gratitude to Mitsubishi Electric Co. Ltd, who kindly showed us the importance of establishing a better database and visualization method in geomorphology.
Special thanks are extended to Mr. H. Nishimura of the Kunii Laboratory of Computer Science, the University of Tokyo, for providing much significant advice.

REFERENCES

Agui T (1990) A Fractal. *Kougakusya Pub.Ltd, Tokyo* p.176

Bernsley M (1988) Fractals Everywhere. *Academic Press, San Diego*, p.453

Brivo PA and Marini D (1991) Fractal Approaches to Digital Terrain Modeling. *Eurographics Workshop on Computer Graphics and Mathematics, Genova* pp.173-19

Burrough PA (1986) Principles of Geographical Information System for Land Resource Assessment *Oxford Press, New York* p.243

Ekoule AB and Peyrin FC (1991) A Triangulation Algorithm from Arbitrary Shaped Multiple Planar Contours. *ACM Tran. on Graphics, Vol.10, No.2* pp.182-199

Ikeda T and Ueda M(1991) Automatic 3-D visualization of Geomorphology, using Homotopy Model. *Proc. of Japan Photogrametry and Remote Sensing, Tokyo* pp.89-94

Nakamae E, Nishita T (1989) Three Dimensional Terrain Generalized Model for Smooth Surface Generation from Cross Sectional Data. *The Visual Computer, Vol.7,No.2-3*pp24-29

Shinagawa Y and Kunii TL (1991) The Homotopy Model: A Generalized Model for Smooth Surface Generation from Cross Sectional Data *The Visual Computer,Vol.7, No.2-3*pp72-86

Shinagawa Y, Kunii T L and Kergosian YL (1991) Surface Coding Based on Morse Theory. *IEEE Computer Graphics & Appli. Vol.11 No.5* pp.66-78

Tukamoto M. (1991) A Representation Method of Cartographic Information Data Using Verbal Representation. *System Control, Vol.4, No.6* pp.226-234

AUTHOR'S BIOGRAPHIES

Minoru Ueda is currently a technical advisor to Wavefront Japan Ltd. and CSK Corp. He started his work in remote sensing and global climatic model projects at NASA Goddard Flight Center for Space Studies NY NY in 1975. Engaged in reservoir modelling workstation project at Nipon Schlumberger Co. Ltd.

Ueda received his BSc and MA in geoscience from Kyoto University in 1966 and 1972. Ph.D in regional science from Columbia University in 1983.

Tetsuya Ikeda is currently a master course graduate student of the University of Tokyo. His research interests include computer graphics, computational geometry and computer animation. He received the B.Sc. degrees in information science from the University of Tokyo in 1991. He is a student member of ACM and IPSJ.
Address: Department of Information Science, Faculty of Science, the University of Tokyo, 7-3-1 Hongo, Bunkyo-Ku, Tokyo, 113 Japan

Tosiyasu L. Kunii is currently Professor of Information and Computer Science, the University of Tokyo. At the University of Tokyo, he started his work in raster computer graphics in 1968 which was let to the Tokyo Raster Technology Project. His research interests include computer graphics, database systems, and software engineering. He authored and edited over 32 computer science books, and published over 120 refereed academic/technical papers in computer science and applications areas.

Dr.Kunii is Founder of the Computer Graphics Society, Editor-in-Chief of *The Visual Computer: An International Journal of Computer Graphics* (Springer-Verlag), Associate Editor-in-Chief of *The Journal of Visualization and Computer Animation* (John Wiley & Sons) and on the Editorial Board of *IEEE Transactions on Knowledge and Data Engineering*, *VLDB Journal* and *IEEE Computer Graphics and Applications.* He is on the IFIP Modeling and Simulation Working Group, the IFIP Data Base Working Group and the IFIP Computer Graphics Working Group. He is on the board of directors of Japan Society of Sports Industry and also of Japan Society of Simulation and Gaming.

He received the B.Sc., M.Sc., and D.Sc. degrees in chemistry all from the University of Tokyo in 1962, 1964, and 1967, respectively. He is a fellow of IEEE and a member of ACM, BCS, IPSJ and IEICE.

Address: Department of Information Science, Faculty of Science, the University of Tokyo, 7-3-1 Hongo, Bunkyo-Ku, Tokyo, 113 Japan

Yoshihisa Shinagawa is currently a Pesearch Associate of the Department of Information Science of the University of Tokyo. His research interests include computer graphics and its applications. He received the B.Sc. and M.Sc. degrees in information science from the University of Tokyo in 1987 and 1990 respectively. He is a member of the IEEE Computer Society, ACM, IPSJ and IEICE.
Address: Department of Information Science, Faculty of Science, the University of Tokyo, 7-3-1 Hongo, Bunkyo-Ku, Tokyo, 113 Japan

Using Surface Coding to Detect Errors in Surface Reconstruction

Yoshihisa Shinagawa and Tosiyasu L. Kunii

ABSTRACT

To reconstruct a surface of an object from a given series of cross-sectional contours, it is necessary to decide between which contours surface patches should be generated. Contemporary methods use only local information between consecutive contours and do not consider global information such as the topology of an object. This paper presents error detection and correction in surface reconstruction based on the topological information. The reconstructed surfaces are checked to see whether they are topologically legal using the surface coding method. The detected errors are heuristically corrected.

Keywords: surface reconstruction, surface coding, error detection, error correction, Morse theory

INTRODUCTION

There are many surface reconstruction systems that utilize cross-sectional contours of 3-dimensional (3D) objects (Fuchs, Kedem and Uselton 1977; Christiansen and Sederberg 1978; Boissonnat 1988; Shinagawa and Kunii 1991b) .When the distance between adjacent cross-sectional planes is large compared with the complexity of the object, it is not easy to decide between which contours surface patches should be generated. There have been several approaches to automating this process, including branch handling method. Shantz (1981) proposed a multiple-branching procedure based on a concatenation of contours. Ekoulé, Peyrin and Odet (1991) proposed a heuristic method of detecting branching using the overlap of consecutive contours. Shaw and Schwarz (1989) used the voxel adjacency for the detection. This method, however, assumes that sampling in the z direction (perpendicular to the cross-sectional planes) is very dense. These methods use only local information between consecutive contours and do not consider global information such as the topology of an object. To reduce errors in surface reconstruction, it is necessary to consider the global structure of objects as described, for example, in (Kergosien 1987; Kergosien 1991) . This paper proposes a method that makes this decision based on the surface coding method described in (Shinagawa, Kergosien and Kunii 1991) . The result can be directly fed to the surface reconstruction system using cross sectional data; i.e., the surface of an object is automatically reconstructed and visualized when the cross sectional contours are given.

First of all, we construct a tree representing the containment relation of the contours on each cross sectional plane. Each contour is then identified with a contour on its adjacent cross sectional plane based on a criteria such as the distance between the two contours. When the tree structure changes between two adjacent cross sectional planes, we check whether the change is legally based on the coding method. When it is legal, we call this change **acceptable**. If it is not acceptable, as is shown in Figure 1, the identification process is backtracked.

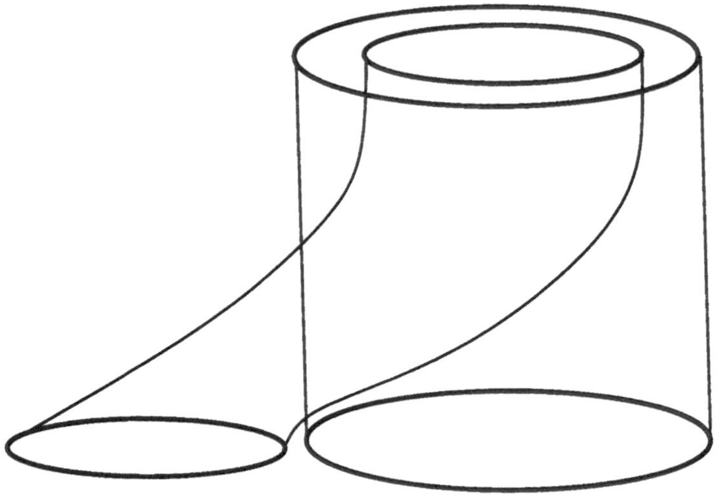

Fig. 1. Unacceptable change in the contour structure

OUTLINE OF THE SURFACE CODING METHOD

The surface coding method based on Morse theory (Shinagawa, Kergosien and Kunii 1991) enables coding of complex shaped objects such as human organs. This method codes the surface by describing the cells that form the surfaces. To decide the sequence of pasting cells, a user specifies the skeleton of the object called the Reeb graph (Reeb 1946) using the icons. In the system, we use three kinds of cells: 1D, 2D and 3D cells. They are called 1-cell, 2-cell and 3-cell. Simply speaking, a 0-cell is a point, a 1-cell is a chip of a string and a 2-cell is a patch of a surface. Figure 2 shows how the cells are pasted to form the surface of a torus. According to Morse theory, there is a one-to-one correspondence between a cell and a non-degenerate singular point of a Morse function defined on the object surface that is a C^2 2-manifold. In our system, we use the height function that gives the height of a point on the object surface embedded in $\boldsymbol{R}^3$. In this case, there are three kinds of non-degenerate singular points: peaks, saddle points and pits (see Figure 3a). A peak corresponds to a 2-cell, a saddle point to a 1-cell and a pit to a 0-cell. (A description of Morse theory can be found, for example, in (Milnor 1963) .) Scanning from top to bottom, codes are generated by listing the operations of attaching cells that correspond to the singular points. There are four kinds of operators: *put_e2*, *put_e1_divide*, *put_e1_merge* and *put_e0* (k-cell is abbreviated to *ek* above). Each operator has several parameters. To attach a 1-cell, there are two operators (*put_e1_divide* and *put_e1_merge*): one for dividing a contour and the other for merging two contours.

To specify the sequence of attaching cells, the Reeb graph (Reeb 1946) is used. The Reeb graph of the height function is obtained by considering the cross-sectional contours of the object (see Fig. 23b). A cross-sectional contour is represented by a point in the Reeb graph as shown in Fig. 23c. Users define the Reeb graph using icons.

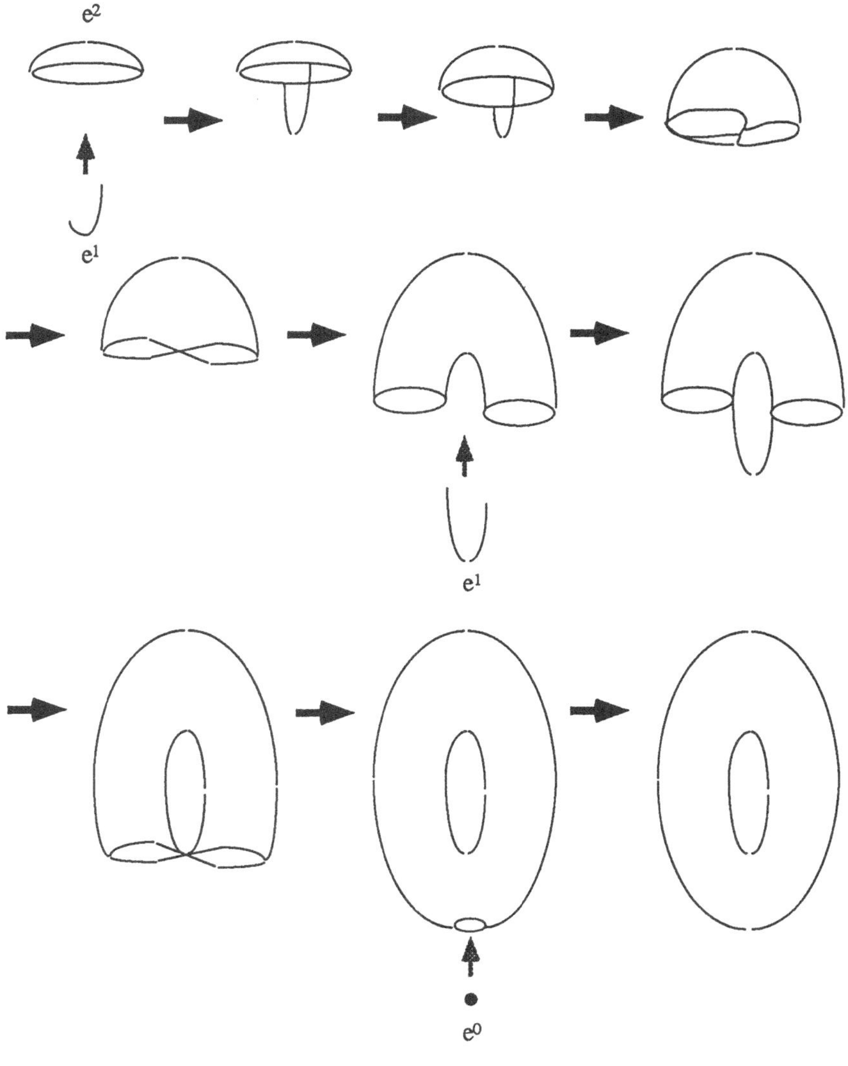

Fig. 2. Surface Construction of a torus

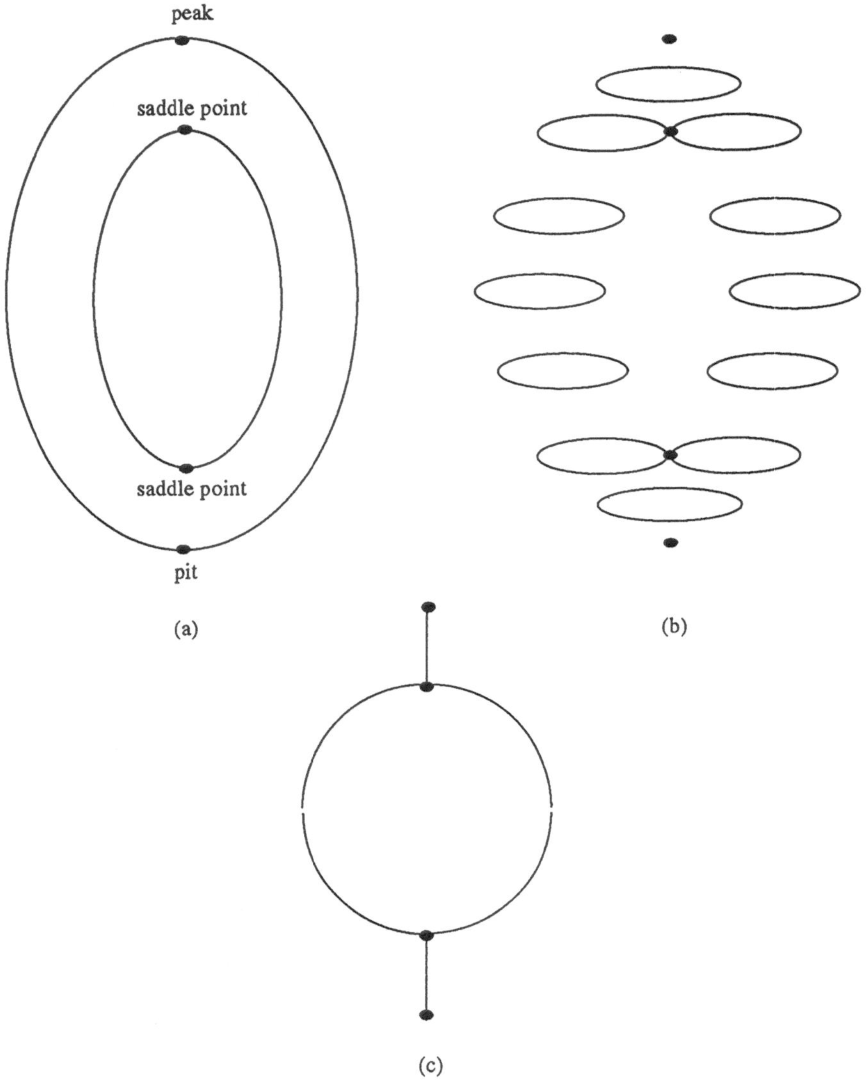

Fig. 3. (a) A torus, (b) its cross sections and (c) its Reeb graph (Shinagawa et al. 1991)

GRAPH CONSTRUCTION

Contour Identification

The containment relation of the contours on each cross-sectional plane is nested and can be represented by a tree as shown in Figure 4. This relation is called the "parent-child" relation. We introduce a virtual contour #0 as the root of the tree. In this paper, the tree structure is constructed using the spatial containment check described in (Dobkin, Guibas, Hershberger and Snoeyink 1988; Guibas, Ramshaw and Stolfi 1983) .

We construct a graph corresponding to the Reeb graph. In the graph, each cross sectional contour is represented by a node. For each node, an edge corresponding to a part of an edge of the Reeb graph is then spanned between a node representing a contour on its adjacent cross-sectional plane based on a criterion. In this paper, the 'average distance' d between two contours was used; i.e., for each contour, an edge is spanned to a contour on its adjacent plane with the smallest distance. When there is more than one edge incident to a node, it is either rejected or accepted according to a criterion such as described in (Shinagawa and Kunii 1991a) or by using some threshold values. Each contour is given a number as an identifier. When the upper and lower contours are spanned by an edge, the two have the same identifier. When there is more than one edge incident to a node or when a new contour appears or a contour vanishes, the identifier is provided by the coding system as is discussed later.

Average Distance

The 'average distance' is defined as follows. We denote by L_i^j the i-th contour on the j-th cross-sectional plane and by $d(L_i^j, L_k^{j+1})$ the average distance of the edge that corresponds to the surface patch generated between L_i^j and L_k^{j+1}. We denote by N^j the number of contours in the j-th cross-sectional plane and N_{frame} is the number of cross-sectional planes. We assume that the contours are approximated by polygons and use

$$d(L_i^j, L_k^{j+1}) = n_i^j D_j / \sum_{m=0}^{n_i^j} f(\boldsymbol{x}_{i,m}^j, L_k^{j+1}). \tag{1}$$

Here, D_j is the distance between the j-th and $j+1$-th cross-sectional planes. $\boldsymbol{x}_{i,m}^j$ is the m-th vertex of the polygon that approximates L_i^j which has n_i^j vertices,

$$f(\boldsymbol{x}, A) = \min_{\boldsymbol{y} \in A} d(\boldsymbol{x}, \boldsymbol{y})$$

where d is the distance function and $\boldsymbol{x}, \boldsymbol{y} \in \boldsymbol{R}^3$. f gives the minimum distance between $\boldsymbol{x}$ and points in set A.

ERROR DETECTING AND CORRECTING PROCEDURE

After the edges are spanned, the reconstructed surface is checked to see whether it uses only legal change in the contour structure allowed by the coding method. To be precise, the nested contour structure at the lower level is compared with that obtained by applying the corresponding operator to the contours on its upper level. When they are not the same, the edges are modified.

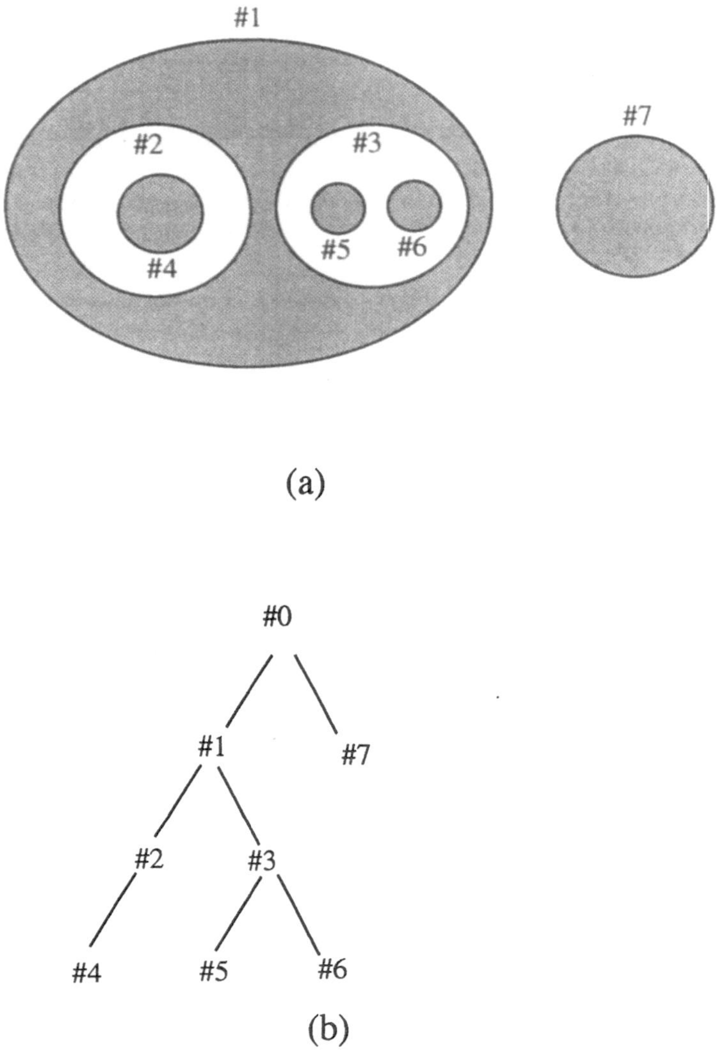

Fig. 4. (a) The parent-child relation of contours and (b) its tree representation

Derivation of Operators

First of all, the change in the contour structure is coded. The singular points are assumed to be non-degenerate and no two singular points are assumed to be at the same height. The procedure for the coding is as follows. It scans the graph from top to bottom.

- When a node to which no edge from the upper level is incident first appears at a certain level, the corresponding code is *PUT_E2*. When it is contained in an existing contour (let it be contour #n), the corresponding code is *PUT_E2(n)*. The identifier of the new contour is the smallest positive integer that has not yet been used.
- When a node of the graph disappears at a certain level, the corresponding code is *PUT_E0*.
- When two edges are merged, the coding is *PUT_E0_MERGE*. When the child contours of the new contour do not coincide with the child contours of the two contours that have been merged, an error is reported. The identifier of the merged contour is the smaller of the two identifiers.
- When an edge splits, the corresponding code is *PUT_E0_DIVIDE*. The children of the split contour (the second parameter *clist* described in (Shinagawa, Kergosien and Kunii 1991)) are decided by checking the containment relation of contours. When the contour of one of the branches (let it be #m) is contained in the other (let it be #n), the third parameter described in (Shinagawa, Kergosien and Kunii 1991) is *OUTSIDE*, otherwise (a sibling contour) it is *INSIDE*. In the case of *OUTSIDE*, the child contours of #m are checked to see if they have become the children of #n. In the case of *INSIDE*, the child contours of #m and #m are checked to see if they coincide with the child contours of the old contour. The identifier of the new contour is the smallest positive integer that has not yet been used.

Error Detection

After the code at that level is derived, the parent-child relation of contours at that level is checked to see if they coincide with the result of applying the derived operator to the tree structure of contours at its upper level. If it does not, there is an error.

Let the former tree be T_1 and the latter be T_2. The detection procedure is detailed below. Let the current position indicator of T_1 be p_1 and that of T_2 be p_2. Let us denote the height of p_1 and p_2 from the root by h_1 and h_2 respectively. The comparison starts from the root of T_1. (p_1 is at the root). For each child of p_1, we search for a contour in T_2 at height h_1 with the same identifier. If there is none, the contour is marked. In Figure 5, marked contours are represented by putting * before the contour number. For each subtree with the children of p_1 that are not marked as the roots, the procedure is continued. This procedure is applied recursively. When the procedure finishes and there are marked contours, then the surface reconstruction is unacceptable.

Error Correction

The error thus detected is heuristically corrected. First of all, we define a procedure called *INTERCHANGE*(#k, #l). For a contour #k and a contour #l on #k's upper level, let us assume that an edge spans #k and #m and another edge spans #n and #l, *INTERCHANGE*(#k, #l) interchanges the two edges so that the edges (#k, #m) and (#n, #l) become (#k, #l) and (#n, #m) (see Figure 6). Note that $k = m$ and $n = l$ when there is no branching. When there is no edge incident to #l, it simply changes (#k, #m) into (#k, #l). After this, contour identifiers are recomputed. We also use a function *NEAREST*(#k, i) that gives the i-th nearest contour on #k's upper level.

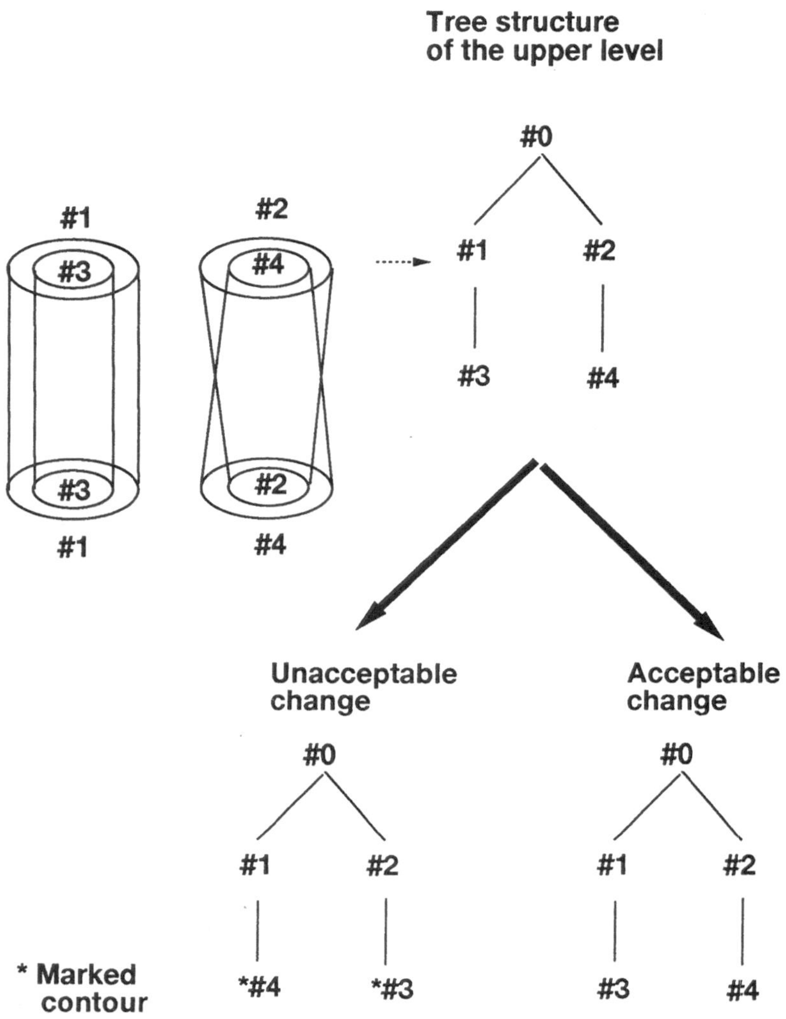

Fig. 5. Error Detection

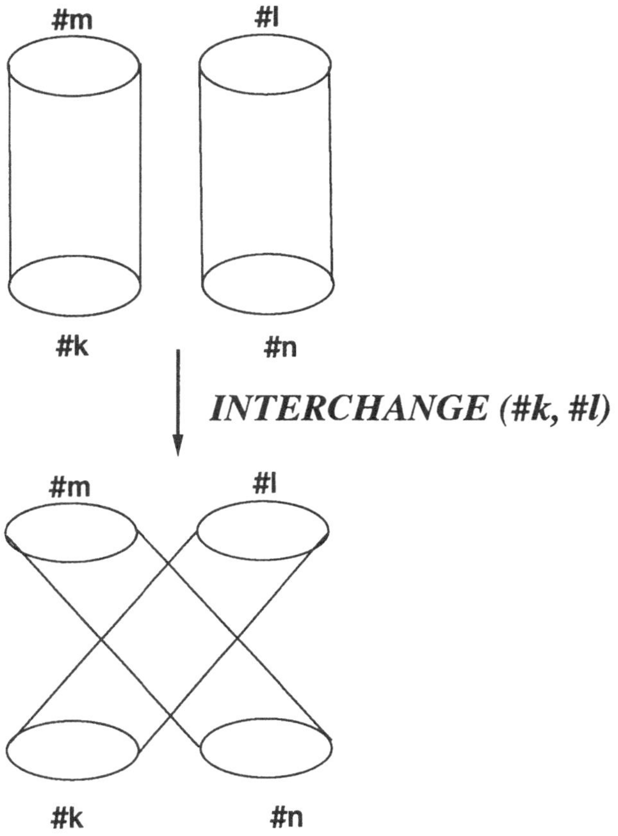

Fig. 6. INTERCHANGE

The procedure for error correction is as follows:

Case A When there is only one marked contour (say, $\#k$), use *INTERCHANGE*(parent of $\#k$, *NEAREST*($\#k, 2$)) (see Figure 7).

Case B When $\#k$ and $\#l$ are both marked and $\#l$ = *NEAREST*($\#k, 2$), use *INTERCHANGE*($\#k, \#l$) is performed (see Figure 8).

Case C Otherwise, for each marked contour, use *INTERCHANGE*($\#k$,*NEAREST*($\#k, 2$)).

For cases A and B, it is probable that the error will be corrected. Otherwise, the situation is more complicated and the errors might not be corrected. Also, there are cases where the correction is ambiguous if we use topological information represented by the tree structure only (see Figure 9). As the coding method cannot use the information regarding embedding, the error detection system cannot detect errors as shown in Figure 10.

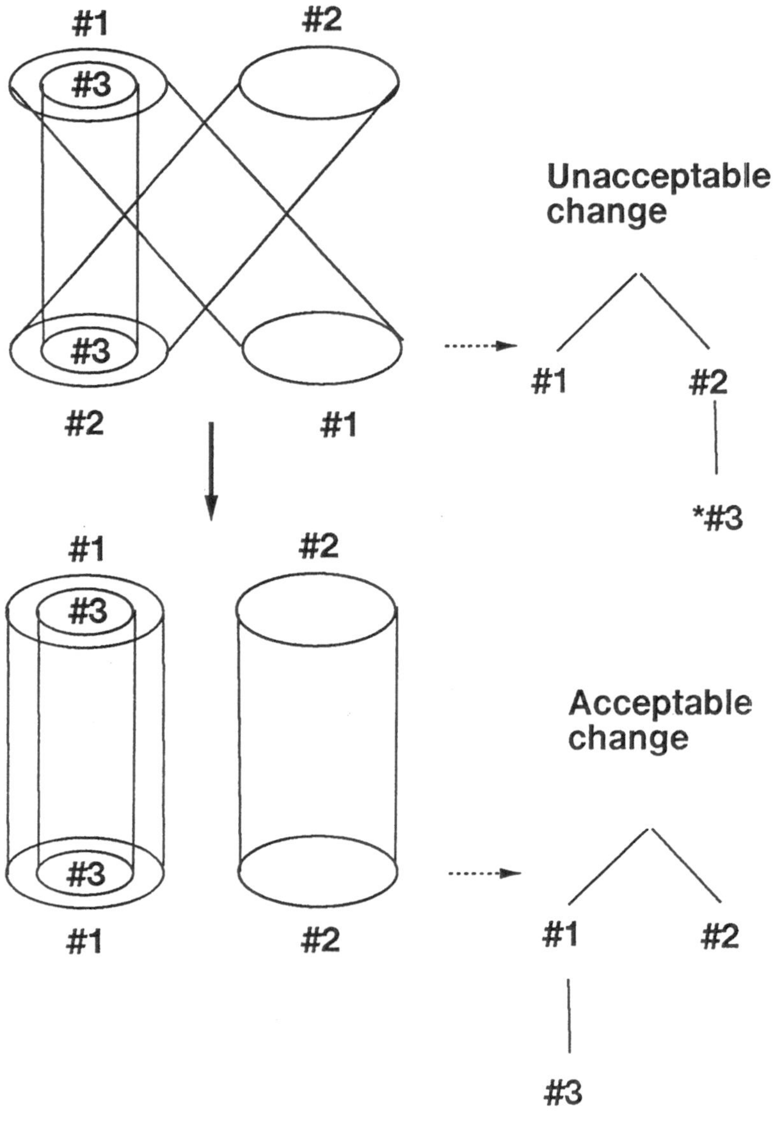

Fig. 7. Error correction for Case A

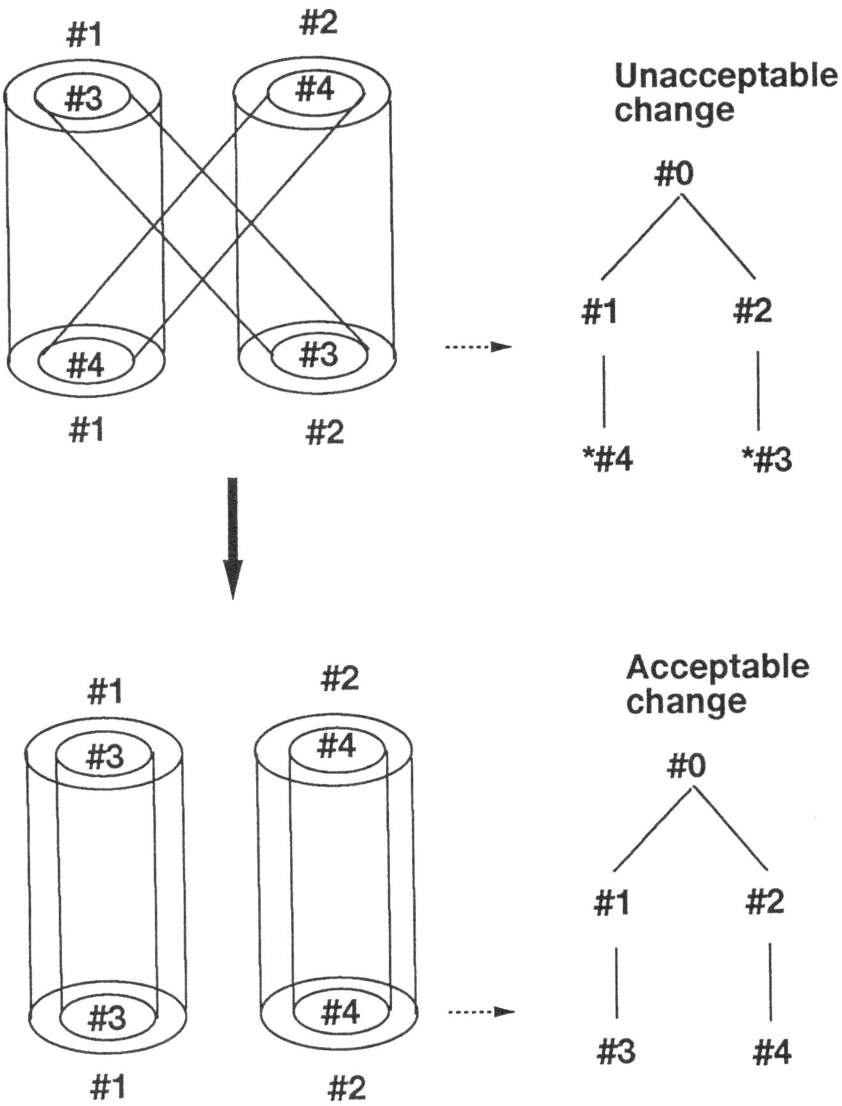

Fig. 8. Error correction for Case B

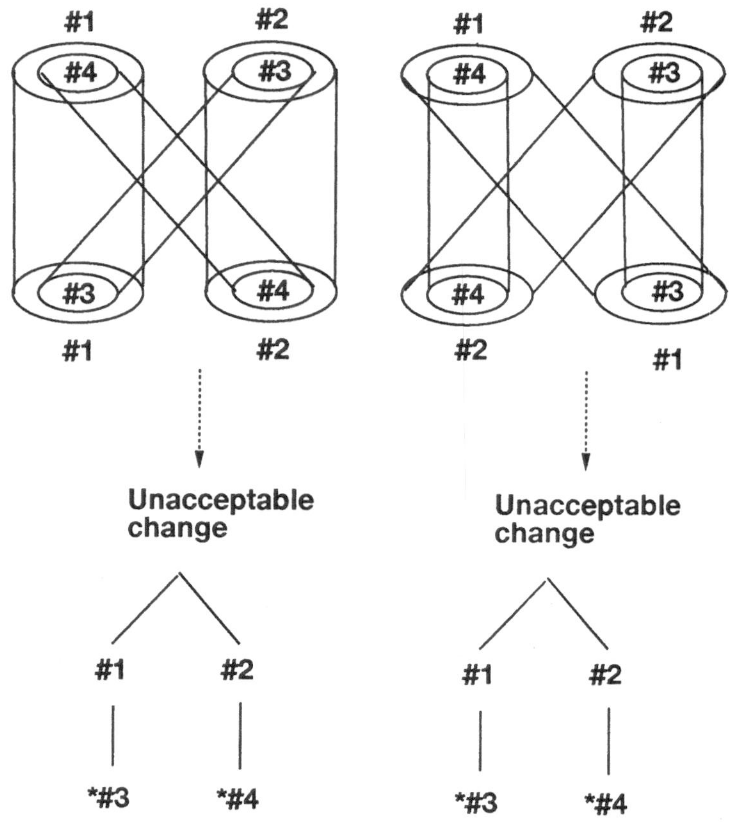

Fig. 9. Ambiguity of Error Detection

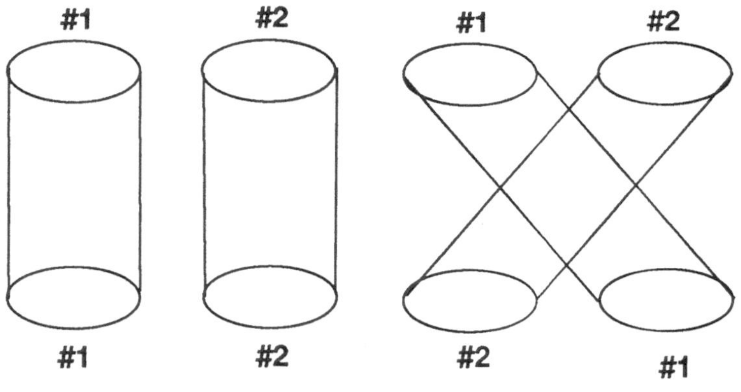

Fig. 10. Two configurations that cannot be distinguished

SUMMARY

This paper has presented error detection and correction for the surface reconstruction systems that use cross-sectional contours. The method uses the topological information represented by the surface coding described in (Shinagawa, Kergosien and Kunii 1991) . Error correction for more complicated cases is left as future research. To remove errors completely, the result of the correction procedure must be fed back to the detection procedure. The procedure can be iterated until all the errors are removed. The analysis of the convergence of this iteration is another task of the future.

ACKNOWLEDGMENTS

We wish to express our gratitude to Dr. Kansei Iwata, the president of Graphica Co., Ltd. and Mr. Norimasa Koyama, the executive director of Cadtech Inc. for offering the drum scanner, G-225C, to Yokogawa Hewlet Packard Co., Ltd. for HP9000 model 550 and to Silicon Graphics Co., Ltd. for IRIS 4D/70GT. Special thanks are extended to Dr. Yannick L. Kergosien of Mathématiques, Université de Paris-Sud for information on the Reeb graph and his precious comments on our papers.

REFERENCES

Boissonnat JD (1988) Shape reconstruction from planar cross sections. *Computer Vision, Graphics, and Image Processing*, 44(1):1–29.

Christiansen HN, Sederberg TW (1978) Conversion of complex contour line definitions into polygonal element mosaics. *Computer Graphics (Proc. Siggraph)*, 12(3):187–192.

Dobkin D, Guibas L, Hershberger J, Snoeyink J (1988) An efficient algorithm for finding the csg representation of a simple polygon. *Computer Graphics (Proc. ACM SIGGRAPH'88)*, 22(4):31–40.

Ekoule AB, Peyrin FC, Odet CL (1991) A triangulation algorithm from arbitrary shaped multiple planar contours. *ACM Transactions on Graphics*, 10(2):182–199.

Fuchs H, Kedem ZM, Uselton SP (1977) Optimal surface reconstruction from planar contours. *Communications of the ACM*, 20(10):693–702.

Guibas L, Ramshaw L, Stolfi J (1983) A kinetic framework for computational geometry. In: *Proc. 24th Annual IEEE Symposium on Foundations of Computer Science*, pp. 100–111.

Kergosien YL (1987) Projections of smooth surfaces : Stable primitives. In: *Proc. Cognitiva-MARI*, CESTA. Paris, pp. 447–454.

Kergosien YL (1991) Generic sign systems in medical imaging. *IEEE Computer Graphics and Applications*, 11(5):46–65.

Milnor J (1963) *Morse Theory.* Princeton University Press, New Jersey.

Reeb G (1946) Sur les points singuliers d'une forme de pfaff completement integrable ou d'une fonction numerique. *Comptes Rendus Acad. Sciences Paris*, 222:847–849.

Shantz M (1981) Surface definition for branching, contour-defined objects. *Computer Graphics*, 15(2):242–270.

Shaw A, Schwartz EL (1989) Construction of polyhedral surfaces from serial secions: Exact and heuristic solutions. *SPIE Medical Imaging III: Image Capture and Display*, 1091:221–233.

Shinagawa Y, Kunii TL (1991) Constructing a Reeb graph automatically from cross sections. *IEEE Computer Graphics and Applications*, 11(6):44—51.

Shinagawa Y, Kunii TL (1991) The Homotopy model: A generalized model for smooth surface generation from cross sectional data. *The Visual Computer*, 7(2–3):72–86.

Shinagawa Y, Kergosien YL, Kunii TL (1991) Surface coding based on Morse theory. *IEEE Computer Graphics and Applications*, 11(5):66–78.

AUTHOR'S BIOGRAPHIES

Yoshihisa Shinagawa is currently a research associate of the Department of Information Science at the University of Tokyo. His research interests include computer graphics and its applications. He received his B.Sc. (in 1987), M.Sc. (in 1990) and D.Sc. (in 1992) degrees in information science from the University of Tokyo. He is a member of the IEEE Computer Society, ACM, IPSJ and IEICE.

Tosiyasu L. Kunii is currently Professor of Information and Computer Science at the University of Tokyo.
He authored and edited more than 32 computer science books, and published more than 140 refereed academic/technical papers in computer science and applications areas.
Dr. Kunii is Founder of the Computer Graphics Society, Editor-in-Chief of *The Visual Computer: An International Journal of Computer Graphics* (Springer-Verlag), Associate Editor-in-Chief of *The Journal of Visualization and Computer Animation* (John Wiley & Sons) and on the Editorial Board of *IEEE Transactions on Knowledge and Data Engineering*, *VLDB Journal* and *IEEE Computer Graphics and Applications*. He is on the IFIP Modeling and Simulation Working Group, the IFIP Data Base Working Group and the IFIP Computer Graphics Working Group. He is on the board of directors of the Japan Society of Sports Industry and also of the Japan Society of Simulation and Gaming.
He received his B.Sc. (in 1962), M.Sc. (1964), and D.Sc. (in 1967) degrees in chemistry from the University of Tokyo. He is a fellow of IEEE and a member of ACM, BCS, IPSJ and IEICE.

Address: Department of Information Science, Faculty of Science, University of Tokyo, 7-3-1 Hongo, Bunkyo-Ku, Tokyo, 113 Japan

Chapter 4
Supercomputing for Modern Geometry

The Development of the Supercomputer System Electronica SS BIS

Vladimir A. Melnikov and Yuri I. Mitropolski

ABSTRACT

The paper describes the prehistory of Electronica SS BIS development, the system main development concepts and architecture.

Keyword:supercomputer system vector pipelined processor supercomputer arhitecture, hardware, memory system

1.ELECTRONICA SS BIS DEVELOPMENT PREHISTORY

The most famous original high performance computer in the USSR was BESM-6 introduced in 1967. The computer was designed for scientific computations and had quite a high performance - 1 MIPS. A number of factors contributed to the successful usage of the computer:

- a combined approach to the design of construction,architectuer and circuitry;

-an application of original high frequency circuits on current switches;

-a high density electronic curcuits packaging, providing short links between logical circuits;

-a pipeline organization both on register transfer and instruction execution levels;

-CPU buffer memory original organization scheme;

-an effective and compact input/output subsystem;

-a multiprogram computer organization;

-a highly effective operational and programming system;

-large volume of application programs;

-a system of circuitry engineering documentation representation,convinient for design, manufacture and maintanance process.

During 15 years Besm-6 systems were the main instrument in large computer centres of the country.

Record duration of this system manufacture and employment proves on one hand the success of the design and on the other hand - the lack of serious competitive developments.

In the beginning of 70ies the emergence of new problems, connected with complex objects real time control became the reason of creating AS-6 data processing system. The system had several stages of development - from interface hardware to multimachine heterogeneous computer system, in which Besm-6 computer itself was one of the components. In AS-6 system the following ideas were realized for the first time (at least in the USSR):

-subsystems and seperate devices specialization;

-two-level structure of intrasystem channels for joining up machines, processsors and main memory devices on the first level and peripheral input/output devices, external memory, remote terminals and objects, including seperate computers on the second level;

-the development of CPU new architecture to optimize the high level languages program translation and execution;

- the development of a new peripheral machine architecture, based on joining up multichannel exchange device (channelers) and a peripheral processor;

-the development of a number of controllers for various peripheral equipment;

-the development of a simulation complex,which provides the possibility of creating software simultaneously with designing, manufacturing and debugging of hardware;

-the creating of a CAD system on the base of circuitry engineering representation system used during BESM-6 design.

AS-6 system was realized on a modernized BESM-6 component set and construction, that resulted in a large hardware volume. So less than 20 systems with various sets of hardware were produced.

The accumulated scientific potentcial made it real to raise a problem of creating a system compatible with AS-6 on new constructive conceptions using ICs. However the project (called BESM-10) proposed in 1974 didn't get any support from administrative structures and thus wasn't realized.

In 1979 a problem of creating a high performance system was raised. Naturally the expierience of AS-6 development and application was laid in the base of a future project.CRAY-1 by Cray Research[1] and Cyber 205 by CDC [2] - the supercomputers already put on the market in the USA, were carefully examined as well.Vector processing together with pipelined structure, high speed ICs application as well as new solutions in construction,cooling and power supply systems were the most important and interesting features of these supercomputers.

The comparative analysis of these two systems showed that the most perspective was the approach, used in Cray 1 computer and later it was proved in practice - the success of Cray 1 and further models on its base is widely known [3].

2.THE MAIN CONCEPTIONS OF ELECTRONICA SS BIS DEVELOPMENT

The stated above preconditions of the considering development served for formulation of the following main conceptions:

1.Problem orientation of the main computing facilities. Due to this conception processor and machine architecture is best optimised from the point of view of application problems algorithms. But there are considerable technical and economic difficulties on the way of this conception realization. The development of the machines for a narrow class of algorithms results in the neccesity of creating a great number of different machines joining them into a united system and the development of problem assignment automatic aids.

The technological possibillities of designing and manufacturing such systems would probably appear in the future. Systems with limited degree of specialization were analized (vector, array, combinatorial, etc).Vector pipelined version was chosen for the first stage of realization.

2.Functional specialisation of auxiliary computing facilities. This conception is connected with increasing efficiency and flexibility of a computing system as a whole, firstly due to the release of the main computing facilities from the routine auxiliary and nonproductive work and, secondly, due to the auxiliary facilities performance raise owing to the specialization.

Among such subsystems we can name the following: IC external memory, magnetic disk memory, data base subsystems, communication subsystems, graphic subsystems, subsystems for operational system functions execution, etc.

3.Flexible and open architecture for joining the mentioned facilities into a united sustem. The availability of the facilities so different in functions and data transfer rates presupposes the usage of a whole hierarchy of channels and relative protocols.

4.Combined approach to integrated system design.The optimization of construction, circuitry and technological means are possible only due to such approach.

3.CONSTRUCTION AND TECHNOLOGY

A high degree of the vector processor parallelism leads to it's large volume of hardware - about 1 million gates.

The urge towards the highest speed dictates the usage of the most high frequency circuits - ECL. In due course the problem of developing gate array LSI with about 200 gates was raised and solved. Besides LSI medium scale integration is used in the system. Quite a large power of LSI - up to 5W, their compact placement on boards and LSI temperature mode requirements lead to the necessity of LSI packages mounting on heat removing pipe, in which freon is circulating. To provide the sufficient pressure of the packages to the pipe the construction of contacting device with a pressure spring is used. Leadless packages are in contact with the spring contacts in the device. There are 50 blocks in the processor construction, each of them has 144 placing sites for LSI. The blocks are put into corresponding cells in horizontal plane. To supply freon and to provide the access to the block ICs there are flexible hoses, which allow to pull out the block while debugging and repairing.

It is possible to use specially designed heat pipes to draw off the heat in the main memory construction due to less power (about 1W) of LSI memory. Heat pipes were used in such hardware for the first time and proved high efficiency.

Considerable supplied and removed power required the development of new power supplies and cooling devices. Processor unit power is about 15 kW, memory unit - 40 kW. The aggregate two processor system power - 150 kW. Special attention was paid to the development of power supply and cooling system, as well as control subsystem. This subsystem, based on the usage of the microcomputer and some specialized controllers with sensing elements, allows to have constant observation of block supply voltage levels and temperature in many points of the construction. The exceeding of admissible values leads to the formation of warning signals, breakdown signals and automatical switching off the power.

The development of a high frequency construction required the design of new interconnection means.They include already mentioned contacting devices, in which contacts have little values of mutual capacitance and induction. High frequency coaxial connectors with 72 contacts with contact pair step - 2,5 mm were specially designed. Besides multilayer printed circuit boards with strip terminated transmission lines specially was designed microcable which provides less delay, then links on PCB and the possibility of calibrated delay in synchronization circuits is used.

4.ELECTRONICA SSBIS SYSTEM ARCHITECTURE

Electronica SSBIS system block scheme is presented in fig.1. There is one main computer in minimal configuration and also there is a possibility to connect two main computers to the external solid state memory . Each machine has its own main memory. Naturally the communication of the main computer with the external solid state memory is less tight than with a common main memory, but the availability of a specialized processor with a corresponding software in the external memory controller provides editing during the exchange. In fact from the application program point of view the external solid state memory is an expansion of main memory, that allows to relate the system to an intermediate class between two-processor and two-computer system.

To provide the main computers operation there is an external memory on magnetic disks, front-end computers, local network to join up abonents with PCs, and also service computers subsystem for control, test and diagnostics.

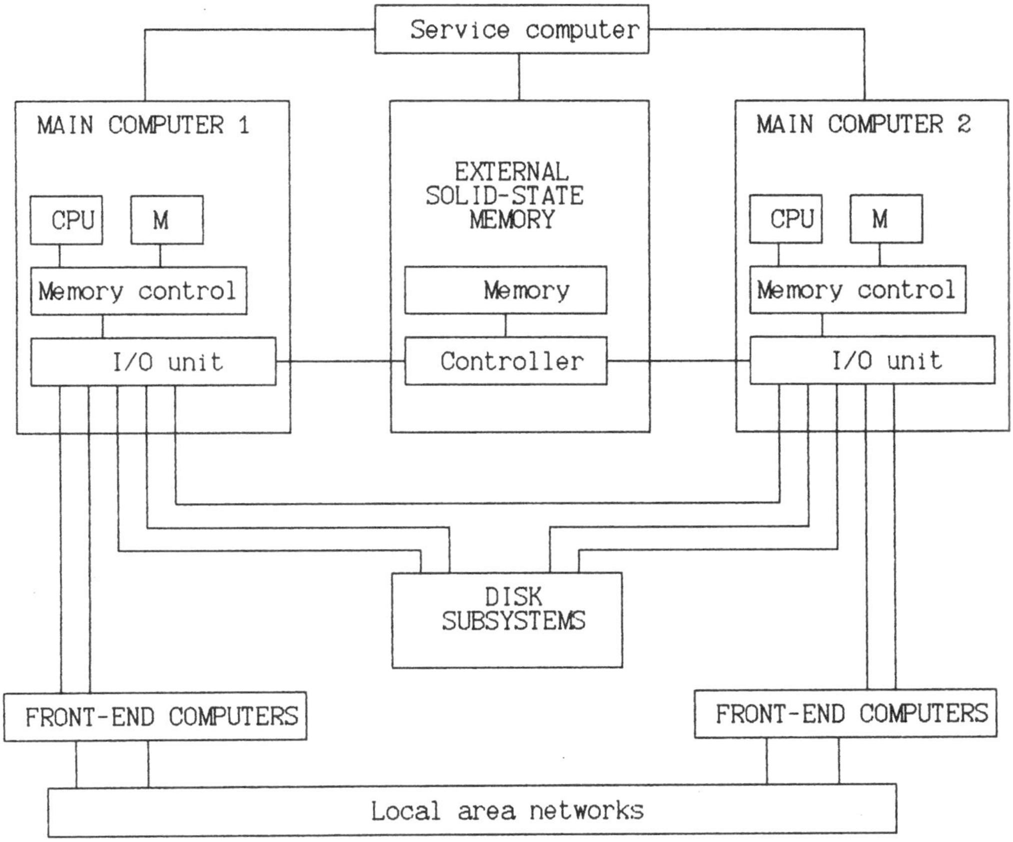

Fig. 1 ELECTRONICA SS BIS ARCHITECTURE

4.1.The Main Computer Subsystem

The main computer subsystem includes processor, a main memory and an exchange unit.

There is an addressable memory for 8 vector operands in the processor each of them consists of 64 64-bit words, addressable two-level memory for scalar and address operands registers. There are 8 64-bit scalar operands registers and 8 24-bit address operands on the first level, and 64 scalar and 64 address operands registers.Processor functional devices have pipe lined structure, which provides the receipt of each operation result, including the reciprocal approximation in each clock period. There are seven independent devices for scalar processing and also seven devices for vector processing

A chain mode is provided in vector devices, that allows to get up to 3 results during one clock period. The processor pick performance is 250 MFLOPS with 13,5 ns clock rate.

Instruction buffer is organized in the form of 4-section cache memory and has 256 64-bit words volume.

The main memory has 1 or 4 million words volume, and is divided into 16 independently operating blocks, that allows to transmit 4 words in a clock period during the buffer loading. The data transmition rate is one word per a clock period.

The exchange device provides the operation of up to 15 pairs of input/output channels of four types with a throughput from 6 to 150 MB/s.

4.2.External Solid-state Memory Subsystem

External solid-state memory has the volume of 256 MB. To increase its usage efficiency an intellectual controller, controlled by the main computer processor was realized instead of usual in such cases operation mode as fast "solid state disk".

The application program determines the structure of the data, which located in the external memory and defines the method of access to the portion of information transmitted during each exchange session. For example, if the array is kept in the external memory then while forming its lines and columns it's necessary to compute elements addresses in accordance with the array placement in the memory. The specialized processor in controller serves for such address computation.

When there is a call from an application problem main computer operational system forms the so called directive consistsing of a set of words, in which there is an information about data location in external memory,specialized processor program locations and other auxiliary information, particularly program parameters. After getting the directive the controller starts the program named in it. With this the exchange between the main memory and the the external memory is carried out. The mainframe memory address is computed with the help of an exchange device by increasing each following address by 1.External memory addresses computation depends on program algorithm.

These algorithms may be both the simplest, for example, with constant address increment and rather complex - with addresses computed according to the formula or to the table.

The described system increases the performance because, firstly, reduces volume of the main memory used, secondly, releases the main computer from the routine job of data editing and , thirdly, decreases the data flow between the main computer and the external memory. It results in rather high efficiency during data bulk processing.

There are two interface sets in the controller for a high-speed synchronous channel, that permits to connect two main computers. The exchange rate in the channel - 150 MB/s.

4.3 Disk Subsystem

The disk subsystem occupies the next level of memory hierarchy. There are two possibilities of connecting disk subsystems.

In the first variant the disk subsystem is built on a base of the specialized controller . Up to 4 controllers may be connected to the main computer, each of the controllers may be connected up to 8 317,5 MB disks. Disk controllers are connected to the main computer by means of input/output synchronous channels. Controllers include memory for a current data block storage and a microprogramed specialized processor.

In the second variant the disk subsystem is constructed on a base of the disk server.4 GB disk server is realized on a base of the BESTA workstation.Disk servers are connected to the main computer by means of asynchronious channels. Each main computer may be connected up to 8 disk servers.

4.4.Front-end Computers Subsystem

The front-end computers subsystem serves as an interface between the main computers and users. All peripheral devices are connected by means of front-end computers. The front-end computers can execute the functions of a system console, local problem batch input/output station, concentrator of data, received from some terminals or workstations, interactive workstation, etc.

There is a set of controllers for connecting different computers - BESM-6, Electronica-79, Electronica-82, SM computer, BESTA. The controllers are connected to the main computers by means of asynchronious channels. The front-end computers operate under their own operational systems control with additional drivers controlling their exchange with the main computer .

Various local networks and remote abonents connection aids are included into front-end computers peripheral equipment.

5.DESING,DEBUGGING AND MAINTENANCE SYSTEM

The complex of CAD, module functional test installations, as well as build-in control,test and diagnostics hardware form a united system, designed for providing error detection and correction on all stages of design, debugging and maintenance.

All the devices are checked out with the help of the logic modeling system on the logic design stage.During the modeling separate devices and modules tests are generated.Then they are used in functional test installation to check the manufactured modules.

Functional test installation unites a specialized hardware and a control computer. The nuclear of this hardware is a buffer memory for the storage of test sequences of signals sent on the module and responses. By means of comparing the responses received and expected, executed by the control computer errors and failures in the module are detected.

While debugging the device (a processor or a controller) the service computer is used. It permits to send a control and test information and receive an information about the device registers state. The comparing and analysis of this information allows to localize faults with separate IC accuracy.

The test system consists of functional tests - computer programs, detecting the fault operation fact and diagnostic tests - computer programs cooperating with a diagnostic system, that allows to localize the error.

Electronica 79 computer or BESTA workstation is used as a service computer.

6.SOFTWARE STRUCTURE

The system software includes main and front-end computers operational systems, Autocode, Fortran 77, C,Pascal languages translators, scientific library program and library complex.

The main computer simulation complex, realized on BESM -6, IBM PC/AT as instrumental computers is intended for the developing and debugging of the main computer programs.

7.PERSPECTIVES OF DEVELOPMENT

Presently the works on the system modernization and perspective system development are carried out. The modernization is connected with the improvement of a number of parameters, first of all the increase of external and mainframe memory capacity and construction and manufacture technology perfection.

The new design is oriented on the development of a series of models - from a 300 MFLOPs one-processor system to a multiprocessor system with 5 GFLOPs performance. A gate array chip of ECL type with 10.000 gates is a basis for this new development.

REFERENCES

1.R.M.Russell. “The Cray-1 Computer System“. Com.ACM, Vol.21,N1,January 1978

2.N.R.Lincoln. “Technology and Design Tradeoffs on the Creation of a Modern Supercomputer“,IEEE Trans.Computers,Vol.C-31,N5,May 1982

3.W.Schatz. “Who's Winning the Supercomputer Race?“. Datamation, Vol.35, N14, July 15,1989

AUTHORS BIOGRAPHIES

Vladimir A.Melnikov is a Director of the Institute for Cybernetics Problems Russian Academy of Sciences, Professor and Chairman of the Department of Mathematical Logic of Moscow State University and Chairman of Department of Optoelectronics and Computing of Moscow Physics and Technical Institute. The Member of Expert Council for Russian Goverment.

Graduated from Moscow Power Institute in 1951. He received his Candidate of Science in 1958 and Doctor of Science in 1968 (both were received in computers). In 1981 elected to be the Full Member of Russian Academy of Sciences.

From 1950 worked in the Institute of Precision Mechanichs and Computing. From 1978 he had heading the Department of Electronic Instruments and Computing of the Ministry of Electronic Manufacturing.

His research interests include the creation of high perfomance computer, architecture, computer and software engeeniring, computer automation design.

He has authored and edited more than 20 computer science related books and published more than 100 refereed academic papers in computer science and application areas.

Founding President of Supercomputer Society of Academy of Sciences, Editor-in-Cheif of "Informatics and Education" journal, "Computer Science Referative Journal", "Cybernetics and Computing" collection.

Address: The Institute for Problems of Cybernetics Russian Academy of Sciences
Vavilova st.,37,Moscow,Russia

Yuri I. Mitropolsky heading the Supercomputer Architecture and Hardware Department in the Institute of Cybernetics Problems of Russian Academy of Sciences, Professor of Moscow Institute of Physics and Technics.

Graduated from Moscow Power Institute in 1958. Received his Candidate of Science in 1972, Doctor of Science in 1985 (both in computers). Elected to be Corresponding Member of Russian Academy of Sciences in 1990.

He took part in working out the project of Computer systems BESM-6, AS-6, Elecronica SS BIS (as a vice-head designer).

From 1958 worked in the Institute of Precision Mechanics and Computing of Russian Academy of Sciences, from 1978 – in the Department of Electronic Instruments and Computing of Ministry of Electronic Manufacturing, from 1991 he is the Head of the Department of the Institute of Cybernetics Problems RAS.

His research interest are in the field of architecture, hardware, methods of design and debugging of high performance computer systems.

Address: The Institute for Problems of Cybernetics Russian Academy of Sciences Vavilova st., 37, Moscow, Russia

Automatic Parallelization of Programs for MIMD Computers

Vladimir A. Melnikov, Boris M. Shabanov, Paul N. Telegin, and Alexander P. Chernjaev

ABSTRACT

Large-grain parallelization of programs is needed for efficient use of multiprocessors. An approach based on program structurization allows top down parallelization to obtain larger parallel segments of code. This approach was adopted for design and implementation of C source-to-source converter for multitransputer as object architecture. Signal/image processing are typical multitransputer applications.

Keywords: multiprocessors, automatic parallelization, structured programming, dependence analysis, C programming language, source-to-source converter, multitransputer

INTRODUCTION

MIMD (i.e. multiprocessor) concept is becoming wide-spread, because it allows to create reliable high performance computers with relatively low cost/performance coefficient (Melnikov 1991). For achieving high performance it is necessary to present programs in parallel way. Programming languages ANSI C and ANSI FORTRAN contain no elements which express parallelism explicitly.

There are a plenty of C and FORTRAN application programs and their amount is increasing. The most of the programs are oriented to uniprocessors and portability to MIMD computers with efficient execution is cost-expensive. Tools for automatic parallelization can greatly reduce efforts for program portability, simplify development of parallel programs and be good means for teaching parallel programming methods.

Today some tools for automatic or semi-automatic parallelization are already implemented, e.g. automatic systems Parafrase (Polychronopoulos 1986), PTRAN (Allen 1988), semi-automatic SUPERB (Zima 1988), PTOOL (Allen 1986) and others.

In this paper approach for constructing automatic systems is described. In section 2 the basic definitions are given. Section 3 describes how does top down parallelization of structured programs works. In section 4 capabilities of parallelizer are explained with an example of simple program transformation. Examples of programs are presented in extended C.

Source-to-source converter for C programming language is now under development at the Institute for Problems of Cybernetics (Russia Academy of Sciences). Top-down approach is the keystone of our project. Resulting parallel program is generated for 3L Parallel C (3L 1989) and then can be run on multitransputer (Inmos 1988).

1. DESIGN CONSIDERATIONS

Automatic parallelization systems can be implemented in two ways: a source-to-source converter (i.e. preprocessor) or a specific optimization stage of a particular compiler. Converter output text includes either special function call or extended language constructs which are "understandable" by the compiler for object parallel computer. Parallelizing compiler outputs already object file with parallelism hidden in it. Parallelization stage of compiler should be developed together with compiler itself. Converter is much cheaper than parallelizing compiler and allows better tuning for different parallel computers. If a C or FORTRAN compiler already exists for parallel computer it is preferable to develop a converter rather than compiler.

Parallelization systems can be automatic or semi-automatic. Semi-automatic parallelyzer organizes dialogue with the user who can control the process of parallelization. Fully automatic systems assume "the worst case" when it is very hard or impossible to extract automatically some semantic information. Thus coefficient of parallelization is decreased and execution rate of parallel program is slow down. Special pragmas in users' programs can give such semantic information. Such pragmas are also required to make parallel programs understandable for users.

Parallel programs can be generated for static and dynamic execution modes. Dynamic mode cause overheads for organization of parallel execution, but may achieve better load-balancing between parallel branches when execution time is unpredictable.

In addition to static program analysis a dynamic analysis with window interface is very desirable. It makes possible parallel programs debugging and profiling.

2. GENERAL APPROACH

Only few commercial parallelization systems (mainly oriented to FORTRAN) are known today. This fact can be explained with high complexity of the kernel of any parallelizing system - the block for searching and analyzing dependencies. For C programs such a block is even more sophisticated than for FORTRAN programs. For distributed memory systems memory optimization is also needed.

Dependence analysis needs obtaining information on usage of program memory and logical precedence of program components. This needs analyzing of both control graph of program and usage of data. In contrast to vectorizing systems the analysis always should be *global*. Hence, the interprocedural analysis is needed. Dependencies can be obtained directly from the graph of program or indirectly by using structured representation of program. Such a representation reduces computer resources on program analysis and also makes the parallelizing system less cost-expensive.

Let's follow Dijkstra structural approach (Dahl 1972). A program S is an ordered set of structures: $S_1, \ldots, S_m$. Each structure can consist of a subset of structures. Before analysis user's program can be automatically structured or a simple detection of existing program structures may be implemented. Some languages do not contain GOTO statements and the program is always structured. The presentation with structures simplifies the control graph of program (Smirnov 1988).

Let's denote:

IN(S) - the set of variables that are possibly read by the structure S during its execution;

OUT(S)- the set of variables that are possibly modified by the structure S;

DEF(S)- the set of variables that are modified on every execution of the structure S.

E.g., for the structure S

```
if(L) { Z=Y*Y; X[I]=Z; } else X[I]=Y;
```

the sets are the following:

$IN(S) = \{L,Y\}$
$OUT(S)= \{Z,X[I]\}$
$DEF(S)= \{X[I]\}$

In general case dependence of two structures S_1 and S_2 (S_1 precedes $S2$) can be determined by the formula:

$$IN(S_1) \cap OUT(S_2) \cup OUT(S_1) \cap (IN(S_2) \cup OUT(S_2) \setminus DEF(S_2)) \cup OUT(S_1) \cap DEF(S_2) \neq \phi$$

(here '$\cap$' denotes intersection of sets, '$\cup$' denotes union of sets, '$\setminus$' denotes difference of sets, 'ϕ' denotes the empty set).

$OUT(S_1) \cap (IN(S_2) \cup OUT(S_2) \setminus DEF(S_2))$ is a true (flow) dependence,
$IN(S_1) \cap OUT(S_2)$ is an antidependence,
$OUT(S_1) \cap DEF(S_2)$ is an output dependence.

Antidependencies and output dependencies can be avoided by common technique (Padua 1986).

True dependence consists of two parts. $OUT(S_1) \cap IN(S_2)$ - is important dependence and $OUT(S_1) \cap (OUT(S_2) \setminus DEF(S_2))$ is important in the case when a variable v from the set $OUT(S_1)) \setminus DEF(S_2)$ belongs to the set $IN(M)$ where M is the part of program that is executed after $S2$; otherwise this case is similar to the output dependence. To distinguish this problem a down top backward pass of program analysis can be implemented to find the sets of variables that will be read after executing each structure.

Some results on semantic independence investigation are described in (Best 1989/90).

3. AUTOMATIC PARALLELIZATION

3.1. Calculation of Sets *IN*, *OUT* and *DEF*

It is easy to prove that if a structure S is a sequence of two structures S_1 and S_2, S_1 precedes S_2 ($S=S_1 \| S_2$) then

$IN(S) = IN(S_1) \cup (IN(S_2) \setminus DEF(S_1))$
$OUT(S)=OUT(S_1) \cup OUT(S_2)$
$DEF(S)=DEF(S_1) \cup DEF(S_2)$

Using the formula above the rules were constructed for definition the sets *IN*, *OUT* and *DEF* for different types of program structures. The structures are the following: **SEQUENCE, ALTERNATIVE STRUCTURE, LOOP** and **UNKNOWN**, i.e. the case of a program fragment with one entrance, one exit and non-structured body. The rules are presented in (Smirnov 1988).

3.2. Pseudovariables

For eliminating analysis of the control graph of the program some dummy variables are used. Let's call these dummy variables as pseudovariables. Pseudovaraibles do not correspond to any program variables and they are used only during program analysis.

The need of pseudovariables occurs on parallelization of program, especially on analysis of DO loops. Also the three types of pseudovariables are always used. Let's exam a general case loop in extended C :

```
WHILE(w);
 {
  P1;LEAVE(L1);
  ...
  Pk;LEAVE(Lk);
  Pk+1;
 }
UNTIL(u);
```

Here the structures **WHILE(w)**, **LEAVE(L_i)** and **UNTIL(u)** are the control parts of the loop. The **LEAVE** structure contains instructions that break the loop if L_i condition is true. The **LEAVE** can be used in any kind of structure, not only in loop. Structures **WHILE**, **LEAVE** and **UNTIL** form a control part of the loop. Structures *Pi* form a functional part of loop. Control part usually can contain its own control and functional parts. During the analysis of the loop body one or more pseudovariables can be added to the set of variables. They are called *CONTROL* variables. Each structure of the loop body uses control variable as an *IN* variable. The **LEAVE** structures use control variables as *OUT* variables. In this case control dependencies are reduced to data dependencies. *CONTROL* variables exist only inside the structure which is interrupted.

The same situation occurs, for example, with functions. All the structures containing RETURN statement are the **LEAVE** structures.

For each instruction a global *STOP* pseudovariable is added to the *IN* set. For each structure that finishes the program the *STOP* pseudovariable is added to the *OUT* set. Occurence of pseudovariables *CONTROL* and *STOP* can break the calculation of the *DEF* set.

When we have file operations a *FILE* pseudovariable is used. For each file operation that pseudovariable belongs to the sets *IN* and *OUT*, because the file operations always use and modify the file pointer. If it is known that a set of different streams refers to a corresponding set of different files several file pseudovariables can be used.

Pseudovariables *CONTROL*, *FILE* and *STOP* are never added to the *DEF* set.

3.3. Parallelization of Structures

The main idea of parallelization is the following. The control part of a structure is copied to different parallel processes (and possibly modified). The functional part of a structure is divided among parallel processes. The process runs recursively on inner structures until a good parallel scheme is found for terminal structure (i.e. language instruction) is reached.

LINE	PROGRAM	STRUCTURES
1	`SX=0.;`	S2, S1
2	`SY=0.;`	S3, S1
3	`for (I=1;I<=N;I++){`	S5, S4
4	`J=K[I];`	S7, S6, S4
5	`if(J==0) break;`	S8, S6, S4
6	`SX=SX+X[J]*X[J];`	S10, S9, S6, S4
7	`SY=SY+Y[J]*Y[J];`	S11, S9, S6, S4
8	`}`	S4
9	`S=sqrt(SX)+sqrt(SY);`	S12

Figure 1a. Example of C program structure

E.g., let's have a look to the program fragment on fig. 1a.

The program consists of the following structures: **SEQUENCE** (lines 1 and 2), **LOOP** (lines 3 to 8) and **SEQUENCE** (line 9). The loop contains inner structures. Statement *break* (line 5) can finish execution of the loop, hence it is a **LEAVE** structure.

The loop body contains two independent parts: lines no. 6 and 7 (structures S10 and S11). The loop is split. The value J (line 4) can be either transferred or evaluated (depending on the transfer and calculation times).

The parallel version of this program for two processors is presented on fig. 1b.

PROCESS 1

```
SX=0.;
for(I=1;I<=N;I++)
 {
   J=K[I];
   if(J==O) break;
   SX=SX+X[J]*X[J];
 }
receive SY;
S=sqrt(SX)+sqrt(SY);
```

PROCESS 2

```
SY=0.;
for(I=1;I<=N;I++)
 {
   J=K[I];
   if(J==O) break;
   SY=SY+Y[J]*Y[J];
 }
send SY;
```

Figure 1b. Parallel (two-processor) version of C program

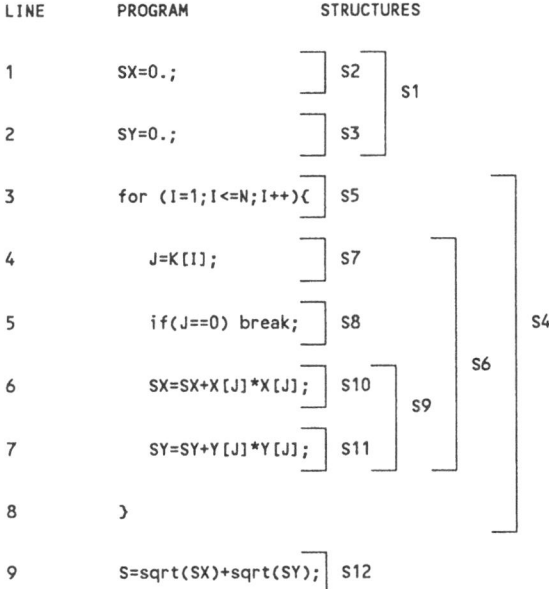

For estimation the transfer time (T_R) of N data elements to the neighbour the following function is used:

$$T_R(N)=T_1+T_2*\lceil N/L\rceil+T_3*N$$

where
T_1 - is time for transfer initialization,
T_2 - time for organization a message buffer and initialization of its transfer,
L - buffer size (maximal message length),
T_3 - time for transferring one element.

Constant values T_1, T_2 and T_3 are determined experimentally and are dependent upon the certain object computer architecture and software. When N varies some symbolic computations can be made, as number of transferred elements usually depends of the number of loops iterations.

3.4. DO loops

Of course, parallelization of loops is the most important part of program parallelization. If possible, implicit loops should be reconstructed to DO loops (i.e. explicit loops). Note that in this consideration FORTRAN DO loop corresponds to C FOR loop with loop-invariant boundary values.

Four types of DO loops are taken in account.

1. *FULLY PARALLEL LOOPS* (or *DOALL* (Padua 1986)). All iterations of such a loop are independent. The problem of detection such loops can be solved by using common technique of finding loop cycles. Pseudovariables are also taken into account as if they are true variables. Analysis starts for one node representing the loop body. Diophantian equations should be solved only if a cycle is found. If the cycle does not disappear the representation of the structure of loop body is taken in account. This process runs recursively until terminal nodes in the tree of program structures are reached. Only the structures that appear in the cycles are analyzed deeper. In general case it is possible to find cycles in subroutines (once for each module) and then use that tree if necessary. Some useful techniques exist to avoid dependencies (loop splitting, increasing number of dimensions, induction variables recognition, constant and variable propagation etc (Chernjaev 1990)).

2. *RECONSTRUCTABLE LOOPS*. Often a loop has some instructions that makes a cycle, but parallelism is hidden in reduction constructions such as associative operations (e.g. summation) or linear recursion (e.g., recursive doubling algorithm for reconstructing linear recursion x[i]=a[i]*x[i-1]+b[i] (Kogge 1973)). Practically this means that the loop has some essential sequential part. Complexity of such reduction construction is logarithm of number of processors if the system provides good routing. In the worst cases of connection the complexity with large number of processors is a square root of the problem dimension. In fact, organization of sequential operation may significantly slow down loop execution on distributed memory computers.

3. *LOOPS WITH PARTIAL DEPENDENCE OF ITERATIONS*. When *successive* iterations of a nested DO loop are dependent sometimes it is possible to parallelize the nest of two or more loops. Vectorization of such loops is discussed in (Lamport 1974). In (Konoshenko 1989) a method for multiprocessors is discussed. The space of iterations is split into blocks. The nested DO loop is reconstructed in the way that allows macropipelining in processing space of iterations. Time estimation with data transfers

shows that complexity of the parallelized loop is the root of n-th degree of the problem size.

4. *DOACROSS LOOPS*. When *all* loop iterations are dependent it may be possible to overlap execution of iterations (Cytron 1986). Statements in such a loop should be reordered to minimize sequential execution. Speedup of the loop is limited with T_P/T_S, where T_P is time for execution of parallel part and T_S is corresponding time for sequential part (time for wait of initialization). Main problems with *DOACROSS* loops on distributed memory computers are following. Usually the best array distribution is *cyclic* for *DOACROSS* loops but for other types of loops it is *block*. This may cause runtime array redistribution and loss of performance. Small *DOACROSS* loops may be inefficient because of data transfers. That's why execution time should be carefully estimated before parallelizing. But in some cases usage of *DOACROSS* is the only way to speedup the program.

3.5. Data Distribution

To increase memory using efficiency large data arrays should be physically distributed among local memories. Arrays can be overlapped for time efficient processing. Execution of some sequential loops is also distributed according to data distribution and data transferrings are required between local memories. Pointer variables can be used in C, Pascal and FORTRAN-90 languages for access to arrays but in many cases pointers can be reduced to explicit arrays.

Distribution of one array can influence the distribution of other arrays. Parallel and sequential execution times should be estimated for each array dimension with estimation of redistribution overhead. Physical array distribution can be built with help of some heuristics. The limitations are speedup and correspondence of distributed arrays to each other. The task becomes much more complicated when using non-linear distribution or distribution of arrays onto a subset of local memories. The user defined distribution like in Vienna FORTRAN (Chapman 1991) can be useful.

4. PROGRAM PORTABILITY AND MODIFICATIONS

When a source-to-source parallelizing converter is created it is useful to generate parallel program in some base language extension and use a preprocessor to create parallel program for certain implementation (different compilers or even different systems). The following language extensions are suggested. An additional data type *MASK* is used to describe index decomposition. Variables of *MASK* type are used to spread arrays and loops among processors. *PARFOR* is language extension for parallel loop specification description. Extended C language example is presented on fig. 2.

It is meant here that array x of 100 elements is physically distributed among 2 local memories (52 elements in the first local memory and 51 in the second one). *linear* is a distribution function and means block distribution. *-1,+2* are array overlaps. *M–L* means logical distribution (elements from x[1] to x[n/2+2] in the first local memory and from x[n/2] to x[n] in the second local memory). *PARFOR* means execution of iterations with index i ranges from 2 to n/2 on the first processor and from n/2+1 to n-1 on the second processor.

Mask value can be passed as a parameter to a subroutine. Some C basic operations can be applied to mask. Let's explore an example of computing all sums of an array elements. The sequential version of program is presented on fig. 3a. The parallel one (fig. 3b) can be generated automatically from sequential version by using a pattern .

```
void main(void)
{
    MASK M–X=\1:2;1:100;-1,+2;linear\,M–L;
    double x[M–X];
    int i;
    ...
    M–L=\1:2;1:n;-1,+2;linear\;
    read (handler,x[M–L],n);
    PARFOR ( i, M–L, noover ) (i=2; i<n; ++i)
            x[i[M–L]]=x[i[M–L]]+x[(i+2) [M–L]];
    ...
}
```

Figure 2. Example of *MASK* and *PARFOR* language extensions

```
void main(void)
{
    double a[10000];
        ...
    allsums(a,n);
        ...
}
allsums (double a[], int n)
{
    for (i=2;i<=n;i++)        a[i]=a[i-1]+a[i];
}
```

Figure 3a. Sequential version of program for all sums calculation

5. CONCLUSIONS

The central idea of the structural approach to parallelization based on program structurization is already implemented. Semi-automatic parallelyzer needs an experienced user. On the other hand, fully automatic system not always allows to achieve good parallelization coefficient because of some semantic information is lost during program analyzing. That's why future parallelization system should provide the both modes.

Further efforts on source-to-source converter for C programming language at the Institute for Problems of Cybernetics will be connected with increasing of runtime efficiency. Efficient algorithms for data distribution, analysis and parallelization of dynamic memory allocation (such as pointer usage) and program recursion are still needed. It is useful to extract automatically some elements of program semantics for eliminating unnecessary data dependencies and reconstructing source programs for parallelization. The converter will allow usage optional pragmas. The execution mode of parallel programs will be static because of parallel programs efficiency. User's interface will allow understanding of parallel program structure and behavior.

```
void main(void)
{
   MASK M-P=\1:N-PROC;1:10000;-1\;
                          /**** M-P is a mask for physical distribution.
                           **** Missing values are set by default.
                           **** N-PROC is number of processors/local memories */
   double A[M-P];
   MASK M-A;               /**** M-A is a mask for logical distribution */
      ...
   M-A=\1:N-PROC;1:n;-1\;
   allsums(A,n,M-A);
      ...
}
allsums ( double a[M-A], int n, MASK M-A )
{
   int i,j,np;
   a [first-index(M-A,over)] = 0.;/**** function first-index(MASK,over) returns
                                    **** the first index value for current
                                    **** processor with array overlap  */
   PARFOR ( i, M-A, noover ) (i=2;i<n;++i)  a[i]=a[i-1]+a[i];
      for (j=0; j<=(int)(log((double)(2*N-PROC-1)); j++)
       {
                              /***** Repeat for number of algorithm steps */
         np=pow(2.,(double)(j-1))+1+.01;
                              /**** np is the number of first working processor
                               **** .01 constant is needed for correct rounding */
         if ( CURRENT-PROC >= pow((double)2,(double)J)+.01 )
           {                  /**** CURRENT-PROC is the current
                               **** processor number */
             if ((j>0) && (CURRENT-PROC>=np))
               {
                 receive a [ first-index ( M-A, over ) ]
                      from CURRENT-PROC-(int)(pow((double)2,(double)(j-1))+.01);
               }
               else
               {
                if ( CURRENT-PROC != 1 )   a [ first-index ( M-A, over ) ] =0.
               }
             PARFOR (i, M-A, noover)(i=max(2,first-index(M-A,np,noover));i<=n; ++i)
                              /**** function first-index(MASK,np,over) returns
                               **** the first index value for  processor np
                               **** without array overlap  */
               {  a[i]=a[i-1]+a[i];   }
             if (( CURRENT-PROC + pow ((double)2,(double)j)+.01 ) <= N-PROC)
              {
            send a [last-index (M-A, noover)]
                to CURRENT-PROC+(int)(pow((double)2,(double)j)+.01);
           } }
       } /**************** End of loop for number of algorithm steps */
}
```

Figure 3b. Parallel version of program for all sums calculation

REFERENCES

Allen F, Burke M, Charles P, Cytron R, Ferrante J (1988) An overview of the PTRAN analysis system for multiprocessing. J. Parallel and Distrib. Comput. 5 (5): 617-640

Allen R, Baumgartner D, Kennedy K, Porterfield A (1986) PTOOL: a semi-automatic parallel programming assistant. In : Proc. Int. Conf. Parallel Process., Aug. 19-22, Washington D.C., pp 164- 170

Best E, Lengauer C (1989/90) Semantic Independence. In : Science of Computer Programming, 13, Elsevier Science Publishers B.V. (North-Holland), pp 23-50

Chapman BM, Mehrotra P, Zima H (1991) VIENNA FORTRAN - a FORTRAN Language Extension for Distributed Memory Multiprocessors. Technical Report. Austrian Center for Parallel Computations, September

Chernjaev AP (1990) Programming systems for high performance computers. Annuals of Science and Engineering. Series Computer Science, 3. Moscow, VINITI (in Russian)

Cytron R (1986) DoAcross: beyond vectorization for multiprocessors (extended abstract). In : Proc. of Int. Conf. Parallel Process. , Aug.19-22. Washington D.C. pp 836-844

Dahl OJ, Dijkstra EW, Hoare CAR (1972) Structured Programming, N.Y., Academic Press, 1972.

Inmos (1988) Transputer Instruction Set. A compiler writer's guide. Prentice Hall, New York London Toronto Sydney Tokyo

Kogge PM, Stone HS (1973) A parallel algorithm for the efficient solution of a general class of recurrence equation. IEEE Trans. on Computers C-22 (8) : 786-792

Konoshenko MP, Telegin PN (1989) Parallelization of nested DO-loops for multiprocessors. Programmirowanie 2 (In Russian)

Lamport L (1974) The parallel execution of DO loops. CACM 17 (2) : 83-93

Melnikov VA (1991) Keynote remarks. In : Mirenkov NN (ed) Proc. of the Int. Conf. on Parallel Computing Technology "PaCT-91", Novosibirsk, USSR, Sept. 7-11, pp 17-19

Padua DA, Wolfe MA (1986) Advanced compiler optimizations for supercomputers. CACM 29(12) : pp 1184-1201

Polychronopoulos CD, Kuck DJ, Padua DA (1986) Execution of parallel loops on parallel processor systems. In : Proc. Int. Conf. Parallel Process., Aug. 19-22. Washington D.C. pp 519-527

Smirnov AD, Telegin PN (1988) Analyzer of parallel programs written in FORTRAN-4 . Programmirowanie 2 : 95-99 (in Russian)

Zima HP, Bast HJ, Gerndt M (1988) SUPERB: A tool for semiautomatic MIMD/SIMD parallelization. Parallel Computing 6 (1)

3L (1989) Parallel C User Guide

AUTHORS BIOGRAPHIES

Vladimir A.Melnikov is a Director of the Institute for Cybernetics Problems Russian Academy of Sciences, Professor and Chairman of the Department of Mathematical Logic of Moscow State University and Chairman of Department of Optoelectronics and Computing of Moscow Physics and Technical Institute. The Member of Expert Council for Russian Government.

Graduated from Moscow Power Institute in 1951. He received his Candidate of Science in 1958 and Doctor of Science in 1968 (both were received in computers). In 1981 elected to be the Full Member of Russian Academy of Sciences.

From 1950 worked in the Institute of Precision Mechanichs and Computing. From 1978 he had heading the Department of Electronic Instruments and Computing of the Ministry of Electronic Manufacturing.

His research interests include the creation of high perfomance computer, architecture, computer and software engeeniring, computer automation design.

He has authored and edited more than 20 computer science related books and published more than 100 refereed academic papers in computer science and application areas.

Founding President of Supercomputer Society of Academy of Sciences, Editor-in-Cheif of "Informatics and Education" journal, "Computer Science Referative Journal", "Cybernetics and Computing" collection.

Alexander P. Chernjaev is currently a senior research worker at the Institute of Cybernetics Problems of the Russian Academy of Sciences. He started work in system programming in 1977. His research interests include program development systems, compiler construction; debuggers and parallel computing. He has authored monography on supercomputer programming systems and more than 10 technical papers in supercomputer system programming.
Chernjaev received his MSc in applied mathematics from the Electronic Machinery Institute of Moscow in 1977 and DSc in computer science from the Scientific Council for Cybernetics of the USSR Academy of Sciences in 1987.

Address : Institute of Cybernetics Problems,
37, Vavilova St., Moscow, 117312, Russia
E-mail : gna @ ipk.msk.su
Fax : (007)-(095) 125 43 80

Boris M. Shabanov is currently a deputy director at the Institute of Cybernetics Problems of the Russian Academy of Sciences. He started work in computer hardware and architecture in 1977 on Elbrus MIMD Supercomputer Project . Then he was a member of design team of an Electronica SSBIS Vector-Pipelined Supercomputer Project. His research interests include computer architecture, computer components, vector/parallel processing. He has authored more than 10 technical papers in supercomputer systems.

Shabanov is a member of Scientific Council on Supercomputing of the Russian Academy of Sciences.

Shabanov received his MSc in computer systems from the Electronic Machinery Institute of Moscow in 1977 and DSc in computer science from the Institute of Cybernetics Problems of the Russian Academy of Sciences in 1991.

Address : Institute of Cybernetics Problems,
Vavilova St., 37, Moscow, 117312, Russia

E-mail : sbm @ ipk.msk.su
Fax : (007)-(095) 125 43 80

Paul N. Telegin is currently a senior research worker at the Institute of Cybernetics Problems of the Russian Academy of Sciences. He started work in system programming in 1983. His research interests include program development systems, automatic parallelizing and parallel computing. He has authored more than 10 academic/technical papers in parallel programming (system software and applications). Telegin received his MSc in applied mathematics from the Electronic Machinery Institute of Moscow in 1983 and DSc in computer science from the Physics and Technology Institute of Moscow in 1989.

Address : Institute of Cybernetics Problems,
Vavilova St., 37, Moscow, 117312, Russia

E-mail : gna @ ipk.msk.su
Fax : (007)-(095) 125 43 80

Workshop Organization

Organized by :

Computer Graphics Society

Kogakuin University

Japan Personal Computer Software Association

Department of Information Science, The University of Tokyo

In coorporation with

Information Processing Society of Japan

The Institute of Electronics, Information and Communication Engineers

Supported by:

Nihon Silicon Graphics International

The Aizu Area Foundation for the Promotion of Education and Science

Kubota Computer Inc.

Program Committee

Program Chairperson

T. L. Kunii (Japan)

Members

Y.L. Kergosien (France)
S. Kojima (Japan)
V.A. Melnikov (Russia)
T. Oshima (Japan)
N.M. Patrikalakis (U.S.A.)
Y. Shinagawa (Japan)

List of External Reviewers

V.B. Britkov (Russia)

H. Gotoda (Japan)

T.C. Lan (Singapore)

T. Noma (Japan)

M. Lucas (France)

H. Saji (Japan)

K. Yoshida (Japan)

Special thanks to:

T. Takahashi (Japan)

H. Yamamura (Japan)

T. Tsukioka (Japan)

H. Hioki (Japan)

S. Takahashi (Japan)

Author Index

Citation Index

Keyword Index